# FLEET AIR ARM BOYS

## VOLUME ONE

# FLEET AIR ARM BOYS

## VOLUME ONE: AIR DEFENCE FIGHTER AIRCRAFT SINCE 1945

TRUE TALES FROM ROYAL NAVY AIRCREW,

MAINTAINERS AND HANDLERS

STEVE BOND

GRUB STREET • LONDON

Published by
Grub Street
4 Rainham Close
London SW11 6SS

Copyright © Grub Street 2020
Copyright text © Steve Bond 2020

A CIP record for this title is available from the British library

ISBN-13: 978-1-911621-98-0

Design by Lucy Thorne

Printed and bound by Finidr, Czech Republic

**DEDICATION**
To the memory of the 1,544 Fleet Air Arm personnel
who have lost their lives in the service of their country since August 1945

# CONTENTS

# PREFACE
## ADMIRAL SIR MICHAEL LAYARD KCB CBE

"The lives of a naval fighter pilot and his observer are hugely challenging, and dangerous at the best of times. As a crew operating from an aircraft carrier brings new dimensions – the ship is always on the move, never where you last saw it, and in rough seas forever pitching, rolling and cork screwing – an even bigger challenge at night of course. All this breeds some very special people with a vital suit of talents.

"This book illustrates the whole Fleet Air Arm family, aircrew, maintainers and aircraft handlers alike in their own words. It is an important historical record and tells a story that is long overdue in the telling."

Michael Layard was commissioned into the Royal Navy in 1954 and trained as a pilot. He flew Sea Venoms with 891 Squadron, and in 1970 he took command of 899 Squadron with Sea Vixens aboard HMS *Eagle*. He became commander (air) in HMS *Ark Royal* in 1977 and chief staff officer to the flag officer, Naval Air Command in 1979. During the Falklands War he was Senior Naval Officer aboard the *Atlantic Conveyor* which was hit by Exocet missiles and sunk.

He was appointed commander of RNAS (Royal Naval Air Station) Culdrose in 1982, captain of the destroyer HMS *Cardiff* in 1984 and director Naval Warfare

(Air) at the Ministry of Defence in 1985. He became Flag Officer Naval Air Command in 1988, director general Naval Manpower and Training in 1990 and Second Sea Lord and chief of Naval Personnel in 1992 (and, concurrently, president of the Royal Naval College, Greenwich from 1993). From 1994 he combined this role with that of Commander-in-Chief Naval Home Command. He is a trustee of the Fleet Air Arm Museum, and a past governor of Pangbourne College.

*Admiral Sir Michael Layard.*

# INTRODUCTION AND ACKNOWLEDGEMENTS

If you ask the 'man in the street' who flies military jets in the UK, most people will automatically say "the Royal Air Force" (RAF). Generally, there is little understanding of the role played by the Royal Navy's (RN) Fleet Air Arm (FAA) in maintaining a British military aviation presence around the world. The aim of this book is to introduce the FAA to a wider audience, and to give the service the higher profile it so richly deserves. Flying high performance aircraft off an aircraft carrier demands not only a high level of skill, but also a considerable amount of courage and determination, not least when landing back on a very small piece of real estate bobbing about in a rough sea, at night, with no possibility of diversion. The nature of these operations meant that the accident rate and aircrew losses were very high – but 'accepted' as part of the job.

Since the FAA carries out most of its operations at sea, this has naturally led to low public awareness. What makes the FAA different from the RAF? Why is it not better known by the public? Both services fly fast jets, but that does not mean they have the same ethos; personal accounts within these pages illustrate this very well.

*Fleet Air Arm Boys* is intended as a tribute to the brave personnel, of all ranks, who operated and maintained FAA aircraft, especially those – far too many – who lost their lives doing so. This book concentrates on the post-1945 era of British naval, mainly carrier, aviation during which it saw action in crises and wars worldwide. It concentrates on personal accounts by former aircrew, maintainers and aircraft handlers – giving a taste of what life on board and in the air was like. The development and service of the aircraft types is also summarised.

Focussing on fixed-wing aircraft, this first volume looks at the fighter types in their air defence role, whilst the second volume considers the types used for strike, anti-submarine and airborne early warning (AEW). Both volumes also include some other, land-based fixed-wing types. Mention must be made here of helicopters, which have become important FAA assets in their own right since the 1950s. Initially employed on carriers alongside fixed-wing aircraft, they were later deployed on those smaller ships fitted with flight decks. Today at least one helicopter is carried on all ships of frigate size and larger. From 2010, following the withdrawal of the Harrier force, until 2020, the front-line element of the FAA was all rotary-wing.

### THE FAA POST-WORLD WAR 2

During World War 2 the battleship was replaced as the 'capital' ship of the fleet by the aircraft carrier – and its aircraft were its principal weapons. At the end of that

*HMS* Ocean *taken from USS* Lowry *1952.*

war the strength of the FAA stood at 57 aircraft carriers, 3,700 aircraft (the majority of which were US lend-lease and subsequently returned), 72,000 personnel and 65 naval air stations around the world.

By the late 1940s four new light fleet carriers – Her Majesty's Ship (HMS) *Triumph*, *Theseus, Glory* and *Ocean* – had entered service alongside the six remaining wartime aircraft carriers (the others, the great majority of which were of the small escort type, had been disposed of). All of these operated piston-engined aircraft. A Vampire had made the world's first jet deck landing on 3 December 1945, but it was not until August 1951 that the first operational British naval jet fighter, the Attacker, entered service.

Early jets were considerably more difficult to handle at the low speeds required for landing aboard a carrier which resulted in high accident rates. The FAA continued to operate high-powered piston-engined aircraft such as the Sea Fury, Seafire, Sea Hornet and Firefly. In June 1950 these were the carriers' 'teeth' when, following North Korea's invasion of the south, the Korean War broke out. They were the only British-operated combat types 'in-theatre' and flew sorties in support of United Nations (UN) forces (the RAF employed flying boats for some reconnaissance missions). Despite their disadvantage in performance compared with jets, four Sea Furies successfully engaged a flight of eight MiG 15s, shooting one down and damaging others in an air combat engagement. They suffered no losses to themselves. *Triumph, Theseus, Glory* and *Ocean* all participated in this war which continued until May 1953.

As jets became larger, more powerful and faster, they required more deck space from which to operate. The US Navy simply built much larger carriers, whilst two large 'fleet' carriers – *Eagle* and *Ark Royal* – entered RN service in 1951 and 1954 respectively. However, modifications had to be devised to make jet operations much safer, not least because all serving carriers had axial (i.e. straight) flight decks. The solutions were all developed by the FAA, and comprised three major contributions to naval aviation. These were:

*Angled Flight Deck.* The port side of the flight deck was extended outwards to accommodate a landing area laid out at an angle to the left of the main deck axis. This allowed a landing aircraft to 'go around', if its hook missed the arrestor wires, and make another approach.

*Deck Landing Sight.* This provided accurate glidepath information. RAdm

Nicholas Goodhart RN invented what was the first version of the sight using a mirror. Jets, particularly those with a slower throttle response, suffered high accident rates because landing safety officers (LSOs) were not always able to give pilots adequate warning to correct for glidepath errors. Goodhart's solution was to position a concave mirror on the deck's port side, flanked by green datum lights. A powerful beam directed at the mirror created a bright yellow ball of light visible to approaching aircraft. By keeping this 'meatball' centred between the datum lights pilots could be sure of the correct glidepath. Goodhart developed his idea with the aid of his secretary, a Wren, and her make-up compact. He asked her to draw a horizontal line with her lipstick across the mirror of her opened compact and place it on a table. He then rigged a torch with a pencil beam at the end of the table and shining directly at the mirror. He asked the Wren to walk towards the table whilst keeping the beam's spot on the mirror on the lipstick line. As she did so she progressively had to stoop, eventually coming to a halt with her chin resting on the table several inches in from the edge. The Fresnel Lens, an American development of the sight, employs a system of lights rather than a mirror to create this 'meatball' and its effect.

*Steam-Powered Catapult.* Hydraulic catapults had previously been used on carriers for launching aircraft. However for the newer, larger and heavier aircraft, especially jets, a more powerful steam-powered version was required.

These modifications were also enthusiastically adopted by the US Navy. In 1952 the USS *Antietam* was the very first carrier to be converted with an angled deck. *Eagle* was subsequently modified, as was *Victorious*, both also being fitted with steam catapults and deck landing sights. *Ark Royal* received all these modifications in major changes to her design during construction, and *Centaur*, *Albion*, *Bulwark* and *Hermes* were all completed to this latest standard. Between 1954 and 1955, all the remaining World War 2-era carriers (except *Victorious*) were scrapped. With the introduction of the first mirror deck landing sights it was deemed by the FAA that LSOs would no longer be needed – a major error. However with many personnel continuing

*Top: Mirror landing sight on HMS* Albion.

*Bottom: Later projector sight.*

to be killed in carrier-landing accidents, the great majority being aircrew, LSOs were re-introduced.

Newer, more powerful aircraft, mainly jets, entered service throughout the 1950s, replacing the remaining piston-engined types and the Attacker. The Wyvern, Sea Hawk, Gannet and Sea Venom were followed by the Scimitar and Sea Vixen from 1957 onwards, the last two being the first twin-engined jets to be operated by the FAA. During the same period, Dragonfly helicopters entered service in the search and rescue/plane guard role, along with Whirlwinds for anti-submarine warfare (ASW) and troop-carrying operations.

Following nationalisation of the Suez Canal by Egypt in 1956 an Anglo-French-led invasion, Operation Musketeer, was undertaken to retain its control. The Allied governments viewed the takeover as a threat to their economic and strategic interests (especially those of the British and French 'East of Suez'). There was also the need for oil tankers and other ships to be able to pass through the canal unhindered. Due to the lack of suitable airfields from which to mount air operations, British carrier-borne aircraft played a crucial role. Sea Hawks, Sea Venoms, Wyverns and Skyraiders, all wearing invasion stripes to aid Allied recognition, operated from *Eagle*, *Albion* and *Bulwark*; whereas Whirlwind helicopters operated from *Ocean* and *Theseus* in the commando role. A ceasefire came into effect in November 1956 with *Eagle* and *Albion* providing air cover for the Allied withdrawal.

A further test for the FAA came in the summer of 1961. Iraq laid claim to the oil-rich territory of Kuwait, a former British Protected State. The only way to avoid a direct Iraqi invasion – which might be triggered by a build-up of British and Allied forces in Kuwait and nearby friendly countries – was to build up forces at sea. *Bulwark*, by then a commando carrier, and *Victorious* were dispatched to the area. After a short waiting game, it became apparent that Iraq was moving forces closer to the Kuwaiti border. Following a request from Kuwait's ruler *Bulwark*'s Whirlwinds landed commandos at the airport to prevent any Iraqi airborne assault and thus keep the runways open for reinforcements. *Victorious* arrived nearly two weeks later and started to provide air defence cover, as well as air traffic control of the Kuwaiti skies (RAF aircraft were by now also operating from the airport). *Centaur* had transited the Suez Canal in early July, but stood off at Aden awaiting further developments. Iraq backtracked on its claim to Kuwait. With the immediate threat over, *Bulwark* re-embarked her troops.

In the 1960s an AEW version of the Gannet replaced the Skyraider, and the Wessex superseded the Whirlwind in both ASW and commando roles. The general-purpose Wasp also entered service, operating from frigates and destroyers. Eventually the Buccaneer and the Phantom were introduced to replace the Scimitar and Sea Vixen. In July 1963 plans were announced for a new aircraft carrier, designated CVA-01 with a displacement of 50,000 tons. It was to be named *Queen Elizabeth* and would be vastly more capable than any of the existing carriers.

Between 1962 and 1965 *Bulwark* and *Albion*, the latter also having been converted for the helicopter-carrying commando role, were heavily involved in the Indonesian Confrontation; *Eagle*, *Victorious* and *Centaur* also played their part at various times. Although a rebellion in the Sultanate of Brunei had been quickly suppressed, rebels had taken refuge in the jungle, with some

CVA-01 HMS Queen Elizabeth.

crossing the Indonesian border. Re-armed, trained and bolstered by the Indonesians they initiated a guerrilla infiltration into Sarawak. British, Australian, New Zealand and Malaysian forces, supported by *Bulwark* and *Albion*, were engaged in the confrontation. Strike carriers deterred any attempts by the Indonesian navy from playing any serious part in the confrontation, which ended with an abortive *coup d'état* and subsequent military takeover in Indonesia in the autumn of 1965.

In 1963 Britain had adopted a policy of maintaining two strike and one commando carriers 'East of Suez', thus retaining a potent strike and amphibious force in the Indian Ocean and South East Asia. It could be called upon quickly when trouble brewed, as it did in Yemen. A civil war created a requirement for land and air forces to patrol the frontiers of the Aden Protectorate and the South Arabian Federation. This was largely carried out by land-based forces, although they were heavily dependent on sea-borne logistic and air support.

Another crisis erupted in January 1964 in eastern Africa involving revolutions, mutinies and rebel uprisings in Zanzibar, Tanganyika, Kenya and Uganda (all members of the British Commonwealth). Initially airfields were not available so aircraft carriers were essential for these operations. The strike carrier *Centaur* had just arrived at Aden where she embarked Royal Marines, and two troop-carrying RAF Belvedere helicopters. Once on station her helicopters landed troops ashore in order to secure strategic points such as airfields so that reinforcements could be flown in by the RAF, with air cover provided by her Sea Vixens. *Victorious* and *Albion* arrived later. After five weeks all the miscreants had been routed and defeated. These operations served as an excellent example of an aircraft carrier's inherent flexibility.

In November 1965 Rhodesia (now Zimbabwe) declared independence from Britain. This action was considered to be illegal and treasonable and an economic blockade of the 'new' nation was sought. Rhodesia's most critical import was oil. This normally reached the land-locked country via the port of Beira in Mozambique.

Britain imposed an oil blockade of the port, an operation known as the 'Beira Patrol'. Permission was granted to base RAF Shackletons in Madagascar. Limitations at their host base meant they were only able to fly in daylight; therefore carrier air power was deemed essential for the task. *Ark Royal* was detached from the Far East, taking up station to monitor merchant shipping, particularly oil tankers. This involved her aircraft flying long sorties in order to probe vast areas of the Indian Ocean. She was relieved by *Eagle*. Because land diversions couldn't be secured due to diplomatic issues, the carriers had to conduct non-diversion flying on a continuous 24-hour basis, averaging more than 20 sorties per day.

## DEMISE OF THE CONVENTIONAL CARRIERS AND THEIR FIXED-WING AIRCRAFT

In February 1966 whilst the Beira Patrol was still in operation, and being undertaken by 'indispensable' aircraft carriers, the British Labour government released its Defence White Paper with their commitment to withdraw forces from east of Suez (a reflection of the shrinking British Empire). It called for widescale reductions across the armed forces during the '60s and '70s. Amongst other things it stated that in future land-based aircraft would carry out all the airborne tasks required. It envisaged that Britain would only undertake major operations in concert with her allies. This White Paper sounded the death knell for the aircraft carriers and their fixed-wing aircraft, and construction of CVA-01 was immediately cancelled. The Minister of Defence for the RN, Christopher Mayhew, and the First Sea Lord, Adm Sir David Luce, both resigned.

In the interim British carriers continued to offer essential support to various

Victorious, Ark Royal *and* Hermes.

operations, including the withdrawal from Aden. As a result of its strategic position Aden had been a British protectorate since 1869, and a Crown Colony since 1937. The south Arabian region had been dogged by years of unrest fuelled by Arab nationalism and anti-colonialism. By late 1967 the federal government in Aden had collapsed, order was lost and British forces were increasingly coming under attack from insurgents. All British civilians and the majority of military personnel had already left the territory and, following negotiations with nationalist groups, the last British troops departed in November 1967. A Task Force was assembled in the Gulf of Aden to cover the withdrawal, including *Eagle*, *Albion* and the commando ship *Fearless*. The publication of the 1966 White Paper, and its consequent defence cuts, led to aircraft carriers becoming dirty words within the government. The RN had no choice but to start the disposal process, with *Centaur* going in 1966 (having been in commission for only 13 years) followed by *Victorious* in 1967. 'Vic' had re-entered service only nine years earlier, having been extensively modernised. However a fire, which broke out during a refit in 1966, provided the excuse needed for scrapping her. Whereas the US Navy designed and constructed its carriers to last anywhere between 30 and 50 years with refits, British carriers were being withdrawn after much shorter periods of service. *Albion* served for 19 years, from 1954 to 1973, and even the large carriers *Eagle* and *Ark Royal* lasted less than 25 years each. *Bulwark*, commissioned in 1954, served until 1981 (27 years). Entering service in 1959, *Hermes* probably gave the most valuable and flexible service – as a conventional, commando, ASW and V/STOL (vertical/short take-off and landing) carrier. She survived until 1986 when, also at the age of 27 years, she was sold to India.

The scrapping of Gannets and Sea Vixens commenced in the early 1970s after which the Phantoms and Buccaneers, as had been ordained in the 1966 White Paper, started being transferred to the RAF. *Ark Royal* continued to operate Phantoms, Buccaneers and Gannets (as well as Sea Kings and Wessex) until late 1978, a Gannet of 849B Flight making the last arrested landing aboard a British carrier on Saturday 18 November. The RAF then took over the remaining RN fast jets.

### V/STOL-CAPABLE CARRIERS AND THEIR AIRCRAFT

Despite the loss of its conventional carriers, and their aircraft, the RN was still faced with a requirement to provide air defence protection of the fleet, a role which could clearly could not be carried out by helicopters. The V/STOL Harrier had entered RAF service in 1969. During its development it had proved its ability to operate from ships' decks, leading to the development of the Sea Harrier. By 1973 the RN had ordered three small CVS carriers which would come to operate Sea Harriers as well as helicopters; for political reasons they were initially called 'Through-Deck Cruisers'. These ships were the brainchild of Lord Mountbatten and were initially derided as not being 'real' aircraft carriers. The first of the class *Invincible* entered service in 1980 – as did the Sea Harrier. The ship had a unique feature – an upswept forward section of the flight deck known as the 'ski jump'. This increased the aircraft's vertical momentum during a non-catapult-assisted launch, enabling heavier weapon and fuel loads to be carried than would have been the case if launching from a flat deck. The concept has been retained on the new *Queen Elizabeth* and *Prince of Wales* ships.

The role and effectiveness of the ski jump/Harrier carrier concept on *Invincible* and *Hermes*, was completely vindicated during the Falklands campaign. This could

*CVS* Ark Royal, Illustrious *and* Invincible.

not have been so successful without tactical and naval air power (there were no friendly airfields within efficient operating range of the Falklands). After the islands had been reclaimed, air defence cover was still needed and *Invincible* remained in the South Atlantic to provide it. Here again was a classic demonstration of the value of the projection of power using sea-borne aircraft. The newly completed *Illustrious* was rapidly deployed – so rapidly in fact that she was commissioned while at sea – and replaced *Invincible* in September 1982. Many lessons were learned as a result of the Falklands campaign, one being the absence of ship-borne AEW. This subsequently led to Sea Kings being modified to perform the role. The new carrier fleet was finally completed when *Ark Royal* was commissioned in 1985.

The next FAA operation was during the 1991 Gulf War, following Iraq's invasion of Kuwait. In the opening days of the conflict the destroyers *Cardiff* and *Gloucester* employed their missile-armed Lynx helicopters to help neutralise Iraqi naval power, whilst Sea Kings provided heavy lift support to British forces ashore. After the war Sea Harriers flew air defence patrols in support of the Anglo-Saudi-American enforcement of the no-fly zone over Southern Iraq.

Meanwhile in the Balkans, the persecution and 'ethnic cleansing' of Kosovo Albanians by Federal Republic of Yugoslavia (FRY, comprising Serbia and Montenegro) forces had started in the early 1990s. The potential for the destabilisation of the region provoked intervention by the UN and NATO. Operation Deny Flight commenced in April 1993 to enforce a no-fly zone over Bosnia and Herzegovina. From February 1998 to June 1999 the mission was expanded, under Operation Allied Force, to include offensive and reconnaissance missions against Bosnian targets. During that period all three *Invincible*-class carriers were involved, at one time or another, employing Sea Harriers for air defence, ground attack and reconnaissance. Sea Kings aided refugee evacuations and supported UN-sponsored troops ashore. Hostilities ended when an agreement was reached that led to the withdrawal of FRY forces from Kosovo.

Throughout the 1990s, and later, *Invincible, Illustrious* and *Ark Royal* were in turn rotated between the Gulf and Balkan theatres of operation. Ironically, in the late 1990s, the Labour government had become so impressed with the flexibility of sea-borne air power that it sanctioned two new large V/STOL aircraft carriers. The philosophy of Joint Operations had already been accepted, and this led to helicopters from all services and RN Sea Harriers/RAF Harriers being operated from carriers.

In April 2000 the Sea Harrier force was merged with the RAF's Harrier GR.7 fleet to form Joint Force Harrier. In that same year *Illustrious* led a task group, comprising several ships, with the aim of restoring peace and stability to Sierra Leone where a civil war had broken out. Her Sea Harriers, RAF Harriers, and helicopters flew in support of operations ashore, including reconnaissance missions and evacuation of British and foreign citizens. The invasion of Iraq in 2003 saw *Ark Royal* returning to the Gulf to support operations, although only with helicopters. Later RN-operated Harriers and RN commando helicopters, also provided air support in Afghanistan flying from land bases.

Budgetary pressures forced the RN to withdraw the Sea Harrier from service in 2006. In March 2007 the Naval Strike Wing was formed, with both RN and RAF pilots flying Harrier GR.7/GR.9s from carriers and shore bases. However, again for economic reasons, all these aircraft were withdrawn from service following the 2010 Strategic Defence and Security Review (SDSR). The last ever Harrier flight from an RN carrier took place on 24 November 2010 from *Ark Royal* flown by Lt Cdr James Blackmore.

## TODAY'S CARRIERS AND AIRCRAFT

The two large V/STOL aircraft carriers, which were sanctioned in the late-1990s, comprise *Queen Elizabeth* and her sister ship *Prince of Wales*. They each have a displacement of 65,000 tons and are the largest ships ever to be operated by the RN. *Queen Elizabeth* was commissioned in December 2017 and is currently working-up with the F-35B version of the stealthy Lightning II strike fighter. *Prince of Wales*, commissioned in December 2019, is also conducting sea trials. As well as the F-35B, these ships will operate Merlin (including AEW variants) and Wildcat helicopters, plus those of the Army and RAF during joint force operations.

The introduction into service of the *Queen Elizabeth* class and the F-35B heralds a renaissance in British fixed-wing carrier air power. While the pros and cons of V/STOL versus 'cat and trap' (conventional carrier) operations will probably be debated ad infinitum, there is no doubt that these new ships and aircraft provide a quantum leap in capability over their predecessors. The current plan is for a force of 139 F-35Bs, of which the UK has committed to 48 to date. No. 809 Naval Air Squadron will be the first FAA and second UK front-line unit (the first being 617 Squadron RAF) to be equipped with the aircraft. All F-35B squadrons,

Queen Elizabeth *and* Prince of Wales *in Portsmouth.*

including the operational conversion unit (207 Squadron, RAF), have a mix of both FAA and RAF air and ground crew, whether operating on board ship or from a shore base.

Running through all the stories in these pages is a mixture of the routine, the exciting, the boring, the funny and inevitably, the tragic times when things went wrong and I have endeavoured to ensure that all these aspects are balanced. One theme that appears in many of the stories is a 'love–hate' relationship between the FAA and the RAF, but the real respect they had for each other was nicely expressed by a former RAF Shackleton pilot Bob Lyall:

> "I shall look forward to reading *Fleet Air Arm Boys* – bloody mad, that lot! But then they had to be to do the job they did, didn't they? March hares the lot of them but, by Golly, I take my hat off to them."

The response to my appeals for contact with Fleet Air Arm 'Boys' was overwhelming with more than 120 coming forward with their memories (sadly not an 'FAA Girl' amongst them). It became clear at an early stage in my research, that in order to ensure that as many of their great stories as possible – be they routine, exciting, humorous or sad – reached a wider audience, more than one volume was essential, hence the content breakdown explained at the start of this introduction. This has only been possible with the help of the following people, who have so enthusiastically allowed me into their homes, burnt the midnight oil writing down their memories, endured lengthy telephone calls, answered interminable questions and granted access to their precious logbooks and private photograph collections.

John Adams, David Allan, Paul Bennett, Chris Bolton, George Brewes, David Brown, Micky Brown, the late Peter Carmichael, Gene Carolan, Paul Chaplin, Ron Chitty, Mike Cole-Hamilton, Colin Coleman, Nick Cook, Dave Cooper, Andy Copeland, Keith Cotton, Bill Covington, John Coward, Bob Crane, John Crossley, John de Winton, Richard Dickinson, John Dixon, Dave Eagles, Bob Edward, David Edwards, Rob Faulkner, Ed Featherstone, Matt Fooks-Bale, John Ford, Harry Frost, Michael Garforth, Tim Gedge, Steve George, Tim Goetz, Peter Goodwin, Nathan Gray, Julie Halford, the late Tony Hayward, Peter Hiles, Vernon Hopcroft, Chris James,

Mervyn Jones, John Keenan, Lou Kemp, Alan Key, Jeremy Kyd, Michael Layard, Stuart Leeming, Douglas Macdonald, Murdo Macleod, Reg Maitland, Jock Mancais, Terry McDonald, Roger Meecham, Richard Moody, Ian Moor, Dave Morgan, Colin Morris, Pat Mountain, Andrew Neofytou, Mike Norman, Brent Owen, Henry Parker, Graham Peck, Brian Phillips, Noel Pinder, Tony Pinney, Graham Pitchfork, Chris Pugsley, Keith Quilter, Peter Randall, Alan Reed, John Roberts, Jack Routley, David Rye, Tony Sanders, Sandy Saunders, Robert Scott, Dick Searles, Arnold Sedgewick, Kim Sharman, the late Pete Sheppard, Richard Sheridan, Tony Smith, Jim Speirs, Anthony Stephens, Digby Stephenson, Bill Stocker, John Sturgeon, Allan Tarver, Tony Tayler, Mark Thomson, Tim Thorley, Jonathan Tod, Robin Trewinnard-Boyle, Adrian Tuite, the late Doug Turner, Richard Vandervord, Stuart Wakefield, Nigel 'Sharkey' Ward, Paul Waterhouse, Simon Watts, David Webb, Jonathon Whaley and Denis Woodhams. Gentlemen, I thank and salute you all.

Many others have helped along the way, including: Richard Andrews, Richard Ansley, Adrian Balch, Tony Buttler, Martin Grant, John Hughes, Chris Lofting, Bob Lyall, Pat Martin, Dr Ray Neve who transcribed many interview recordings, Jon Parkinson and Rob Jones of Navy Wings, Jeff Peck, Paul Richards, Martin Rotheram, David Rye, Nick Sellers, Robbie Shaw, Drew Steel, Tim Lewin, Stephen Wolf, and David Winterbottom. I must also express my gratitude to John Davies, Natalie Parker and Lucy Thorne at Grub Street, who continue to support and encourage my literary endeavours. Finally, and most especially, my thanks and love go to my darling wife Heather, who is the driving force and support for this project, providing endless ideas and advice, sense-reading and proof-reading the manuscripts.

I have endeavoured to credit correctly the origins of all the photographs and other material I have used. However, in the internet age, the true origins and source of some material is not always possible to identify with certainty. If I have omitted anyone, please accept my apologies and grateful thanks.

Dr Steve Bond
April 2020

## CHAPTER ONE

# AIRCREW TRAINING

## PILOT TRAINING

A 1950s' recruitment poster for the Royal Navy.

*Prospective navy pilots are initially put through a short flying grading course to assess their suitability. Successful students are then streamed onto fast jets or helicopters depending on their abilities, whilst those who do not make the grade may be offered a transfer to observer training (navigator in the RAF). On 14 June 1960 Britannia Flight was formed at Roborough, Plymouth the nearest airfield to the Britannia Royal Naval College (BRNC) at Dartmouth. Operated by Airwork Ltd, Tiger Moths were used until 1966 when they were replaced by Chipmunks. The operation was later taken over by a civilian contractor, then on 6 December 2001, 727 Naval Air Squadron (NAS) was reformed at Roborough to continue the grading. In 1994 the Chipmunks were replaced by Grob G.115 Herons. The unit moved to Yeovilton in January 2007 where it continues to run three-week courses giving each student 12 hours flying.*

### Mike Cole-Hamilton

Mike Cole-Hamilton.

"As part of our basic training at the Dartmouth Naval College we were introduced to flight. The Tiger Moth was ideally suited to giving us air experience. In the autumn of 1962, I had reached the stage where my civilian instructor reckoned I was safe to solo. It sounds so straightforward – take-off, fly one circuit and land! Logically, it's simple if it weren't for the humans involved (the instructor and the student pilot).

"The student had approximately ten hours dual instruction – always with an instructor to take control if things got dodgy. So much to take in at first – taxiing, take-off, control of power, use of the stick and rudder in three dimensions, descent, approach and landing. But most of all, stalling! Learning what happens when you go too slowly to maintain lift, and therefore flight. Stalling near the ground is not a good thing so it is learnt at a safe height. This, of course, means no obvious visual reference of height lost unless there's a convenient flat bit of cloud around, and there never was. So you have to use the altimeter to see how much height you've lost – and this can be quite startling. Recovery means stick forward instantly, but cautiously, and increase power until flying speed is reached – using rudder not stick to combat any tendency to roll. Then ensure a positive rate of climb.

"With a first solo the instructor has a huge responsibility. He signed for the aircraft but has to be confident he can safely step out and let the student fly it alone. The student's state of mind can vary from 'Let me get at it!' confidence to intense nervousness. Most of us were somewhere in between. Whatever the case this is a monster first step. One's first flight alone in any aircraft is exciting, but pilots agree that their very first solo is incomparable. Mine came on 10 October 1962, a perfect autumn day.

"'OK, you're on your own! Take-off, normal circuit and land – you'll be fine' said Mr Hawkins. I taxied cautiously to the downwind end of the field with the pre-take-off checklist spinning in my head. This is me, alone in the aircraft. No other aircraft on approach, green light from the tower, turn into wind, open the throttle and a much-lightened Tiger Moth surges forward. OK, tail up, take-off speed already, stick back lightly and up into a sunny autumn sky over Devonshire. That's the easy bit and it's exhilarating.

"What a view! But events stop me from looking – 500 feet, turn 90 degrees to port, 1,000 feet (got there quickly!) so throttle back and turn 90 degrees port onto the downwind leg. Downwind checks and take a look at the windsock and the landing T beside the tower to make certain the take-off and landing direction hasn't been changed. A brief look around – Plymouth and Devonport off to my right and over my right shoulder with the sea beyond, the Channel coast and the soft farm-lands of the South Hams ahead to the right. Dartmoor, dark and slightly sinister even in warm sunlight, ahead and left with the deep valley of the River Meavy, sinuous green and wooded in my 10 o'clock position.

"Throttle back and start coming down, turn 90 degrees port and watch for the line of approach to the field. A final 90-degree turn just before the line and the field lies ahead. Keep an eye on airspeed. A bit high, throttle back but watch that airspeed, this is no time for a stall. Houses, trees and hangars regain three dimen-sions and perspective. The drystone wall at the near end of the field takes on a solid aspect, individual blades of grass appear. Floating down to the grass, height looks OK, throttle right back, keep holding the nose up and...BUMP BUMP! Not a perfect three-point landing and a bit solid, but we are back on the ground and slowing down. There was now so much more to learn, but the sensation of having taken that first step alone is incomparable."

## ELEMENTARY AND ADVANCED TRAINING

*The Royal Navy Elementary Flying Training School (RNEFTS) was formed within the RAF's No. 2 Flying Training School (FTS) at Church Fenton in April 1973, moving to Leeming in November 1974 to join 3 FTS, flying the Chipmunk and later the Bulldog. It moved to Linton-on-Ouse in April 1984 and Topcliffe in April 1993. The school combined with army flying training in May 1995 to form the Joint Elementary Training School at Barkston Heath, near Cranwell. Initially flying the Slingsby T67, the unit re-equipped with Grob Tutors and now the Grob Prefect. Since 2003 it has operated as 703 Squadron.*

### Andrew Neofytou

*Andrew Neofytou.*

"I had done a bit of flying before I started flying training with the Royal Navy. As I had an air force flying scholarship when I was 16, I was able to get my private pilot's licence (PPL) when I was only just 17. I continued flying on Manchester and Salford University Air Squadron at Woodvale and had about 100 hours flying by the time I entered elementary flying training.

"I joined the navy at the end of 1996, and started training at Barkston Heath on the T67 Firefly which gave a broad background. By the time we got to the end of elementary training we were streamed to either rotary or fast jet. There were about 20 of us going through the course and just two of us got streamed to fast jet, myself and Tim Flatman, who was the first Royal Navy boss of the F-35 OCU (207 Squadron). We went off to Linton-on-Ouse for jet training – at that stage you needed to have all the credentials to be a fast jet pilot."

*Following operational tours on both the Sea Vixen and Phantom, **Paul Chaplin** was selected for training as a qualified flying instructor (QFI).*

"I went to the Central Flying School (CFS) to qualify as an instructor then off to the RNEFTS at Church Fenton where we trained navy helicopter pilots before they learned to fly helicopters. It was quite a shock for me from flying the Phantom to go to the Chipmunk. I thought I was going to the Gnat or the Jet Provost, but because we didn't have any fixed-wing pilots coming through there were none to train. The posting I went to was normally a 're-tread' helicopter QFI or a Gannet pilot's tour, but now we had Buccaneer and Phantom pilots doing it as well. Once you got back into the Chipmunks it was very enjoyable, you really get back to the basics of flying."

*The RAF's 1 FTS was formed on 23 December 1919 at Netheravon, Wiltshire and was responsible for training officers of the Fleet Air Arm. That task was taken over by RAF Leuchars on 15 February 1928, and then passed back to a reformed 1 FTS on 1 April 1935, still at Leuchars. The unit retained the FAA training task from that point on.*

*On 18 June 1947 1 FTS reformed at Spitalgate, Lincolnshire with Harvards and Tiger Moths, disbanding again on 25 February 1948. It reformed on 1 December 1950 at Oakington, and there followed moves to Moreton-in-Marsh in 1951, Syerston in May 1955 where it absorbed 22 FTS which had also trained navy pilots, and finally on to Linton-on-Ouse in November 1957. During that period the aircraft used went from the Prentice to Piston Provost, plus Chipmunk and Vampire, then Jet Provosts from 1961. From December 1966 the unit was also referred to as 1 (Naval) FTS. In 1995 the Tucano arrived. From October 2019, pilot training transferred to 4 FTS Valley with the T-6C Texan followed by the Hawk for the advanced stage to wings, and after 100 years 1 FTS ceased to be.*

## SYERSTON

### Nick Cook

"I was sent off to join No.18 Pilots' Course at Donibristle in September '49 to do the three months pre-flight schooling. The course finished at Christmas and in January '50 we went to 22 FTS at Syerston. This was the designated unit which trained pilots for the navy under the Inskip Defence Review of 1937, whereby the navy got back control of its aviation (although training to wings standard was still done by the RAF). At Syerston I did six months on the Percival Prentice – it had replaced the Tiger Moth in early '49.

*Nick Cook.*

"The Prentice had the advantage of being a side-by-side trainer. It had a six-cylinder Gipsy Queen engine which gave a much better performance than the Tiger Moth. Halfway through 1950 we went onto the Harvard, which was very demanding as a training aircraft. I reckon if you could fly a Harvard you could fly anything. It was a high-performance aeroplane and had toe brakes, unlike the British pneumatic ones on the stick. It could ground-loop at the drop of a hat if you let it swing. A third of the instructors at Syerston were navy who'd been through CFS; the rest were all RAF hard-bitten QFIs. The RAF could never – nor could the navy – get to terms with the right career structure. You had men who'd commanded Lancasters in the sergeants' mess when the navigator might have been a pilot officer (Plt Off) or a flying officer (Fg Off) – it was all topsy-turvy. In the late '40s they got to grips with it and created the P-branch (P1 to P3) – it was a mad idea. Quite a few of the instructors were P3s. I had one for a time but they were generally flying officers, flight lieutenants (Flt Lt) or naval lieutenants (Lt), some of whom went on to distinction because the QFI qualification was regarded as a good career step for a young aviator."

## Jock Mancais

*Jock Mancais.*

"During our early professional courses as a sub lieutenant (Sub-Lt) we were given 25 hours flying in Tiger Moths at HMS Siskin Gosport. We had to pay for five hours if we wanted a certificate, but that started me off and I was assessed as average and capable of flying without breaking my b\*\*\*dy neck. When I was serving as a junior lieutenant on the destroyer *Crossbow* in 1951 I really got the bug when we were 'plane guard watching all these chaps making a 'Horlicks' of landing Sea Furies aboard *Indomitable*. I thought I could do better than that – and decided to go for it. I went to Syerston for basic flying training on the Prentice. You sat up front side-by-side with each other. This was very useful for the station commander who would fly away at the weekend, putting his dog in the other seat! They asked whether you'd like to go to fighters or anti-submarine. There was no guarantee that you'd get what you asked for, but I asked for fighters – it suited my temperament."

## Rob Faulkner

"I did my flying training on the Provost at Syerston. We went along at a nice pace, and then there was a ten- or 12-hour progress check at around solo time. There was a 50-hour progress check with the flight commander, an independent instructor, a progress check and then you were into final nav and final handling. Then there were instrument ratings and things like that but there were very few check-rides or 'chop-rides', as they were known. There didn't seem to be the same pressure at all."

*Rob Faulkner with Vampire FB.5 or 9, 7 FTS Valley, 1956.*

# LINTON-ON-OUSE

### Jonathan Tod

"I started off on the first ever Jet Provost course at 1
FTS Linton-on-Ouse – in the navy we boast that we
did jet training before the air force did. Then I went
on from the Jet Provost to the Vampire, when I got my
wings. Next to Lossiemouth and started flying Sea
Hawks (we also had Vampire trainers), on 736 and
738 Squadrons."

*Jonathan Tod.*

### Mike Cole-Hamilton

"Linton-on-Ouse was run by the RAF for the benefit
of the Royal Navy. Apart from the naval fixed-wing students on the Jet Provost and
Vampire, and naval helicopter student pilots in Chipmunks, there were plenty of
dark blues all over the place. Linton was commanded by a group captain but also
had a senior naval officer (SNO), a commander (Cdr) with his own staff. A chief
ground instructor kept us up to the mark for parades – we hoisted the White Ensign every morning.

"At every wings parade 'Groupie' and the SNO were up front, backed by RAF
and RN instructors and staff. In 1963 Bill Hawley took over as SNO. He was a man
of strong opinions, outgoing, not afraid to speak up and an intensely loyal and
wise commanding officer. The VIP awarding wings on this occasion was the may-
or of York. A nice man but like so many, not fully aware of the navy's air branch.
In his speech he managed to drop two superb bricks in the first few words of a
sentence: 'You young raff boys' – 'Groupie' flinched visibly – 'of the Fleet Arm' – Bill
Hawley went purple. The rest of us on parade facing the VIPs stood rigidly to attention and did our best to keep straight faces. To this day when people hear that
I flew they assume that it was with the Royal Air Force. I tell them proudly I was
with the Fleet Air Arm – some get it."

### Kim Sharman

"There was a naval flight at Linton with both navy and RAF QFIs. My QFI was a
really nice chap, a flight lieutenant called Pat Kidgell. The early days were pretty
hectic with people being 'chopped' left, right, and centre. In March '67 came the
presentation of our wings. I was awarded the trophy that everybody wanted, the
Aerobatic Trophy. I was flying against a guy called Ken Lamprey – he and I had
shared a cabin at Dartmouth. Whilst I was standing in the flight line hut Ken came
in – he'd obviously been at a p***-up the night before. I've got this trophy in the
bag I thought – which I had."

# VALLEY

### Rob Faulkner

"Valley for 7 FTS and Vampire T.11s. We were the last course to graduate from there, the next course No.64 went to Linton. It was marvellous and far more relaxed in those days.

"My main recollection of flying the Vampire was how smooth and quiet it felt after the Tiger Moth and the Provost. The acceleration was far greater and you could see the runway streaming past under the nose. It was a beautiful aeroplane to fly, a bit cramped in the side-by-side cockpit (which was never designed for ejection seats), but light on the controls, well balanced for aerobatics, and very sensitive for formation flying. There was a short period after take-off when you were too slow to turn back, and too low to eject, with very little choice if you had an engine failure – but at 19 years old you know no fear and these sorts of possibilities didn't worry you.

"My primary instructor was a wonderful master pilot (later Flt Lt) Pete Quinton, who claimed to have more hours on Vampires than the rest of the instructors put together. He was very quiet and unassuming but made it clear that he expected perfection – he could make the T.11 eat out of his hand. I arrived back near the threshold one day on a practice flame-out approach, far too high to get down on the runway. Pete took over saying 'don't try this unless you are desperate'. He slowed right down to near stalling, did a very steep descending 'S' turn, and placed it right on the numbers at the beginning of the runway.

"We also flew single-seat Vampire FB.5s and 9s – real front-line fighters. They had no ejection seat, which made it much easier to strap in but which gave pause for thought when we went off to practise a high-speed run. Climb to 40,000 feet, roll into a 30-degree dive at full throttle and experience compressibility (at about Mach .8). At this sort of speed you felt the buffeting. The shock waves blanketed the tailplane so, with an indicated speed of probably about 300 knots at 30,000 feet, you could move the elevators from full up to full down with no effect whatsoever…this with the ground below getting rapidly larger in the windscreen! Everybody said 'close the throttle, pop the airbrakes, and you will be OK when you reach 20,000 feet and the air gets thicker', but you did start to wonder if they were right.

"Night flying took place in July, right at the height of the tourist holiday season, and couldn't start until about 11 o'clock because until then it was still daylight. Valley is on Anglesey between Rhosneigr and Trearddur Bay, and the circuit is always on the south side. This means that you climb out over one of them at 100 per cent throttle and approach over the other at about 90 per cent throttle. By about midnight the station commander got fed up answering the complaints so they routed them through to us down at the squadron. We were not particularly sympathetic – we were working and didn't see why everybody else shouldn't suffer with us.

"Accidents were unfortunately regular in those days. One member of the course ahead of ours, in a Vampire 5, failed to stop on the short runway and finished up in the middle of the pond next to the officers' mess. The pond was only a few feet deep and we were very impressed when he managed to paddle ashore in his dinghy before the rescue boys got to him. Another student, on the same course, had an engine failure on a cross country somewhere in mid Wales – he and his instructor managed to eject safely and came down in a farmyard.

"I made a visit in a Vampire 9 to the gliding club where I originally learned to fly. I was en route from Worksop back to Valley at 2,000 feet and couldn't resist a quick flyby. I saw the resident steward walking his dog up the airfield and managed to make him lie down flat on his face – he never forgave me for that.

"We lost three people off our course. One was number three in a tail-chase, flying a Vampire 5, and he probably blacked out trying to follow the first two round a loop and sadly failed to pull out. They later discovered he'd had nothing for breakfast – you've got to have a solid breakfast before flying. The other two were killed in Sea Hawks, from Lossie, just after they left Valley. Jackie Veres was doing a cross country to Valley, was too tight on finals and went in. Dave Hicks did the same thing doing dummy deck landings at Milltown. One Vampire had an engine flame-out on the course in front of us – they banged out. Apart from that I've managed to avoid any excitement due to my superior skills to avoid them!

"Towards the end of the course they asked who wanted to go where. The alternatives were Sea Venom, Sea Hawk or Gannet. We were the first course to be invited to go onto the Sea Venom. Previously, progress to night fighters had always been a second-tourist job, but two of us who'd passed out well volunteered for Venoms. At Lossiemouth we were the first to do the day fighter course flying the Sea Venom – it was brand new and totally unfamiliar to them. We found it to be a better weapons platform than the Sea Hawk – this didn't go down at all well with the day fighter boys. It had just that bit of extra span, and therefore a slightly lower wing loading, so it was not quite as manoeuvrable but steadier. We got better than average results on air-to-air and air-to-ground."

### Andy Copeland

"The Vampire T.11 was a huge learning curve for me. Newly graduated from Syerston in Provosts, No. 51 Course of Royal Navy trainee pilots arrived at Valley in November 1955 for jet conversion and training to wings standards. This aircraft was cumbersome and cramped (a very tight fit for anyone but a dwarf), however, it was our first jet and therefore very exciting. It certainly proved to be an adequate two-seat training aircraft and I accumulated 46 hours on type during this period. If I was to summarise my feelings about flying it the word that comes to mind is – 'boring'. Later in my career I would

*Andy Copeland.*

never volunteer to fly this aircraft if there was something more interesting to fly.

"Our FB.5s were well-used ex-front-line fighter aircraft with the gunsight and cannons removed and no ejection seat. We were introduced to the marvels of jet flight with eight sorties with an instructor in the T.11, followed by a solo. All being well we were then strapped into the FB.5 and told to go and fly it. My turn came on 21 December 1955.

"To me this little aircraft was wondrous and in complete contrast to the cramped, ponderous T.11. In the FB.5 the cockpit was roomy, the visibility all-round was superb and the controls were light and responsive. It was easy to fly, to land, to fly in formation and an absolute joy when doing aerobatics; more so than any other aircraft that I have flown. It must have had some vices; we lost a couple of course mates to fatal crashes and I remember the briefing on bailing out which was, basically, DON'T! The chances of clearing the tailplane were reckoned to be zero.

"I got my wings in May 1956 having accumulated 44.45 hours on the FB.5. This brought to an end my love affair with this aircraft, except for one flight a few months later when a volunteer was wanted to take an FB.5 from Ford up to Lossiemouth. I jumped at the chance and flew it with drop-tanks for the first time."

## TYPE CONVERSION AND OPERATIONAL TRAINING

*Conversion to fly an operational type was split into two parts, Operational Flying School (OFS) I and II. These were initially flown at a variety of different units, but in August 1952 736 Squadron reformed at Culdrose as an Advanced Jet Flying School with Attackers and Meteors, moving to Lossiemouth in November 1953 – later flying Sea Vampires and Sea Hawks, with Scimitars arriving in June 1959. In March 1965 the squadron changed roles to become the Jet Strike Training Squadron.*

*Other units that played a major part in OFS included 738 Squadron which reformed at Culdrose in May 1950, with Seafires and Sea Furies, moving to Lossiemouth in 1953 where it received Sea Vampires and Sea Hawks. Sea Venoms arrived in late 1957 followed by Hunters in June 1962. In 1964 the unit moved to Brawdy to continue training in fighter tactics and weapon release until disbandment in May 1970. Similarly 759 Squadron reformed in 1951 at Culdrose with Seafires and Firebrands, adding Meteors and Sea Vampires in 1952 before disbanding in 1954. It reformed at Brawdy in 1963 for Part I of the Advanced Flying Training Course with Hunter T.8s, remaining there until disbandment on 24 December 1969.*

*Lossiemouth housed 764 Squadron from 1957 until 1972. Primarily equipped with Hunter T.8s and GA.11s for air weapons and air warfare instructor (AWI) training, Scimitars were briefly added in 1965 for type conversion.*

## John Roberts

"Twenty of us went up to the north of Scotland to Rattray Head, north of Aberdeen, and converted to the Firefly for operational training Part 1. Then we flew all the aircraft down to St Merryn in Cornwall to do Part 2. That was firing the guns and the rockets! – taking me up to the end of 1946. In January 1947 I was at Eglinton in Northern Ireland and converted to the Seafire Mk.3, which was very similar to the early Spitfire – it was a very light aircraft. I was there for three months and was then appointed to 800 Squadron with the Seafire 17 to join *Triumph* for my first tour out in the Med."

## Nick Cook

"We got our wings at the end of 1950 and went off to Lossiemouth for operational flying school Part 1. This was three months on Seafire 17s with the Griffon engine. It had a bubble canopy, which was a great improvement, and three of us teamed up with a naval flying instructor. My three were an engineer pilot, a short-service midshipman, Tommy Tomlinson, and me, an RNVR (Royal Navy Volunteer Reserve). The instructors weren't necessarily QFIs but they were very hardened squadron pilots. So we did flight drill the whole time – navigation, low level and high level. When I volunteered for flying I'd already done 18 months as a naval airman 2nd Class and had to renounce that to have two years clear for the pilot's course.

"The Seafire was wonderful – I did 107 hours in three months. My instructor was Peter Hutton, a highly decorated wartime service fellow. Of the three students Tommy Tomlinson was killed in an Attacker two years later, and Ken McDonald, the engineer pilot, was shot down in Korea on his first sortie and killed. Neither of them made 24 years old – appalling!

"At the end of March '51 we started OFS Part 2 at Culdrose on the Sea Fury, which had only come into service in 1947. This was weapons training involving low-level bombing with 25-lb practice bombs and a lot of rocketing. They had four old Sherman tanks perched on a cliff in north Cornwall, just to the east of Newquay on Treligga range. The range had a retired fisherman in a hut who would plot your dive, and the fall of shots of the four-inch rockets, registering the hits. There was a lot of camera gun work and then some air-to-air firing. The last month was taken up with assisted dummy deck landings (ADDL). These were done at Predannack on the western side of the Lizard, which had been a Beaufighter airfield during the war. Vickers had a presence there trying to perfect something all very secret (Barnes Wallis's Swallow project). We did ADDLs on the runway, round and round and round, with the highly trained batsmen who would eventually take you to deck. You did eight, had a break, then eight more. I must have done over a hundred landings. You didn't bother to do your parachute up because you never got above 200 feet. By the end of it all you could fly it really accurately to one knot."

## David Edwards

*David Edwards.*

"I arrived at HMS Seahawk (Culdrose) for conversion to Firefly T.2s, AS.6s and T.7s. The Firefly was a bit of a 'work-horse', especially the T.7 with two in the back, but the Griffon engines were superb. The AS.6 was better to fly, but compared with jets their performance was somewhat lacking. After this I only had another three months until the end of my two years National Service so I joined 1844 Squadron of the Midland Air Division (RNVR) at HMS Gamecock, Bramcote. Here I flew the Firefly and Sea Fury until the end of my National Service in November 1955, however I then continued as a 'weekend flyer' in the RNVR. In early 1956 there was a call for jet-trained pilots to join sister squadron 1833 to fly Sea Vampire T.22s and Attackers at RAF Honiley. I accepted, and after a couple of hours re-familiarisation in a Sea Vampire T.22 I was 'introduced' to the Attacker – the first single-seater I had flown which didn't have a similar two-seat trainer."

## Richard Sheridan

"I went to Lossiemouth to do the OFS on 736 Squadron Sea Hawks. We did weaponry, air-to-air camera, then live ammunition and bombing/rocketing. By then the Sea Hawk was at the end of its career and used exclusively for ground attack. It was a great little aeroplane and very easy to fly. It had powered ailerons and quite a large stick so you got a good pull on it. In about September or October '59 I eventually joined 806 Squadron at Brawdy where I continued to train (I was a 'sprog' pilot). As we were going to sea in January, we worked up a lot. We had quite a few new-ish pilots who hadn't been to the deck before, so when we did eventually embark there were quite a lot of us milling around not knowing what we were doing.

"We'd done lots of MADDLs (mirror-assisted dummy deck landings) of course

*Richard Sheridan.*

– they said that deck landings improved your MADDLs no end. We did some at Lossie and some at Brawdy. We embarked in *Albion* in January 1960, and did a couple of approaches with the hook up, arrestor wires down, and a couple of 'touch-and-goes'. On the first pass I was nowhere near the deck, floating past the whole lot; I was somewhere amongst the wires on the second 'go'. They said 'hook down' on the next circuit and I managed to grab a wire. Very frightening, the first time you did it.

"Night landings – I was petrified. Being a day fighter squadron, our boss made us night fly once a month. So one night we would do a dusk take-off, and then a night landing – the anticipation was horrific. Later I was on an all-weather squadron, where we did a lot of night flying and I got used to it. But when you only do it once a month it's very off putting."

### Andy Copeland

"In 1956 I went to Lossiemouth to join 738 Squadron flying Sea Hawks. This was preparing us for service at sea, and for intensive instrument flying and air weaponry training we also had a couple of Sea Vampire T.22s. As a gun platform the Sea Hawk was very steady. Advanced fighter and ground-attack tactics were then learned in 764 Squadron, again in Sea Hawks and Sea Vampire T.22s. From Lossiemouth I went to Ford to join 767 Squadron, again in Sea Hawks with the T.22 for dual training and instrument flying checks."

### Mike Layard

"During the operational flying training, which I was doing at Lossiemouth, you had the choice of either staying in the ground-attack world or going to the fighter world. Ground attack would have meant staying at Lossiemouth, whereas the fighter boys were at Yeovilton. I was driven by my social life as much as anything else. If anything I'd quite like to be down south. My connections to London and friends were almost the deciding factor. That's how I ended up as a fighter pilot, the Sea Venom to start with. I was in the very last Sea Venom squadron with a delightful boss called Micky Brown and then converted to the Vixen – and the Hunter, of course."

### Jonathan Tod

"The first time I flew a Sea Hawk was on 15 December 1961, when I was on 736 Squadron for six months. The Sea Hawk was probably the nicest aeroplane I have ever flown, absolutely lovely – it was so forgiving. You could do a quick spin on the downwind leg and still recover and do a good landing at the end of it. You could do tail-slides in it, you could do anything. I loved it so much I actually had a Sea Hawk on top of my wedding cake when I got married. It was such a change – before that we had the Attacker, our first jet fighter and an absolute disaster.

"From the Sea Hawk we flew the Hunter T.8 which was a better performance aircraft, before going on to the Scimitar. The Hunter is a beautiful aeroplane to fly. There were two versions of the two-seater of which one had the conventional instruments. When we got the Buccaneer we put its instruments into the T.8 so you could learn to fly on those. It was nicknamed the Chinese Hunter."

**Anon pilot**

"I went to Brawdy for fighter training Part 1 (759 Squadron) on the two-seat Hunter T.8, and Part 2 (738 Squadron) on the single-seat Hunter GA.11. The good sorties were brilliant, but not worthy of note. We were taught new skills, particularly on sorties like low-level strikes on GA.11s. This consisted of four strike aircraft, four escorts and two 'bounces' with virtually the whole of Wales as our playground. When we landed, hyped up wasn't the word for it, there was so much adrenaline pumping round our systems – and this was in peacetime.

"Towards the end of 738 Squadron the decision was made about who was going to fly what next. It could be strike aircraft (Buccaneers), fighters (Sea Vixens) or AEW (Gannets). About 34 of us started at Dartmouth and by the end of our training there was one pilot (me) on the Sea Vixen, three Buccaneer pilots, two observers, an air traffic controller and one who joined to be a helicopter pilot (which some of us thought a bit strange at the time). Most of us started off wanting to be pilots, but then the whittling down process began. If you failed a phase such as instrument or night flying, you might be given a choice to continue flying helicopters, or as an observer, or become an air traffic controller – or leave altogether. It was somewhat unnerving watching your fellow course mates disappear one by one. Had I known the odds of passing I sometimes wonder if I would have bothered to apply – being young, I expect so."

*Doug Macdonald was a Phantom observer who went to 764 Squadron for his AWI course.*

"I was picked to do the AWI course at Lossiemouth on 764 Squadron, which had nine or ten Hunter GA.11s and four or five T.8s. I flew in the right-hand seat of the T.8 and had a safety pilot instructor with me – it was the most amazing thing I ever did. First I had to go to Portsmouth to learn all about weaponry. This lasted about two-and-a-half months and included the nuclear bit. I got to Lossie about the beginning of September, and flew non-stop until the second week in December. I flew four or five 30-minute sorties a day, dropping four 25-lb practice bombs, coming back to get some fuel, then dropping another four bombs, using the Tain range. Eventually the culmination was at Garvie Island, where we were allowed to drop live ones. It was a very, very intense course, a bit of air-to-air, lots of theory and putting it into operation – but mostly it was strike. It ended up as four against four amongst the mountains and lochs of Scotland (the weather was good). I look at my logbook and ask myself how I managed to do five sorties in a day. They were only 30 minutes each, but it was still very tiring when you add on time for briefing, debriefing and then off again – it was fantastic flying though."

**Richard Moody**

"Lossie was an ideal location to practise air combat manoeuvring down to a low level in the mountains since the north of Scotland was scarcely populated and we had free range of the majority of the Highlands in which to practise our manoeuvres. I'm amazed that there were so few complaints about our antics – and even fewer accidents. These antics often involved a four-plane strike flight of Hunters, escorted by two other Hunters, flying at low level along a tortuous route to attack a simulated target. The escort's role was to seek out the enemy and engage them – the enemy being two further Hunters who were lurking hidden in the hills along the attack route. Inevitably, when the strike flight was intercepted, all hell would break loose and the ensuing engagement would result in four Hunters at perhaps 50 feet above the ground engaging each other in high G slashing attacks as the four-aircraft strike force endeavoured to reach it's intended target.

"The AWI Course took first-class pilots from their front-line squadrons and trained them to a high level before sending them back to their squadron to instruct the other pilots in fighter combat and air-to-ground manoeuvres. The course was founded ten years before the USN's Top Gun school was formed at Miramar by an Act of Congress as a result of the initial poor fighter combat kill ratios with the North Vietnamese. As a subsequent staff member with the first cadre of Top Gun pilots in California, I have always felt that the concept of Top Gun was taken from the programme developed by the Royal Navy's AWI course. Naturally, many of my fellow USN pilots still object to this suggestion and we now good naturedly agree to disagree!"

**DON'T LET YOUR FLYING EFFECT THE SURROUNDING COUNTRYSIDE**

*"Not that low Sir, I'm too chicken!"*

The work of the navy's own cartoonist 'Tugg' Wilson.

*The huge increase in aircrew requirements, with the onset of the Cold War and the coming Korean War, led to the hurried establishment of additional training units. For example, twin conversion, and some early jet conversion on Meteors, was provided by civilian contractor Airwork at St Davids, a satellite of Brawdy.*

### Doug Turner

"After leaving the air force (although I was still a flight lieutenant reservist) I joined Airwork at St Davids in 1950 to run the outfit. It was then realised that if a war came along running the unit as a civilian would no longer be possible, so I would have to rejoin the military as a naval officer. However, about a fortnight after I arrived they said, 'Oh it's all right, we're not going to do that anymore, you can go back to being a flight lieutenant.' It was an awful lot of fun. One section was teaching people who had to do a 'heavy' twin conversion to fly Mosquitoes – it was the only aircraft we had to do it."

### Peter Hiles

"I did the heavy twin conversion course in the Mosquito T.3 run by Airwork at St Davids in July and August 1950, totalling 29 hours dual and solo. This was required before jet conversion. My civilian instructors were Mr Fopp and Mr Tapper, while the chief flying instructor Mr Hackney did my final handling check."

*The civilian training at St Davids ceased after a few short years as the FAA's own training system adapted to the rate of student intake, followed by the arrival into service of higher performance aircraft. For example, following OFS II, type conversion for the Sea Vixen was*

*Peter Hiles.*

*carried out on 766 Squadron at Yeovilton. Similarly, when the Phantom arrived at the end of the '60s, 767 Squadron undertook the same task.*

### Kim Sharman

"I just wanted to fly fighters, but the Vixen was a pretty grim aeroplane. You just had to look at the 38 per cent loss rate. There were a lot of young men killed in peacetime – it was a very dangerous role. Vixen training was at Yeovilton. Here we met up with our observers who'd come through their own training. There was no forced pairing up, we simply sorted out amongst ourselves who we'd like to fly with. My 'looker' was Flt Lt Dave Trotter. There were no dual-control Vixens and your first flight was effectively a solo. The guy in the right-hand seat was a staff looker – brave man.

"We did all the usual stuff – bombing and rocketing, primarily air intercepts, culminating in our first deck landings. First we went to have a look at the deck in a Hunter T.8 with a QFI. We made approaches to *Hermes* using the deck landing sight, then did a low wave-off (go around). The most difficult thing was lining up – it's a very short runway and quite easy to get off the centreline. It was important to stay lined up because if you veered off to the right you'd hit parked aircraft and blokes. If you went left you'd be in the catwalk, or over the side!

"I did my deck qualification on *Eagle* in the Moray Firth. We flew up to Lossie, then out to the ship and did several approaches with the hook up. You were talked down all the time, and once they thought you'd got the hang of it they would say 'hook down', so you put the hook down and landed on. The observer would always be reading out the speed. With reference to the landing speed he would be saying 'plus 5', 'plus 6' or whatever. I hooked on and taxied forward putting my hand down in the hole between us and shaking hands with Dave. Then they put us on the catapult and blasted us off. That was two firsts within about four minutes.

"We had done catapult training at RAE Bedford, where they had a catapult raised above ground. But you can't turn Bedford into wind. So the launch was unbelievably harsh. What was disconcerting was that to get to the catapult you had to go up a ramp, and you don't often taxi an aircraft up a slope and then try to stop it at the top. Once that was done we were all clear, had our certificates, and off we went to our first embarked trip on *Eagle*."

### Tony Smith

"On 9 February 1966 I made my first flight in a Sea Vixen from Yeovilton. We'd had ground school lectures and using a basic simulator we learnt and practised all the necessary checks such as pre-start-up, pre-take-off etc., plus a whole range of emergency procedures – though this was not a flight simulator.

"The take-off and subsequent familiarisation flight went OK, including two or three 'touch-and-goes'. Then came the final landing. We had been briefed that the brakes were not man enough to brake the aircraft from its initial touchdown speed of between 120 and 130 knots, so we were briefed to use aerodynamic braking with the wings until the speed dropped back to 80-90 knots – then lower the nose onto the runway and start braking. As we touched down, I let the nose go down onto the runway, and then tried to bring it back for aerodynamic braking. Being a little ham-fisted I brought it too far back and the nose was too high, so we lifted off again. So down went the nose again – but we

*Tony Smith.*

*Sea Vixen FAW.2 XP957 VL-720 766 Squadron at Yeovilton on 9 September 1967.*

were still going too fast for the brakes! By this time we were getting a bit close to the end of the runway, so I whacked down the arrestor hook and picked up the SPRAG (spray arrestor gear) wire which brought us to a pleasant halt. SPRAG was similar to carrier arrestor wires and was strung across the runway.

"The landing on my second trip didn't go much better, but at least I didn't use the SPRAG. On the third trip I had cottoned on to the right way to handle aerodynamic braking. As one touched down you did not lower the nose at all, you just closed both throttles and held the nose up at the same attitude, then slowly you brought it further back until the tail bumpers on the booms either just touched the runway, or preferably stayed just above it. When the speed came down to 90 knots you lowered the nose and commenced braking. I certainly learnt something from those first flights."

### Jonathon Whaley

"You made a request for the type of front-line aircraft you wanted, basically a bomber or fighter. The dice rolled in my favour and I set off for Yeovilton and 766 Squadron. After the Hunter the Vixen was a *big* aircraft, and took a crew of two to operate in any role other than a ferry flight. It had systems all with flight reference cards that were like a small novel rather than the Hunter's handful of pages.

*Jonathon Whaley.*

"Preparation were the normal lectures, tests on the systems and five sessions in the static simulator. The principal task on the first flight (apart from putting the aircraft back on the flight line in one piece, preferably with your observer's nerves only partially shredded) was to climb at full power, and then level the aircraft at 10,000 feet. Demerit points were awarded depending on how many hundreds, or some cases thousands of feet you overshot flight level 100. There were then eight FAM (familiarisation) flights before you started high-level air-intercept training, after five of those you started doing it at night as well. Every landing was made on the dummy deck marked out on the runway, using the mirror landing sight, unless doing a pairs formation landing. Take-offs were conventional but almost always as a pair. I 'strapped my first Sea Vixen on' at the age of 19 and I overshot by 100 feet. I learnt that the trick was for your observer to ask you to make a turn and look for a 'contact' he had on the radar as you passed 9,500 feet – that sense of humour again.

*Sea Vixen observer's coal hole. (Kim Sharman)*

"Observers needed to have a sense of humour in 'spades' (not playing with a full deck was probably also a necessity). His seat was in what was called the coal hole, to the right, below and aft of the pilot. His only view out was through a window some 7 inches by 10 inches normally covered with a blind. When we were playing at being fighter pilots he spent all the time leaning forward with his head buried in the radar, while the pilot threw the aircraft about in macho mode. When we were playing at being strike pilots he had little to do other than watch the fuel (only the pilot could reach any of the switches and levers!), and call the height and speed during the dive. Deck launches and landings were also a stressful time for him, however I always liked doing them, especially at night, in the rain. You couldn't see anything once into the cloud at 500 feet anyway. Sadly, I know we pilots were all guilty to some degree of not giving recognition of the observer's spirit – I can recall several pilots who refused to climb into the coal hole. Another thing the observer could do was make sure the pilot saw the rusty pair of dividers in the ob's nav bag. The pilot's right thigh was nicely placed should he not heed his observer's plea to cease and desist whatever was turning the ob's knuckles white. Having rusty ones was just their little joke."

> *Into the 1980s and with the advent of the Sea Harrier, and given the significant differences between this and the RAF Harriers, it was decided to reform 899 Squadron at Yeovilton to carry out type conversion and operational training.*

## Andrew Neofytou

"I finished jet training on the Tucano in '99 and then went off to Valley. There were probably about four or five navy guys there, among 50-odd air force, and I got my wings in 2001. Not enough navy students were being recommended for single-seat jets. The navy had an agreement with the air force where they would go and fly the Tornado for a tour (possibly changing to the air force) and then convert to the Sea Harrier. There were only small numbers that did that, maybe only two or three a year joining the Sea Harrier Operational Conversion Unit (OCU), 899 Squadron at Yeovilton.

"You joined the Sea Harrier from the Hawk, which is a pretty basic aeroplane to fly, and it really was a baptism of fire. We did a couple of simulator sorties, then two flights in a Harrier T.8, then first solo in a Sea Harrier, so you'd only flown two hours in a real jet. The performance of the Sea Harrier next to a T.8 was insane. The Sea Harrier was a very powerful aeroplane with a big engine. When you were flying it lightweight, without any drop tanks or stores, the first time you accelerated it was mind-blowingly quick – it could out-accelerate an F/A-18 at low level.

"The first solo is a great experience. You get airborne and just climb up to do some general handling. I remember looking back in the mirror and seeing these two swept-back wings, the intake and the exhaust – the whole lot shrouded in vapour as you were climbing through 24,000 feet. But you'd flown for so little time, so you really felt out of your depth to start with. The next time you stepped into an aircraft it was a two-seat Harrier to go and do vertical take-offs, 'press-ups', we'd do three with an instructor. Prior to joining 899 I'd done a very brief hover course on a Squirrel helicopter at Shawbury – all navy Harrier pilots did that. After flying it for half an hour I was doing auto-rotations – 'easy' I thought. Then you got to Sea Harrier, you'd do two dual flights, first solo, then those three press-ups, probably hovering for about three minutes on each. Then your second solo is a vertical take-off to the hover.

*Harrier T.8 ZD993 VL-723 of 899 Squadron Yeovilton, at Biggin Hill on 26 June 1999. (Adrian Balch)*

"After doing just a handful of flights at Yeovilton we went to Wittering to do the V/STOL work. They'd got various short runways and taxiways you could land on, and they'd also got a pad on which you could land in a wooded clearing. Unfortunately, there was an accident on my course whilst out at Wittering. Nathan Gray was flying with Lt Cdr Martin 'Jak' London and they had engine failure on take-off. I was first to the scene to aid Nathan – not a great way to start the OCU. There was about a two- or three-month break while the accident investigation took place, and then the course carried on."

> *The accident occurred on 5 December 2002 and the aircraft involved was Harrier T.8 ZB605 of 899 Squadron. Both crew ejected, Lt Cdr London losing his life, and the aircraft crashed inverted. Nathan Gray survived and rejoined the Sea Harrier world later.*

## TRAINING IN THE UNITED STATES

*During World War 2 many thousands of British aircrew trained in the United States. This continued, to a decreasing degree, well into the post-war period, up to and including F-4 Phantom training.*

### Peter Hiles

"I started flying in 1943 with the grading school, then I went to America and learnt to fly with 5 BFTS (British Flying Training School) at Clewiston, Florida. Having got my wings and commission, I came back to the 'Harrogate air force' – you do nothing except courses and I could *not* get on a squadron. I tried very hard, and the weeks just went by. This was August 1944, when the war had a year to run, and I was getting nowhere in the RAF. Finally the navy came up with a signal requesting volunteer pilots to join them. Then all sorts of funny things happened – I went to the navy and they told me to sit down! They measured my inside leg, and that apparently was a bit too long for a Seafire, so they said they would train me on Corsairs. I finished the training course at Yeovilton, and the war ended."

### Another anon pilot

"Yellow paddles stand out clearly against the drab grey paint. The waters of the Mexican Gulf close below as the Pratt and Witney in

*US Navy SNJ-6 in Florida. (Dave Eagles)*

fine pitch howls away in front dragging the aircraft along, hanging on its propeller. First carrier deck landing coming up. The paddles signal cut, and with throttle closed the SNJ (Texan/Harvard) flops down on the deck.

"Flat hatting – a US Navy term for low flying – in an F9F-2 Panther over the Texas scrub lands close to the Mexican border. Only one head of cattle per couple of square miles. Strictly forbidden in the Training Command but the instructor in the lead ship is a real fighter Jock, just back from Korea. What the hell! Rules are made to be broken (so he says)."

## John de Winton

*John de Winton.*

"I joined my first front-line outfit, 809 Squadron Sea Venoms, exactly two years after going solo in the SNJ with the US Navy at Pensacola. After the SNJ we flew the T-28 Trojan, Lockheed TV-2 and Grumman Panther, returning to the UK with our wings (and USN wings) for further RN training on the Vampire and Sea Hawk. I had expected to go to a Sea Hawk squadron but was selected as an early 'guinea pig' to go straight to night fighters. Prospective pilots did a night-fighter course with the RAF, so I had a few months flying the Meteor T.7 towing targets at Lossie, before starting at RAF North Luffenham and crewing up with my observer to fly the Meteor NF.12 and 14."

## Dave Eagles

*Dave Eagles.*

"I joined the navy from grammar school in 1953 as a cadet. I was 17 and had to do two years National Service. In my school there was a booklet about the Fleet Air Arm, and at the same time there was an advert in the *Radio Times* for the Fleet Air Arm – 'See the world'. My headmaster said, 'Ee lad, they don't take grammar school lads'.

"I went through all the routines and joined *Indefatigable*, a World War 2 carrier in the Pacific Fleet. It had a crease in the island where it had been hit by a kamikaze. There were no aircraft on her except one non-airworthy Seafire for training aircraft handlers. There were 20 of us cadets, called National Service upper-yard men, and we learned seamanship, anchors and cables, communications, some naval history, and how to be a naval officer. The course lasted six months. On graduating we were told that half of us would stay in the UK for flying training with the RAF and the rest would go to America.

"To my delight I went to Pensacola, an enormous US Navy installation. Six small airfields, all within about 25 square miles, all flying the SNJ. We went through the American training programme; the strange thing was that you shifted 'field as you went through each phase. You qualified up to solo standard in two months, and then changed airfield to learn formation flying, then on to Barin Field to do gunnery and bombing. It was an amazing thing to do, but it worked very well. At Barin we also learned deck landing. The SNJ-5 had a hook and we did about 15 trips of FCLP (field carrier landing practice) with a batsman. Then we went out to the USS *Monterey*, a 15,000-ton ex-wartime convoy escort carrier with a wooden deck, where we had to do six successful landings on. We then shifted to the T-28 Trojan for our instrument phase and tactics, then went onto jet conversion on the TV-2, which was the navy version of the T-33. Finally on to the so-called advanced trainer, the F9F-2 Panther, which had only just come back from the Korean War two years earlier. It had four 20-mm cannon, and we did all the usual exercises, including air-to-air firing on a banner, a wonderful sport."

## Bob Edward

"As part of the Mutual Defence Aid Programme approximately 40 FAA students a year were trained by the USN during and after the Korean War, the last group of ten going in June 1955. The training was very different from that of the RAF. US Naval Air Training Command was a vast organisation turning out 3,000 qualified pilots a year, a new course starting every week.

"Six weeks of ground school at Pensacola, and assimilation into the combined USN/USMC environment. Basic flying training was with the SNJ. This included day and night flying, formation flying, instrument flying, air-to-air gunnery with a .5 inch machine gun firing through the prop, dive bombing and six arrested deck landings on board USS *Saipan*.

"Advanced flying training was in Texas. It commenced with instrument training in the T-28B Trojan, which included airways navigation and civil-controlled airspace. Jet conversion on the Lockheed TV-2 was followed by the F9F-5 Panther. This included air-to-air gunnery, strafing, dive bombing and rocket firing. For me, the whole programme lasted 17 months – it was enormous fun.

"I view my time with the USN/USMC as the most formative time of my life. I went as an

*Bob Edward.*

Jetstream T.2 XX481 750 Squadron, Fairford in July 2006. (Richard Andrews)

18-year-old midshipman and came home as a qualified sub lieutenant pilot. In my group were five ex-Dartmouth-trained officers (three lieutenants and two subs), three short-service subs, and two midshipmen of which I was the younger – all passed the course. Three were killed in accidents, one on his first tour in a Sea Hawk, one as commanding officer (CO) of 736 Squadron in a Buccaneer and one as commander (Air) Yeovilton in a Phantom."

## OBSERVER TRAINING

*Since its formation on 24 May 1939, 750 Squadron has been synonymous with training observers for both the fixed-wing and rotary-wing fleets. It was disbanded in October 1945. The upsurge in aircrew requirements with the onset of the Cold War and the Korean conflict saw it reformed on 1 February 1952 at St Merryn, Cornwall, with Barracudas and Ansons.*

*The squadron re-equipped with Sea Princes and Fireflies in early 1953, moving to Culdrose that November. Here it joined 796 Squadron which performed a similar role with Fireflies, then Gannets, until that unit disbanded in 1958. No. 750 went over exclusively to the Sea Prince in March 1955 and moved to Hal Far, Malta in October 1959 to take advantage of the better weather conditions. Sea Venoms were added to the squadron in 1960, for high-level navigation, and the unit returned to the UK in the summer of 1965 to make its new home at Lossiemouth.*

*No. 750 Squadron returned to Culdrose in September 1972, and six years later Jetstreams began arriving to replace the by now rather tired Sea Princes – which were all gone by 1979. The Jetstreams were themselves replaced in 2011 when four Beech King Air 350s (officially known as the*

*Avenger T.1) arrived. These continue to fly with the squadron today.*

## Tony Tayler

"Observer flying training took place at four different air-
fields. The main part was at St Merryn, Cornwall and the
last part at Eglinton, Northern Ireland. We started flying
in Ansons, progressing to Barracudas and Fireflies. Many
of the pilots were themselves inexperienced, and some
were taking up flying again after leaving the navy at the
end of the war. Several times in flight I was asked 'Do you
smell burning?' or 'Does that engine sound all right to
you?' though I could never note any change in the acrid
smells or the deafening roar of the engine. On the Barra-

*Tony Tayler.*

cuda we did half the sorties in the observer's seat (which
seemed roomy) and half, sending Morse, in the TAG (telegraphist/air gunner) seat.
One aspect which I found impossible to come to terms with was the death of friends
in flying accidents. It often seemed to be the nicest people who were killed."

## Tony Pinney

"I was supposed to join the Scimitar trials squadron as the sprog pilot, but as the
aircraft was delayed by the need to upgrade the hydraulics I was, at two days' notice, sent to 750 Squadron at Culdrose 'driving' U/T (under training) observers
around. That was not ideal for me at just 21 with 650 hours and 184 deck landings.
The average age of the pilots in 750 was over 35, and most were time serving lieutenant commanders! The idea was to have some pilots in the squadron closer in
age to the students.

"After two dual sorties in the Sea Devon I did three solo familiarisations, and
then five in the Sea Prince. I was 'driving' observers around a week later. Sadly, at
that time, we were losing Sea Venom crews at a high rate. At the end of July I went
to the boss and handed in my application to volunteer for the next all-weather
fighter course. It was accepted, and after two weeks and overseas service leave
which was owed to me, I joined 766 Squadron at Yeovilton."

## Stuart Leeming

"After my Buccaneer tours I converted onto the Sea Prince. It was a very casual
conversion, I think the chap who instructed me didn't know much about propellers either – he kept talking about things like 'crisps and lollipops' instead of RPM
levers and throttles! The Sea Prince squadron was attached to the navy's Observer
Training School at Lossiemouth initially, but was later relocated to Culdrose. After
18 months of pleasant Sea Prince flying I joined 809 Squadron at RAF Honington."

*Sea Prince T.1 WP309 750 Squadron at Greenham Common in June 1977. (Richard Vandervord)*

## Kim Sharman – pilot

"I flew Sea Princes with 750 Squadron at Lossiemouth doing observer training, which was average to boring. But it was quite good for racking up the hours prior to leaving the navy, and you also got your twin-engine rating. Then 750 moved down to Culdrose, which was a long flight in a Sea Prince. We used the Prince occasionally for communications work – 'Can you go to Wittering and collect stuff?' or whatever. One such job came up and there was massive jockeying to do it for a change. The guys were saying 'But you did it last time'. 'I'm senior to you'. I thought 'b\*\*\*\*r this; I can do this every day of the week if I want to' so I put my letter in and left the navy."

## Anthony Stephens – air electrics

*Anthony Stephens.*

"I went to Hal Far to join 750 Squadron with Sea Princes and Sea Venoms. In about September 1962 a Sea Venom had crashed on take-off at Hal Far diving into the LOX (liquid oxygen) plant. The crew survived, but the burns they received from their melted nylon socks were horrendous. Although it was not my aircraft, nor had I worked on it, I was intrigued by the cause.

"On take-off Sea Venoms opened the 'Full Flo' valve which gave maximum fuel availability to the engine for launch. The crash investigation showed that the valve's electrical cable had parted from its connection due to fatigue. I recommended a new type of terminal should be adopted as standard, and it was, appearing as a Fleet Electrical Review. I saw the review (my name didn't appear), and its title was 'Crimping Techniques in the Royal Navy'. I often wondered if any Sea Venoms crashed as a result of the failure of this electrical connection after the publication of the report in about 1963/64."

> *After many years on various helicopter squadrons, including eight postings as a training officer, pilot **John Adams** got his first fixed-wing job at Culdrose instructing observers.*

"I arrived on 750 Squadron at Culdrose in 1990, and did a three-month conversion course onto the Jetstream. I struggled a bit at first. Some aspects of fixed-wing aviation didn't come naturally, but thanks to the perseverance of my QFI, Sqn Ldr Hooper, I qualified and enjoyed the flying. One of the biggest buzzes for me was the ability to punch straight into cloud over Culdrose, go through the airways system and become visual at Berlin, hundreds of miles away. Unlike rotary flying, air traffic control had done all the hard work en route and all you had to do was manage the aircraft.

*John Adams.*

"I left 750 Squadron in 1993 and continued to fly the Jetstream in the FAA and for civilian operators. After 15 years, I ended up back on 750 flying for Serco as a contractor. In 2011 the Jetstreams were replaced by four King Airs (Avengers in FAA speak) and I was lucky enough to fly those for my last year or so. The flying

*Avenger T.1 ZZ503 750 Squadron, Fairford in July 2017. (Richard Andrews)*

characteristics and operation of the two types were quite different. We all thought the Jetstream was wonderful, but once acquainted with the King Air, there is nothing to touch it. The PT-6 engine is just about bulletproof, and they are lovely to fly.

"The 750 observer's course is generally recognised as the second most difficult in the RN, the first being the 'Perisher' Submarine command course. All of us pilots had a great respect for these young men and women when they qualified. Training sorties were generally an hour-and-a-half to two hours, and the students progressed through phases. The first thing they did was basic plotting with a Dalton computer – the 'Wiz Wheel' – which was about producing very accurate log cards. Then they started working with radar – a 1950s' ex-weather radar in the nose of the Jetstream – that was challenging, to say the least. We would then go to sea and do low-level intercepts of any unsuspecting ships they could find. They directed the aircraft on an approach pattern, talking the pilot down as if making an approach to 'mother'. It was quite exciting. You would descend through cloud and once visual fly alongside some large ships at 50 feet before over shooting. Then it was high-level navigation, using a combination of map and radar to plot where they were, followed by low-level, sitting in the front right-hand seat 250 feet–500 feet in the King Air.

"The last phase was tactical navigation, and then the dreaded TACNAV 0, a two-hour final test which was a combination of everything they had learnt. They didn't have a clue what was going to happen, the mission brief would simply be, for example: 'You are going to take Admiral so-and-so from Culdrose to Southampton.' You'd get airborne and set course only for a 'message' to be received that a 'plane had crashed somewhere along a given route. They'd have to go and set up a search and rescue (SAR) pattern, then perhaps low level out to sea to find a ship in distress and so on. The scenarios were never the same to keep the students guessing and you couldn't help feeling for them – they never got a moment to relax. The instructor deliberately kept the scenario secret, even from us up the front. The student was the notional aircraft commander – obviously if they got it wrong they were 'going round again'. Generally the observer instructor was the mission commander and quite often the aircraft captain, which made sense given the nature of the sortie. We just made sure what we were doing was safe.

"One advantage of the Avenger was that it had something like nine hours endurance – although we never used it. The main thing was that its state-of-the-art 360-degree belly radar which unfortunately turned out not to be that great. Often when the students were trying to find small ships in the 'gloup', the instructor would come up front and look at our weather radar to find out where the ship was. He'd then go back and pretend he had suddenly identified a contact on the students' radar."

*Having successfully survived the lengthy training programme, the newly fledged pilot or observer was ready to join an operational squadron and embark on an aircraft carrier.*

# CHAPTER TWO

# GROUND CREW TRAINING

## ARTIFICER

*An artificer – known to all as a 'tiff' or 'tiffy' – was a highly skilled naval rating who entered the RN directly as an apprentice, either from school or from the RN training establishment HMS Ganges near Ipswich without becoming basic naval ratings. The five-year apprenticeship included specialist knowledge training such as electrical, electronic, electro-mechanical and mechanical devices.*

*From December 1946 new entrants joined HMS Fisgard at Torpoint in Cornwall, for four terms of general engineering training. Apprentices were then allowed to choose one of five trades, depending on merit and demand, as follows: aircraft artificers (AA), specialising in aero engines and airframes went to Condor, Arbroath. Engine room artificers (ERA) and shipwright artificers went to Caledonia, Rosyth, electrical artificers (EA) and radio electrical artificers (REA) to Collingwood, Gosport. The split engineering training schools were combined from 1971. The fourth year of training was spent 'in the field' gaining practical hands-on experience; for all trades except AA, this was on board ship – AAs went to an air station. The final year was back at the training establishment and apprentices were rated up to the grade of leading hand or 'Killick'.*

*In the 1980s Daedalus at Lee-on-the-Solent became the centre for the air electrical engineering specialisation. When that station closed in December 1983 the function was taken over by HMS Raleigh. The training of artificers continued until the decision was taken to end the role in 2010 when it was superseded by the introduction of air engineering technicians.*

**John Coward**
"I finished my four-year engineering apprenticeship in 1948, followed by three years of practice in Malta. There, after three months of working at Kalafrana on a Sea Otter (Kalafrana was part of HMS Falcon at Hal Far), I joined 728 (Fleet Requirements) Squadron which had one or two Seafires, three Miles Martinet target tugs, one or two ordinary Mosquitoes, a couple of target-towing Mossies and two Short Sturgeons. It was a very mixed fleet and my job was to maintain the Martinets and attach towed-targets to them – although for my first task I was given an ordinary Mosquito and told to paint it. The Martinets towed drogues, with the larger

*John Coward.*

targets being towed by the Sturgeons and Mosquitoes. There were two types of large towed target, one with a wingspan of eight to ten feet and the other of 16 feet which, I seem to remember, were used for radar tracking and being shot at. The next time I served in Malta, which was on 750 Squadron, targets were towed by Meteors. Lt Cdr 'Monty' Mellor was the CO.

"The Mosquitoes were TT.35s but I can't remember the marks of the Sturgeons [TT.2 and TT.3]. The only other time I saw Sturgeons was after starting my pilot training at Portland. Following that I moved to Gosport which had Brigands, though I had nothing to do with them as I was undergoing my pre-flight training. The only other aircraft I came in contact with early on was an Oxford during my apprenticeship at Arbroath.

"It was during my time on 728 Squadron that a Mosquito took off, on the long south-westerly runway at Hal Far, losing an engine and ditching in the bay. Another pilot jumped into a Sea Otter amphibian, took off and landed in the bay even though the sea was very rough. Although the Mosquito pilot got out OK his aircrewman didn't. The Sea Otter then suffered an engine failure whilst taxiing in the bay and was washed up on the rocks and destroyed. Fortunately the aircrewman was the only fatality during this whole incident. Normally you entered, and exited, a Mosquito through a door on the nose. In a ditched situation you had to evacuate through the top of the canopy which was quite difficult to do. When I was at RNAS Ford the duty electrician had to do some checks on a Mosquito and asked me, a petty officer (PO), to run the engines because no one else was available to do it. I'd never climbed into one before and I remember how difficult it was to get through that door, let alone exiting through the canopy."

## Alan Reed

*Alan Reed.*

"I trained at RNAY (Royal Naval Aircraft Yard) Fleetlands, Gosport from September 1960 to September 1965, a five-year craft apprenticeship in airframe and engines – I won the top apprentice award every year, and stayed on for six months as an aircraft fitter. I was awarded paid leave to obtain an A and B gliding licence, and a private pilot's licence (learning on Austers).

"During training I worked on the Scimitar, Sea Hawk, Dragonfly and Rolls-Royce Avon engine, as well as many other engines and components. I spent a number of months working on Whirlwind, Wasp and Wessex helicopters, and the repair and rebuilding of

Avon, Gazelle, Gyron Junior and Gnome engines. I also spent six months in the drawing office, and flew from Fleetlands' heliport in a variety of helicopters.

"While still an apprentice, working in the Scimitar area, I was invited to join the Final Functional Trials Department (FFTD). This was totally unheard of. No apprentice had ever been allowed to join this highly selective, highly skilled, team. I was soon on day or night shifts all aimed at rapidly producing finished aircraft for service, and this meant much higher pay. There was also a bonus incentive to get the job done. Bonuses were only paid once the aircraft had passed flight test from Lee-on-the-Solent. Thus I received cheques through the post when I was well into my subsequent RAF service. This proved to be vital, since my mess bills often exceeded my salary!

"Scimitar functional tests were extremely exacting, and I was fortunate to be working with the most skilful and experienced tradesmen. My final day in the Scimitar hangar was a most emotional experience, since I was 'hammered out' on departure. This involved the whole workforce hammering on their toolboxes as a farewell to the departing, and was normally reserved only for long-serving members who were retiring.

"My life at Fleetlands was a very happy time during which I made many friends. I represented Fleetlands apprentices at the opening ceremony and parade for the FAA Museum at Yeovilton, and was honoured to be spoken to by HRH Prince Philip. He considered our civilian group to be an 'old comrades' reunion, until he saw me. There was much laughter when he asked the shortest, fattest sailor where he would rather be if he were not standing on this parade? The sailor replied 'Standing where you are sir!'

"On joining the RAF as an engineering officer in 1966, I was pleasantly surprised that my training compared well to that provided for RAF technicians. I also had a distinct advantage in having dual trade experience, which stood me in good stead on the flight lines at Coastal Command stations on Shackletons, and at 4 FTS Valley on Gnats."

### Henry Parker

"My father Henry Herbert Parker served in the RN through the First World War. He was aboard HMS *Weymouth* chasing SMS *Emden*, HMS *Phaeton* at Gallipoli and Jutland. He retired having completed time for pension as a chief engine room mechanician. It was pretty well accepted that in 1960 I would take the Admiralty Artificer apprentice examination (equivalent to five 'O' levels, a year before I would have sat them). Unfortunately Dad died that November, so he didn't see me entering Fisgard, which was the initial artificer apprentice training college in May 1961.

"Moving on in 1962 to Collingwood, the electrical training establishment, I was first categorised 'computer/weapons', (who knew about computers then?) From Collingwood on to Ariel at Lee-on-the-Solent as an air electrical artificer apprentice, followed by Heron, Yeovilton, for field training."

## Mike Norman

*Mike Norman.*

"I arrived in Malta in September 1963 for the fourth year of my aircraft apprenticeship, to get hands-on experience of an operational FAA squadron. I was to spend six months on 750 Squadron, which provided aircraft for the flying training of observers, working on Sea Venoms, Sea Vampires and Sea Princes.

"I was understudying Leading Airman Barry Strangleman, changing wheels on a Sea Venom due to tyre wear. All went well and the job was signed off by a supervisory senior rate. The next day the aircraft was to be flown by Lt (later VAdm) Jonathan Tod. Barry and I did the pre-flight inspection, and it wasn't long before the pilot and observer came out to the aircraft; the observer weighed down with a large nav bag and an expression of impending doom. The pilot noted the wheel change, and carried out his walkround of the aircraft before strapping in.

"I manned the fire extinguisher as the engine was started by cartridge with a bang and a cloud of black smoke. Barry marshalled the aircraft out, and we returned to the line hut for a smoke. We briefly glanced at the aircraft with some indifference, as the engine was wound up for take-off. My curiosity got the better of me, as I wanted to see where the aircraft would lift off and I saw with incredulity one of the mainwheels leave the aircraft as it did so. I tried to say something to Barry, who wasn't watching, but the words didn't come out of my mouth. I was frozen to the spot with a sinking feeling in the pit of my stomach. Would this be the end of my short-lived naval career? I became mesmerised by the bouncing wheel, happily making its way towards the airfield perimeter fence, and elbowed Barry pointing at the aircraft as it climbed away – his jaw dropped!

"Having detached from the aircraft at something in excess of 100 knots, the bouncing wheel was a missile. It smashed its way through the fence, across the road, and straight through the Lyster Barracks main gate, narrowly missing the master at arms who was crossing the road to his office! All hell broke loose with lots of shouting and the airfield tannoy announcing what had happened. The AEO (air engineering officer) appeared at the line hut demanding to see the A700 (aircraft log), which was impounded. What could possibly have gone wrong? We had followed the book and done everything correctly as far as I could remember. Then I remembered the split pin that prevented the wheel nut from undoing. I had handed new ones to Barry, and was called away. I said to him 'You did fit those split pins, didn't you?' He didn't answer.

"Lt Tod elected to bring the aircraft back to land because he was too long in the leg to safely eject. Fire trucks came from Luqa to lay a foam carpet as the

*Sea Venom FAW.22 XG721 750 Squadron, Hal Far, 1965.*

aircraft jettisoned fuel over the sea. An hour passed, and it seemed the whole air station had turned out to watch. Should I have double checked the spit pins when I got back? But I was under training and still learning, I could not possibly be held responsible, surely.

"The aircraft approached, close to stalling speed with a pronounced nose-up attitude and flaps down. The pilot did a wheels-up landing and it skidded along the runway with foam flying everywhere – there was a crescendo of clapping and whooping. The observer climbed out while the aircraft was still travelling at some speed, ran along the wing and launched himself into the foam. The aircraft came to a stop, Lt Tod stood up to put the safety pins in his ejection seat, climbed down and walked across the grass to where everyone was assembled. He stopped in front of the station CO, saluted him followed by a handshake and simply said: 'Aircraft recovered safely sir.'

"A Board of Inquiry was held a week later. I was summoned to appear, and answered the questions as best I could. The officers could see I was nervous and were sympathetic. It was concluded that a missing split pin was probably the cause of the wheel coming off. Some disciplinary measures were handed out, but I was in the clear. Lt Tod was awarded a Green Endorsement[1] for exemplary airmanship in safely recovering his aircraft. I was involved in the repairs, though the damage was mostly superficial, and the aircraft was flying again in three weeks."

*This took place on 12 May 1964 and involved Sea Venom FAW.22 XG721 HF-592. The student observer was Midshipman David Thompson. This was his first ever trip in a jet aircraft. He later served with Jonathan Tod in Buccaneers and ended up as the naval attaché in Paris, retiring as a captain.*

---

1. A Green Endorsement is a recorded recognition of a job well done in avoiding damage or loss of an aircraft and crew by exceptional flying skill.

## Tony Sanders

"The FAA realised it couldn't have large numbers of service personnel – engineers, mechanics, etc. – on board ship because there wasn't enough room for them. Where you might have 200 guys on an RAF squadron you had 80 on an FAA squadron.

"When I first joined up, we had three large fixed-wing aircraft carriers. We were just beginning to withdraw the Scimitar, we had the Sea Vixen, and later the Buccaneer followed by the Phantom. With the Bucc and Phantom came a whole new range of equipment and weapon systems. All aspiring maintainers underwent the same initial training. At the end you were assessed as to whether you possessed an electrical or mechanical aptitude, and then they would try to fit you to the correct trade for specific training.

"I was streamed for general service electrical at first, but whilst going through initial training I was told that four of us were required for the FAA for a new trade. I was interviewed by a Wren officer who said that a new branch system was being established, a mixture of electrical and mechanical, for the maintenance and operation of weapon systems. When I arrived for technical training I found out that it wasn't just weapon systems, it was the preparation of a variety of weapon types, and as well as bombs it included air defence missiles such as Red Top and Sidewinder. The work included weapon-release systems, mechanical and electro-mechanical plus explosives – you dealt with every explosive item including ejection seats, canopy systems and flotation systems requiring an explosive cartridge.

"All the armourers, subsequently called 'ordinance electrical (air)', started courses at Arbroath. It was a large FAA school specialising in mechanical airframes, engines, gearboxes, ground equipment and armament systems. My course did basic electrics, control systems plus mechanical work and specialised in armament. We were also responsible for small arms and our training was on the .38 Webley, the Lee–Enfield .303 and machine guns as well as Very pistols and life-raft flares. We did range-shoots followed by strip-down and cleaning, and learnt about cannons and machine guns on both fixed and rotary-wing aircraft."

## NAVAL AIR MECHANICS AND MECHANICIANS

*Naval air mechanics were engineers trained in a single specialisation (airframe, engines, electrics, radio/radar, armament, etc.) depending primarily on their academic abilities. Further training led to achieving the highly skilled mechanician status.*

### George Brewes – airframes

"I joined the navy in July 1947 for two years' National Service and was demobbed in July 1949. We went to Gamecock, Bramcote to do our technical training, which lasted from September 1947 to March 1948 – I was a rigger (airframes). We were doing fabric repairs, metal repairs, hydraulics, pneumat-ics, everything – a day on aviation so we learnt about things like ADDLs (approach and dummy deck landings), and fire-fighting. The last bit of the course was about aircrew – beware of aircrew urinating on the tailwheels of the aircraft as they get in! One of the interesting things on the course was when the instructors asked a Yorkshire lad what stitch to use on the trailing edge of a wing fab-ric. Deathly silence. So he was asked, 'What do you wear when you go to work?' 'Oh, it's a clock stitch'. The answer

*George Brewes.*

was a boot stitch. When it was my turn, the PO was reeking of rum bless him. He said 'what's that?' and I said 'gravity switch. It's a switch which is activated if the aircraft crashes.' 'What does it do?' 'It blows up the radio so the enemy cannot find any secrets on the radio.' He says 'Well don't you think if it's crashed there won't be much left?' – so I got that one wrong. The other question was about a lap joint. 'What kind of joint is that?' I couldn't think. 'All right you've done a circuit in a race – think of it as a race, a motor race' – 'Oh a lap joint'…passed that one."

### John Keenan

"My father was in the RAF. I passed the RAF ap-prentice exam – which startled him witless, and he decided to put me in the navy as a sailor! I went down to Raleigh on 12 February 1963 as a sailor, but immediately realised I wanted to join the FAA for which you had to take exams. Having com-pleted those, I trained at Arbroath for 16 weeks as a mechanic. I was barely 16 and was therefore a junior because you didn't become a naval air mechanic until you were 17½. Arbroath was a wonderful place. In those days, the chief instruc-tor (and people like him) were all ex-World War

*John Keenan.*

2 chaps. They were coming to the end of their careers and didn't take any prison-ers – they used to say: 'If you can't hack it you can join the rotary wing world'.

"I was pretty much top of the class and they offered me the appointment of my choice, so I chose Buccaneers, of which the Mk.1 was then brand spanking new. I joined RNAS Lossiemouth in Easter '63. My first squadron was 809, which had just changed from being 700Z (trials) Squadron with Buccaneers. In those days we didn't have the WOs (warrant officer) of course. There was an old chief AA there called Smith, who had an enormous pot belly. The chief AA was called the chief 'Tiff' or chief mech, anyway he was a formidable man to a young junior naval airman 1.

"As I was under 17 years old I was in the juniors' division. I went in front of Chief AA Smith – and he said, 'Keenan!'. 'Yes, Chief', said I. 'You're going to work on my Buccaneers, and let me tell you that if you don't come up to scratch you'll be on ground equipment, and if you can't fix my ground equipment it's helicopters for you boy, down at Culdrose.' That's how it was in those days."

### Vernon Hopcroft – airframes

"From 1946 to 1947 I served as an AMA (air mechanic airframe) on 804 Squadron on *Theseus*. I joined as a boy entrant in 1945, and was demobilised in 1947. We were the first navy entry there. Originally the majority of Fleet Air Arm mechanics were trained at Hednesford, not far from Birmingham. I come from Redditch, Worcestershire, so I hoped that when I'd done my square-bashing I was going to complete my training near to home. They sent me down to RAF St Athan near Cardiff – the biggest air force base in the country at the time! They said it covered 26 acres.

"I trained on Airspeed Oxfords and Avro Ansons. That's more or less all we played about with. I was an air mechanic and we did 20 weeks of training. Air fitters were one step above us; they did much longer training. They wore square caps, we wore bell-bottoms. You could tell the difference and we all had different messes in the navy. When I finished training I worked on the Station Flight's Anson, and before I went on board ship I worked on Oxfords, Ansons and Mosquitoes at Goldcrest, Brawdy."

### Terry McDonald – radio/radar mechanic

*Terry McDonald.*

"I joined up on 7 January 1958 at St Vincent, Gosport as a JEM2 (junior engineering mechanic). When you joined up as a junior you joined the electrical branch, which was ships/electrics, ships/radio and radar, and then air/electrics and air/radio and radar. You were eventually chosen for a branch depending on your academic abilities. They sent a Wren officer to interview you to determine what you were going to be. I simply told her that if I couldn't do aircraft/ radio and radar I was out. That was what I got, so on 12 September I was rated a JREM – not *air* at that stage.

"In March '59 I went to Ariel, which was Lee-on-the-Solent then, until 27 September when I was rated REM2. Then I went to the ATU (Air Trials Unit) at Daedalus, and in October '59 I went up to Lossiemouth."

### Arnold Sedgewick – engines

"I joined the navy under National Service in Feb 1947 – it said 'stoker' on the en-rolment form. I'd been in the sea cadets. When I went down for the induction in Wiltshire, I told the interviewing officer that I was an apprentice motor mechanic. He said that I could join the FAA as an air mechanic (engines) – I thought that that was very 'enthusiastic' for a young lad. My training was carried out at Bramcote, just outside Birmingham – we had wartime-standard training. I was lucky or unlucky, depending on how you viewed it. Most of the aircraft were still prop-driven, jets were hovering about in the background. We were qualified to sign the Form 700 (aircraft technical log) but they wanted artificers trained on jets. So after training I went into workshops for quite a while, and they kept us in National Service for three months longer. I think this was because of the Korean War. I was only released to the reserves, so I was still liable for call-up. After finishing training I was told I could go to a station nearest my home and I was sent to Blackcap, Stretton to base workshops."

## Denis Woodhams – engines

"My memories of Bramcote in the late 1950s are of a very well organised base for the training of air mechanics in all three trades, engines, airframes and ordnance. Set in the Warwickshire countryside, with a grass airfield, we had very comfortable accommodation in rooms of eight. It was a revelation after our initial training establishments with 40 plus to a mess deck.

"The excitement heightened when we got to our classrooms and the hangars and met our instructors, most of whom were senior chief petty officers (CPO) with vast experience and wartime service. Then the aircraft – Seafires, Fireflies, Sea Furies, Skyraiders, Gannets, Wyverns, Attackers and Sea Hawks; the toy box was full of wonderful and exciting assets. Merlin, Griffon, Eagle, Cyclone, Wasp, Goblin, Gnome, Double Mamba and Python were some of the engines on stands around the hangars.

"This was at a time when the FAA was considering amalgamating the engine and airframe trades into one, and resulted in all of us getting instruction on hydraulics, pneumatics, fabric and stressed skins as well as our engine training. I decided I wanted to be an engine mechanic, then known as a fitter, as opposed to airframes, known as a rigger, but nothing was guaranteed. We had a lot of instruction on all the engines mentioned, but the most interesting was a long period on the Bristol Centaurus, an 18-cylinder sleeve-valve radial producing 2,520 hp and powering the Sea Fury.

"We were under the supervision of a superb senior chief air fitter. Our first task was to take the engine out of the Sea Fury, then to remove many of its ancillaries including several of the front row of cylinders. There seemed to be hundreds of parts laid out on benches, the mysteries of which were explained to us before we re-assembled them and fitted the engine back on the aircraft. The most exciting part came next, when the aircraft was wheeled outside and the tail secured to massive ring bolts on the hardstanding. Each trainee, after a thorough briefing, sat in the cockpit with the chief standing on the wing (brave man!). The trainer was then allowed to start the engine, and give it a ground run for about five minutes. We obviously had to limit the power, or we could have blown chiefy off the wing.

Another very thrilling exercise was learning to put the aircraft on jacks, especially in the shooting butts. The armourers then zeroed the guns and we were allowed to fire a few rounds.

"After six months we passed out in October 1958 as air mechanics airframes and engines 2nd Class. The irony was there were no badges available at this time, so we were issued with an 'A' or 'E' and to my disappointment I was given an 'A'. My posting was to Yeovilton, onto Station Flight, where I worked on and flew in the Dragonfly helicopter. In 1960 I was sent off to Arbroath to complete a SAMCO (short aircraft maintenance course) on the newly introduced Sea Vixen FAW.1. This gave me some idea of what was coming next – a front-line squadron and some sea time. In August 1960 I joined 893 Squadron on its formation under Lt Cdr F D Stanley."

## ENGINEERING OFFICERS

*Until 1995 HMS Thunderer, the Royal Naval Engineering College (RNEC), Manadon, Plymouth was responsible for training all the navy's engineering officers. Closed that year, this training is now concentrated in a combination of university courses, followed by specialist training at various naval establishments.*

### Henry Parker

"Having seen predecessors starting at 'tech' college to do HNC or HND (Higher National Certificate/Diploma) then being drafted to sea and having to give up, I started a correspondence course for the graduateship examinations of the Institute of Electronic and Radio Engineers (IERE). Along with several others of my apprentice entry I had previously applied to be considered to go to RNEC for promotion as an untrained entry supplementary list engineering officer. In due course I attended the interview board at Sultan. By then I had passed the IERE Part 1 examination, so the admiral said I might get three months off the course, and my boss, the workshops officer, called me in to say I'd been accepted. The signal said I was to appear at Dartmouth the week prior with uniform. By then I was well into studies for the finals, Part 2 and decided I would wait to try for trained entry.

"However in late 1966, with several of my chums already on a world cruise on *Eagle*, someone came from the drafters and asked for volunteers to go to the States for training as key support personnel on the Phantom F-4K. My mate Terry Russell and I couldn't refuse. In 1967 with several others, mainly CPOs, as a nominal CPO I went to NAS Miramar, San Diego for several months. I was christened the 'tame workshop boffin' having shown the Yanks how to use the transistor analyser in the avionic workshop. This was so they could repair auto-throttle units (not fitted to our Phantoms).

"On return to Yeovilton I helped set up the Phantom avionic workshops but otherwise didn't have a heavy workload as the kit in our aircraft was holding up well. I was later appointed as commander's assistant at Victory Barracks until AE-O(L) application courses commenced at Lee and Arbroath. My first brief appointment was as air stores usage control officer at Lossiemouth (Fulmar), rationalising the stores by removing thousands of parts for aircraft types no longer in service."

## AIRCRAFT HANDLERS

*Whilst carrier flight operations are a highly hazardous undertaking for the aircrew, they are equally so for the flight-deck crew – not least of all for the aircraft handlers. Working in very close proximity to moving aircraft, in all weather and sea state conditions, and with a permanent gale blowing along what is often a slippery deck, is not something for the faint hearted. As a former commander (Air) on Ark Royal said:*

"This was a demanding task, requiring great skill and the young aircraft handlers who did this work carried a heavy responsibility and worked under considerable personal risk. Death stalked the flight deck, there were so many dangers from jet blast and being blown over the side, walking into propellers or turning rotors, being trapped by ammunition lifts, caught between moving aircraft or being sucked into jet intakes."

*The aircraft handling branch was formed on 9 April 1945. Handlers are responsible for the safe movement, launching and recovering of aircraft on board ships. They are also responsible for aircraft crash rescue fire-fighting duties both on board ships, and at air stations. All handlers undergo six months' training at the Royal Naval School of Flight Deck Operations (RNS-FDO) at Culdrose.*

*Universally referred to as 'Chockheads', aircraft handlers are readily identified on a flight deck by the wearing of a blue surcoat or tabard. Other personnel on the flight deck wear differentiating colours as follows:*

**Armourers** *(known as 'Bombheads') – red*
**Stokers** *(marine engineers) 'Badgers', who looked after catapults, arrestor wires and aircraft refuelling. White with a black stripe (hence 'Badgers')*
**Electrical branch** *'Greenies' – green*
**Radar and radio artificers** *'Pinkies' – pink*
**Aircraft engineers** *– white*
**Aircraft engineering mechanics and officers** *'Grubbers' – brown*
**Flight deck directors** *(officers, petty officers and leading airmen) – yellow*
**Medics** *– red cross on white*

## Richard Dickinson

"I joined in 1974 as a 16-year-old and did my training at Ganges, and then down to Culdrose. I finished training in December that year and went to Osprey, Portland where, as a junior, I was in ATC (air traffic control) as a radar assistant to the officers and petty officers. The three main areas we worked in ATC in our branch were the control tower itself, the radar room and the flight-planning office. All this was in addition to our roles in fire-fighting and aircraft movements.

"In early '76 I joined *Ark Royal* and we went to the States; it was a fantastic trip. I started in admin for the air department and was in the regulator's office for a short time. We had a newspaper called *Noah's News*, and my role was to deliver it around the ship – a sort of paper boy! Then I moved up to the flight deck, which was quite a scary environment – I was a 'chockman' at first. In the latter part of '76 we were exercising off Norway around the oil rigs – that was when it got really scary because we had an incident with a Gannet.

"We had all three Gannets flying. When they landed and came off the wires, we put a steering arm on the nosewheel for two people manually to guide the aircraft up to Fly 1 (forward parking area) because the Gannet did not have nosewheel steering. We had two steering arms. Two Gannets had landed and the steering arms were with them. The third one landed, no steering arm, and he decided to try and make his own way up to Fly 1. As it was taxiing the front wheels turned through 180 degrees, the Gannet turned round and started heading for the island. I was sitting on a tractor with another guy plus the driver, and it was coming straight towards us. I and the other guy jumped off, but the driver didn't – he was mesmerised – our leading airman dragged him off the tractor. The Gannet hit the rear of the tractor, chopping an attached towing arm in half and coming to a stop.

"At one point during our States trip, the weather was so bad that the waves were coming over the flight deck. They needed to get a man off in a Gannet because someone in his family was seriously ill. It took off from the flight deck without the aid of a catapult – the only time I ever saw that!"

## Michael Garforth

"At Culdrose in the summer of 1973, I was doing aircraft handling training on the dummy deck when I was directed by one of the training officers (leading airman/ PO) to chock up a Gannet. The Gannet had two sets of nose props, one had already stopped turning but the other was spinning, so I was sent in to chock it up. I should have gone in via the wings – only I didn't. I went towards the spinning nose props and unbeknown to me they just missed my head. I was ordered to FlyCo (flying control) where PO Chris Horspool gave me a 'reet' dressing down, and threatened if I ever did that again I would be kicked off the course. I was ordered to run around the perimeter of the dummy deck with a pair of chocks in the hot August sunshine. I never did that again, however I was christened with the nickname 'Gannet Garforth' which stayed with me even after my naval service. I served on *Ark Royal* in

1976/77. On the flight deck one day I was speaking to Chris Horspool and noticed he had a gash on his forehead. Asking how that had happened, he replied, 'I walked into the Gannet props'. Jokingly I said, 'Chris, you see those chocks over there, go and pick them up and run around the flight deck.' I don't think Chris thought that was funny. The Gannet aircraft and I had many run-ins together."

## Chris Pugsley

"I joined the navy in 1963 to be an aircraft handler. I had always been interested in aeroplanes, and to work with them – yes! I went to Raleigh first for basic seaman-ship training, learning to swim, etc. Then it was down to Culdrose to the School of Aircraft Handling where they had a dummy deck. We had Sea Hawks to train with. Some of the staff instructors had been passed out allowing them to taxi them around, folding the wings, etc. We also trained in fire-fighting. When I finished there I was held for some months awaiting my draft. When it came through I was sent to join *Albion* (which was in dry dock at Pompey on a 10-month refit). I was basically employed as a runner until we put to sea with 848 Squadron, which had the Wessex 5."

*Chris Pugsley.*

*The new aircraft carriers,* Queen Elizabeth *and* Prince of Wales, *both have female air group members on board including aircraft engineers and handlers – Fleet Air Arm Girls!*

*Air Engineering Technician Marli Norman, a member of the air engineering department on* Queen Elizabeth. *(Royal Navy)*

## CHAPTER THREE

# LIFE ON BOARD A CARRIER

*Living and working together in an enclosed environment for months at a time, the ship's company and air group aboard an aircraft carrier certainly led a life that in many ways was very different from their RAF counterparts ashore.*

### Mike Cole-Hamilton – pilot

*Celebrating the wedding of Prince Charles and Diana in the chiefs' mess* Invincible. *Jim Speirs getting his tot from Eddie Jones the Buffer. (Jim Speirs)*

### Graham Peck – flight deck officer

"A ship at sea is independent of the world in many ways. Days of the week, and time of day, can be adjusted to suit the situation. In *Centaur* off Gibraltar in '65 we altered the clocks by three hours for ten days or so, allowing all aircrew to get night qualified and allow most of the ship's company to be in bed at a reasonable hour – and it worked.

"But the best was an alleged pipe during one of those endless patrols off East Africa in the mid '60s. Over the Tannoy came: 'There will be no Thursday this week. Thursday next week will be on Sunday as usual'."

#### 'THE ROOF RATS'

"In 1970 I was drafted at short notice to *Ark Royal* as the FDO3 (flight deck officer 3). As the ship was in refit the skeleton crew were billeted ashore. The refit eventually reached the stage when we transferred to the ship. Our daily routines became increasingly involved with final preparations for the sea trials. During this time the 'roof rats' attended the Flight Deck Handling School at Culdrose, as a refresher for the experienced hands and an eye opener for the first timers like myself. This gave everyone a taste of what the job involved, and provided instruction and practice on moving aircraft around a confined deck. It also included a flight deck machinery course for the FDOs giving an insight into the workings of the steam catapult and arrestor gear. Although I'd flown off the deck on *Victorious* during my time as a Sea Vixen pilot, I had no real appreciation of what it actually took to load an aircraft onto the catapult and launch it, yet alone recover it and park it safely on its return.

"The Handling Team was made up as follows: four officers (FDO plus FDOs 2, 3 and 4), CPO captain of the flight deck, four POs and handlers (leading and ordinary seaman) placed into port and starboard watches. Each watch comprised two FDOs (FDO and FDO3 in one watch and FDO2 and FDO4 in the other); two POs

*Graham Peck and Paul Jewell of 893 Squadron after making the 1,000th landing of* Victorious's *1967 commission, with commander (air).*

and the chief PO who maintained a roving routine across both watches. The handlers (junior rates) were split equally into the two watches.

"Good communications with the handling team were vital, and a 'loop' system ensured that only those within the loop could hear one another. Anyone outside the loop, such as the invariable Russian 'escort', were unable to hear what was going on. The FDOs, CPO and POs were able to transmit and receive – the handlers could only receive. This was done to avoid excessive chat, ensuring that orders were not drowned out. The system worked extremely well, and issues were rare. Wings and Little 'F' ran the flying operations from FlyCo overlooking the flight deck communicating to the handling team through the loop. In order to identify the numerous 'trades' working on the deck all personnel wore a colour-coded

*Hermes flight deck crew 1966. (Tim Lewin)*

*Foreign object sweep – a 'FOD Plod'. (David Lanham)*

jersey or tabard to allow easy identification (see Chapter 2).

"During flying operations we operated a four hours on/four off routine, with the two watches reciprocating. This represented a continuous cycle that lasted for as long as flying operations were taking place – I was amazed how well everyone adapted to the routine. This watch interval was for safety reasons – concentration could fall off beyond four hours. Lapses could result in injury due to jet blast and/or propellers, both lethal in the extreme, particularly at night. I witnessed a very unpleasant injury when an aircraft was brought out of the pre-launch park. As it turned towards the catapult hot jet exhaust gas, containing searing hot unburnt fuel, covered one of the handlers. It blew his flight deck jersey up his back, and his skin bubbled off causing serious burns. When on passage (non-flying), the handlers maintained a normal daily routine. Together with movements of the aircraft, the time was used to practise emergencies and carry out cleaning, painting, routine maintenance and equipment repairs.

"I was responsible for the bow catapult and carried out all the related launches during my watch period. Having been on the receiving end of a cat shot that fired as the bow was pitching down, I was very careful to ensure that the bow was travelling upward when I launched somebody. There was a delay of several seconds from the point of signalling to the launch actually occurring. The technique was to look at the stern of the ship, and as it reached its zenith (during the pitch cycle), signal the launch. The bow would then be rising as the catapult fired. The launch sequence was:

- Aircraft start engines at given signal under individual squadron engineering control.
- Handlers bring aircraft out of the park in sequence and direct them towards the catapults.
- Aircraft queue behind the relevant jet blast deflector (JBD).
- Following the launch of the aircraft ahead the JBD is lowered and the next aircraft is brought forward by the handlers and directed onto the rollers that centre the aircraft on the catapult.
- The 'badgers' (flight deck engineers) attach the 'hold back' that secures the aircraft until the point of launch. The 'shuttle' is repositioned from the end of

the catapult (following the previous launch) and the 'strop' is attached to the aircraft and looped around the shuttle. When secured the badgers signal for the aircraft to be tensioned and the 'shuttle' is moved forward to a pre-determined position holding the aircraft against the 'holdback'.

- Once all personnel are clear the FDO confirms that he has the 'launch light' and signals the pilot to apply full power. Once the pilot is happy he is at full power and in a 'go' condition he signals the FDO that he is ready to launch. The FDO will assess the deck pitch and drop his flag at the appropriate time to launch the aircraft at the optimum angle.

"Following launch the deck was prepared for the aircraft recovery sequence. The ship invariably steamed downwind during this process; this having the effect of reducing the wind over the deck and improving the working environment. All aircraft and machinery remaining on the landing area had to be positioned behind the landing safety line, or moved into the hangar deck below. The aircraft in the air were given a landing time. At the last minute the ship turned into wind on the 'flying course', as the first aircraft in the landing sequence arrived on the deck. As soon as it cleared the arrestor wire the aircraft was picked up by the handlers and directed into the allotted parking spot. The arrestor wire was reset, and as the next aircraft began its final approach the flight deck engineer checked it for damage/broken strands etc. If damage was found it was immediately cut out with hydraulic shears, removed from the landing area and replaced.

"Aircraft were lashed down at all times, and even when taxiing would be accompanied by handlers with chocks and tie-downs ready to secure it in the event of sliding. The deck became progressively slippery during flying operations; as little as a six-degree roll could cause the aircraft to slide."

### Chris Bolton – pilot
"In the island superstructure there's an operations room, the captain's day cabin, the captain's bridge, FlyCo and air traffic for visual circuits, CCAs (radar let-downs – no ILS in those days), and fighter controllers ('Ds' – directing officers). There were 2,700 people on board *Ark Royal* of whom about 1,000 were the air group.

"The air group didn't get the best accommodation, that was reserved for the ship's company. I had a cabin on seven deck which was three decks below the waterline, and there were four of us in there, all junior officers. You had your own bunk above your writing desk and a chest of drawers for your possessions. A place to write a letter, read a book and get some sleep. With the lights out it was pitch-black and there were lots of sounds to lull you to sleep – the ship's shafts turning, air conditioning, water flowing, all sorts of noises. When you're not flying, or sleeping, there's a bit of eating in the ACRB (aircrew refreshment buffet), and sometimes drinking in the wardroom bar. The wardroom was on five deck, just below the waterline, a big bar in a popular spot. We'd meet up by general agreement at 6:00 p.m. every evening if we were eating early. The wardroom dining room wasn't big enough for two big squadrons so we made an agreement with the Buccs and alternated to eat early or late.

"There were a couple of gambling games – 'horsing' and 'spoofing'. Horsing decided who was buying the wine. We'd go round with some coins in our hand until someone correctly guessed the number of coins – he paid for the wine with the meal. It could be as cheap as 10d (old pence) for a bottle – especially if we'd been to Malta. Drinking was fairly heavily policed as the commander liked to keep an eye on what we were up to. There was a limit of £20 per month (66 old pence per day). My boss said, 'this is a limit, not a target'. Drinking at 66 pence per day meant you could have 22 measures of vodka (not many did), or 5½ pints if you were a beer drinker. Courage Export was the draft beer which was strong stuff. I got one of the RAF navs' wine bill because you just sign for it and I used his. One night I must have lost my judgement slightly because he got a warning for excessive drinking – he was teetotal."

"Drinking wasn't excessive during the flying 'week' – nine days of flying then a day of maintenance. If you 'hit the bottle hard' on the evening of the ninth day, the worst that was going to happen was you'd have to sit through boring lectures the next day in the squadron ready room during a thing called 'shareholders'. This is an all-aircrew meeting where the QFI and AWI do their bits and so on, including the executive officer reading out notices."

### Anon pilot
"Life on board ship for aircrew was pretty cushy compared with what the rest of

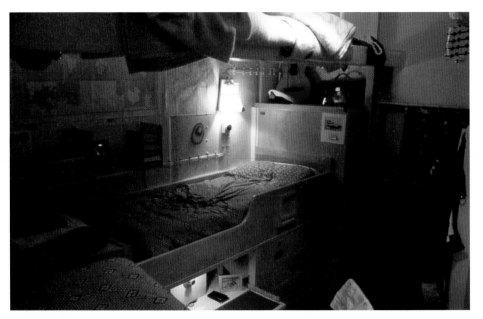

*Tony Smith's 'scruffy cabin, just below the point aircraft landed on'* Eagle *off the Maldives in 1968.*

the ship's company had to put up with. We were accommodated aft in cabins of varying sizes and 'depth' below 1 deck, which was the flight deck. Decks above were 01, 02 etc. – the island. Below were 2, 3, 4, etc. down to 10 or 11 deck. On *Hermes* almost all the cabins were single, mine was on 2 deck. On *Eagle* and *Ark Royal* we shared cabins, the more junior you were, the more people you shared with. On both I shared a three-berth cabin; on 4 deck on *Eagle* and 6 deck on *Ark Royal*. Each type of cabin had its pros and cons. On 2 deck you were just below the flight deck – understandably noisy with aeroplanes landing on the roof. On 4 deck you might have a scuttle (small window) if the cabin was against the ship's side. However most of the time it was clipped shut because if there was any sea at all the scuttle would have been awash. On 6 deck, you were closer to the four huge propellers. Most of the time they were making a 'tac-a tac, tac-a tac' sound as the blades rotated, the amplitude of which varied depending on whether the stern was rising or falling – quite soothing as one drifted off to sleep. There were a lot of other noises; generators, air conditioning, tannoy announcements, the wires being pulled as aircraft landed on, thumps reverberating throughout the ship as the catapults fired. Communication was tested from the emergency steering room; this happened to be on the same flat/deck (always at 02:00 and by a chap with what seemed a north country accent). *Eagle* also had four pairs of 4.5 guns housed in barbettes on the edge of the flight deck, and the ammunition hoist for one of them ran in a large tube partly intruding through our cabin. Every morning at 06:00 the gunnery department started the hoist which buzzed annoyingly – although this was nothing compared to the noise when they actually fired the things! It could have been worse, we could have been living in a senior rate's mess with the waist catapult track running through the deckhead (ceiling).

"We aircrew did what the RAF called 'secondary duties'. We never viewed them in this manner, we did whatever was needed – or the commander perceived to be needed – to run the ship, our home. The commander decided what he wanted in cahoots with commander air (wings), the squadron COs and the 1st lieutenant. Most of us had a division of ratings of our own squadron, and when the ship was in harbour and even at sea at one point on *Hermes*, we were OOW (officer of the watch). We participated in some of the essential dirty jobs, e.g. cleaning aircraft; even the boss would put in an appearance – he didn't stay too long, but then nobody expected him to.

"One day on *Eagle* I ended up, together with other junior officers, painting the ship's side; hanging in boarding nets with the Indian Ocean slipping by underneath. It was quite a refreshing change provided one didn't have to do it all the time. There is an anchor from *Eagle* outside the Fleet Air Arm Museum and every time I drive past I see in my mind's eye, that anchor hanging just to the right of my head!

"When we joined a ship we always made a point of scouring it from bow to stern to find out where everything was, not only out of natural curiosity but also because passageways were always being blocked off for transferring stores, oiling, varnishing the deck etc. – you had to know your way around. The USS *Forrestal* fire casualties were largely attributed to the fact that the aircrew, in particular, did not know alternative ways of escape. I doubt that that would have applied to any of us. We were shown the film of the fire before we embarked on *Ark Royal*, with the message 'know your alternative routes of escape'. This would have been fine except that from 6 deck, where we were accommodated, there was only one way in or out, a vertical ladder through a hatch onto 5 deck.

"One of the highlights of any visit to a major port was the official cocktail party, normally held on the first or second evening. The upper hangar was cleared of aircraft which were ranged on deck, the hangar deck polished and the sides disguised with flags and bunting. The invitations were arranged in part by UK embassy/consular staff to include local dignitaries and the expat community. The guests were guided to the hangar deck by junior officers and midshipmen to be handed over to those more senior – that was the theory but similar age groups attracted each other. We were in mess kit, which looked quite smart, and copious amounts of G&T, and brandy and dry were brought round in jugs by the ship's stewards. As capital ships the carriers had a full Royal Marine band which, to finish off the 'official' party, would descend on the after lift to march up and down 'Beating the Retreat' – the guests having been ushered to the sides of the hangar. They finished with 'Sunset' followed after a suitable pause by Reveille, all this while a large illuminated white ensign, visible through the open lift well, floated gently in the evening breeze. Pure theatre and capable of bringing a lump to one's throat

*No. 899 aircrew, Eagle wardroom. Jonathon Whaley looking at the camera behind 'Wiggy' Bennet, talking with Marcus Edwards. (Jonathon Whaley)*

– even those of us who were used to it. The guests were often visibly moved, and this display helped in no small way to promote UK Plc. Selected guests might then be invited to the wardroom (by us this time) to continue the party.

"My last flight from the deck was not without its humorous side. We were disembarking to the UK, which we normally did in the Bay of Biscay as soon as we were within range. Unfortunately the boss's aircraft went unserviceable, so he took ours – not humorous for me or my observer. We were stuck on board for nearly a week while the maintenance team worked like dervishes to fix the problem. It was evidently quite a difficult job, as the ship steamed ever more slowly up the channel, passing Devonport, our home port. During the last 24 hours on board we had been getting updates on a French trawler which had been caught illegally fishing somewhere near the Scilly Isles, and had 'done a runner'. By the time we launched, the fishing vessel, still trying to evade our fishery patrol vessels, was somewhere in Lyme Bay – and so were we. We launched in only half-a-mile visibility, about three miles from his position. We overflew him at mast height (not very high on a trawler) – in reheat – which must have given him a shock! Shortly after, the largest warship in the Royal Navy hove into view through the mist. He surrendered, no doubt with an 'Alors, vous gagnez' ('So, you win') preceded by some choice Gallic epithets."

### John Keenan – artificer

"*Victorious* was a beautiful ship. She had served during World War 2, including the action against the *Bismarck*. Our skipper was a wonderful chap whom everybody admired and 1966 was the best year of my life – young chap, single, great ship, great squadron, touring the Far East. The only problem was that you lived directly below the flight deck. On 2 deck not only did you have to put up with all the noise from the catapults and arrestor gear from aircraft launching and recovering, you also had to suffer the heat of the Far East. There was no air conditioning on these old carriers, and because the ship was operating 24 hours a day they used to turn the fire hoses on the flight deck just letting them run to cool the deck and the mess decks below. When off-duty it was so hot you just lay in your bunk and cooked. The mess decks were pretty dire places as there were about 50 or 60 guys in there, all living in intensely close proximity.

"The only good thing about it was the rum 'tot'.

Albion's no. 2n44 mess. (Chris Pugsley)

We drew our tot every day but only when off-watch, never when you were about to go on duty. The day's mess sweeper (cleaner) had to collect the mess deck's rum from the weather deck, from a wooden tub with 'The Queen God Bless Her' in brass letters on its side. You marched up to the OOW, saluted and said '8A Mess, Sir', to which he replied, '70 gills' (or whatever), everything was in old volume measures. The biggest mortal sin you could commit – you could sleep with the admiral's wife – was to spill the rum! You never ever did; the punishment was tantamount to receiving the death sentence. You brought the tot ration up to the mess deck, where there was a board with all the names of those who were 'G' (Grog) on it.

"The 'Bubbly Bosun' (BB) was the chap who collected the ration. Watched like a hawk, to ensure there was no spillage, he issued each of us a measure which he poured into a half-pint glass. When you'd been given this glass, your tot, you spilled some back into the 'fanny' – that was 'Queen's' – and you offered the BB a sip. There were definitive terms – 'sippers', 'gulpers', 'lower finger'. A sip was wetting your lips. Holding the glass with one or two fingers indicated the measure of rum you're prepared to give someone for doing your duty – everything had a value in rum. 'Sandy bottoms' to 'see it off' (the bottom of the glass – the sea bed) only happened to me once. After receiving our tots we'd sit around drinking and chewing the fat. You also toasted the Queen. The BB then distributed the rum left over (the 'Queen's') into glasses and passed them around for everybody to sip until it had all gone. Some would drink three or four tots, others would have their own tot and then a

*Watery tot.*

beer. Then you all filed up to the forward dining room, where food was put aside for the 'rum rats'. We always arrived about ten minutes before the meal was due to finish. Having had a tot or more of rum you were ready to eat anything – so it was a good way for the cooks to get rid of the leftovers! I saw two drunk senior 'killicks' doing handstands on the cable deck before toppling over the side into the sea. This was in the middle of flying stations which had to be cancelled, aircraft recovered, 'man overboard' declared and dinghies deployed to rescue them. They were severely dealt with but managed to hold their rates. Such was the fun of rum; it was all part of life on the lower deck.

"We had water rationing. On the old carriers, fresh water was at a premium. The first priority was for the boilers, second the catapults, then the sick bay, and finally the galleys. Somewhere near the bottom were our showers. In the Far East they put enormous canvas bag tanks on the cable deck, full of sea water from the fire mains system, in which you could wash and bathe. You didn't shave, you can't with sea water, so you'd turn in salt encrusted but clean.

"We then moved onto *Hermes*, known as the 'Happy H', but what a bucketful of doleful misery that ship was. We had to reduce our compliment of aircraft from 12 to eight as *Hermes* was very small. The fishheads ran the ship and it didn't make any difference if you were a WAFU. There were no allowances given to our watch-keeping routine or anything. *Hermes* was the worst ship I ever served on. They ran a watch-keeping system, when tied up alongside, in such a way that it affected when you could go ashore. As a WAFU you work a watch-keeping routine which allowed you to go ashore at say, 12.30 (no matter where you are in the world). We were told 'No shore leave until 3 o'clock' – this really ticked us off. We would be itching to get ashore, but even when we were alongside, we were required to 'get the liberty boat' (leave the ship) at three o'clock."

## Bob Crane – observer

"Throughout my time at sea, which included two one-month work-ups in the Moray Firth and a five-month Mediterranean cruise ('commission' in RN parlance), my constant thoughts were very much with home and family. That may sound obvious but those who join the RN expect long periods away from family, regardless of whether they are married or not. Deploying on a long-ish cruise year after year is a fact of life. RN personnel must, and do, develop the mindset to cope with a near-continuous working life away from their families – it's a lifestyle choice. Those who are married in the RAF spend some time away but, largely, life is spent going home after work. There is, therefore, a big difference between RN and RAF personnel in their outlook and the balance they strike between work and family life. A stronger camaraderie is fostered by a greater time spent away on detachment/deployment. Because of this the *esprit de corps* on RN squadrons is, on the whole, stronger than on their RAF equivalents.

### TYPICAL FLYING DAY

"05:30 – steward wakes you with a cup of tea. After getting washed, shaved and dressed, have a quick self-service breakfast in 'dirty shirt' wardroom 2 ('dirty shirt' dining room), thus working dress, i.e. flying suit, or overalls for engineers. 06:30 – briefing room for an 07:30 launch (normally the first of the day). As the briefing/ crew room, a couple of decks below the flight deck, is shared with all fixed-wing aircrew, there may be some present who are not on this wave (on *Hermes* there was a separate one for the helo guys). Briefing content is much the same as ashore and includes met, domestics and task/mission, and the all-important addition of 'charlie' time, your expected recovery time; when you need to be abeam the ship's round-down at about 600 feet, at the correct fuel weight, about to enter the break. There is also other important info such as 'deck slippery and pitching/rolling'. 07:00 – collect life jacket and 'bone dome' [helmet], then walk/climb ladders to the aircraft, via the air engineering 'shack' in the island to check the F700.

"Exit the island, locate your aircraft (you've been briefed where it is) on the flight deck, taking care not to trip over anything such as a tie-down chain, or get blown over the side of the ship by another aircraft running up/taxiing, or falling down the open lift shaft because the elevator had been lowered to bring up another aircraft. Unlike US carriers there were no guard rails – automatically raised when the lift was lowered.

"After the aircraft walk-round, strap in, check in and, when cleared to do, so start up. There is a pre-planned order in which aircraft are taxied to the catapults – you do not 'make' the launch time yourself. Normally a Gannet would be first, so as to provide AEW cover soonest. Taxi when directed (a marshaller's commands are mandatory), unfold and lock the wings when directed, otherwise you might hit someone else in the confined space. Configure the aircraft for launch and get linked up to the catapult; launch strop and hold-back connected, and catapult tensioned. When directed, run up the engines to 100 per cent – hopefully ASAP. Being linked to a 'cocked' catapult, with the engines at idle, you are very vulnerable should the catapult be fired accidentally. Complete final checks outside as well as inside the aircraft – there are also 'badgers' watching/checking. To confirm that the aircraft is ready for launch, with the crew's heads firmly against their headrests, the pilot salutes (at night he switches the anti-collision lights on). The FDO does a final check around him – ensuring for example, he's not going to launch you into a wave if the deck is pitching. The FDO lowers his flag (a lighted wand at night) to the deck and....nothing happens!...at least not for about half a second which seems like an eternity, then the catapult fires. After a 'theme park ride' along 180 feet of deck with acceleration to 135 knots in one-and-a-half seconds, pinned to the back of your ejection seat, you are airborne. Night flying follows the same level of activity, but with everything done at a slightly slower pace.

"At the end of a sortie the aircraft 'recovers' aboard. By day, and in clear weath-

*Sea Vixen FAW.2 XJ571 893 Squadron launching from* Hermes *on 20 July 1966. (Tim Lewin)*

er, the aircraft flies down the starboard side of the ship at about 600 feet, breaks, and turns downwind, lowering its undercarriage and hook. The pilot calls 'finals, four greens' as he flies the aircraft 'into the groove', aiming to line up with the centreline and assume the correct 4° glidepath. To assist the pilot in the latter, the optical landing sight provides a system of fixed horizontal green datum lights, and a moving vertical red light; when the red lines up with the greens you are on glide-path. The sight is manned by the LSO who will help guide the aircraft down by making various calls such as 'slightly high' or 'slightly fast', indicated to him by lights on the nosewheel door of the aircraft. At night or in bad weather, all approaches are made via CCA (carrier-controlled approach).

"An actual arrestment, day or night, was stark: the aircraft hits the deck hard. The pilot doesn't flair as in landing on a runway – he 'plants' it on a carrier – often described as a 'controlled crash'. Aircrew strain against their locked harnesses as the aircraft pulls out the arrestor cable, decelerating very quickly to a stop. The feeling is immediate once the arrestor hook catches the cable, coupled with the wheels hitting the deck. No immediate deceleration means a 'bolter' – the hook has not caught a wire; sometimes it will have bounced on the deck and skipped over the wires. The pilot pushes the throttles to full power so that the aircraft can get airborne again for another approach. FlyCo also transmits 'Bolter, Bolter', but the pilot obviously doesn't rely on this as it may delay getting those throttles to 100 per cent leaving him with insufficient flying speed off the deck. The US Navy procedure is to go to full throttle as soon as the wheels hit the deck, so it's quite usual to see an aircraft which has 'trapped' straining against the arrestor wire in full afterburner!

"After the aircraft stops the arrestor wire is retracted a little, then halted; this has the effect of pulling the aircraft slowly backwards so that the hook disengages the wire and can be raised. The aircraft then taxis clear of the landing area, 'cleaning up' and folding its wings as it does so.

"The aircrew head back to the engineers' 'shack' to complete the F700 and report any defects, and then to the crew room for debrief. As there is no tea/coffee available there the next destination post-debrief is the ACRB 'greasy spoon', where a drink plus a bacon/egg (or both) sarnie awaits. After night flying a meal would be provided in wardroom 2. On average you would fly three sorties in two days – equating to about 20-25 hours per month. A cycle of four continuous flying days, with the fifth day non-flying, plus time in port.

"If you were not on the flying programme, or involved as duty ops officer or other some such, you were free to go about your business, resting/relaxing or undertaking secondary or other duties. You could even change into uniform, if you wished, to enjoy waiter service at lunch in the wardroom – it generally had better food than wardroom 2. One of the things about resting/relaxing aboard ship is putting up with the constant noise of machinery/air conditioning, tannoy announcements etc., and of course the huge, crash-like thud of aircraft hitting the deck during recovery; occupying a cabin one deck below the flight deck didn't help. Equally living in close confines with others, even when occupying single cabins as on *Hermes*, generates its own noise (the disturbance factor must be worse on other carriers where officers reside in two or three-man cabins). But you get used to the 'din', and can quite easily nod off to sleep when the mood takes you – a couple of hours 'combat nap' or 'speed sleep' at will. This is especially useful when you are due to night fly, having been on the early day flying programme.

"There was always the 'banter' in the crew room to keep you occupied and amused, or reading a (probably well out-of-date) newspaper in the wardroom anteroom, rather than going solo in your cabin. Carrier flying provides an eternal

action-packed spectacle, so there was always the option of watching flying ops from 'goofers', a small open platform above the bridge which provided a clear, all-round view of the action. It was also quite common to see aircrew racing up to 'goofers' following an announcement that Vixens were conducting 'Bravo' at-

'Bravo' attack, 1970. (Bob Crane)

tacks, or that an aircraft had a 'problem' and was about to make an approach.

## AT THE END OF THE 'WORKING DAY'

"Shower, change into 'Red Sea Rig', comprising white short-sleeved open neck shirt with epaulettes, cummerbund, uniform trousers and shoes. Drinks at the wardroom anteroom bar then dinner. The quality of food aboard was, on the whole, good; anybody who disagrees with this has to remember it was a warship, not a cruise liner. Wine was served with the meal, and a 'horse' was often held to decide who paid for it. Someone chose two digits from the serial number on their wristwatch, and each in the group would take it in turn to guess the combined number, whilst the wristwatch owner called 'higher' or 'lower'. Eventually the numbers are whittled down to one individual, and it is he who pays for the wine. This was unusual in the RN which has a tradition of individuals ordering only for themselves using their exclusive bar numbers; sometimes noting the bar numbers of others!

"Post-dinner activities – boys will be boys, especially when away from home. *esprit de corps* was very much to the fore – 'live for today 'cos tomorrow may never come'. More drinks – some drank beer, others shorts including liqueurs. Beer/ soft drinks were relatively expensive, but whisky, brandy, rum etc. were duty-free and therefore cheap. If you wanted a really cheap drink, a pink gin comprised gin and angostura bitters.

"On the fourth night of flying ops (i.e. before the fifth, non-flying day) things could get somewhat riotous; ripping the pockets off 'Red Sea Rig' shirts was quite common or, with a little pre-planning, such as when an 'oppo' is in the shower, re-attaching the epaulette boards on his shirt the wrong way round – this means he forfeits a round of drinks when 'caught out' by those in on the jape. Another was filling balloons with water and attaching them to one of the deck head fans.

"Uckers – a board game similar to Ludo, but where you can 'double up' with counters to 'take' those of your opponents (a bit like in chequers); cheating was rife but all in good fun. To add extra enjoyment glasses of liqueurs replaced the counters – crème de menthe for the greens – so that when you entered 'home' you drank the appropriate glass. Cards – including poker for real money, but in very small amounts. Watching a movie; with the wardroom re-configured appropriately, the same movie was run on two nights to make sure most had a chance to see it. On *Hermes*, with the night-flying team recovering, the crash-like noise and ensuing vibration often sent the projector haywire.

"Sing-song around the wardroom piano. Songs were, of course, of a highly sexual or morbid nature (the latter usually involving flying):

> 'High on the glidepath, throttled back
> That was the end of Andy and Mac
> We're movin' on, we're movin' on

The sea'll always get'cha if the Lord can't protect ya
We're movin' on'
(sung to ...er... We're Movin' On)

"On *Hermes*, the piano would ordinarily have taken a ride down the catapult at the end of the cruise, but it had to be retained for her future use as a commando/ASW/Harrier carrier.

"Each junior officer took it in turn to act as aircrew officer of the day (AOD). This involved attending to a myriad of matters which arose, such as: getting aircrew out of bed if they'd overslept and were late for briefing, or had to replace somebody who was ill and couldn't fly; apprising the boss of aircraft serviceability at the start of the flying day; or in my case rising at 'O-crack-sparrows' to monitor a damaged aircraft being craned onto a lighter when we were anchored in Limassol Bay, Cyprus, then transported away for deep repair. One of the last duties of the AOD took place late into the evening, when he and one of the ground crew, would check that all the aircraft – every single one – were correctly tied down on the flight and hangar decks. After all, you didn't want to wake up in the morning and find one had rolled over the side or into another. There you were, in 'Red Sea Rig', getting your hands dirty tugging at each tie-down chain to ensure it was tensioned. This chore was especially risky when an aircraft on the corner of the flight deck was half hanging over a choppy sea, in little or no light!

*Catapulting the wardroom piano off* Ark Royal *at the end of the final commission. (Steve Shirley)*

## TYPICAL NON-FLYING DAY

"07:30 – steward wakes you with a cup of tea. Breakfast in the main wardroom (for those who didn't get too drunk the night before). 09:00 – 'shareholders', which typically lasted an hour or two, comprised op/admin briefings, presentations and parish notices by the squadron hierarchy (boss, senior pilot and senior observer). Shareholders was held, even when in port, to stop officers having a lie-in, ensuring an orderly and timely start to the day. If there were no formal activities planned after shareholders, the hierarchy would declare a 'make and mend', what the RN called personal administration.

"11:00 – occasionally aircrew would help clean their assigned aircraft – to the great amusement of the ground crew. Air-

Eagle, 'hands to bathe'.

crew getting their hands dirty? Never heard of such a thing! At other times all non-duty personnel would be required on the flight deck for a fitness session. It was quite impressive to see hundreds of officers and sailors exercising together, jumping up and down, running on the spot etc., often wearing anti-flash gear in order to 'get the sweat flowing'. When sea conditions allowed, 'hands to bathe' was declared. The carrier was stopped dead in the water, a rear boarding ladder lowered, a sea boat crew launched to act as safety watch, and officers and sailors invited to jump off the quarterdeck and go swimming. On *Hermes* in 1969/70 there were no facilities available for sports or other pastimes – it is untrue that there was a 'rough sea' billiard table with cube-shaped 'balls'.

"A RAS (replenishment at sea) was performed on every non-flying day to ensure the carrier was re-stocked as necessary; everything from fuel (both ship and aircraft), aircraft/equipment spares and other equipment, to food/drink etc. Intensive aircraft maintenance was also carried out, and aircrew were encouraged to 'visit' their assigned aircraft and learn from the maintainers what work they were doing.

"Midday and onwards. Following lunch in the main wardroom, your time was your own to attend to secondary duties, mail, hobbies etc., and to catch up with sleep (referred to as 'stringing the Zzzzzs') – the on board working/living/playing cycle could be very tiring. The all-important mail (the only method of contact with home, unless you were in port), was delivered and sent every couple of days or so via the COD (carrier on board delivery) Gannet which would have flown to an airfield ashore. Mail was also collected/sent when in port. The RN had a very

impressive worldwide arrangement with other countries ensuring mail reached ships in almost every corner of the globe. As to hobbies, I carried on with the equivalent of the tradition of mariners carving objects out of wood. In my case this was building plastic model aircraft. In a lovely little hobbies shop in Gibraltar I bought a kit of the original 'Frog' DH.110, and converted it into a Sea Vixen. All these personal activities took place when not flying on any day.

"At the end of the non-working day, the format was much the same as for a working one, i.e. shower, change into 'Red Sea Rig', dinner, drinks etc. – somewhat toned down because of flying the next day.

*Mail from home. Ark's quarterdeck, January 1972.*

"There were numerous port visits during the cruise. Officers and sailors could enjoy the various local 'delights' and purchase 'rabbits' (gifts) to take home. Being in port allowed the ship to re-stock with fresh food such as eggs and milk. A RAS did not supply these, and the powdered variety could only be endured for so long. Also there was the 'Cockers P' (cocktail party) held on the first evening in port, where the ship's officers hosted local dignitaries and their ladies. It also enabled those of a certain disposition to meet, and get fixed up with, some of the local 'talent'. The aircraft would have been ranged in a pretty pattern on the flight deck and the RM band would beat the retreat – always most enjoyable. For certain port calls, particularly those lasting more than a few days (e.g. Malta and Cyprus on *Hermes*' last commission) some aircraft would be flown ashore so that continuity flying could take place."

*Deck hockey on board Ark in the 1970s.*

**Anon – commander (air)**
"The highly competitive hockey matches on the flight deck deserve a mention. Many people on board, working in store rooms at lower levels, never saw daylight unless able to go on the flight deck. Use of the deck was a contentious issue between the demands of sufficient flying time, the requirement for endless engine running and moving aircraft, and the health

and morale of other members of the ship's company. This had to be fairly agreed between the commander (air) and the ship's executive commander. It usually resulted in an open deck for an hour and half between the end of day flying, and the first night launch. Then teams came up to play hockey with rope pucks and reversed walking sticks! Others did individual exercises or just walked up and down listening to the Royal Marines band playing popular music."

### Tony Hayward – observer

"Since our 'Fishhead' brethren considered that we 'Flyboys' did b***** all at sea, we used to be landed with OOW in harbour. There were two brows, one forward for the 'troops' and one aft for the officers. This did have its moments....in the early hours, alongside in Singapore, the OOW on the aft brow heard a 'clip clop' coming towards the ship. Eventually there hove into sight a very happy stoker on board a horse. He had found it (God knows where) in the city, and had liberated it because he couldn't find a taxi. The duo came to a halt at the bottom of the after officers' brow, and the stoker dismounted. The OOW moved to the top of the brow with his telescope under his arm, hoping that 'Jack' would realise his mistake, but he kept on coming...finally, face to face, he crouched and said 'Draw!'

"On the flight deck there are safety lines to keep ground equipment clear of the angled deck and landing aircraft. With the first land-on downwind, the FDO, Bob Ponter, noticed a fork lift parked over the line and leapt onto it to move it back. Unfortunately it was in gear and when he hit the starter he shot smartly backwards and over the side. To the tannoy and radio shout of 'man overboard!' the 'plane guard chopper laughingly radioed that it was the FDO and he was OK. That evening the ship's tannoy announced, 'fork lift flying for today is completed, stand down from flying stations'.

"When the ship was on passage, with no flying, there were a number of card schools including dealer's choice poker and chemmy. I still recall the blind baseball version of poker and the dealer's ritual chant, 'whores, fours, one-eyed jacks and king with the axe are wild'. There were movies, magic shows (Roger Squires, last heard of as a crossword compiler on the *Daily Telegraph*, was an observer with 849 Squadron and an amateur magician who kept doves in his cabin). Special dates, such as Trafalgar, and especially Taranto (the FAA's Trafalgar), merited a formal mess dinner, (as a hangover from the days when deckheads were lethally low, the loyal toast was made sitting) and with energetic and fairly violent after-dinner games.

"Booze and fags of course were duty free, and measures were the equivalent of civilian doubles; in old money whisky was 4d, gin 2d (cheap gin 1d), brandy 5d, beer 10d, so everyone drank spirits. Since the booze allowance for officers was £5 a month, we were constantly reminded that it was an allowance, not a target. Brandy and ginger ale Horse's Neck had taken over from pink gin as the beverage of choice. Pusser's Rum issue, and beer, were available to the lower deck; whereas the officers only saw the rum if the order was given to 'splice the mainbrace' as a

*'Crossing the Line'. (Ray Day, Chockheads)*

reward for a job well done. As a tightly knit squadron however, we were often the unofficial guests of our chiefs' and petty officers' messes where Pusser's Rum and Double Diamond chasers were offered.

"There were, of course, the traditional 'crossing the line' ceremonies. Also lethal hockey games on the flight deck, lethal because it had no rules about the height that sticks could be raised and was played on a non-skid armoured flight deck. Some squadron COs banned their aircrew from playing because of the high attrition rate.

"On a much more sober note I will always remember Remembrance Day. At 11:00 hours our carrier and its escorts came to a standstill in the middle of the Indian Ocean for the two-minute silence. It was not all fun and games."

### Peter Hiles – pilot

"What *did* we do when not flying? My first thoughts were nothing, but of course we did many things; briefings and debriefings, watching films of our air-firing exercises and rocketry. We spent time with our ground crews learning the ins and outs of the nuts and bolts of the airframe and engine. We stood the occasional watch, usually one of the night watches. Collateral duties; I was at times the photographic officer, laundry officer, and I did a time and motion study of the engine room. We enjoyed PT and sports when possible, deck hockey, volleyball in the after lift well. We looked after ourselves (after all junior naval officers do not have batmen). Whilst in harbour, officer of the day, officer of the patrol and escort for visitors when the ship was open to them. There was so much more – eating and drinking, all the personal things like writing, drawing, painting, playing music, reading a lot, theatrical jobs and so on."

### Roger Meecham – armourer

"In 1960/61 I had the opportunity to visit, and work on board, two somewhat exotic foreign ships. The first was an ex-World War 2 British aircraft carrier *Vengeance*, which in 1956 had been sold to the Brazilian navy for £9 million. It spent four years in a Rotterdam dockyard being modernised with an angled deck, mirror landing devices and improved steam catapults. In 1960 she was relaunched with a new name, NAeL *Minas Gerais*. She spent three weeks in the English Channel getting the crew to familiarise themselves with, and become properly trained in, the workings of their new vessel, or as they say in the navy 'working up', on her trip to her new home. They had a big problem as this was their first aircraft carrier; no-one had any flight-deck experience and they had no aircraft to practise with. They called on the expertise of the squadron that I was with, 700X Squadron at Yeovilton. This squadron undertook all sorts of different tasks from radar jamming to flight-deck training, with a number of different types including Sea Venoms and Gannets.

From left to right: Roger Meecham, PO unknown, and 700X Lt Cdr Squadron CO.

"A group of us were detailed to join the ship at Portland, and be prepared to stay on board for about three weeks. Once aboard the ship headed for Lyme Bay. The accommodation was very crowded and I ended up slinging a hammock in a passageway which wasn't a problem, but the food on board was. The Brazilian navy seemed to exist on a rice-based dish similar to paella with lamb, while the British sailors were used to potatoes and roast beef. What made it worse was that every now and then you'd come across a sheep's eye. Brazilians considered this to be a delicacy, and if you didn't have one in your meal the very companiable Brazilian sailors would give you one of theirs. It was considered a friendly gesture for them to pick an eye out of their meal, with their fingers, and pop it into your mouth. They were a bit miffed when virtually all the British lads refused these overtures of friendship.

"The lack of experience of the Brazilians working on the flight deck was painful to watch. One man stood up in front of a Sea Venom's air intake and was sucked in. Fortunately the pilot closed the throttle so he wasn't drawn right into the engine, which would have been fatal. A number of other guys were bowled over after walking behind running aircraft. One walked into the jet efflux of a Sea Venom on the catapult. He was rolled down the deck and over the side where he fell onto a gun sponson and was badly injured.

"Another incident was more funny than dangerous. One of the flight-deck firefighters was dressed in a heavy asbestos fire suit, complete with asbestos over-boots. It was the same suit that British firefighters wore, except that we did not use the over-boots, relying on leather sea boots. This Brazilian was called to communicate with the pilot of a Gannet which was on the catapult. To do so he had to climb up the three or four kick-in steps in the side of the aircraft – it was then that the reason the British lads did not use over-shoes became apparent. He got up two steps, and suddenly both his feet were stuck due to the extra bulk of the over-shoes. At first he just hung on looking a bit perplexed, then in an effort to free himself he let go with his hands, fell backwards and hung upside down – his hands not quite touching the deck. The pilot had to abandon the take-off and was livid, he couldn't even get out of the cockpit. With some effort, half a dozen guys managed to extricate the unfortunate upside-down firefighter, and prize his over-shoes out of the steps.

"We did help the Brazilians to become more professional and safety conscious on the flight deck, but realised when we left them that they had a long way to go in becoming competent flight-deck operators. We wished them 'Godspeed and good luck' but were secretly thankful to be seeing the back of their goodwill, friendly gesture sheep's eyes.

"In 1961 we were once again deployed aboard a foreign ship, this time the INS (Indian navy ship) *Vikrant*, formerly the British carrier *Hercules* laid down in 1943 but never commissioned. In 1957 she was bought by India, towed to Belfast and given a modernising refit by Harland & Wolff, including an angled deck. By May 700X personnel were on board to assist with deck-landing trials. I found myself in a messdeck with a load of Sikh sailors, all of whom could speak English, I even had a bunk of my own.

"One afternoon there was no flying as there was some trouble with the forward lift, which was down and being worked on by the engineers. By the door of the island I saw an engineer, who was standing on a temporary staging in the lift well with his upper body showing. He began ringing the 'lift moving' bell, as if he was operating the lever to go down. At that moment, a guy came out onto the flight deck in a bit of a rush. In normal circumstances, if the lift is at flight-deck level and is about to go down the operator turns a lever which sounds a warning bell. Once the bell sounds no-one is to get on or off the lift. However, it doesn't work like that, the bell ringing is a late wake-up call to all those dozy blighters who need to go down to the hangar deck and the few who are standing on the lift but don't want to go down, to either run up and jump on, or scramble off the now lowering lift.

"Well, the guy who had rushed onto the flight deck took the bell and the upper body of the engineer, as signs that the lift was just starting to go down. He ran forward, leaping effortlessly over the big sign that said: 'Lift Down Maintenance in Progress. Keep Clear', and sprinted the few paces to the lift that wasn't there. Everyone realised what was about to happen, but no one was able to stop the accident. I will never forget the look of shock and amazement on the engineer's face, as the guy leapt, glancing over his shoulder with a friendly word followed by a scream, a loud and painful thump, and an even more painful silence. The fall could have killed him, it did in fact break a few bones, but he made a full recovery and became a bit of a celebrity. He was nicknamed 'Birdman', because of his incredible ability to fly.

"Part way through the deployment the guys were having withdrawal symptoms for proper grub such as sausage rolls (known throughout the navy as 'dog rolls'), meat pies and chocolate. The senior pilot agreed to send a Gannet back to Yeovilton for supplies. Being an armourer I didn't have a lot to do, so I volunteered to go back in the rear seat of the Gannet to collect what was wanted. Once the squadron personnel heard I was going, I was inundated with lists of food to buy from the NAAFI, and especially the Women's Voluntary Service canteen which made a particularly good dog roll.

"As we were operating in Lyme Bay, it only took half an hour before we were back at Yeovilton and I was spending in the tuck shops. When it came to flying back, the only way we could accommodate all the boxes of sausage rolls, pies, Mars bars and other goodies was for me to get in, strap myself in, then get the ground crew to load everything in on top of me. This just about filled the cockpit up to the canopy. I contemplated what would have happened if we'd had to bail out. I suppose if I could have found the 'hood jettison' handle and got rid of the canopy, most of the sausage rolls and cardboard boxes would have been sucked out by the slipstream, allowing me a chance to clamber out, if I still had time.

"Back on board ship, just as I was going off to sleep that night, with a belly full of dog rolls, Mars bars and indigestion, I wondered what the local residents would have thought if we had bailed out over land and all those dog rolls, meat pies, chocolate bars, (known as 'nutty' in the navy) and filled rolls, had landed in some village."

### Richard Moody – pilot

"One of my non-flying roles in *Eagle* was that of horse racing correspondent for the ship's newspaper – the *Eagle Express* – my nom de plume being Captain Cuttle. Captain Cuttle had won the Epsom Derby in 1922 ridden by the legendary jockey Steve Donaghue.

"I've always loved horse racing. That autumn there was an excellent Irish two-year-old called Sir Ivo, which I told the entire ship's company to back at all costs for next June's Epsom Derby. At the time I also ran the ship's squash team, and in Hong Kong we played a number of matches at the Hong Kong Cricket Club. The opposing teams were organised by a judge – Sir Ivo Rigby. It was just too much of a coincidence, and Sir Ivo duly won the Epsom Derby. I was feted by all and sundry on board for my tip in the ship's newspaper.

"But earlier in the same year, while at sea without any radio news contact, I had pretended to be the official commentator for the Grand National steeplechase. Needless to say, my 'winner' – Dagmar Gittell – did not distinguish itself in the real Grand National, and my pretence was rapidly rumbled."

### Colin Morris – pilot

"As officers, aircrew were expected to do normal ships' duties as well as squadron duties. We were also allocated groups of men to cater for their promotion and welfare et cetera. To help prepare me for this, sometime back in 1963, I was sent on the divisional officers' course at Whale Island, Portsmouth. It was a man-management course specialising in leadership qualities with reference to naval ratings and it wasn't particularly memorable. Except for the occasion when we were taken out on a Saturday night with the shore patrol.

"'Jolly Jack' gets himself into trouble when he has had a few beverages; it was the job of the shore patrol to keep the peace and round them up to return them to their ships, or to the cells, depending upon their indiscretions. It was most illuminating. When I was a lieutenant in 899 Squadron, I was responsible for the radio and electrician sailors of the squadron; in general, a bright and intelligent bunch of lads though not always matched by their actions. This was a major responsibility, getting to know one's men and writing up their reports. Those hauls backwards and forwards across the Indian Ocean were good times to catch up with paperwork and report writing. So, life wasn't entirely flying and socialising. In many ways, it was a bit like being a Citizens Advice Bureau worker. It was amazing the scrapes into which some of the sailors would get themselves. Another job was being on watch on the gangway, which could be a little tedious."

### Tony Sanders – air ordnance electrical

"After the Falklands War *Invincible* was pulled out for a two-week rest and recuperation. We were resting up, and Captain J J Black had his first sleep for days. We all just shut down, had a nice kip and some decent food. As nobody drank at all during the conflict the RAF sent over some extra beer – so we all had a decent beer for a change. We had one of the ENSA (Entertainments National Service Association) groups come on board. They'd been to a couple of other ships prior to ours, and now they'd come to the big one. The lead comedian was Bobby Crush along with a couple of very nice girls, and a few other people; it wasn't a big troop but it was brilliant. There were two performances, one in the afternoon and one in the evening. All the senior rates went to the one in the evening; we let the young lads go first. Bobby Crush said it was good and they enjoyed themselves but, 'By gum, weren't they all quiet'; they'd expected a lot more noise. Then he walked on in the evening and asked the senior rates – what the hell were we like? Were we the grizzled old lot; were we the old growler bears, or something like that? That was brilliant, in

fact he over-extended the show, especially his comedian's slots, with singing, dancing and extra jokes. It was a brilliant evening."

### Kim Sharman – pilot

"As a WAFU we didn't really have any experience or training as seaman officers. Consequently we were not regarded as 'real' naval officers – a situation we were not un-

*WO and CPO mess function,* Invincible *1980. (Tony Sanders)*

happy about! It left us plenty of time and opportunity to do other things whilst we were at sea. In between flying duties (more or less continuous whilst at sea) we were left with little time to do anything else. WAFUs are typically portrayed as having a very close relationship with their bunk. Not entirely untrue!

"In fact we all had a division of sailors to be responsible for. On a day-to-day basis this was not arduous as the divisional petty officer did the real work in communicating with the troops. The only exception to this would be if one of the sailors had misbehaved in some way, ending up being subject to some form of official investigation – thus we became involved. This would be at the commander's 'table' where the misdemeanour was appraised and punishment issued. If the charge was not particularly serious the sailor was asked if he would accept the commander's findings and punishment, or opt for court martial – which very few did given the choice. We had other jobs within the squadron. The most unpopular was confidential books officer, who had to keep tabs on the secret books, and account for them.

"Whilst in harbour things changed. Suddenly we were considered competent enough to man the gangway – especially in the midnight watches! Our role there was to ensure that 'Jack', after a good run ashore, got back on board safely and down to their mess deck. Of course he could be in various stages of intoxication. I remember being OOW when a rating turned up at the bottom of the gangway dressed only in his underpants. I watched closely as he made his way up to the ship, where he stood and saluted smartly. I didn't say a word as he looked at me and said: 'It was a bloody good run ashore Sir.' I just replied, 'Get below' and he did. There was no point in instigating any form of punishment as no-one had suffered.

"The most serious aspect of 'Jack' returning drunk was if they were generally fed up with the navy and, through drink, had lost their inhibitions enough to have a swing at the OOW. This would result in a very serious charge of assault. To protect the drunken sailor from this possibility, there was a 'knuckle party' of Royal Marines, just inboard of the ship whose job it was to prevent this happening. Very pragmatic and comforting to a 20-year-old 'sprog' aviator!

"Naval squadrons are composed of all trades. Aside from engineers, we had our own handlers, safety equipment people, fighter directors and even cooks and stewards. There would be occasional squadron runs ashore where everyone would go out together for beers and grub. These were enjoyable events where the rigid formality of rank was relaxed, but not forgotten. On one run ashore in Gibraltar everyone soon got very relaxed. Towards the end of the evening, I was chatting to a young naval airman who complimented me by saying: 'You're the only good one amongst them, Sir. All the rest are bastards!' 'Yes, all right Bloggs. Enjoy the rest of the evening.' He then moved on to the next aviator. 'You're the only good one amongst them, Sir. All the rest are bastards!'

"Sometimes you'd invite a naval officer to dinner in what was known as a 'grippo'. My wife and I were invited to a cocktail party on *Ark Royal* in Hong Kong during the 1980s, so later I found myself hosting two naval officers to dinner – known as a 'reverse grippo'. The first evening after leaving a port visit, an important award was given. This was the 'Ropey Trophy' for the guy who had escorted the least attractive woman ashore. Cruelly, after leaving one port, this was awarded to someone who had flown his wife out!

"Whilst at sea in the '60s and '70s, there was very little chance to communicate directly with loved ones at home. Consequently mail became very important; the navy was very good at organising this. An aircraft was sent ashore at various places to collect mail for the ship. When it arrived back on the ship, the arrival of the mail was announced. It was a bad day if you didn't get a letter. During a postal strike in the UK in the 1960s, mail that had been posted at Portsmouth, Plymouth and the various air stations, was amazingly delivered to the ship off Aden within 24 hours!

"Telephone calls from the ship were virtually impossible, and from ashore had to be booked in advance and were expensive. It was not uncommon to go months without speaking to the 'significant other' in your life. My wife flew out to Hong Kong after eight months apart, and I found that I had forgotten how she sounded!"

### Jim Speirs – aircraft handler

"Whilst I was on watch in the hangar on *Eagle* a fire broke out in the LOX plant; one or two guys were killed in the explosion. We could smell smoke, the plant was just the other side of the bulkhead which became red hot. We shot water at it from hoses and it turned the water to steam – that's how hot it was. The metal was actually burning because the LOX was in contact with it. The ship went to emergency stations. Everybody disappeared to their allotted places. There were six Buccaneers in the lower hangar; one of them was on jacks. Because they were all full of fuel, they had to be moved up to the flight deck. Most of the maintainers had disappeared, leaving myself and two others to move them – there was nobody to ride the brakes. I attached a strop around the hook of the aircraft on jacks and pulled it off using a mechanical handler (the undercarriage was down). The only damage was where

*Jim Speirs front and centre squatting down,* Eagle *FD party 1965.*

it had moved off of the jacks.

"If we hadn't got the aircraft out of the hangar, and they had caught fire, we would probably have lost the ship. I received a 'recommend' from the ship's air engineering officer for that. There was a lot of damage on the port side of the ship, from 3 deck down. One of the mess decks filled with smoke. The handlers, having been trained in fire-fighting, entered the mess deck, extinguished the fire and got everybody out – they were considered to be heroes."

## Allan Tarver – pilot

"I joined 893 Sea Vixen Squadron on *Victorious* in October 1964. On my arrival the most important thing was not getting used to the ship or aircraft; it was whether I was going to invest my money in the squadron speedboat. Before leaving the UK it had been bought by a syndicate of 25 aircrew who each paid £25. The deal was that each month the on-paper value of the boat was assumed to reduce by £1. When somebody left the squadron they were paid off using the current on-paper value – this kept everybody happy. The only problem, on the way home from the commission, was how we could get rid of the damn thing. We managed to sell it to some gullible soldiers in Gibraltar, quite keen to take the wreck off our hands!

"The boat was a great thing to have in the Far East. Periodically the carrier would anchor off a small island and lower the boats, including ours, so we could get to one of the local beaches. My abiding memory was of the number of flip-flops floating around – forget plastic rubbish, this was something on a much greater scale.

"I returned to the UK nine months later and, after three enjoyable months at Greenwich, I joined *Ark Royal* in February '66. The *Ark* had a problem with its boilers and we were holed up in Singapore in April. We were waiting to sail across the Indian Ocean to join the Beira Patrol – for all the good that did. The aircraft had disembarked to Changi with the aircrew dispersed to various hotels along the coast, mostly in the Ocean Park, a name I won't forget in a hurry. On one occasion after attending a farewell cocktail party on *Ark* I returned to the hotel to go to bed. However, there was a competition to select the 'Playboy of Singapore', and whilst having a nightcap, I got collared by Keith Sommerville-Jones who propelled me onto the dance floor.

"I wasn't sure what the judges were

*Playboy of Singapore. (Allan Tarver)*

looking for but, with much encouragement from my colleagues, who were full of booze, they decided I would do. I was instructed to appear one week later at a cinema where the final selection was to be held. It became apparent that *Ark*'s departure from Singapore would be delayed for another couple of weeks as there were still problems with her evaporators, so I duly appeared for the 'final'. All I had to do was walk on stage and light a cigarette. Given that the place was full of sailors, hooting and roaring and cheering me on, I won the competition and, thus, became Playboy of Singapore 1966. That's my sole claim to fame, one which haunted me for years."

### Mark Thomson – pilot

"I served on three carriers in the '60s, *Albion*, *Centaur* and *Victorious*. All three had been laid down not long after the end of World War 2, or 1939 in the case of *Victorious*, so there were similarities about the on-board experience.

"Life on board was hugely different depending on whether we were at flying stations or not. Most of the time we had three operational carriers at sea – two east of Suez, and one west of Suez. The officers' cabins were all in the stern – I remember being in a four-bunk cabin, and as a junior member of the squadron I had the top bunk. When lying in my bunk I could raise my arm and touch the hot flight deck above my head – I also heard every aircraft landing above my head. East of Suez we had to get used to relentless heat and humidity, as the air conditioning was very poor. The noise and smell were always present; an operational carrier is constantly busy 24 hours a day, seven days a week. Life was spent either in the squadron crew room preparing to fly, eating, or unsuccessfully trying to sleep. I remember being constantly tired from lack of sleep – I felt tired for months.

"The introduction into operational service of the Scimitar, Buccaneer and Sea Vixen was a quantum leap in technology and capability, compared to the benign aircraft which they replaced. The price paid for this arms race in the Cold War was that there was also a massive leap in the size and weight of these new aircraft, yet the size of our carriers was still the same. Night-deck landing a Sea Vixen with its 52-foot wingspan on *Centaur* was character-forming stuff! On the starboard side there was not much wing clearance.

Ark Royal *hangar from forward lift shaft.*

## THE SQUADRON GROUND CREWS

"The leap in technology of these new aircraft meant that there was always a high unserviceability rate; the ground crews were caught in the middle between that and the senior pilot always demanding that more aircraft were available to fly. Working through the night in the hangar was often the norm. In all my time flying Sea Vixens I was blessed with excellent reliability; particularly with the Rolls-Royce Avon which was always hammered whenever it flew, and I never even had a cough out of it. What an engine! The squadron engineers were unquestionably the unsung heroes of the piece.

## A VERY SAD ACCIDENT

"It has often been said that a carrier flight deck is the most dangerous place in the world, particularly at night. In pitch black the pilots have to taxi their aircraft onto the catapult, and the ship may well be turning into wind at the same time. A Sea Vixen pilot, my closest friend, was following the marshaller's torch signals to manoeuvre onto the catapult when one of the flight-deck crew ran behind his aircraft and was blown overboard. Everything stopped as the 'man overboard' procedure swung into place, but very sadly, he was never found.

## A SURPRISE!

"A carrier, particularly when carrying nuclear weapons, is always surrounded by its own task force of frigates or destroyers; protecting it, out to perhaps 100 miles, against an air, sea or subsea threat. In *Victorious* in the '60s we were night steaming (no night flying), in the Indian Ocean, in an easterly direction toward Singapore. The following morning there was a buzz that something had happened during the night, but everyone was very tight lipped. It emerged that the task force with their 20 or so radars had tracked something approaching them at about 1,000 mph; it suddenly stopped before flying off at the same speed. Such manoeuvres were certainly unknown to the laws of physics as we knew them.

## WHAT TO LOOK FORWARD TO?

"In those days life on board was an amazing experience, however we used to long to be ashore away from the continuous and inescapable noise, heat and exhaustion. My longest period on board, with a lot of flying round the clock, was ten weeks in the tropics."

### David Webb – observer

"I was a naive fresh-faced 'crab' (navy slang for any member of the RAF), and a really keen squash player. I brought my squash kit with me and in the first few hours on board *Hermes* I was challenged. I countered by saying the carrier did not have a squash court but was swayed by one and all that it did exist. I was given directions on how to find it and at the appointed time, in my kit with racquet in hand, off I went. It was sometime later in the bowels of the ship that a rating looked at me and said: 'I think sir, as a crab, you've been had.' I learnt a hard lesson.

"Embarked evenings in the wardroom, post-dinner, tended to be lively affairs with the Buccaneer or Sea Vixen crews spoiling for a fight. This usually started with the obligatory ripping of a shirt pocket. As the 'fighting' continued the Gannets would join in on the losing side. Things could get quite heated, and some serious injuries did ensue. A broken leg and arm on one evening brought matters to a head as commander (air) could not afford to lose valuable aircrew. Another memorable event was the attempted 'lynching' of the catering officer. We had been at sea for some time and food supplies were low. Rumours circulated that the catering officer was profiteering from his contracts, so one officer produced a toy pistol and, went off with helpers, to kidnap the offender. The catering officer was frog marched to the wardroom where a solitary noose hung from a ceiling fan. As things got out of hand wing commander air appeared just in time to stop the ritual hanging.

"One of our small RAF contingent was nicknamed 'the 18-carat gold extension'. The first evening on reaching port was a sundowner's cocktail party. The officer's party trick was to watch out for any lady who needed to light a cigarette. Before she could get a lighter an arm would appear, showing off his 18-carat lighter, and matching cufflinks – creating a novel way to get introduced.

"Following night flying, with the squadron safely aboard, wardroom 2 was used for the wind-down. Copious amounts of canned beer downed, with the empties being thrown into the overhead fans to provide extra amusement. The squadron worked and played hard. On one such night in Gibraltar we visited North Front mess. Being a little late for supper, and hungry, we decided to eat the table flowers. Obviously, we were asked to leave and promptly banned from returning."

### Terry McDonald – radio and radar technician

"My pal David Smith and I were ashore at RAF Khormaksar with some aircraft and new pilots. They had to do so many touch-and-goes during the day before they could hook on, and then do the same at night, until everyone thought they could hook on all right. We were looking after the aircraft on shore. We had a Land Rover and were based down in Sheba, the naval base in the harbour. We had to drive up to Khormaksar every day through the Maala trouble area. Ordinarily they never ever gave 'Jolly Jack' a gun except for a ceremonial guard; never any ammunition, except for a funeral firing party. However, they gave us Stirling sub-machine guns with as many ammunition clips as we wanted. When we handed the guns back they weren't interested in the ammunition clips; they never checked them. We were going through Maala with one 'up the spout', ready to fire.

"Four of us leading hands used to play bridge together. As we were coming up to Christmas and I was ashore, they sent me a message asking if I could get some bottles of spirits for Christmas. 'When the Land Rover gets hoisted back on board from the barge, Ted will meet it on the deck. If you put the bottles in the cubby hole at the back of the Land Rover, and put a padlock on it, nobody will know. He can get the bottles out later on when nobody's looking.' So I bought four bottles of spirits and put them in the Land Rover, put the padlock on, and it was sent back out to the ship on a lighter. We distributed the bottles of spirits amongst the four of us. Although we didn't know it at the time, some stupid stoker had broken into the NAAFI stores and stolen some crates of beer. It was announced that if whoever had stolen the beer returned it to the NAAFI, nothing would be said – he had two days to do it. Nothing happened. We were warned that the ship was going to be searched. We loved our spirits, but we could only buy beer on board; we couldn't have any spirit other than our rum ration. What the hell we were going to do?

"We were having a 'sod's opera' variety show, and they used to raise the lift off the hangar floor so it was open to the sky and used as a stage. We had some marvellous shows. I had a jazz band on board, in which I played trombone, so I got my trombone case (a big square box), took out all the rubbish I stored in it, and put two bottles of spirits inside. I locked it and left it on the stage. It was up to the others to try to hide the other stuff somewhere. They opened the vents on some trunking. Although we didn't have air-conditioning, we had some air blasting through and they hid them in the vents. Of course, other people had been saving beer for Christmas; you were each allowed to have two cans of beer a day. Sometimes you could buy more, but not much, and people had been saving it up and hiding beer everywhere – if you were caught with it you were in trouble.

Fortunately, as luck would have it, the master at arms and his team found the stolen beer in the stokers' mess. They'd opened a hatch and slung the beer in a kitbag in the ammunition hoist. – all hell was let loose. The guy responsible was sent back to the UK to DQs (detention quarters).

"We had the BBC

*Purity jazz band on HMS* Eagle, *Terry on trombone. (Terry McDonald)*

on board making a documentary called 'Warship Eagle'. Charlie Squires was the director of the programme. We had them on in the 'sod's opera' second leg (the one I was on) – so my jazz band featured on the show. I had a guy who played guitar who looked and played like Hank Marvin. However we used to have to drag him by the scruff of the neck to come along and rehearse."

## CONTRASTS

### Tim Lewin

"Late on a dark night in mid-Indian Ocean; flying is finished for the day and most of the ship off-watch is sleeping. Junior Seaman Scroggins is preparing for his very first watch on the bridge. He knows not to be late, to announce his presence and all other details. Dead on time he comes to the door of the bridge, the flat (area) outside is brightly lit. He knocks, no response. He opens the door and goes inside. The bridge is completely black to his unadjusted eyes.

'Is there anybody here?' he asks.

'Well, I'm here' replies the captain (Terence Lewin, better known as TTL), sitting in his chair writing up his sea orders under a dim red light.

'OK mate,' says Scroggins 'you can eff off now, I'm here to take over.'

'Splendid,' replies TTL, 'I'm off gentlemen, goodnight.'

It was several minutes before anyone could stop laughing enough to tell Scroggins what had happened."

### Mike Cole-Hamilton

"Grand Harbour at dusk on a perfect summer evening. A cluster of dghajsas and ships' boats around *Centaur* for an official reception, cocktail dresses and 'mess undress' on the flight deck. G&T, Horse's Necks, the ancient, tawny battlements in the afterglow and Malta's bells heard across the still water. The Royal Marines band playing quietly in the background before the full splendour of 'Retreat' and 'Sunset'. And then the news that a close friend had been killed in an accident. My wife Jane turned to me and said, 'Tragedy, to the sound of trumpets'. Yes, it was."

CHAPTER FOUR

# THE LAST PISTON-ENGINED FIGHTERS

*Following the Japanese surrender in August 1945, there was a rapid run-down of the carrier fleet, matched by the quick disposal of the lend-lease American aircraft types. As far as fighters went the Vought Corsair and Grumman Hellcat had only about a year remaining (although one Hellcat lingered on as a station 'hack' at Lossiemouth until January 1962).*

**Jack Routley** *flew operations with both types, but had a soft spot for the Hellcat:*

"It was an absolutely wonderful carrier aircraft. A big wide undercarriage, it sat down contentedly on a deck when you arrived. It had the performance to out-perform the Japanese Zero; it had speed and altitude advantage. It was

*Hellcat II(NF) JZ893 G 892 Squadron, Drem, autumn 1945.*

good value, having six .5 calibre machine guns and rocket rails (it was a rocket-launching platform), and could carry 500-lb bombs. A versatile aircraft and a good one for its theatre of operations.

"Under the lease-lend agreement we had to return the Hellcats in our squadron. After the Japanese surrender, our aircraft had to be ditched in deep waters, so they were unceremoniously dumped somewhere off Australia. The aircraft carrier was returned to the United States and made into saucepans or something. Sadly, there was no further use for either the ship or these aircraft."

*Jack Routley.*

*This left the Seafire and to a lesser extent the Firefly, to carry the fighter burden until the arrival, within a few years, of the Sea Fury and Sea Hornet.*

## FAIREY FIREFLY

*Entering service in 1943, the Firefly was designed as a fighter with an anti-shipping strike capability. After the war its strike capabilities came more to the fore and its role was expanded to encompass anti-submarine work. Its deployment in post-war years as a fighter was quite limited, and it never really adopted an air defence role. However, it was briefly employed as an interim night fighter as the NF.1.*

### Peter Hiles

"I went to Culdrose on a night-fighter course on Firefly Mk.1s, however a lot of the course was done on Ansons – trying to be a fighter pilot on Ansons needed some effort. I then went to the Mediterranean for a tour on *Ocean*, *Glory* and *Triumph*, which included a trip to the Far East. We had two squadrons of Mk.5s on board plus Black Flight. This was us in our four night-fighter Mk.1s.

"We were getting a bit of air experience because we hadn't flown during the long passage out east, and I decided to give my mechanic a trip in the back. He climbed in and off we went. We enjoyed ourselves, returned to the carrier, lowered the hook, came round to the downwind leg and the undercarriage and flaps wouldn't come down. They thought I ought not to ditch, 'Fly ashore and land at Sembawang'. It suddenly occurred to me that RNAS Sembawang didn't have a hard runway; it was Sommerfeld tracking, full of holes, and I had a hook down! So I made the decision to go and belly-land at an RAF station, where they had grass. I landed with no trouble at all – that was a very exciting flight for my mechanic.

"While we were in Singapore the Korean War started. The Admiralty, in their

*Firefly TT.4 TW722 FD-513 771 Squadron Ford, Gibraltar, 1954. (Steve Bond collection)*

wisdom, sent Black Flight (and us) back to the Mediterranean, because they wanted all Fireflies on board to be the same type, to simplify maintenance, although we were perfectly capable of flying the ship's Firefly Mk.5s."

## SUPERMARINE SEAFIRE

*Squadrons post-war: 700, 701, 703, 706, 709, 715, 718, 721, 727, 728, 731, 733, 736, 737, 738, 741, 744, 746, 748, 751, 757, 759, 760, 761, 764, 766, 767, 768, 770, 771, 772, 773, 775, 776, 777, 778, 780, 781, 782, 787, 790, 791, 794, 799, 800, 801, 802, 804, 805, 806, 807, 809, 879, 880, 883, 887, 894, 899, 1830, 1831, 1832, 1833.*

*Squadrons numbered in the 700s are second-line units, 800s are front-line operational units and 1800s were RNVR units – the 'weekend fliers'.*

*Post-war the Seafire continued to serve primarily in its Mks. 15, 17, 45, 46, then the final variant, the Mk. 47, which entered service in 1948. 800 Squadron took them to sea in Triumph and they flew operations in Malaya and Korea. The last Seafire users were 1833 RNVR Squadron, which gave up its Mk. 47s in May 1954, followed by 764 Squadron's Mk. 17s in November.*

### Peter Hiles

"The Seafire 47, compared to the Seafire 3, was at least 2,000 feet/min better in rate of climb, much more manoeuvrable, had much better visibility, was more stable on landing and was better built for landing. The Seafire 3 was not a good aeroplane. The undercarriage wasn't up to it; not only was it very narrow but the oleos weren't up to a deck landing – the 17s had a 1½-inch-longer and much stiffer oleo. The 47 had a slightly different wing, but a very different sort of loopy tail.

"I spent two years flying Seafires in the Mediterranean – totalling 277 hours. I was appointed to 805 Squadron, which was on *Ocean* and that was a good move, because not only did I get on well with all the chaps but we had Seafire 17s with bubble cockpit canopies, whereas *Triumph* had the Seafire 15. Ours were a much nicer aeroplane to fly in.

"Two squadrons did a 'raid' on *Triumph*, which was a hundred-odd miles

*Seafire F.17 SX235 1833 Squadron Bramcote, landing on* Illustrious. *(RNVR Air Branch FB)*

away, and at the same time they were doing another 'raid' on *Ocean* so we had fighters covering both – I was on the *Triumph* one. If you were in 'finger four' formation when you returned you came alongside with hooks down, and the ship checked you because you didn't have any indication in the cockpit of the hook position. It was rather jury-rigged with a sort of golf ball pull for it in the cockpit, and 'it came orf in me 'and!' The hook wasn't down so I was left with options: I could try to get ashore if it was near enough, I could ditch (not advisable with the Seafire) or I could bail out. *Ocean* were trying to make up their minds what they wanted me to do – I was getting higher and higher and closer to Greece. They asked me if I could reach Greece. I said I'd have zero petrol when I arrived, but I would do my best. I kept the speed at maximum cruise, managing to get down on the runway, which was when the engine gave up – no petrol – and I was stuck on the runway intersection. I looked up, and coming towards me on the other runway was a Constellation! I had never heard of reverse pitch propellers but he stopped way before he got to me. By then I think I had beaten the 100-yards record with a parachute still on my back.

"I couldn't speak any Greek, and the maintenance people didn't speak any English, however we managed to get the aircraft refuelled, with the right kind of fuel, and jury-rigged the hook with a little toggle that I could pull. I flew back to the ship and landed. Climbing out of the cockpit I heard a loud-hailer message 'Lt Hiles to report to the bridge'. I was given a terrible dressing down because I hadn't been carrying a map. Nobody else had a map either because the flight we were doing was entirely over the sea, and the map would just have been a piece of white paper."

## Jock Mancais

"At Lossiemouth we had one trip in a dual-control Firefly – there were no dual-control Seafires. You had one flight to get used to the extra power, then we were let loose in the Seafire – an education in itself. I did all the wrong things except kill myself! I took off with the hood open, wearing my white flying scarf with my goggles above my eyes on my flying helmet. My goggles flew off, my scarf ended up by the tail, and I was up at 3,000 feet before I got the undercarriage up. It was all a bit hairy. Flying training was such that there weren't many professionally qualified flying instructors. My instructor would say, 'Here's a Seafire, go and amuse yourself'.

"We were sitting on our parachutes at Milltown. There were no Seafires but there was a Firefly. Hugh Montague decided to take it up without authorisation, stalled it, ending up in a ditch without a scratch on him. By way of punishment he was told that he wouldn't be playing cricket for the navy the following week, and his wine bill was stopped for a month.

"The Seafire was a lovely aircraft to fly, not so good to land. We had quite a lot of ground loops because of the torque of the powerful Griffon engine. I only got 50 hours on them."

*1832 Squadron Culham.*

## Keith Quilter

"In 1947 the Royal Navy formed reserve squadrons. Together with a guy who had been a student with me at de Havilland's, we joined the Culham squadron flying Seafire 17s and 46s. The 17 had a four-bladed prop, and the 46s had contra-rotating props. That summer we took the 46s down to Culdrose to do a fortnight's continuous flying. In subsequent years the 46s were taken from us. We ended up with 17s which I preferred and for our summer training took them for deck landings. On the 46 it was lovely to be able to open up the throttles and not have any torque to worry about, but it did seem a bit heavy compared to the 17. I stupidly said I'd stop flying when I got married in 1952 so I only flew them until then."

## John Roberts

"I did two years in the Med with 800 Squadron on *Triumph*. The Seafire 17 was a lovely aircraft to fly. In comparison to the Sea Fury, which was really designed for carrier operations and was a sturdy aircraft, the Seafire was really just a Spitfire with a hook and folding wings.

"When Israel came into being in 1948, the Palestinians were trying to grab as much land as they could before the Israelis arrived. We were anchored in Haifa harbour and with a catapult we could still launch Seafires. On 30 June 1948 (the day before Israel's creation) I carried out the last ever British armed 'recce' over Palestine. I was catapulted at five minute's notice from the ship, and recovered 90 minutes later when the ship was at sea. They said that if aircraft were needed you could catapult out any time you liked, as the nearest RAF aircraft were in Cyprus. When you take off from sea level you put your altimeter at 0. I flew with the altimeter reading 100 feet below sea level because I was flying down the Dead Sea.

"Nos. 800 and 827 Squadrons embarked from Hal Far to *Triumph*, led by the air group commander (he was not very popular with 'sprogs'). *Ocean* was at sea at the time, and when the leading flight broke formation to enter the landing circuit a voice on the radio said 'That's *Ocean!*' The leading flight slowly resumed position in front of group and all proceeded 15 miles to *Triumph*. After landing on, all pilots were ordered to report to the briefing room. The group commander demanded to know who said 'That's *Ocean*'. Lt 'Bur' Knight, grinning from ear to ear, proudly said it was him, whereupon the group commander said, 'Write out 100 times 'I must not transmit without giving my call sign.' Another reason why the group commander was not popular."

## HAWKER SEA FURY

*Sea Fury FB.11 VR943 R-105 804 Squadron HMS Glory 1950-51.*

*Squadrons: 700, 703, 736, 738, 739, 744, 751, 759, 766, 767, 771, 773, 778, 781, 782, 787, 799, 801, 802, 803, 804, 805, 806, 807, 809, 810, 811, 898, 1830, 1831, 1832, 1833, 1834, 1835, 1836. Embarked on the following carriers:* Centaur, Glory, Illustrious, Indomitable, Ocean, Theseus, Vengeance, Warrior. *Airwork Fleet Requirements Unit (FRU).*

*Considered by many to be the finest piston-engined fighter of all time the Sea Fury was a navalised version of the Fury, which essentially was a development of the Tempest II. Entering FAA service in 1947 Sea Fury squadrons distinguished themselves in Korea, being replaced in the front line by 1955. The last squadron was 1832 Squadron at Benson, which retired them in June 1956. However a few lingered on beyond that at Hurn – as we shall see.*

### Nick Cook

"The Sea Fury was the ultimate piston-engine aeroplane. When you got into it, after flying the Seafire which made a load of noise and smoke and vibration, it was like operating a sewing machine. It had a sleeve-valve engine – you couldn't believe how smooth it was. It was also much more powerful, giving about 2,500 hp. The aircraft had spring tabs and a laminar-flow wing – it was really a breakthrough. The maximum speed was about 450 mph straight and level.

"I was demobbed to the London RNVR squadron based at Culham, near Abingdon. They still had Seafire 17s, and also had an initial batch of Furies. It was the best flying club in the world. We all did as much continuous training as we could because we got paid for it.

"In December 1951 I volunteered for continuous service and joined 802 Squadron. I flew out to Malta in a Viking – the squadron was coming out in *Theseus*. I had 11 days in Malta on my own, and there was a brand-new Sea Fury trainer there. Every morning I authorised myself to fly down to the North African coast, or round Sicily and had a wonderful time. Then the squadron arrived so we embarked on *Ocean*, and we went off to Korea for nearly the whole of '52. Up until we got back for Christmas leave I did 600 hours in Furies.

"No. 802 reformed at Arbroath under a new CO. Donald Dick (the former CO) along with 32 other naval aircrew, had been killed in Korea – 11 of them in accidents. Donald had been my flight commander, and was shot down attacking a bridge. The new CO was an ex-Royal Marine, Lt Cdr Steer, a marvellous man. Nearly all of us had been through the Korean tour. We dropped down from 20 pilots to eight and worked up at Arbroath and Brawdy, flying in the 1953 Coronation flypast.

"We embarked on *Theseus*. Whilst exercising in the channel I had catapult failure and went over the bow with full power on. I passed under the ship and surfaced abeam the propellers. It was so cold I couldn't get the hook from the 'plane guard Dragonfly onto the Mae West straps. I was picked up by a sea boat from the

Sea Fury FB.11 WG596 144 807 Squadron HMS Theseus, *being ferried ashore at Malta in September 1952 on its way home from Korean waters. (Steve Bond collection)*

destroyer HMS *Cadiz*. We deployed to Malta and spent the rest of 1953 with the Mediterranean fleet. This was the last operational deployment of piston-engine fighters in the navy.

### MEMORIES OF KOREA

"After some hopeless rocket attacks, it was all bombing – we mainly used two 500-lb bombs. It was all wartime stock and some didn't go off, but when they did they were quite effective – we were bombing bridges. We attacked the famous bridge north of Sinuiju. We 'threw the book away' about diving and angle of dive. We worked out that a 400 dive with a fixed gunsight was a very good way of hitting the target. Donald Dick, who was leading the flight, was hit on the way down and went straight in. Generally you flew three times a day and did one defensive sortie just orbiting the ship, one offensive and one mixed. I did eight patrols because the ship did eight days at sea (with a break in the middle for replenishment).

"At the start of the war in 1950 the North Koreans didn't have any aeroplanes, or good anti-aircraft weapons. But by '52 we were very vulnerable because the Russians had supplied MiGs and heavy machine guns – they were lethal. I was hit three times at 5,000 feet and was amazed at the kinetic energy in the bloody things. Compared to what was available in World War 2, the energy was extraordinary. A hole in the wing made a terrible noise and that's just one bullet hitting you. You're just ambling along and then suddenly bingo! The bridges were surrounded by high ground and the guns were emplaced in strategic positions – generally you couldn't see them.

"If you were hit you tried to make it to the coast. Luckily I got away with it, every time I was hit I managed to get back to the ship. I got out and looked at the holes – there were three bad ones. One 20-mm went through an elevator hinge, if it had been half an inch to the left or right it would have taken the hinge with it. A second went through the hood rails, transversely across my shoulder blades. It went through the left-hand rail, which was toughened steel alloy, and out the far side. I heard it of course, this terrible clunk. The third one went through the starboard wing. I was actually looking at the wing when it hit! You didn't feel anything, you looked at it with a sense of wonderment.

"No. 802 had 20 aircraft and could field five flights of four, a lot of hitting power. I did about eight sorties with two 1,000-lb bombs for which you had to have rocket-assisted take-off gear (RATOG). We'd practised in Malta, the gear was quite complicated, six cordite rockets in a frame which in themselves weighed 500 lbs. As soon as you had taken off and the rockets had burned out, you jettisoned them. When we started doing RATOG Frazer Shotton, the CO, did the first one and went off the bow without firing them. Somehow he got airborne, an unbeliev-able feat of airmanship. There was a bow wave coming from the wash of the aeroplane. He rode the air cushion I suppose, and accelerated away – quite extraordinary. He called back and said, 'Oh my God – I forgot to throw the master switch'. That night in the bar we all teased him and asked why he didn't ditch the bombs. He said he had given it a moment's thought but as one bomb always comes off before, at that height he would have gone straight in – good point.

"For the first two sorties with 1,000-lb bombs, we were catapulted off. With two 1,000-lb bombs, full internal ammunition and two 45-gallon drop tanks the total came to 15,200 lbs. We didn't realise we were outside the weight limits, and the main spar was suffering from distortion. So then we went for RATOG, which got you off quite easily, provided you held the stick forward as there was a tendency for the nose to rise.

"I was still a sub lieutenant RNVR and three more of the Benson RNVR guys had volunteered to come out, all ex-World War 2, so then we had five reservists in *Ocean*. The captain said to one of them, Ralph Clark, 'You've done RATOG before, haven't you?' Clark concurred and off he went. He fired the button but he let the stick come back, went into a vertical climb and almost did a stall turn above the funnel. He went vertically into the water with the rockets still burning and was under the water for 90 seconds. The helicopter hovered and then up he bobbed. He had completely lost control of the aircraft, it was a very close call but he got away with it. The three elderly RNVRs were teamed up in one flight with a regular navy flight leader. On their first sortie they were attacked, and Ralph was hit in one of the mainplanes starting a miniature fire. He jettisoned the hood and the side panel with a view to getting out but the fire went out and he managed to get back to the ship."

### Peter 'Hoagy' Carmichael

"On 3 April 1952 I landed on *Ocean* en route for Korea, and during that cruise I flew 93 missions. Most of these were combat air patrols (CAP) and offensive patrols against enemy bridges (dropping 1,000-lb bombs), troop concentrations and the like – opposing aircraft were seldom met.

"On 14 May we suffered an early casualty when Lt Kenneth 'Mac' MacDonald was bombing a gun position, and hit by flak, exploding on impact. On the 19th I used RATOG to get airborne carrying two 1,000-lb bombs, which I dropped on a bridge. On 1 June Sub-Lt Carl Haines wrote my aircraft off when he taxied into me while I was parked on the forward end of the flight deck. Three days later I was hit by flak while bombing another bridge, but it still flew OK. On 6 June I escorted a chopper that was sent out to rescue someone, and on 22 June I led a strike against a concentration of Chinese troops hidden in woods. On 11 July we attacked the railway at Pyongyang, and then on the 27th we encountered MiGs for the first time but did not get into a fight.

"On my birthday, 9 August, four of us took off early in the morning. With me were Sub-Lt Brian 'Smoo' Ellis, Lt Toby Davis and Carl Haines. After checking some

*Brian Ellis, Toby Davis, Peter Carmichael and Carl Haines, 802 Squadron* Ocean *9 August 1952.*

bridges, we patrolled in formation at 3,500 feet. We were north-west of Chinnam-po when my number 2 called out 'MiGs, five o'clock, coming in!' We all spotted them. I thought what beautiful jobs the MiG 15s were, just gliding through the air. There were eight of them, coming out of the sun. We turned to meet the attack and I found myself head-on at two of them. I saw tracer shells from the leader and Carl, who was with me, sustained some hits. I then spotted a third flying in the same direction but lower down. I dived to attack, getting in a short burst at about 300 yards before I lost sight of it. After what must have been only a few seconds, I saw the crash of an aircraft hitting the ground, and at first I thought that one of the Sea Furies had gone in – possibly my number 2. But then, someone shouted 'Wizard, you got him!' To be sure I called for the pilots to 'tell off' and as they all replied I knew they were safe. By this time the remaining MiGs had left us and hurried away at low altitude.

"We were not impressed by the North Korean tactics. They seemed to have no idea at all about basic air-to-air fighting – we even thought they might have been student pilots. In addition to the MiG shot down, two others had been damaged, although two of our aircraft had also been hit; one of them had to put down on Chodo Island en route back to *Ocean*. When the three of us landed back on, one hour and 45 minutes after taking off, we found that the news had gone ahead of us and a champagne reception was waiting."

*Some 60 years later, Brian Ellis admitted that it was he who had shot the MiG down rather than 'Hoagy' Carmichael, but at the time he had felt* *obliged to defer to his boss. '**Hoagy**' again:*

"The next day a MiG encounter happened again south of Sariwon, but this time one of the eight MiGs got behind me. Luckily, Carl forced him to break off. Our dogfight must have lasted for about ten minutes, during which I got in bursts at two of them at about 600 yards range with no visible result. We saw one of the other MiGs was trailing smoke and heading away – Toby Davis was credited with a 'probable'."

## Peter Sheppard

*Peter Sheppard.*

"I volunteered for service in Korea and was transferred to the Sea Fury – the beginning of a love affair. I joined 807 Squadron which was working-up at Hal Far. We were due to embark on *Ocean* but its refit had not yet been completed so we carried out further training on *Indomitable*. My first catapult launch was on 30 March 1953 and I had just reached full power when the catapult hold-back broke and I trundled over the side in my Sea Fury. I scrambled clear as it started to sink and was quickly picked up by the helicopter and taken to the bar!

"We eventually embarked in *Ocean* which arrived off Korea in May 1953 to take over from *Glory*. We were soon in action attacking railway lines and roads, and on one mission I was tasked to take photographs of other aircraft in the formation bombing a target before I attacked it. When we got back to *Ocean*, I was getting low on fuel only to find that the carrier was shrouded in sea mist, so I had to do a CCA. My first attempt had to be aborted and I went round again. As I did so a small gap appeared in the mist and I managed to land off a somewhat unconventional approach with just 90 seconds of fuel remaining. We had to practise RATOG take-offs. A Dutch pilot on exchange with us had a partial failure of one rocket, staggering ahead at wavetop height, as he broadcast 'This is b****y dangerous!'

"The Korean War ceasefire took effect on 27 July and our carrier air group did a flypast. That was almost the end of my time on the squadron and just that October, having just celebrated my 21st birthday, I began conversion to the Sea Hawk, which I flew for quite a long time. However, it turned out not to be the last time I would fly the Sea Fury.

"In 1972 I was converting to the Phantom on 767 Squadron at Yeovilton. The RN Historic Flight had acquired a Sea Fury FB.11 (TF956) from Hawker's at Dunsfold, and their test pilot Duncan Simpson came to Yeovilton to give it a test flight. Subsequently, I was nominated to test it on the basis that I was the only Sea Fury qualified pilot around, even though I had not flown one for 20 years.

"Over the next ten years I displayed the aircraft widely, including flying in formation with a Concorde and the Red Arrows Gnats. At the end of the first day of a two-day air show, I agreed to fly in formation the next day with the Rollason Turbulents of the Tiger Club. The Turbulents flew at their maximum speed of just under 100 knots and I joined on with full flap and close to the stall as they swept by. On another occasion I led the Rothmans team's Pitts Specials as they trailed smoke. It was fun, but they couldn't hold on when I entered a loop. Although I flew in a lot of formations, my solo displays were the real fun, keeping the aircraft low and fast.

"I was preparing to take off from Yeovilton to fly to Farnborough and practise for their air show, but a swarm of bees had settled on the tailplane. After a few hours a beekeeper was found who caught the bees and left me free to set off for Farnborough. Having started my display, I was inverted in a four-point roll when a lone bee appeared in the cockpit. My subsequent manoeuvres were difficult to explain after I'd landed.

"I occasionally flew other civilian-owned Sea Furies, and my last flight in one was in 1981, by which time I had accumulated 600 hours on type."[2]

### John Roberts

"My first Sea Fury hours were flown from the back seat of the trainer version giving instrument flying training to the pilots in a Firebrand squadron at Ford. The Sea Fury was a good all-round aircraft and nice to fly. Later – in 1953-54 – I was the senior pilot of 850 Squadron at RANAS (Royal Australian Navy Air Station) Nowra. During 12 months there we worked up on *Vengeance* and *Sydney*, followed by six months in *Sydney* off Korea. One morning a young pilot asked if the statement in the Pilot's Notes was correct. 'What statement?' 'The one that says you can't fold the wings in flight.' He met his end another way. While transferring from an unserviceable 'plane to the spare, with ten aircraft running up on flight deck, he walked into a propeller – messy."

## POST-KOREA

### Dave Eagles

"I was appointed to a Royal Australian Navy (RAN) Sea Fury squadron, which was heaven. I got about 400 hours in it – a superb aircraft, for many years my favourite. There were lots of good things about it – a true fighter. It had a single-lever throttle system in that you could pull the pitch lever back to 'auto' and, through a series of linkages, when you moved the throttle after that, it would give you the

---

2. Adapted from 'Fast and Furious' by Graham Pitchfork, *FlyPast* 2017 with the permission of Peter Sheppard.

*Sea Fury FB.11 805 Squadron RAN Nowra 1956-57. (Dave Eagles)*

minimum rpm selection for the boost you had. That was a delightful thing if you were on your own. If you were flying in formation you couldn't do that because a single-lever movement would be altering the pitch so you got a slightly odd acceleration. It wasn't like a jet engine single lever and it wasn't like varying boost with a fixed pitch. It had a fighter cockpit (the Sea Hawk cockpit was developed from it). We had an aerobatic team; it was a highly manoeuvrable aircraft and had a spring-tab aileron so at high speed you were actually moving the tabs as well as the aileron. A torque tube would wind up and the ailerons would stay where they were but you got through to the tabs. You had quite a reasonable roll rate at high speed. It had a gear change to bring in a supercharger, to maintain boost in the climb – just a lovely thing to fly.

"The Sea Fury was probably coloured for me by having been very impressed by jet aeroplanes, having flown F-9s and Sea Hawks, then been so disappointed by the old Firefly. Being put in a Fury squadron was a delight; I loved every second of being in that aeroplane."

### Harry Frost

"I got posted onto Sea Furies in VF871 Royal Canadian Navy (RCN) and did the majority of my flying in them, mostly at sea on HMCS *Magnificent* – 'Maggie'. Our NATO role was fighter cover for anti-submarine warfare. I was having fun and absolutely loved the Sea Fury, a most magnificent machine. It was a great platform, great for rocketing and dive bombing. It had four 20-mm cannons, and was a good

*From left to right: Harry Frost, Archie Benton and Benny Oxholm. (Harry Frost)*

all-round ground-attack and fighter aircraft, even when the early jets were coming in.

"In 1952 'Maggie' set sail to Europe with us and VF-881 Avengers on board. We made for Gibraltar where we joined the RN Med fleet under Adm Lord Louis Mountbatten. He had asked Canada if he could borrow 'Maggie' as no RN carrier was available for a war game with the US 6th fleet. We were to defend Malta, and they were to take it. The Americans had the Panther, their first carrier-borne jet – we beat the crap out of them.

"We flew ashore to Ta Kali, on Malta, to defend the island, engaging the Panthers using camera guns. At the end we had a debriefing ashore with the Americans. We had pictures of them in our gun sights every time we engaged – it was quite something. The Americans just couldn't believe how they were outgunned by this snubby-nosed aircraft with a propeller!

"Prior to the Malta 'hostilities' the fleet had cruised towards Greece where we were to gather in Piraeus for a few days of partying. Approaching the west of Greece I was in a flight of four led by our USN exchange pilot Archie Benton. His wingman was Joe Becket, who was commissioned from the lower deck and thus older and 'wiser'. My wingman was a Danish/Canadian, Benny Oxholm, who later commanded the Canadian Air Group in Germany.

"We received a signal from the carrier that they were becalmed. Its maximum speed was 22 knots – we needed 28 to 30 to get on board. We were directed to a Greek air force field on the west coast at Araxos. The field was sand and we had removed our engine sand filters. The Greek airmen spoke no English, we no Greek and we had to get to Athens over the mountains. They had a wind-up magneto-driven radio and we tried to get them to radio Athens that we would arrive later that day. To take off without sucking sand into our intakes, we got a Greek airman to lie on each tailplane to put weight on our tails. As each of us gathered speed, in three-point attitude, we waved off the Greeks with a hand signal from the cockpit and we all got airborne successfully.

"We had a beautiful flying day. On arrival at Athens, a combined commercial and military airport, we were met by military police brandishing machine guns. We were relieved of our 45s and ushered into custody. Greece and Turkey were nearly at war, and as no notice had been received of our coming, they mistook us for Turkish Fw 190s which did look like Sea Furies. We were rescued by the Canadian embassy and taken to the finest hotel in Athens, the Grande Bretagne. I was elected paymaster and received 400 Drachma – it lasted one day. Inflation was rife so our US exchange pilot took us to their PX [the US equivalent of the NAAFI] where we all became USAF officers! We had five days in Athens awaiting our fleet and flew every day exploring Greece.

"The following year we were based at Shearwater, across the harbour from Halifax, and doing rocket training against a sea target about 75 or 80 miles east along the coast. It wasn't in a sea lane, so we could rocket at our leisure. I was in a flight of four and the last one on the range. After I'd let go my rockets I wheeled around to come back to base and the fog came in, which was typical in Nova Scotia. The three chaps ahead of me had all landed safely, but I was completely fogbound right down to the ground. I climbed and found a break between the cumulus and cirrus. But I'd lost my radio, had no contact and the compass was going all over the place – I had lost virtually all instruments. I knew I was in deep trouble.

"I decided to fly south to see how far this 'clag' went out to sea. Then if I could get down on the water, come in at 20 feet and hit the shoreline – risking running into trees. As I came in the fog was coming down and down, and I had no idea where the land was. I was in trouble. Whilst watching my fuel I went back up into the intermediate area (about 15,000 feet) to see if I could find a gap. Rolling over to bail out, the death rate was very high (because of the risk of getting caught up in the harness) or if I was to ditch in the sea – where the hell would I go? They'd lose me on radar when I got right down onto the sea, so they probably would not know where I was; I was in despair.

"My CO had taken off with another pilot as a pair, and they were vectored onto me – all of a sudden, there was one on either wing! These two guys took me miles away to the commercial airfield at St John's, New Brunswick. We landed, and it was the only time I ever ground-looped. I did a perfectly good landing, but then decided to turn off onto the grass. All I wanted to do was shut down, get out and kiss the ground."

> *The last Sea Furies served with the FRU at Hurn, Bournemouth. The final three were withdrawn from use in April 1961.* **Peter Goodwin**, *who had previously flown Venoms in the RAF, unexpectedly found himself confronted with a Sea Fury when he arrived at Hurn in the summer of 1958 to fly their Sea Hawks.*

"The Sea Fury was a great aircraft for a jet-jockey! I'd not been at Hurn long and the man said, 'Oi, there you are' and I said, 'What did you give me these Pilot's Notes for?' He replied, 'You're airborne at eleven'. 'What? The last bloody tailwheel aircraft I flew was a Harvard, years ago'. He repeated: 'Airborne at eleven'.

"I walked out to this Sea Fury and there was a bloke to strap me in. I asked him

*Peter Goodwin*

how to start the aircraft, and he said, 'Stop p*****g around. Open the throttle ¼ inch, pitch fine…' this and that – he got down. To start the thing there was a piece of wire which you pull to fire a cartridge – bloody hell! With a 2,500-hp Centaurus engine the whole thing was shaking and vibrating. I taxied out and at least remembered to put the wings down. I got to the end of the runway, locked the tailwheel and because I knew about propeller torque, wound it up very slowly. When I got airborne I said to myself: 'That was very clever Goodwin, now get it down!' It had a two-stage supercharger and went like s**t off a shovel. I did some aerobatics, roared around, then came in and did quite a good landing. You had to do a curved approach because if you came straight in you couldn't see where you were going."

**Paul Chaplin** *came to the Sea Fury as a historic aircraft, display flying with the Royal Navy Historic Flight (RNHF) at Yeovilton.*

"I'd got back into prop and tailwheel aircraft on the Chipmunk, and thought it would be nice to get my hands on a big piston aircraft. So I took the Yeovilton tour and volunteered for the RNHF, which was my last two years in the navy.

"As well as flying the Hunter, Sea Devon, Heron and Chipmunk, I was tasked to qualify and display the Firefly for my first air display season. The second season they liked you to qualify on a second aircraft – I said I'd rather fly the Sea Fury. It was effortlessly powerful, you could be cruising along, do a loop, and as the power to weight ratio was so good – carry on again. I had the deepest respect for the young FAA crews operating those earlier generation types from the deck with less training and emphasis on safety than I had."

## DE HAVILLAND SEA HORNET

*Squadrons: 703, 728, 739, 759, 771, 778, 792, 801, 809. Embarked on:*
Eagle, Illustrious, Implacable, Indomitable, Perseus, Vengeance. *Airwork FRU.*

*Developed from the RAF's Hornet, the Sea Hornet F.20 joined FAA service with 801 Squadron in 1947, being followed two years later by the NF.21 two-seat night-fighter variant in 809 Squadron. They only lasted in front-line service until early 1954, but some second-line units continued to operate them until 1957. Like the Sea Fury, it turned out to be a firm favourite amongst those who flew it.*

*Sea Hornet F.20 TT197 703 Squadron Lee-on-the-Solent, deck-landing trials on HMS* Implacable, *July 1948.*

## Peter Hiles

"At Ford we had a range of aircraft including the Sea Hornet, the Mosquito's younger brother, far and away a better aircraft. It was my No.1 favourite of all the aircraft I flew. 'Winkle' Brown said exactly the same and, according to his logbook, he flew 470 aircraft types and his No.1 was the Sea Hornet. My unqualified comment is that it was pure delight to fly – it was a splendid aeroplane. I only flew it for a few 'stooging' missions – the joy of it!"

## Brian Phillips

"I was a radio/radar mech and joined 809 Squadron at Culdrose just before Christmas 1953. The squadron was in turmoil as we were due to join *Eagle* in the new year. We made an uneventful departure on our 'cruise' to Gibraltar, the aircraft joined the ship and our work-up started, deck-landing practice being the order of the day. The Sea Hornet was quite a large aircraft and not many of the aircrew had deck-landing experience, especially in a twin-engined aircraft. We had very little problem with the radar, it was a well-established type.

"All went well until the third day. It was lunchtime, and we were in the Bay of Biscay, with all the aircraft aboard. It was not the practice to tie aircraft down during lunchtimes, but rather to have the squadron duty watch keep one person sitting in the cockpit of each one, ready to apply the brakes as needed. I was duty radio

*Brian Phillips.*

mech and I drew the short straw to sit in one of the aircraft. With the ship's movement my aircraft started to roll back and forth, about 18 inches to two feet. I applied the brakes and called for another man to re-chock the wheels. There was a bang from the port brake – the brake bag had burst. Without brakes it was no good staying in the cockpit, and I was told to exit sharply – which I did. The ship started to roll far more, and the chocks were pushed apart again – now it was getting dangerous.

"To get the aircraft under control the flight deck party was instructed to take it down into the hangar deck. The guys fitted a towing arm to the tailwheel, took the chocks away and started to move the aircraft towards the aft lift. The carrier then took a particularly heavy roll to starboard, the Hornet slithered across the deck and hit an Attacker. The ship then rolled to port and the luckless Sea Hornet reversed its direction, but this time there were no aircraft to hit. It bounced its mainwheels into the walkway at the side of the deck. Both legs snapped off and the aircraft took a leisurely dive over the side and into Davy Jones' Locker. This was bad enough, but when the squadron muster was called one man was missing. It was thought he might have been skiving in the rear cockpit of the aircraft and gone down with it. The ship was searched from stem to stern, no easy job on a carrier. He was eventually found asleep in a storeroom; to say he was unpopular was an understatement[3].

"We subsequently operated from North Front, Gibraltar where flying was leisurely, and boredom soon set in. After a pleasant couple of months operating from the RAF-run airfield we packed everything up for shipment back to the UK. The aircraft were flown direct to Culdrose and then on to Northern Ireland. We never saw them again. Sometime later they were all chopped up, hence there is no longer a Sea Hornet NF.21 in existence."

## Doug Turner

"We had Sea Hornets at Airwork's FRU at St Davids. We co-operated with Kete (HMS Harrier, operated in conjunction with RNAS Dale as the aircraft direction centre), and did all their flying for them. One would go out as a target, another would go out as a fighter. You got plenty of flying in as they directed one onto the other, about 200 miles out into the Atlantic. The Hornet was lovely."

---

3. The Sea Hornet lost over the side (10 February 1954) was VW955 J-483. The Attacker it hit was WK325.

## John Coward

"I was on *Implacable* when we lost a Sea Hornet, flown by the squadron commander, off the catapult. When the wings were unfolded, the flight deck officer had to check that an indicating pin was in the correct place, on this occasion he somehow missed it. Consequently, as the aircraft came off the catapult the port wing folded and it went straight in."

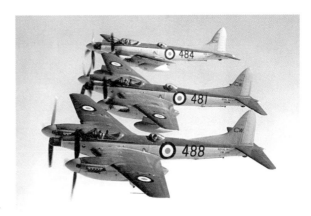

*Sea Hornet NF.21 VW956 CW-488 809 Squadron Culdrose. (Culdrose FB)*

*This accident occurred to Sea Hornet PR.20 VR862 of 801 Squadron on 12 June 1950 off St Kilda. The pilot Lt Keith Shepherd, lost his life.*

*By 1954 piston-engined fighters were a thing of the past in the FAA's front-line squadrons. Jets had already started to arrive a few years earlier, and were now flying from all the carriers. This would start to bring its own problems due to the small size of some of the ships, and the need to make changes to them to cope with higher performance aircraft.*

*Final words from Harry Frost:*

"We did our ops training at Lossiemouth in Scotland with the RN. We had one Brit, five Indians, four Aussies, one Kiwi and five Canadians. I'm the only one left of those five. One crashed in a Seafire by torque-stalling as he was coming in at Lossiemouth – he gave it too much gun and turned upside down. Another chap was landing on *Bonaventure* in a Banshee, lost his brakes, went over the sharp end and was run down by the ship. He had ejected when he knew he was in trouble, but he wasn't high enough. We lost another chap in a diving accident in the Med. The fourth one torque-stalled in the Irish Sea on his first deck landing during deck trials with Sea Furies. He survived, but was a nervous wreck and left the navy."

## CHAPTER FIVE

# THE FIRST JETS

## DE HAVILLAND SEA VAMPIRE

*Sea Vampire F.20 landing on HMS* Illustrious. *(Edward Jones)*

*The Vampire was the first jet aircraft in the world to operate from an aircraft carrier when Lt Cdr Eric 'Winkle' Brown landed a prototype aboard Ocean on 3 December 1945. Thereafter the navy acquired a modest fleet of unmodified Vampires F.1, F.3 and FB.5, plus 18 additional FB.5s navalised as the Sea Vampire F.20. These saw limited service from 1947 until 1957 for jet familiarisation.*

*Squadrons: 700, 702, 703, 764, 778, 787, 806, embarked mostly for trials, on Ark Royal, Bulwark, Glory, Illustrious, Implacable, Indomitable, Ocean, Theseus, Warrior and HMCS Magnificent, Warrior.*

*The largest FAA fleet of the type was the T.22 trainer of which 74 were delivered, serving from 1953 to 1970.*

### Peter Hiles

"Our job in the Service Trials Unit (703 Squadron Ford) was split between the utterly boring, and the utterly exciting. Most of our flying was calibrating ships' radars, flying up and down various courses; as far as possible we tried to do it at night. One absolutely splendid night, it was fabulous visibility. We were flying up and down the French coast for a ship which was calibrating in Portsmouth and I could see Manchester, Paris and Brest! I was at 40,000 feet, on a line north of Calais to north of Ushant, and the distant sightings were more of a glow than an actual view of the cities themselves. I had drop tanks and had to cruise up and down in a Vampire for two hours. The Vampire was a nice little aeroplane, but a bit of a toy. I thought it should never go into action."

# GLOSTER METEOR

*Two navalised examples of the F.3 variant of Britain's first jet fighter were flown by 703 Squadron at Lee-on-the-Solent in 1948 and '49, with deck-landing trials being conducted on* Implacable *and* Illustrious. *The Meteor T.7 and TT.20 later served in some numbers in the pilot-training and target-tug roles.*

## SUPERMARINE ATTACKER

*Meteor F.3 EE387 doing touch-and-goes on HMS* Illustrious, *July 1952. (Edward Jones)*

*The FAA's first operational jet could hardly be described as a great success. The Attacker utilised the wing and undercarriage of the Spiteful (hence the tailwheel configuration), coupled with a new fuselage housing a Nene engine. Entering service in 1951, its first-line career was over in 1954, although it lingered on in some RNVR squadrons until they all disbanded in 1957.*

*Squadrons: 700, 702, 703, 718, 736, 767, 787, 800, 803, 890, 1831, 1832, 1833, embarked on* Bulwark, *and* Eagle *(deck-landing practice on* Illustrious). *Airwork FRU, RN Test Squadron ('C' Squadron A&AEE).*

### Nick Cook

"In the middle of 1955, at the annual 'summer camp' deployment for the RNVR Benson squadron, we were flying the Attacker (the most awful aeroplane!). We landed on *Bulwark*, which by then had an angled deck and a mirror sight, much less onerous than the old type of deck landing. Some of the chaps had never landed on a deck before, and I didn't enjoy it either – it was very unpleasant. We all got away with it except one reservist doing mirror sight practice at Ford who stalled and was killed.

"The aeroplane was ghastly. Imagine designing a jet with a tailwheel. The funny thing was that when you were descending, with power off, it creaked like an old building. It was a real heap and had some nasty characteristics. It had a Spiteful wing tacked on to a jet fuselage – all a

*Attacker FB.1 WA527 deck-landing practice on HMS* Illustrious. *(Edward Jones)*

*Attacker FB.2 J-142 803 Squadron on* Eagle.

last-minute thing. Between 1953 and '55 there were so many fatalities in front-line service. In the Mediterranean fleet, on *Eagle*, they had two squadrons of Attackers. They were getting fuel leaks into the plenum chambers which could explode with no warning – Pete Ree and David Berry were both killed that way. C-in-C Mediterranean Adm Guy Grantham grounded the aircraft, saying he was not going to have any more young men killed while he was in charge – the Admiralty threw a fit. He said if they didn't like it they could have his resignation, and that would mean it would hit the press. They backed down and the Attackers were withdrawn."

*Between 1951 and 1956, 19 RN pilots lost their lives in Attackers, the worst years being 1953 (7 killed) and 1954 (6). A further 11 aircraft were written off in non-fatal accidents. Lt Pete Ree's accident occurred on 11 March 1953 when Attacker FB.2 WK335 of 800 Squadron caught fire, and exploded during a flypast off Gibraltar over the Yugoslav training ship* Galeb. *The fuel cap panel was missing allowing fuel to leak out. His body was never found. Lt David Berry was lost on 2 April 1954 when WK340's engine caught fire on take-off from* Eagle *and he ejected outside the ejection seat's envelope.* **Nick Cook**:

"When President Tito of Yugoslavia visited England, it was an absolute breakthrough with a Cold War leader coming to see us, so they laid on an air display as he got to Gibraltar. Two Sea Hornets collided, three people being killed, and then an Attacker flew past and exploded into a ball of fire; the pilot was killed [see above]. When Tito got to England, the RAF laid on a Meteor display for him at Wattisham and had another accident, with the pilot being killed – extraordinary."

*The two Sea Hornet NF.21s belonged to 809 Squadron. It is believed the pilot of VW952 was blinded by the sun and hit VZ697. The pilot of '952 was Lt John Rankin who was lost, while Aircraftman E J Dingley bailed out and was rescued. In '697 Commissioned Pilot Dennis Martin and Lt Bernard Waygood were both lost.* **Nick Cook** *again:*

"In June 1956 I left to become the CO of one of the RNVR squadrons, as a temporary lieutenant commander. That carried on until the RNVR and Royal Auxiliary
Air Force were disbanded by Duncan Sandys' Defence Review in January 1957. All
the squadrons went, they just locked the hangars – that was it! I have to say it was
the right decision because the equipment coming into service, the Vixen, the Javelin, weren't suitable for weekend fliers. I did 1,841 hours (921 on Furies), with
331 deck landings. It was a golden period which defined my life."

### David Edwards

"Having studied the Attacker Pilot's Notes they always sat in the cockpit with me
for future reference. On the ground the sense was not unlike being in a Firefly, as
it had a tailwheel. However the cockpit was in the nose so you could see where
you were going when taxiing. A problem with this arrangement was that, with the
jet pipe just above the ground, what you didn't blow away got burnt. Concrete
pads had to be set into holding points to stop the tarmac melting. With the wide
wheelbase, and barely adequate brakes, manoeuvring on the ground at low speed
was not easy. Once airborne the Attacker was easy enough to fly, but initially endurance was a problem due to the lack of space for fuel in the wing. An additional 'saddle' tank was placed behind the cockpit – too near the engine for comfort. I
achieved one and a half hours on a couple of occasions, which is not bad for a
single-seat, single-engine jet.

"It was said that if the fire warning light came on you didn't wait to see if it was
an electrical fault, you ejected immediately. For this reason our Attackers had this
saddle tank removed and a belly drop tank fitted. Whilst this greatly improved
safety and flight duration, it spoilt performance. 'Getting the hours in' was the main
objective of weekend flying. After initial familiarisation, hours were spent formation
flying, carrying out aerobatics and tail-chases, as well as flying in IFR (instrument
flight rules) conditions using the aids available. As we were due to go on board
*Bulwark* for two weeks annual training we carried out dummy-deck landings at
Honiley. Sadly the 1956 Suez crisis put paid to our joining *Bulwark* in the Mediterranean, so we went to Ford for two weeks instead. Here we practised air-to-air
firing, rocket firing at floating targets, as well as general instrument and formation
flying, aerobatics, controlled let-downs, etc. All this was brought to a halt in January 1957 when the RNVR squadrons were disbanded. It was only some years
later I discovered that we were in reserve for the Cold War!

"My experience flying the Attacker was generally good, and unlike some squadron pilots I never suffered any unexpected problems. It must be said that it was not
an attractive aircraft, compared for instance to the Sea Hawk, and its performance
was not outstanding. These years were some of the best in my life. Naval life as a
National Service upper yardman (NSUY) was difficult at first and there was a lot to
be learnt. But the like-minded people I met, and continued to train with, made life
both interesting and enjoyable."

## Peter Hiles

"I never flew an Attacker but we had one in the Special Trials Unit. They were do-ing fairly rapid deck-landing tests, and they selected about four pilots to do them. George Baldwin was a famous pilot, having been wing leader of the Fourth Naval Air Wing on HMS *Hunter* during the invasion of southern France in August 1944. He was the captain of the first Attacker squadron, and had a bad landing. The hook was pulled out, and he went into the redesigned barriers, which were nylon strips and they took the wings off. By now like a cigar, he went straight into all the aircraft that were parked at the far end. I was watching it from the 'goofers' gallery'."

> *Lt Cdr Baldwin's accident was on* Eagle *21 September 1952 in Attacker F.1 WA498 J-103 of 800 Squadron. The aircraft was written off.*

## Jock Mancais

"Four of us got one flight each in a two-seat Sea Fury before we were seconded to the Attacker. I did my first jet deck landing in an Attacker – that was an experience – indeed I was the first student to do so. It was on *Illustrious*, the training carrier, in 1952. I missed the wires, probably being a bit high and fast. There was a guy with a red flag who waved it at you to tell you to 'wave off' if you missed the wires, so you then applied throttle and went round again. Why we cut the throttles in a jet I don't know [jet engines are slow to respond to the throttle], the batsman still gave you the 'cut' signal as if you were still working with propellers. You 'floated' like anything with the clean wing [trying to lose lift]. As a tail-dragger you came in nose-high, there was no torque to get the tail down. Speed was of the essence, we'd come in at 110 knots and if you were the slightest bit too fast the hook wouldn't get down near the wires. Although we had a clear deck for initial landings, there were a lot of accidents. When the barriers were up a lot of guys went straight into them. On *Illustrious* we did free take-offs, no catapult, they just ranged us aft and off we went. I did about 20 deck landings, four of which were hooked, the others were 'touch-and-goes'.

"I then went to 800 Squadron at Ford, the navy's first operational jet squadron. From a handling point of view the Attacker was very heavy on the controls, above 400 knots very heavy indeed. As we were unpressurised we all had to undertake pressurisation tests (high-altitude simulation test [HAST]) at Seafield Park. A num-ber of chaps failed, so they went to choppers."

## John Roberts

"I was the boss in the RNVR squadron at Benson and flew the Attacker – we were known as 'weekend flyers'. The Attacker was a bit like flying a bullet. I had my own little air force. I had four Harvards, that I could give people dual instruction on, two or three Vampire trainers and two or three Sea Balliols. We were given the latter because they had air brakes, and it was thought that the RNVR pilots con-

*Attacker F.1 WK320 838 1833 Squadron Midland Air Division Bramcote, Honiley 15 September 1956.*
*(Air Britain)*

verting to jets ought to learn about air brakes. We also had six Attackers, about eight Sea Hawks and about 12 Sea Furies. In all I had 36 aircraft – which is virtually the entire current Fleet Air Arm.

"I did six deck landings with the Attacker on *Bulwark*. The RNVRs used to do two weeks continuous training every summer – 'summer camps' – and I was there for three summers. The third year we went to Ford, and that's where I did my six Attacker landings. *Centaur* had the first of the angled decks at that time, and that put the barrier out of your mind. I had gone into the barrier twice in a Seafire and once in a Sea Fury!"

## HAWKER SEA HAWK

*In marked contrast to the Attacker its successor the Sea Hawk was universally liked by those who flew it although, as we shall see, it was not without its issues. Developed by Hawker Aircraft in response to Specification N.7/46 to replace the Attacker, it entered service in 1954. The Sea Hawk acquitted itself well in the 1956 Suez campaign, finally leaving the front line in 1960. Thereafter it lingered on in second-line units until the FRU at Hurn gave up its final examples in 1969.*

*Squadrons: 700, 703, 738, 764, 767, 781, 787, 800, 801, 802, 803,*

*Sea Hawk F.1s 898 Squadron Ocean, February 1956. (Adrian Balch collection)*

*804, 806, 807, 810, 811, 895, 897, 898, 899, 1832, embarked on* Albion, Ark Royal, Bulwark, Centaur, Eagle, *(deck-landing practice* Illustrious*). FRU, RN Test Squadron ('C' Squadron A&AEE).*

### Nick Cook

"I was appointed to 804, a newly formed squadron with Sea Hawks, in January 1954 at Lossiemouth with 'Winkle' Brown being appointed CO at the same time. Ray Lygo was an A1 instructor and he turned up with Bill Newton, another very good egg, and converted us all to jets. This took about an afternoon because it was so easy. Ray appreciated that, and we formed up with 'Winkle' in command – I flew as his No.2.

"Then there was an experiment to copy the RAF, who were making all their squadron COs wing commanders. The navy followed suit. 'Winkle' was the only one they tried it with – it didn't work. There was always a conflict with the commander flying, and 'Winkle' was relieved in the last quarter of '54. A new CO, the wonderful and very welcome Dougie Price, who was a two-and-a-half ringer lieutenant commander). He had won the DFC with the RAF, flying Mosquitoes – that separates the men from the boys – he was a superb CO."

### Andy Copeland

"In June 1956, a couple of weeks after receiving my 'wings' at Valley, I was introduced to the Sea Hawk. As a sub lieutenant RNVR doing my two years of National Service

I was elated to be sent off to fly fighters. There were five months to go before I would become a civilian once again, but then I would remain in the reserves as a weekend flyer. I was sent to 738 Squadron at Lossiemouth, which had Sea Hawks and a couple of Sea Vampire T.22s. The instructors were all seasoned aviators and included a couple who had

*Sea Hawk WF302 E-184 with Andy Copeland aboard. (Andy Copeland)*

participated in the Korean War. Their job was to turn us into effective fighter pilots. After a short check flight in a Sea Vampire, and a half-hour briefing on the Sea Hawk I found myself being strapped into this awesome machine, then taxiing off to do my familiarisation flight. This was the first aircraft I flew with hydraulic controls, which were very responsive. I staggered up off the runway, wobbling away as I tried to get used to the ailerons.

"The Sea Hawk was a delight to fly, with virtually no vices. In my seven weeks with 738 Squadron I learnt fighter tactics, fired off hundreds of cannon shells at towed and ground targets, was introduced to formation aerobatics and did numerous DDLs. I was having a wonderful time and applied to transfer from the RNVR to the Royal Navy on an eight-year short service commission. While waiting for this to come through I was attached temporarily to 764 Squadron for a couple of weeks, and then sent down to Ford to join 767 Squadron, which was a holding squadron for pilots waiting to join front-line Sea Hawk squadrons. Here I continued weapons training which included dive and low-level bombing, air-to-ground rockets, day and night DDLs.

"I discovered an old and completely neglected 1929 Rolls-Royce. It had been in a barn since 1939 but a talented friend got it running within days. I could fly the latest navy fighter – but couldn't drive, and had no licence. It was a steep learning curve but intensive instruction soon had me transporting all 12 squadron pilots, and assorted female companions on pub crawls! This amazing car commanded huge respect from policemen, and nightclub bouncers. It was completely reliable and in the four years I owned it the only major expense was a new set of tyres.

"In November '56 my longed-for front-line appointment came. I joined 806 Squadron which was re-forming at Lossiemouth under Lt Cdr Bill MacDonald. I had by then 355 flying hours, 135 of them in Sea Hawks. The squadron was to join *Eagle* in August 1957. Meanwhile I qualified as an instrument rating instructor, and completed a photo-recce course.

"One never forgets one's first deck landing. Regardless of endless training ashore the shock of seeing the tiny deck as one flies the downwind leg, the doubts that threaten to overwhelm when on finals, the determination not to make a fool of oneself, and the relief when the hook catches and one is hauled onto the flight deck are lasting memories. Then there is the steam catapult. After being carefully marshalled onto the cat, and being hooked up, the engine is wound up to full throttle. The OK signal is given by the pilot who braces…then wham! In an instant, a massive jolt in the back – and one is airborne. One has to gather one's wits rather rapidly and take back control. While deck landings and cat take-offs became routine, they were always thrilling. Particularly so at night and in really bad weather when the ship would pitch up and down 50 to 60 feet. In reasonable weather our deck landings were only about 25-30 seconds apart. After stopping one raised the hook to release the wire, gave a quick blast on the engine to get forward out of the way of the next 'plane, meanwhile raising flaps and folding the wings.

"*Eagle* had undergone a major refit to accommodate jets, having an angled flight deck, steam catapults and mirror landing aid fitted. On re-commissioning in 1957 there were two Sea Hawk squadrons, 803 and 806; 894 with Sea Venoms; 813 with Wyverns; assorted Skyraider AEW and anti-submarine aircraft and a couple of choppers. We took part in NATO exercises, ranging from the high Arctic to the eastern Mediterranean. We worked hard and played hard, giving weapon demonstrations to allied navies and aerobatic displays to their civilians. The ship visited many foreign ports and I have happy memories of runs ashore in Oslo, Istanbul, Barcelona and Cadiz. We flew ashore for short periods when the carrier docked in Malta and Gibraltar, and in November 1957 I was promoted lieutenant RN.

"All too soon my turn came for a new job. In June 1958 I left 806 and reported to Yeovilton to start training in the Sea Venom. By then I had totalled 535 hours and 111 deck landings in the Sea Hawk, which I continued to fly whenever I could find one. I volunteered for delivery flights, in particular to Lee-on-the-Solent where major servicing was carried out. There were always Sea Hawks waiting to be flown there, and others waiting to be returned to their squadrons. My home was in Seaview, on the Isle of Wight, just across the Solent, and I would beat up the yacht club there before landing at Lee. This was the signal for the club secretary to put my name down for the weekend of racing. I was usually given a lift on one of the SAR choppers based at Lee, and dropped off on the beach close to home. This continued until I left the navy in 1962, as my final job was as QFI in 764 Squadron, flying Hunters from Lossiemouth. On the other side of the airfield 738 Squadron were still equipped with Sea Hawks, so my weekends on the south coast continued. I was loaned to them for two months early in 1962 when the German navy were taking delivery of their Sea Hawks, and I helped instruct them."

## Rob Faulkner

"I did a couple of months on 700 Trials Squadron (at Merryfield) before I left the

*Sea Hawk FGA.6 WV921 516 700 Squadron Merryfield, 1959. (Rob Faulkner)*

navy, doing anything that came up. I was there because I was a Venom driver, and they had a couple of them which they used for any trials involving a Venom and radar. But they also let me fly the Sea Hawk, so I got about 10 to 15 hours on them doing a low-level map trial. They were designing a map for a rolling map system, emphasising the vertical features rather than the horizontal ones. That was great, because with drop tanks I had an hour-and-a-half's fuel so I could fly around the whole of the south of England, going as fast and low as I wanted to."

### Peter Hiles

"I went to Lossiemouth to do the Fighter Leaders' Course, sometimes called the Air Warfare Course, on the Sea Hawk. We did aerial gunnery, and all sorts of things including aerobatics and landing on *Ark Royal*. The difference between Hawker aircraft and other aircraft in gunnery was quite extraordinary. Admittedly the guns were all just under my feet in the Sea Hawk. Having done the gunnery course in the Corsair at St Merryn, the hits on the drogue worked out at about 3 per cent – not far off average. On the Sea Hawk, with the banner target (which I admit was a bit larger), Geoff Tuke scored 74 per cent – my own score was somewhere in the 65 per cent area. We were pouring them straight into it.

"My most spectacular flight of all time was on an absolutely filthy night in a Sea Hawk when I was at Lossiemouth. I climbed up through literally 30,000 feet of cloud, all the way up without any break at all. All I could see were my ghostly wing lights, then I suddenly popped out at the top into the most spectacular Northern Lights – something I had never really seen before. I'd seen vague little bits of it but this was all around me and for at least two seconds I was frightened to death. What a wonderful experience."

## Jock Mancais

"On 806 Squadron we were earmarked to be the first Sea Hawk squadron at Brawdy. It was a very nice aircraft, although there were problems with the early ones. Those we had at Brawdy were made by Armstrong Whitworth, the cannons didn't fire properly and we had problems with hydraulic pipes bursting. The CO Pat Chilton, a very experienced test pilot, said we could amuse ourselves by forming an aerobatic team – it became the 'Ace of Diamonds'! He had just come from the States and thought we needed an insignia. I said, 'We're an ace squadron, what about four aces?' I went to the hangar and spoke to a young leading seaman who suggested an ace of diamonds – that was it. Very basic, just four aircraft in the team. Nice aircraft for aeros (and to deck land as well). We did quite a number of air shows in Europe and the Middle East, Cyprus with the RAF on Battle of Britain Day, at El Adem in Libya and with NATO.

"The Sea Hawk was fairly benign, but it had one big weakness. The fuel tank, I think it was 42 gallons, was behind the pilot. It had a filler cap and if that cap came off the fuel would go into the engine intakes and blow up. I watched it happen to the CO of 801 Squadron, he came off the catapult, cleared the bow and just blew up because the filler cap hadn't been put on properly. We lost quite a few chaps like that. Our CO and senior pilot told us to 'check the bloody thing', but it was too high to reach when you were on the ground doing your pre-flight. They finally put a locking device on it."

*No. 806 Squadron Sea Hawk pilots at Brawdy c.1958-59. Arthur Stewart far left kneeling, Dave Howard seated and Dave Clark standing right.*

**Terry McDonald – radio and radar technician**

"From October 1959 until July 1962 I was at Lossiemouth working on a second-line squadron. This was mainly with Sea Hawks, and some Sea Vampire T.22s, fitted with VHF (very high frequency) radios. We had a problem with one Sea Hawk, every time it went into a high 'g' turn it stopped transmitting. We tried everything – changed radios, the racks, the mic leads, the aerials, the aerial blocks, we changed everything we could sensibly change! At first, the only thing we didn't change was the cabling, but they even did that in the end – and still this damn thing would not transmit in a high 'g' turn! Eventually it was flown down to Culdrose where it was used for ground training the aircraft handlers. You just couldn't fly it in formation, and they never did find out what was wrong with it."

**Tony Pinney**

"On 1 April 1957 I joined 802 Squadron, with Sea Hawk Mks 3 and 5, which along with 804 Squadron were the two allocated squadrons for *Ark Royal* in her second commission. We embarked in the Moray Firth on 6 May which was when I did my first deck landing. I was 19 years 11 months old with 360 hours flying time. After a short work-up we sailed for the massive naval review in Jamestown, Virginia to celebrate the first UK settlement there. We night deck qualified on the way over, with no diversion. In the autumn we were involved in Exercise Strikeback, the largest ever carrier-involved NATO

*Carrier ops in extreme conditions for Exercise Strikeback in the Arctic. (Andy Copeland)*

exercise, which took us north of the Arctic circle. We had three carriers in it, and the Americans six which included *Forrestal* and *Saratoga* on their first deployments.

"That was followed by Exercise Phoenix 2 with the same ships but a different scenario, again up north. The weather was awful but we were able to operate for longer than the Americans as we had pitch recorders on the ships. It was somewhat interesting to be landing on with the ship heaving in the massive swell, and the back-end pitching through a calculated 120 feet. It was eventually stopped as it was very difficult, and dangerous, to control the aircraft taxiing on deck. There was no way that the Dragonfly 'plane guard with a Sproule net pick-up system could have got us out of the water had we ditched – Ha! Ha! – or ejected. In the spring we went out to the Med. Following the deposing of King Faisal of Iraq and problems in the Lebanon, we were on standby in June and sat off Cyprus for a month. We flew a lot of sorties but never got involved."

## Sandy Saunders – air traffic control

*Sandy Saunders.*

"The closest I got to the Sea Hawk, this most beautiful of aircraft, (albeit perhaps under powered) was painting invasion stripes on their wings at Brawdy immediately before the Suez campaign. Sadly, I never flew the aircraft, as I was grounded within a dozen or so flying hours of going solo on Provosts at Syerston. This was due to the after-effects of cerebral spinal meningitis. I retrained at Shawbury in air traffic control, later specialising in GCA (ground-controlled approach).

"This training proved invaluable when a squadron of Sea Hawks was unable to land back on *Eagle* due to fog in the English Channel, and were desperately short of fuel. Their Mayday call was relayed to me as duty officer at Brawdy which was also closed by fog, as were all other airfields in the south of England. As a midshipman, I had no authority to re-open the airfield. However, I was the only officer available who was qualified to talk down aircraft in such conditions. Given that the pilots would have no alternative but to eject, I risked the penalties of ignoring standing orders, and gave instructions to alert the fire and rescue crew, switch on the runway lights, and power up the radar equipment.

"I drove out to the GCA truck. With a now precarious fuel state the squadron commander formed the aircraft into four pairs. Normally there would have been two controllers on watch, but with the airfield closed I was now solo, so I had to use both the search and precision radar screens simultaneously. Talking far more calmly than I felt, I guided the aircraft onto the glidepath, giving instructions continuously to each pilot as to course, speed and rate of descent until the aircraft 'went visual' 60 yards from touchdown – all landed safely. Many years later, one of the pilots involved wrote to me about it:

'A Sea Hawk landing at Brawdy in bad weather strikes a chord in my rather rusty memory. At a distance of some 60 years it cannot be taken for granted, but I have a vivid memory of a superb GCA to a landing at Brawdy in very low visibility. This saved us all from 'Martin-Baker descents' into the Irish Sea. I cannot say for certain that it was on this particular flight, because bad weather is not an uncommon occurrence out on the edge of Wales. My recall of this experience could be from some earlier occasion. On the other hand, this flight was from a carrier, and it was the only landing I made at Brawdy during the relevant period. Whenever it was, if you were involved in the GCA, I hope I shook your hand afterwards because it was a truly magnificent effort.'

"On another occasion, still only a midshipman, I crossed swords with Ted Anson (later to become a rear admiral), who was at the time senior pilot of 897 Squadron. His flight plan was that his pilots should take off in pairs at two-second intervals, and meet up above cloud; the cloud base was less than 300 feet. As the duty officer in the tower I refused the necessary approvals, and restricted the aircraft to take off at not less than five-second intervals. He was furious, and was not prepared to allow the decision to remain unchallenged. Especially a decision made by a **** pipsqueak of a midshipman, telling him how to run his squadron! He took his complaint to Eric 'Winkle' Brown, commander air, who upheld my decision. Anson then appealed to flag officer flying training, Adm Charles 'Crash' Evans, at Yeovilton. He chaired the subsequent enquiry, where 'Winkle' Brown agreed to be my 'prisoner's friend'. Adm Evans vindicated my action, but concluded that in future a watchkeeping officer in the control tower must have a minimum of three years in as a lieutenant. In effect his decision castrated my career, denying me the right to practise my new profession because of my youth."

## Anon pilot

"No. 802 Squadron formed in January 1956 with 12 Sea Hawk FB.3s. The practice then was to start from scratch with a totally new complement of aircrew and maintenance staff. The squadron would then work up ashore for four or five months, in this case at Lossiemouth, then embark in a designated carrier for a deployment which might last 12 to 18 months.

"It was a mix of more experienced aviators led by the CO, Lt Cdr Roy Everleigh, and a number of young pilots recently completing flying training. I was one of those who had returned to the UK after training with the US Navy. We had been given a brief conversion course and were trying to become accustomed to flying in European weather conditions, after the sunny skies of the US. The work-up first commenced with exercises to hone individual skills, and familiarise us with the Sea Hawk – it was a delightful aircraft to fly. Practice was then extended into more tactical uses of the aeroplane, formation climbs through cloud, battle drills at high altitude, ground control interceptions, individual combat and low-level navigation. We often took off in Scottish gloom, the ground disappearing as the aircraft plunged into cloud, to burst out through the tops into dazzling sunshine, a level world spread out as far as the eye could see. Climbing higher the lazy condensation trails fanned out behind each aircraft. The final stage found us with live ammunition and rockets, attacking ground targets on the range at Tain across the Moray Firth, or swooping in on a quarter attack to shoot at a sleeve target towed serenely along by the tug at 20 knots. The cannon shells were painted with individual colours so that hits on the sleeve could be attributed to individual pilots. Sometimes there were no hits.

"A pilot in our companion squadron, working up alongside us, ejected from his aircraft after a fire warning. His parachute was seen to open, but sadly he had drowned by the time a rescue helicopter could reach him. On another occasion, after landing at Ford, we were watching the arrival of another squadron as they followed us in. Pairs were appearing from the low overcast under GCA control – the next to arrive was a lone Sea Hawk. It had grass and bits of crop stuck in the wing-tip and wrapped around the undercarriage legs. This was the leader of a pair. They had hit the top of the South Downs but he incredibly managed to climb away. His wingman was not so lucky and the wreckage was found spread over the hills.

"There was much still to do to weld an inexperienced squadron to a newly commissioned carrier. Both teams needed to start working up slowly in order to gain complete confidence in the other. *Albion* steamed fast to the Straits of Gibraltar and had a short harbour break, allowing the ship to rectify a number of mechanical problems, before sailing on to Malta. Exercises continued daily while proceeding along the North African coastline. Most pilots admit to experiencing a strange feeling of detachment when flying at high altitude; cocooned in a warm cockpit there is a sense of calm and no sensation of movement. The curvature of the earth is prominent, and far away to the south the snow-covered Atlas Mountains made a theatrical backdrop to our world. Visibility was often so good that our home, the carrier, a tiny speck below on the pale sea, could be seen from more than 50 miles away.

"My aircraft required a compass swing, so I was catapulted off to fly ashore to Hal Far. There had been heavy thunderstorms during the night, and unknown to me the pitot head, which measured airspeed, was flooded with water. After take-off the ASI (air speed indicator) reacted only sluggishly – this was going to make accurate speed control difficult during landing. The safe procedure was to join in formation with another aircraft which would lead both in to land. This we did, but the leader failed to tell me during the approach, which was over the vertical cliffs near Hal Far, that his aircraft had also suffered the same problem! The Sea Hawk felt slow and both aircraft stalled just after crossing the runway threshold. Being slightly higher mine fell heavily, hitting the concrete on one wheel. The landing force drove the oleo up to the extent of buckling the wing, and it was only just possible to keep it on the runway during the ensuing swerve. Some hard words were said between us – it was fortunate that the stall had not occurred while still over the cliffs.

"With daily practice deck landing had now become more familiar. The requirement to extend this ability to launch, and recover to the carrier in the dark, was pushing our skill boundaries a big step further. The more experienced pilots were sent off first. The technique was to use the same circuit pattern as for a day landing. This meant flying at 500 feet downwind over the sea, with the only visual aid a cluster of lights far out on the beam. It was difficult to assess the carrier's heading, and then make the required 180-degree turn to end up directly astern. The constant transition from monitoring the instruments to looking outside keeping the ship in sight, was both disorienting and dangerous. The danger of flying into the sea, which was unseen but very close below, was ever present. In later years accepted safe practice was to line up with the ship at a distance of some miles, and make a radar-guided approach from directly astern.

"My turn to explore this new, and not very welcome experience, came a few days later. It was a particularly dark night with a half-overcast sky. None of the new boys found night deck landing easy. There was the combined requirement to line up correctly with the deck, maintain an accurate glidepath and exact speed, while reluctantly descending the final few feet into what appeared to be a black hole. Not being correctly lined up I was forced to make a couple of overshoots, which were followed by bolters. The aircraft shot off the front of the flight deck into darkness, with the urgent need to transfer attention to the flight instruments. I was deemed operationally qualified only after another session of deck-landing practice, finally logging a total of five night deck landings. No one ever enjoyed night carrier operations. It was just part of the job.

"One night the CO Roy Everleigh's aircraft [24 October 1956 Sea Hawk FB.3 WM922 O-132] was tensioned for launch, but when the catapult fired horrified watchers saw it disappear on fire over the bows. It staggered on for a few hundred yards before crashing into the sea. The ship's helm was put over, and engines reversed in an attempt to avoid the rapidly sinking wreckage. Roy afterwards told us his cockpit canopy shattered on hitting the water, and the aircraft sank almost immediately. He managed to unstrap himself with great difficulty, finally getting clear of the cockpit from well below the surface. His head hit a solid object on the way up, which for one horrifying moment, he believed to be the hull of the carrier. It was in fact a piece of aircraft wreckage. *Albion* and our attendant destroyer started a search, not knowing whether he had survived. Nothing was seen for about 30 minutes, until a faint pinprick of light appeared amongst the waves. We all carried a pencil torch in case of complete cockpit electrical failure, and it was Roy's torch which finally attracted attention. Miraculously uninjured he flew again the next day.

"The cause was a known defect of the fuel filler cap. This allowed fuel to escape and enter the engine intake during catapult acceleration. An unofficial local modification, a strap screwed down over the tank cover, was fitted to all aircraft before next flight. During the same period one of our young pilots was forced to eject when the fire warning light came on, landing on a Maltese dry-stone wall with only minor scratches.

"*Albion* entered Grand Harbour for a very necessary eight-day maintenance period. Malta was the collecting

*Sea Hawk FB.5 WM995 Z-138 802 Squadron landing on* Albion *with damage after Suez strike.*

base for every kind of war equipment, harbours crowded with naval ships, Royal Fleet auxiliaries, landing ship tanks and groups of minesweepers. Army troops ashore were camped in every part of the island, together with great parks of tanks and vehicles, while there was a constant stream of trucks and dispatch riders. RAF Canberras and Valiants arrived from the UK. The official explanation for all this activity was preparation for a major exercise off Cyprus. Young officers did not keep up too closely with international news, but obviously our work-up was related to some kind of international tension. How we might be employed was certainly unclear to us.

"It was always something of a relief when the squadron disembarked to a shore base. It was a doddle to land on a runway after the deck. There was also the welcome escape from the constant noise, ship machinery running, the endless rushing sound of the fresh air system, the clang of heavy tools dropped on steel decks, and the never-ending movement of people. Business on board a warship goes on seven days a week.

"*Albion* had just been released after a long period of operations supporting the Suez adventure, and everyone was tired. A disembarkation to Hal Far in Malta was a much welcome rest. For ten days the squadron flew a few training sorties and test flights during the morning, and everyone packed up at lunchtime to enjoy the amusements which Malta could offer. Our carrier was destined to return to the UK in a month's time, so the Sea Hawk squadron received orders to fly on to Gibraltar independently – giving the operational and maintenance teams on board a longer break. The squadron would pick her up later, and re-embark for the final passage home.

"The plan called for a refuelling stop at Bizerta, Tunisia, then another stop for fuel at the French air force base at Blida, Algeria, with a final leg to Gibraltar to complete a good day's work. The 12 aircraft took off from Malta and flew in relaxed formation to make a successful landing at Bizerta. The next leg, in good weather, also went to plan and the formation eventually landed at Blida in the late morning. The crews then set about supervising the refuelling and pre-flighting of their aircraft for the final stage to Gibraltar.

"The French commandant, and pilots from the squadrons based there, arrived to welcome us in very friendly fashion. They insisted that we should accept the hospitality of their mess. Our rather sweat-stained flying overalls were dismissed as irrelevant, and we were led to a shaded area outside the building where aperitifs were served. This entertainment became somewhat protracted with 'entente cordiale' growing stronger by the minute. Eventually the maitre d'hotel or mess sergeant announced that dejeuner was served. The crews trooped into the dining room to discover long tables laden with silver, glass and set with innumerable dishes. White and red wine arrived, glasses being regularly refilled. The commandant stood up and made an emotional speech in barely understandable English – our CO replied in courteous, but somewhat laboured, schoolboy French.

"After coffee the commandant rose again and announced that we would now be shown to our quarters for the siesta, and he looked forward to meeting us all again for dinner. 'Siesta?' said the boss, 'Je regret non, mon commandant, we must fly on'.

'Mon Dieu, C'est impossible.' These and several other emphatic exclamations were understood, by the better educated, to indicate his alarm and consternation at this news. 'C'est les orders' insisted the boss who, marching out a little unsteadily, called his troops together. 'Chaps, we are going to give them a bit of a show in return for all this hospitality. Squadron to form up in three divisions close line astern, and let's give them a real Fleet Air Arm beat up!'

"Few remember much about the take-off and the subsequent confusion surrounding the join up in formation. Division's line astern meant that the leading four aircraft held close formation. The following four aircraft had to step down behind the leading group to avoid their jet efflux. Lastly the third division were forced to fly even lower to clear the turbulent slipstream. There was not perhaps quite the immaculate formation-keeping on this occasion which the squadron could produce in normal circumstances, but it was better than a gaggle. The leader turned and pointing at the distant airfield, put his nose down and increased speed. All hung on as best able, close behind the jet pipe of the Sea Hawk swaying just in front, trying to hold a steady position in the formation. Snatched glances ahead revealed the rapidly approaching airfield and two enormous hangars at which the boss appeared to be aiming.

"The formation got closer and lower. There was a gap between the hangars just wide enough to allow the formation to pass between. It became clear that he intended to lead the squadron between the two buildings, a great idea for a dramatic finale to our visit. The boss seemed to have forgotten however that his rear element was a long way below him. At the back, in the last few seconds, it was horrifyingly certain that there was insufficient airspace to get through without plunging into the ground, and the finale was going to be truly dramatic! A full panic swerve, at the very last moment, just took the rear element clear of the right-hand hangar. People sometimes claim that drink improves their driving skills. I am not sure whether any aviator has ever made a similar claim, but on this occasion adrenaline overcame intoxication in a microsecond of time.

"The outcome of the manoeuvre seemed to have somewhat disconcerted the boss. He decided that we had done enough to demonstrate Fleet Air Arm coolness and verve – under our self-inflicted adversary. The squadron turned away and climbed to 30,000 feet on course to resume its journey to Gibraltar. Oxygen turned up to 100 per cent probably helped a little but it was a very subdued band of naval aviators who climbed out of their aircraft, eager only to reach a hotel bed. Drunk in charge of an aeroplane – never again!"

**Richard Sheridan**
"My first commission with 806 Squadron on *Albion* was a work-up in the Med, and

then through the Suez Canal. We kept one carrier in the Far East – it was all we could afford. We were the Far East carrier, returning in December 1960. Routine flying meant a lot of weaponry on the splash target, towed by the ship. Anywhere we went we'd use a range aiming some ironmongery at the ground. It was all ground attack rather than air-to-air flying.

"I was on finals to the deck one night with a Sea Venom ahead of me. You didn't call finals, 'you've got a ball, four greens' or anything like that, you just called 'downwind' and then you said 'sight' when you saw the mirror sight. The Venom called 'downwind', and I called 'downwind' after him. As I was turning finals, just about to cross the wake to get onto the angle deck centreline, I saw two wheels, his main gear, which was right in front of my cockpit and above me – I was right underneath the Venom! He'd gone a long way downwind, I'd turned in at the normal place and we nearly collided – very frightening. I broke away, he didn't know I was there so I didn't say anything. I came past the island, round again and then called 'downwind'. I reported it when I got back aboard.

"When we got into the Med, one Sea Venom 'went in' off the catapult on the first day of the work-up out of Gibraltar. A Whirlwind also went into the drink. These chaps were in the hover, the engine coughed slightly and they were in the water. They lost another one later on – I thought 'I should have joined the air force!' We worked-up and had an admiral's inspection. They managed to spring a little plate somewhere, below the waterline, by chucking a charge over the side – a 'pretend' torpedo for the inspection. The admiral said, 'What are you going to do about it?' When the ship's plate sprung it leaked fuel oil all the way down through the Suez Canal. It was a very good navigational aid, providing you knew which way to fly when you hit the oil slick.

"We arrived in Singapore and flew ashore to RAF Seletar whilst the ship went into drydock to have the plate fixed. We were there for two weeks and had a great time, doing a lot of weaponry. We also did a lot of drinking, runs ashore, picking up the nurses from the hospital – not me of course, I was an old married man by then.

"We went next to the Philippines – more weaponry. There was a place called Scarborough Reef where there was a ship's bow sticking straight up in the air, a wonderful target. We had two army chaps on board (carrier-borne liaison, known as 'Sea Balls'). We'd all been to a party the night before and missed the last liberty boat back to the ship, so we had to 'borrow' a landing craft from the Philippine army which dropped us off at *Albion*, otherwise we'd have been in the big 'cacky'.

"From there we went to Hong Kong and operated out of Kai Tak. We flew patrols along the border and had been told on no account to fly one inch over it. The previous year, *Centaur* had been there and had been doing battle drill well into China. Then we went to Inchon, Korea, where officers had to go ashore in uniform because of the armistice. We went up to Seoul into some great building for a feast. You took your shoes off before you went in, and one of our Venom observers thought it would be a jolly jape to mix all the shoes up, making three great piles; he was really in the 'dwang'. I walked up to the Officers' Club in my white 'bum-freezer' mess jacket and black tie. As I walked past the Enlisted Men's Club all the Yanks shouted 'hey waiter' – the Americans thought it was very funny. We didn't realise our sailors could use that club – whisky was so cheap!

"Then it was Japan, through the Inland Sea into Yokohama. This was only 15 years after the war. The Japanese were very friendly queuing for about a mile to visit the ship. We attempted to drink in every bar; I think there were about 8,000 of them! We were all very clean, having a bath when we went ashore – and another before coming back aboard – a good time had by all. We visited the USN base at Yokosuka and *Albion* was the only ship in the dockyard with a bar. We went aboard the USS *Bon Homme Richard* for dinner and there were glasses of what looked like Horse's Neck – but it was actually iced tea. Some of their officers would come on board *Albion*, ask for 'Lt Smith', and be told 'The bar is that way, Sir'. When on aircrew rest leave, some of us went to the Hakone National Park, looking across at Mount Fuji with a reflection of the mountain in the lake.

"Finally, back to the Philippines, around the South China Sea, Hong Kong, Singapore and then back to the Med in December. We flew off somewhere around the Balearics, landed at Brawdy and never saw our aeroplanes again."

## Mark Thomson

"My first operational squadron was 806, the last Sea Hawk squadron. On 5 February 1960 the Air Group embarked on *Albion* in the Mediterranean. That day I did my first ever deck landing – I was just 20. My first day in a carrier was particularly memorable as there were three prangs. A Sea Venom had a cold catapult shot, they ejected and were picked up by the Dragonfly 'plane guard. Shortly afterwards the Dragonfly on the port beam had an engine failure – their crew were swimming! Then a Skyraider deck-landed for the first time and ended up in the catwalk.

Mark Thomson.

"With three deck landings under my belt on this first chaotic day, the following day was spent being catapulted off, and doing 'touch-and-goes' with the hook up until FlyCo said 'hook down' for an arrested landing next time. Of the four arrestor wires No.3 was the target. I selected the hook and undercarriage down – the nose and starboard wheels came down but the port leg did not. I reported this to FlyCo, and started all the manoeuvres which might help the stuck leg to come down. I also activated the emergency pneumatic system to blow it down, but it stayed firmly up. Our diversion airfield was Gibraltar where the wind usually blows round the Rock from three different directions at the same time.

"I continued flying round in sight of the ship, reporting my predicament to

FlyCo – followed by silence. I thought 'what's the matter with these people?' and was about to call again. Suddenly over the radio 'Thomson, captain here, now listen very carefully'. I was so stunned that 'God' had called me that, although I was tightly strapped into my ejection seat, I straightened my legs trying to stand to attention!

"The captain continued, 'You've only done three deck landings and your chances of catching a wire are not good. If you don't catch a wire your port wing will touch the deck and you will yaw left into the sea. You can eject now if you wish – let me know your decision.' The Sea Hawk did not have a ground-level ejection seat. If I diverted to Gibraltar the aircraft would swing left on landing, which was where the airport terminal was. I dipped the port wing to look at the sea, very choppy – no ejection I thought.

"I called FlyCo with my decision. Again there was silence for a while until suddenly, 'Thomson, captain here, what is your decision?' I said, 'Yes sir, I'm going to bring it on board'. He said very slowly: 'Are you absolutely sure you've thought about this very carefully?' thinking I was a complete lunatic who, with only three deck landings, had a death wish. The conversation was very short; I landed on and luckily caught the target No.3 wire right on the centreline.

"When there's a crash on the deck there is terrific activity, everyone is colour-coded and knows what to do. With a fire risk, the canopy was opened immediately, the ejection seat was made safe, and two huge firemen in silver fire suits lifted me out. Standing by the cockpit was the medical officer who, like everyone, was much more senior than me. He asked if I was OK and, despite my saying that I was fine, asked me to go to the sick bay with him for a check-up.

"The sick bay was down four decks, near the bow, and I realised that the medical orderly was in front of me and the medical officer behind me. I thought that was strange because the senior officer always went first on a ship. It was a long way to get to the bow, and I was still wondering what was going on when suddenly my legs went from under me. The medical officer had his arms under my shoulders before I hit the deck. He said, 'Got you' – without warning the shock had suddenly hit me as my legs collapsed.

"We got to the sick bay and he laid me on a bed, nearby was a big four-drawer metal filing cabinet. He tried to open the top drawer, but it was jammed. He said, 'This ******* thing never opens when I want it to'. He kept on pulling and suddenly the drawer flew open with a bang – out

*Sea Hawk FGA.5 WV806 A-183 806 Squadron landing on* Albion, *Mark Thomson flying, 1 September 1959. (Mark Thomson)*

came two glasses and a bottle of brandy. He said: 'This is what you need. You're absolutely fine.'

"On a carrier your squadron crew room is where you spend most time when you're ready to fly. When I returned to the crew room I was told the captain wanted to see me on the bridge. I thought 'Oh my God, what have I done wrong now?' After a long climb up to the bridge I met the captain, who was an immensely decorated FAA pilot. He just said, 'That was very good…yes very good.' I turned to leave the bridge as quickly as possible until he said, 'Thomson one more thing, please bring me your logbook.' I rushed all the way back down, somewhat confused about his need for my logbook. In it he wrote, in green ink, my Green Endorsement.

"The Sea Hawk was a very good all-round day fighter for interception and ground attack, as was demonstrated in the Suez campaign. It was remarkable that the straight-winged Mk.6 could achieve Mach 0.8 in level flight at 40,000 feet. Despite the lack of any navigation aids, only one radio and a manual elevator, it was at all times a sheer delight to fly, particularly operating from small carriers. Quite simply this wonderful aircraft never failed to please."

## Peter Goodwin

"I was on the FRU at Hurn flying mainly the Sea Hawk, it was just like flying a Venom (which I had done in the RAF) – great. I was doing carrier approaches and radar calibrations. I also did some simulated strikes on carriers and other naval ships; they got a bit annoyed sometimes. As an ex-ground-attack pilot I would

*Sea Hawk FGA.6 XE339 776 FRU Hurn, 5 June 1968. (Adrian Balch)*

come in, very low and fast, from where they would not expect me to be. Once, to outwit them (and their radar), I climbed to 35,000 feet (in their 'cone of silence') and, with a near-vertical 'beat them up' made a surprise attack. I did not like being fired at with break-up ammunition!

"I worked with the carriers *Ark Royal* and *Victorious*. I flew many approaches, so they could calibrate and practise using the mirror approach system. I never landed on a carrier, although with the hook selected up, I very nearly touched down sometimes."

*The passing of the Sea Hawk meant the FAA was soon to enter an era of much higher performance aircraft. These would bring their own problems for the comparatively small Royal Navy carriers.*

## CHAPTER SIX

# DE HAVILLAND SEA VENOM

*Sea Venom FAW.21 WW286 ADS Yeovilton, Hatfield 5 July 1969. (Adrian Balch)*

*A navalised variant of the RAF's Venom NF.2, the Sea Venom was the navy's first true night/all-weather fighter. Entering service in 1954, it was the first to carry air-to-air guided missiles. Although eventually replaced by the Sea Vixen, the last Venoms leaving the front line in 1961 (831 Squadron flew them in the electronic countermeasures role until 1966), it served on for some years in a variety of second-line roles until the Air Direction Training Unit at Yeovilton retired the last examples in 1970.*

*Sea Venoms flew extensive operations during Operation Musketeer, the 1956 Suez crisis, primarily carrying out ground attacks against Egyptian airfields. On 1 November 1956 an 893 Squadron aircraft from Eagle, flown by Lt Cdr John Willcox with observer Flt Lt Robert Olding, took part in an attack on Almaza airfield. Their aircraft was hit by anti-aircraft fire, holing the cockpit floor and badly injuring Olding's legs. The hydraulics were damaged and Willcox decided to land on, with undercarriage and flaps up; aided by Olding, the landing was successful. Olding then passed out and subsequently had to have his leg amputated. He was awarded the Distinguished Service Cross.*

*Squadrons: 700, 736, 738, 766, 809, 831, 890, 891, 892, 893, 894, embarked on Albion, Ark Royal, Bulwark, Centaur, Eagle, Victorious.*

*Airwork Air Direction Training Unit (ADTU), FRU, and Fleet Requirements
Air Direction Unit (FRADU).*

### Andy Copeland – pilot

"I flew the Venom from July 1958 until March 1960, logging 428 hours in the
FAW.21 and 22. There was a short conversion course, followed by night-fighter
and weaponry training with 766 Squadron at Yeovilton in the Mk. 21. It was there
I was teamed up with Sub-Lt Dirk Breytenbach, from South Africa, as my observer. I think I was paired with him because I was the only one who could understand
his Afrikaner's accent. Dirk was a wonderful partner, with a wicked sense of humour,
and we happily exchanged insults about each other's competence, antecedents and
love lives when we flew together. We shared some pretty hairy experiences, and I
quickly grew to admire his courage and common sense.

"We flew out to Hal Far and joined 894 Squadron flying Sea Venom 22s off
*Eagle*, and I did my first deck landing on 14 October 1958. By the end of my time
in 894 I had accumulated 141 deck landings on *Eagle*, *Victorious* and *Centaur*, and
feel lucky to have walked away intact; the odds were not good and far too many
friends were killed in Sea Venoms.

"This was the height of the Cold War – we were all convinced that a nuclear
war with the Soviets was inevitable. Each side probed the other's defences, and
there were confrontations at sea and in the air continuously. We believed we had
a short-life expectancy. We were flying primitive jets off tiny aircraft carriers almost
regardless of weather conditions, and took risks that would now be unacceptable.
We took pride in being able to 'beat up' our friendly US Navy rivals, flying at night
or in storm conditions when they were unable to. At that time, we still did not
have air-to-air guided missiles; four 20-mm cannon were our sole weapons for
night fighting. We had to be directed on to the tail of 'the enemy', first by a ground
controller and then by your
observer. We had to get very
close on a dark night – usually
under 200 feet – in order to
identify the target visually so
that we could use the gunsight
and loose off a barrage of shells.

"The Sea Venom was greatly disliked by nearly all my fellow pilots. I believe we got it
because it was cheap. The senior officers at the Admiralty
were nearly all seamen, without
the foggiest idea about aircraft.
It had a cramped cockpit with

*Sea Venom FAW.21 WW... 095 893 Squadron wheels-up
HMS* Eagle, *1 November 1956. Lt Cdr Willcox (pilot) observer Flt Lt Olding.*

'Blackie's lot' — 894 Squadron crews, 1958. (Andy Copeland)

poor all-round visibility, sluggish performance and was simply no fun to fly. It was a reasonable weapons platform, and certainly was a successful night and all-weather interceptor for its time. Its huge weakness was at slow speed. If one made a mistake at low altitude, and most accidents occurred when landing or taking off (particularly from a carrier), it was a killer.

"The usual drill was to launch a bunch of aircraft, and then land on others that were at the end of their sortie. All ships would turn in formation onto a heading that was into wind. Their speed was adjusted so that the combination of natural wind, and ship's speed, produced a wind over the deck of 30 to 40 knots. If the natural wind was very strong the carrier might almost stop. Once during Exercise Strikeback in the Arctic *Eagle* steamed backwards to reduce the deck wind! Jets were launched by the cats first, and then the anti-submarine Gannets and Skyraiders did free take-offs. In good conditions we landed on less than a minute apart. Aircraft carriers are very vulnerable to enemy attack when holding a constant heading and speed so launch and recovery periods were kept as brief as possible.

"A carrier landing was the ultimate test of a pilot's skills. There were four arrestor wires strung about 100 feet forward of the round-down across the width of the deck about 15 feet apart. Therefore there were only 45 feet where the tail hook would engage and haul you out of the sky. A yellow centreline was painted from the round-down to the front lip of the angled deck. Following the gyroscopically stabilised mirror landing aid, which gave a visual indication of the glidepath, you approached this touchdown area. The mirror had a horizontal array of green lights on each side; in the centre was a white light, and on final approach you lined up on the yellow deck centreline. You tried to keep the white light lined up with the

*Sea Venom FAW.22 XG687 E-485 894 Squadron* Eagle, *waved off from* Victorious *1958. (Rob Faulkner)*

green 'horizon' lights, and stabilise the speed. In normal weather the mirror gave you a three-degree glidepath. Even in good weather the carrier was always pitching, which became extreme in bad weather. On finals you seemed at one moment to be looking straight down at the deck, the next straight at the stern; in extreme pitching conditions the horizon on the mirror landing aid was adjusted so that our glidepath was three-and-a-half degrees. This gave us additional clearance when the stern reared up in front of us, but made speed control even more critical on finals. Landing on at night in a storm was not fun. In *Eagle* a two-degree pitch resulted in a 60 feet up-and-down movement of the round-down!

"The only way to approach and land on an airfield runway in very low cloud or visibility conditions was by a GCA. A skilled operator talked an aircraft down a glidepath giving heading and height corrections, while the pilot adjusted speed, lowered undercarriage and flaps etc., according to the distance to go. Operating from a carrier could be a problem. Although the observer with his radar was of considerable help, he was busy calling out airspeed and doing landing checks. On finals, when the carrier appeared out of the murk a few seconds before touchdown, we needed to be calm and stabilised. Too often, with minimum fuel, we were diverted to a shore station. Our senior observer, Lt Bob McCullock, suggested that if we parked a Sea Venom at the aft end of the island pointing back towards the glidepath, he could use its radar to give us a proper GCA. I was the squadron instrument rating instructor and flew many of the trials. It worked fantastically well, and we became so confident that we could land on without seeing the ship until the last few seconds.

"A carrier take-off using a steam catapult was another adventure. Being shot off the bow in the Sea Hawk was a 'doddle'. Not so the Sea Venom – it had weights on its elevators to 'balance' them. This was fine and dandy for normal take-offs, but when being shot off the front of a ship you are accelerated, in about 1½ seconds, to 120 knots. The weights on the elevators don't wish to participate, and try to remain stationary, bringing the stick back forcefully. The 'plane, if allowed to do so, would be airborne with bare flying speed, full nose-up elevator and would splash into the sea about 100 feet in front of a ship doing 25 knots. Full co-operation with the observer was needed! Before launching he dug his elbow into the pilot's side, and held it there firmly with his other arm. In order to hold the stick firmly in the straight and level position for the launch, the pilot then braced his elbow against the observer's, so that his arm could not slip backwards.

"Following a successful launch you held the wings level, the nose on the horizon, and 'cleaned up' the wheels and flaps. Normally, in decent conditions, as speed built up, you could start gaining altitude. When the ship was pitching heavily the launch was timed for the bow's rise; you had to remember to ease the nose down after launch. We were all-weather/night fighters, and were expected to fly in almost all conditions – especially when we knew the Yanks couldn't! We had to fly on instruments from the moment the acceleration started, nursing the 'plane off the front of the ship only a few feet above the sea, without any outside reference at all. We relied entirely on instrument flying skills.

"During my training with 766 Squadron I had a couple of incidents. The first was when we were at high altitude, and I was fooling around doing high-Mach stalls when the engine flamed out. I wasn't sure what to expect but bingo! I re-started on first try. Far more serious was a night flight a day later, when I had one of the squadron's instructor observers. We were at altitude doing practice radar interceptions on another Sea Venom piloted by the CO. At the end of the exercise he called for us to 'close up' for the return to base. My partner directed me towards the other aircraft and I picked up his tail light quite quickly. I presumed I would be told when we were getting close in time to match speed with my leader, so continued to pursue the tail light at full throttle. Suddenly we lurched violently downwards, my observer screamed and the radio came to life with a string of invectives from the CO. We must have missed him by inches, such was the violence of this encounter. My partner had, it transpired, dozed off.

"One sortie off *Eagle*, in extremely bad weather, is particularly memorable. We were somewhere south of Sicily, having been launched into low cloud and heavy rain and were climbing up through 25,000 feet when there was a huge flash and bang. We went out of control, the engine lost power and we struggled to calm the thing down to regain level flight; this was not achieved until we had lost a lot of height. The 'plane was buffeting in a very disconcerting way and Dirk reported our problem – we were advised to eject. Unfortunately due to the weather, the ship did not have us on radar, and we both felt that bailing out would give us a minimal chance of being found. We had little power but could maintain level flight when we were down to about 10,000 feet, so headed for Hal Far. As we approached the island their radar found us. Our options were either to bail out close enough to the coast for a chance of rescue, or to try to land. We agreed that ejecting would be the last resort; Dirk had barely passed the 'maximum thigh length' qualification for the observer and didn't relish the idea of leaving his kneecaps behind.

"Hal Far was shut for flying as the runway was flooded, but they tracked down their best GCA controller who waded out to the radar truck and fired everything up. Meanwhile we cautiously slowed down, but found that control was difficult at about 170 knots. We decided not to try the flaps in case only one side operated. Before crossing the coast we put the undercarriage down and got three greens but found that we could not maintain level flight. Fortunately we had height to spare and turned on to our GCA-directed heading, easing down the glidepath trying to maintain a speed of 175-180 knots – we would have just one try. The chap directing us was superb, and the runway appeared ahead. We touched down expecting to need to use the arrestor wire at the end, only to find that the water on the runway brought us to a very rapid stop.

"Lightning or hail had blasted off the entire front section of the aircraft (containing the radar) with some of the debris going into the engine. Another Venom, flown by 'Knobby' Clarke, that was launched at the same time as us also suffered damage, a 12-inch hole in the front of his radar dome, but managed to get back aboard *Eagle*.

"A bit of excitement happened some months later. *Eagle* had lost both its catapults and had to head back to Plymouth for a major refit. No cats meant that the fighter squadrons couldn't fly. A large naval exercise was due to start. The Sea Venom squadron aboard *Centaur* had lost two of its 'planes and needed replacements urgently. The boffins worked out that with 45 knots of breeze over the deck, made

*Sea Venom XG724 after the lightning strike 22 November 1958. (Andy Copeland)*

up of at least 20 knots of natural wind and the ship steaming into it at 25 knots, a very lightly loaded Sea Venom could do a free take-off. This meant starting at the extreme end of the deck with full power on before rolling forward and, hopefully, achieving flying speed before falling off the front end.

"It was flattering to be invited to be one of the two volunteers! Lt Nev Locket was the other. The plan was for only the pilot to be on board, with fuel for ten minutes. *Centaur* would steam a few hundred yards ahead of *Eagle*, we would climb a few feet to achieve a safe approach, and 'plonk' straight down onto *Centaur's* deck. The boffins were right and I duly logged a sortie length of five minutes. The idiotic things we did for Queen and Country! When I was in Sea Venoms we had, statistically, a 90 per cent chance of surviving a year in a front-line squadron. We certainly earned our meagre flying pay."

### Michael Brown – pilot

"I was in 831 Squadron in the early 1960s. One task was the test and evaluation of new ECM equipment for the Buccaneer. I was the squadron trials officer flying Sea Venoms and Gannets which were converted for ECM work. The trials task was largely undertaken on the range north-east of Stornoway. Our aircraft had UHF (ultra-high frequency) radio, but the range was controlled on VHF. The relevant VHF crystals were held by the main users of the range, the

*Michael Brown with his Sea Venom, showing the 'Griff' painting. (Mick Brown)*

V-bomber crews at Finningley. We had to fly Culdrose – Finningley – Stornoway, then fly the range several times, returning to Culdrose via Finningley. This was not a one-day commitment, and weather conditions impacted the best laid plans.

"On 26 March 1962 Lt 'Griff' Griffith and myself took off from Culdrose bound for Finningley, and onward to Stornoway. We flew the range three times the next day, and twice more on the 28th before heading back to Finningley. The weather deteriorated and we were unable to continue, so we parked up and stayed the night courtesy of our Vulcan friends – unbeknown to us, things were about to change. The 'crabs' had 'captured' our navy aircraft whose 'owners' had departed for comfort and food.

"In the 1960s there was a popular act called Miki and Griff. They were a male and female singing act regularly appearing on TV and headlining at working men's clubs (which were very popular in Yorkshire). Miki was the female lead and Griff, her partner. When we returned to our aircraft the following morning, it was adorned with high-quality murals, one each side of the fuselage below the canopy. One was of Miki complete with curls and a bone dome, and on the other side Griff with moustache and bone dome.

"In some commands a dim view is taken of aircrew who permit the 'enemy' to capture, or detain one of their aircraft. I don't recall any comment along those lines when we returned to Culdrose. Years later this Sea Venom was in the static park at a Culdrose Air Day – still wearing those decorations."

## David Cooper – observer

"On 22 June 1958 John Carey and I were carrying out night deck-landing practice in our Sea Venom, I was calling the speed and was totally focussed inside the aircraft. John was either waved off, or had decided to go around when there was a bang and the aircraft lurched. My first impression was that the starboard tip tank had touched the deck as we went round, but in fact the port tank had hit the mirror. We climbed away to a safe altitude, and John checked the aircraft was fully controllable – nothing obvious was not working. We carried out an approach and landing using the starboard mirror – with me calling the speeds in a voice an octave or two above normal. Another 893 crew, 'Kipper' Herringshaw and his looker, landed after us (still using the starboard mirror), but hit the round-down. A third aircraft had to divert to Lod in Israel – very hush-hush at the time due to the political situation. He was so short of fuel that the engine failed just after he cleared the runway.

"My first pilot with 893 Squadron was John Varley. He once said to me, after we had landed at Hal Far very short of fuel (they put in 462 gallons which was the capacity of the aircraft when we were refuelled), that he had thought I was brave. He now realised that I didn't know what was going on – he was right!"

## Dave Eagles – pilot

"I did the all-weather fighter course at Yeovilton in the Sea Venom, joined 893

*Sea Venom FAW.22 893 Squadron HMS* Victorious, *1959. (Dave Eagles)*

Squadron, and did a full tour in *Victorious*. I then did the AWI course at Lossie and was the AWI on 891 Squadron.

"When the Sea Venom squadrons were ashore at Yeovilton, each had a Sea Vampire T.22 added to their complement for instrument flying practice and check flights. The RAF CFS sent standards examiners ('trappers') round to make sure that pilots were maintaining their instrument flying standards. The trappers came un-announced, deliberately. They would wander into a crew room and ask, 'What's your name lad? Come with me.' They then strapped you into their own Vampire and attached what looked like a plastic funnel onto your helmet. You couldn't see out, you could only see the instrument panel immediately in front. You were in the left-hand seat and they taxied you out, putting the aircraft on the runway centreline. They started the take-off leaving you to take over when you had rudder control. Thereafter you followed the trapper's instructions.

"All the observers enjoyed flying with their pilots in the two-stick Sea Vampires, with a lot of them becoming quite good pilots. Willy Stuart was a great character and a very experienced navigator/radar operator. He was also a slightly obnoxious navy type who loved an argument. When word got out that the trappers were in town, we were all in the coffee bar or hiding under our desks. A trapper came into the crew room where the only guy present was Willy, asleep in an armchair. The trapper told him to accompany him, having assumed he was a pilot. He strapped him into the left-hand seat of the Vampire without asking any questions, took him out and lined him up on the runway.

"Willy was a great guy and very experienced so he stuck with this and put on full power. The trapper started the take-off, and announced that he was handing over control after the Vampire had reached about 70 knots. Willy got it airborne and settled roughly onto a likely looking climbing speed, which no doubt varied widely as they progressed. The trapper took him through a series of requested exercises, including 'unusual attitudes' at 40,000 feet, which is awful. You're meant to do a 45-degree banked turn and not lose more than 300 feet – he was up and down by a thousand feet or so! He came back, did a GCA, then the instructor took over and landed, which they always did. As they taxied back in the debrief started. He said, 'That was bloody rough' and Willy made some facetious remark like, 'What do you expect from an observer?' The trapper was very unimpressed with this and returned to Little Rissington. Following this we had a signal to the air station cap-tain complaining about this operation, which should never have been allowed to take place.

"When we joined 893 in *Victorious* in '59, we were all assigned to a more expe-rienced pilot. I had only six deck landings to my name, two years earlier in SNJs. Of the three or four new boys I was the oldest, having done two years in Australia. We were assigned to a more senior pilot who mentored us through daylight deck landings and catapult launches. For night deck landings we were assigned a more experienced chap to hold our hands, and explain the difference. Night deck landings are a fairly intense experience, although I must say the Venom was an ideal aircraft for learning the trade and to build up some confidence. We had a very experienced pilot 'Bunny' Warren, who had been a commissioned pilot at the end of the war. He had now been promoted to Lt 'Bunny' and sat down with me before my first 'Duskers' flight and night landing. He said, 'It's just the same as bloody daytime deck landings; they don't know what they're talking about. All right, it's slightly different at night', and here he used his hands to illustrate. When you think you're over the ship you do this (the left hand came back smartly, signifying the throttle was chopped to idle, at the same time that the right hand went forward, signifying the stick being pushed fully forward.) 'Then you count two, and if nothing's happened (you don't feel deceleration) you reverse it.' (His left hand going fully forward and the right one fully back) – you haven't hooked on, so go round again.

"British carriers were suitable for the Sea Venom, which had about a 42 feet wingspan whereas the Sea Vixen had 50 feet. I used to love deck landings in the Venom, it was very crisp and responsive at approach speed."

### Rob Faulkner – pilot

"Over ten months in 1958, I'd gone through the day and night-fighter courses – we were doing deck-landing practice all the time. As soon as we started on the day-fighter course at Lossiemouth we found that, like all naval air stations, the airfield had a mirror landing aid on the end of the runway. We flew to Milltown where we did nothing but MADDLs.

"The Venom had tip tanks, 75 gallons per side, and Pilot's Notes said that you had to make sure your tip tanks were empty before you started your approach. This was because of the weight on the tips. Standing orders said all jet aircraft must be fully fuelled before take-off. But we were only going five minutes down the coast to Milltown – so we had to dump 150 gallons of fuel! They never did change the rules. Immediately we were over the sea we switched the jettison on to empty the tanks prior to joining the circuit at Milltown. We used to do eight or ten MADDLs in one sortie, and every time we went into Lossie or Yeovilton it was a mirror approach, whether you were in the circuit or on a GCA. I must have done at least a couple of hundred dummy deck landings before I went to a deck. Towards the end of the night-fighter course I was appointed to 893 Squadron on *Victorious*, which was in Lyme Bay. She was embarking the first Scimitar squadron so I was told that whilst she was there, prior to joining, I could do three or four touch-and-goes (not arrested). Then when I had joined, and we had crossed the Bay, they would launch me – I'd be on my own with little choice but to get back on. The day before we were due to go out Des Russell went over the side in the very first Scimitar landing. In the *Illustrated London News* there were photographs of the aircraft sinking for us to read at breakfast. This before our first attempts in the same ship in the same place."

*Lt Cdr John Desmond Russell was the CO of 803 Squadron. On 25 September 1958 he was the first to land on in Scimitar F.1 XD240. The No. 1 arrestor wire failed and he rolled off at low speed into the sea. Unable to release the canopy from the sinking aircraft, he lost his life. The Whirlwind 'plane guard helicopter's diver, on the scene in seconds, actually sat on the sinking aircraft to try and get the canopy open, but to no avail.* **Rob Faulkner** *again:*

"We went out to the ship in 766 Squadron Venoms. It was normally against the observer's union to accompany pilots on their very first deck landings. However, they sent me out with an absolutely brilliant observer Steve Lazenby, and we always flew together. We joined the circuit and the ASI packed up; it had picked up a bee or something. No messing about, back to Yeovilton for a spare 'cab' (navy slang for an aircraft) – you can imagine our state of mind. They were playing hell on the ship because we were holding them up. We finally landed on in the back of a Skyraider. That was my very first arrested landing, not being able to see a damned thing.

"If it was a flying day we worked either a 45-minute, or a one-hour cycle. You had to launch first and as soon as the deck was cleared you could land on. The trouble with that was if you got airborne and had a problem, the deck was crowded so you couldn't land back. We lost a Scimitar in the Moray Firth; as he went off the catapult something burst somewhere – you could see a plume of fuel off both wings. They said, 'No messing about, Lossiemouth is 20 miles away'. He was going to land straight off the sea on the long runway, where there was a big hangar on the right-hand side. They saw the Scimitar curving in behind the hangar, but after a while they realised it hadn't appeared on the other side. They hit the alarm button and the fire engine went off down the runway, through the fence at the end, saw the smoke off to their right, put on full lock and full power, straight across the 14th green of Lossie golf course. As it happened, the pilot was OK. The engines had quit and the hydraulic controls locked solid so he banged out. Lossie Golf Club got a new bunker and a new green out of the navy!

"Somehow life was more fun in those days, and common sense was more prevalent than rules. I managed to set fire to a

*Steve Lazenby and Rob Faulkner 893 Squadron* Victorious, *with their Sea Venom FAW.21 WW140, 1958. (Rob Faulkner)*

*Sea Venom FAW.21 WW279 893 Squadron HMS* Victorious *after its starter fire, 1958. (Rob Faulkner)*

Sea Venom on start-up; when I went to see the boss afterwards there was none of this 'caps on' stuff. He asked me what happened, I told him exactly what I'd done and he said he would've done the same. We were doing a 12-aircraft launch – trying to impress the Americans. I pressed the starter button and nothing happened. The book said switch off and wait 30 seconds, but with the huge pressure of 12 aircraft waiting to get airborne I just switched off, switched on again and pressed the button. There was a God almighty bang and everything wound down. I was carefully unstrapping, because we clearly weren't going anywhere, and suddenly Steve 'woke up'. I looked behind and saw that both cartridges had gone off at once. They'd burst the collector ring so there was fuel spraying out under pressure, with about 15 feet of flames with two full tip tanks in the middle of it. Steve departed stage right, and I departed stage left! They put the fire out without much further damage but they had to replace the engine.

"Landing on wasn't any sort of drama apart from the first few times. We had the angled deck and mirror landing sight – life was dead easy. It got to be so normal that four of us landed on one day, one after the other. We'd gone down below, drinking coffee when Lofty Wreford, the FDO, came down and said, 'OK, chaps, everything all right? Mirror not too bright?' Fortunately the boss was one of us and said that everything was fine. Lofty said, 'Oh that's good, because I forgot to switch it on.' Landing on had become so normal that we hadn't realised that the mirror wasn't on. If it was pitching and a lousy day then you studied things very carefully, but on a normal day it was just like landing on a runway.

"Pressure was the main thing. Once you had landed on and stopped moving, the next guy was only seconds behind you so you had to get clear of the landing area. As soon as you realised that you'd got a wire you closed the throttle, hand down to the hook lever, select hook up, hand back behind the seat to unlock the wings, fold them, then hand forward again and open the throttle wide, which started spinning the engine up. As soon as you stopped the weight of the wire pulled you back, and you started rolling backwards because you had closed the throttle. The wire would drop out of the hook, although there were people on the deck rushing in, just in case it needed help in dropping out. By the time you'd done all that, the engine was spooling up again, so you were accelerating forwards, then turning sharp right to get off the angled deck – you were desperate to get off the landing area.

"A lot of our sorties were at high level. We nearly always flew in pairs, in target and attacker practice interceptions. The ship had a new 984 radar, one of the first with full printout of height etc., so-called three-dimensional radar. It could give you a very good interception, with the chance to get right astern of the target aircraft at four miles or so, all on your own radar. Occasionally we flew low level, and also did rocketing a target towed behind the ship.

"The Sea Venom FAW.20 had no 'bang' seat, but they then introduced the Mk. 21 with a clearer canopy and ejection seats. There was a delay whilst the canopy jettisoned first as you couldn't eject through it. The cockpit was cosy. We were very close together, and as the seats were angled together by several degrees to fit them in, you couldn't eject simultaneously.

"Anyone who is not frightened of night deck landings is not telling the truth. That really was mind-boggling because it was absolutely black. It wasn't like driving a car with headlights on, all you could see was the mirror and the deck centreline of lights. There were meant to be five centreline lights, but you were lucky if three were working at any one time. They were a bit like cat's eyes with a metal cover, right in the middle of the centreline; if you hit one of those with a hook at 140 knots it doesn't do it much good. There were also deck-edge blue glims but you couldn't see those until you were actually on the deck. On a dark night you obviously had no horizon but the mirror had a horizon bar on it so you used that. We also had the advantage of an audio ASI and the observers used to call the speeds, saying '25, 25, 24, 24, 23...' and the pitch of his voice would go up as the speed came off. We had a two-needle ASI which was very accurate so you could read your speed to one or two knots.

"You could see the ship moving. By day the target was such that if you were spot on the mirror you'd get number two wire (there were four wires). By night it was number three. When you came in it was very difficult to know how far away you were, so you carried on until you hit something! Coming across the round-down you had a downward-ident light switched on – you'd be really concentrating on the mirror and the centreline. Suddenly there would be a bright white light underneath you as it reflected on the flight deck – your automatic reaction was to pull back. I don't think I ever got a number one or two wire at night, but I did get several fours. My record was an average of something like 20 per cent bolters at night.

"We were lucky because we had a boss who would fly in anything, regardless of weather and what instrument ratings we had. However, the senior pilot was a real 'old woman' (but an extremely nice bloke to know); if there was a cloud in the sky he wouldn't fly. Between the two of them you got that balance. Occasionally we flew when we were undoubtedly outside the limits, and occasionally we didn't fly when we were outside sun-bathing and wondering why we weren't flying.

"I was flying number 2 to Derek Matthews, our senior pilot, when we arrived back at the ship early. There were perhaps five minutes in which we could entertain the troops, before we landed on – great fun. I was formating on him in echelon

*Sea Venom FAW.22 XG612 V-461 of 893 Squadron* Victorious, *during Blue Jay (Firestreak) missile trials in December 1958. (Rob Faulkner)*

starboard and I could see him beckoning me to come in a bit, so I came in closer and closer towards his wingtip until we were probably less than ten feet apart. I was concentrating hard and aware of having quite a lot of throttle on and fairly shifting. When you get close to the sea, at about ten feet or so, you suddenly feel a 'cobblestone' effect because of the turbulence over the waves. I was sitting there on nearly full throttle, feeling the cobbles, and suddenly the round-down passed over my head. The two of us were underneath the round-down, and this was Derek Matthews, who never took a risk!

"We did the first live Firestreak missile firing trials, flying one aircraft with the weapon and another armed as a back-up in case the target drone went out of control. One day I was flying the armed one and the drone *did* go out of control somewhere over Malta. I was called in to shoot it down but the damned thing crashed before I could do so. I had visions of being able to paint a Firefly profile on the side of my aircraft. I watched them launch one of those radio-controlled Fireflies from Yeovilton – it had a crew on board as they were flying out to Malta. As he set off down the runway, just short of lift-off something went wrong, and he got full right rudder – you have two options. You either keep it on the ground for a certain ground loop, but it was fully loaded with fuel, so not a good option. You can drag it off the ground and try to sort it out – that's what he chose to do, but it didn't work. The starboard wing was dragging along the ground shedding bits, rapidly approaching the control tower next to a long line of Venoms. It spun round, passed through a gap in the line-up of Venoms, and finally came to rest on the concrete. When we got into the bar that evening, the crew were there and not fit to talk to anyone."

*The Firefly was a U.9 VT403 and the accident occurred on 2 September 1958. Fairey's pilot C J Kiss and his passenger H D Joyce, suffered slight burns.* **Rob** *again:*

"Our Mk.21s were fairly ancient. One problem was that the nosewheel swung down forwards against the airstream, and unless you were back to a reasonable speed, they wouldn't come down fully and lock into position. I was downwind with an observer, who had a lot more hours than me, when we had a red light for the nosewheel. I slowed right down – it still didn't come down. I thought we ought to try bouncing it down, so round to finals with only the mainwheels locked, bounced it on the runway, and fortunately it locked down. The instructor observer was as calm as anything, just sitting there unable to do anything with this sprog pilot next to him – Charlie Dwarika, a lovely bloke and a superb instructor.

"Life was different, it was less serious. If one of a pair of aircraft went u/s (unserviceable) they still launched the other one; they'd clear off and do some aerobatics or have fun for an hour. When they got to the next generation with the Sea Vixen, if one went u/s, neither of them flew; it all got more serious."

### Tony Hayward – observer

*Tony Hayward.*

"We had a great maintenance test pilot on 894 Squadron, Jim Fricker. I went off on a test flight with him off Malta. We did the test and Jim said, 'OK, let's see how fast it'll go'. He pointed us vertically down and we got up to .86 Mach (the limiting Mach was .84). He said, 'See, I haven't got any control, they're all ineffective. We'll pop the dive brakes, get the speed back and we'll have control.' He popped the dive brakes and one came off – 'bloody maintainers!' Jim muttered. Nothing dramatic at all, we landed and he went to have a go at the chief about it. Sadly, Jim was later killed trying to force land a Venom wheels-up after an engine failure. The aircraft hit a bump and accidentally fired the ejection seat, which in those days was not 'zero zero'.

"I liked the Sea Venom – although we lost a lot of people before ejection seats were introduced, because then if something went wrong you had to force land it. It had a wooden fuselage; if you were bouncing along when landing with the wheels-up, the cannons would come up through the floor. In a rocket dive, the fabric covering used to come off the nose – one wit suggested we should French polish it instead!"

> *Lt Jim Fricker's loss occurred on 27 February 1960 in FAW.21 WM572 of the Aircraft Holding Unit Abbotsinch after attempting a forced landing in a field at Dreghorn, Ayrshire. Later 'zero zero' seats allowed safe ejection if the aircraft was at a standstill on the ground.*

*Chris James.*

### Chris James – observer

"On the night of 24 February 1960 I was the observer in Sea Venom XG686, with Lt Richard 'Wilky' Wilkinson as pilot. On approach to landing on *Centaur* we experienced a total engine failure at 700 feet. With no time for a Mayday call, I jettisoned the canopy and ejected, followed immediately by Wilky. I don't recall the parachute descent at all...I was in the water, released the parachute and inflated my life jacket.

"In a previous accident, earlier in the cruise, a Sea Venom experienced brake failure on landing and went over the side. Although the observer was able to escape, the pilot was unable to free himself from his life raft and went down with the aircraft. This prompted a squadron procedure that recommended releasing the life raft connections prior to a carrier landing. So I had no life raft and was becoming entangled in my parachute shrouds, which I initially imagined to be a giant octopus. Having freed myself I then decided to kick off my shoes, as they were weighing me down, and as my feet came to the surface I was horrified to see my white socks glowing like beacons in the darkness. Again, my imagination ran wild and I expected every shark within miles would be tempted to investigate. Luckily I was able to activate my TALBE (talk and listen beacon) and started to think about the rescue operation, and how Wilky was getting on. I had seen blue flashes not too far away and presumed it was him trying to connect his TALBE, but we were not in shouting range.

"The ship's SAR Dragonfly helicopter had no night rescue capability so the 'plane guard destroyer *Carysfort* was despatched to search for us and, after what seemed like hours, I saw a searchlight scanning. There was a considerable swell running so every time I rose to the top of a wave I would gesticulate and shout obscenities in the direction of the lights. I was very relieved when the searchlight found me, whereupon a boat was launched and headed towards me. As they reached me the crew were trying to pull me in when a swell swept me under the boat and out the other side, from where I was finally dragged in. In the meantime Wilky had been located and we were soon reunited and taken to the 'plane guard.

"On board *Carysfort* we were treated to a couple of brandies, and then prepared to make a jackstay transfer back to *Centaur*. This almost resulted in another dip in the ocean due to the high swells. Then it was off to the sick bay for a warm bath under medical supervision, and more medicinal brandies, followed by a night flying supper of bacon and eggs.

"Although it seemed like an eternity, we were only in the ocean for about 25 minutes which speaks highly of the skill and efficiency of the rescue team. Also, many thanks to Martin-Baker for the flawless operation of their ejection seats – neither of us suffered any injuries."

## Patrick Mountain – observer

"It is December 1958 and 893 Squadron is embarked in *Victorious*, our nice 'new' aircraft carrier. We are in the Mediterranean visiting a few ports, and having some interesting flying exercises. This is my first front-line squadron, and I am fortunate in being crewed with Lt 'Robbie' Robertson with whom I had not long completed Sea Venom conversion.

"As Robbie was the squadron AWI he was charged with instructing us on using the weaponry, including the Firestreak missile. We were the first squadron to use these weapons, and we were looking forward to the chance of some live firing.

*Patrick Mountain.*

Before we could do this, we carried out trials to ascertain the arc within which the missile would lock on to a target. We did this with a number of different targets, including both piston-engined and jet-powered aircraft. We had to devise our own methods; mine was to use a chinagraph pencil to make marks on the windscreen, and estimate what angle to the target would usually be the limits of acquisition. All this was done to inform the boffins who had embarked with us. They then asked us to try pointing at the sun to see what resulted; at what sort of angle and proximity to the direct line to the sun would the weapon lock on to it, and become useless as a target indicator? The same method was used – the good old chinagraph was perfect for the job. High-tech stuff in those days!

"It was inevitable that our turn to launch from the *Vic*'s deck was invariably too near to midday, and in the Med, even in December, the sun was quite high. We found out, at some discomfort, just how long a Sea Venom could maintain a near vertical climb. Robbie endeavoured to point us close to the sun before we fell out of the sky, recovered and tried again. The boffins seemed quite appreciative of our efforts but we were never told the results.

"The great day arrived when we were briefed to carry out a live firing. The boss Eric Manuel, insisted on being the first as was his right – we were on standby on the other catapult. The boss was absolutely livid when his aircraft, with the senior observer Dave Mather, went u/s on the cat. So we were in the lead. Our target was a Firefly, which was launched from Hal Far, equipped with a heat source mounted under the starboard wing. We duly found it at 10,000 feet, and using my radar we closed in until we had Firestreak acquisition. Range was fine and everything seemed to be right. Robbie fired it off, and we recorded its course with the G90 camera. Satisfyingly the Firestreak homed in on the heat source, exploding with a rather depressingly small puff of smoke. This caused the Firefly to turn steeply to starboard and head for the sea. Duty carried out. Were we the very first in the Royal Navy to carry out a live air-to-air missile firing? We like to think so.

"Late July 1959, same ship, same squadron, same pilot and once again we are in the lead on a live firing exercise. This was an air-to-ship attack off the coast of Virginia, where we had been entertained, between exercises, by the very hospitable USN and their wives and families at Norfolk. We had started our liaison with the usual splendid party on board *Victorious*, where we laid in enough well-fuelled goodwill to ensure that a flood of invitations resulted. Converting our hangar into an English street market complete with bars and seafood stalls, the whole entered via a replica of Anne Hathaway's Cottage was only the start. The 'cottage' was entered at the rear from the after lift well, visitors then came through the 'cottage', out into a small front garden and through a wicket gate into the street market. They were welcomed by Adm 'Crash' Evans, a shortish slender chap with a goatee beard. As the 803 (Scimitar) Squadron line book said, 'the illusion was completed for our visitors by a welcome from a life-sized replica of William Shakespeare'. What the admiral thought of this is unrecorded.

"After an hour or so of drink and seafood, generously dished out for our invitees, officers of the USN and the great and good of Norfolk, the other end of the hangar was illuminated to show the front of a formidable old English castle. A pregnant pause and then down came the drawbridge and out marched the Royal Marines preceded by their splendid band. Lots of martial tunes and a special 'beat the retreat'. There was not a dry eye in the house. The Americans were suitably impressed, and the ground for a really memorable visit was well and truly laid. Our visit was the first to the US by an RN capital ship since World War 2. The USN having (to us), the curious rule of keeping their ships dry, more than offset this drawback by their shoreside hospitality; free-flowing booze and in particular an introduction to the dangerously seductive local speciality, the mint julep.

"We had been operating for some time with the USN and had some problems in trying to indulge in 'combat' with their much quicker aircraft, mostly F8U Crusaders and the very agile Skyhawks. We did though have a much superior carrier-based radar, the 984 system, which was the first to display a height read out straight to the direction officers, so we had some advantage and were able to achieve a reasonable number of 'kills'.

"Come night time however we had a bigger advantage, especially when we were briefed to attack the principal vessel of the US Fleet – the guided-missile cruiser USS *Boston*. It was my fortune to be still crewed with the AWI, and we were to lead a strike of four aircraft; launching after 849 Squadron, whose long-range airborne radar had reported finding, and were tracking, the *Boston* some 150 miles away. We were loaded with four Lepus Flare rockets, and led off our division of four. Guided by the 849 observers we were soon able to get our own radar contact and close in on the ship. We were flying at something under 500 feet at 300+ knots (a goodish speed then).

"Aiming just astern of the *Boston* I told Robbie we were at 2¼ miles and to pull up, and as we got down to 1¾ miles I called 'fire'. In quick succession all four rockets were away, with just a little spread, and we pulled up to about 3,000 feet, winged over and were gratified to see the four flares on their parachutes gloriously illuminating the ship. Our three following aircraft carried out a mock rocket attack which we followed, and we all headed off back to 'mother' again at low level. Duty duly carried out. Robbie carried out our usual immaculate deck landing, and all was well as we hit the deck. We got the familiar sudden jerk as we caught the arrestor wire, but then a sudden release and an almost immediate repeat of the arresting wire taking charge. We instantly realised what had happened, either we had broken the arrestor wire or it had skipped and dropped away. It turned out that the arrestor hook had, by a strange and possibly unique fluke, partially caught the wire, split and broken it, and we had then caught the next but one. We had a very lucky escape as it was estimated that our speed had been down to about 90 knots when the first wire broke, far too low to accelerate and go round again, and probably giving us insufficient time to get rid of the canopy and eject. Back in the crew room we were met by Wings, 'Good show chaps, job well done, and we are told that they never saw you until the very last moment and too late to take any evasive or preventative action. One up to the 'Blues''. Perhaps he was going to buy us a beer? 'I think we will have another go at them, briefing in half an hour', he said. Ah well, who would have a boring civvy job?

"We visited Boston and New York. In both places we were welcomed almost as royalty. The hospitality in Boston was so extreme, and so many invitations were received, that lists would go up in the wardroom detailing officers to attend events; in order to cover all the numerous parties to which we were invited. The freedom of a hotel in Swampscott, run by a member of the Kennedy family, was given to a bunch of us from 893 Squadron. We were chauffeur driven to this palatial place, with private beach and all meals included. One of my fondest memories is one night in New York being detailed as officer of patrol. I was attached to a police precinct with its detachment of US Marines, under a jovial captain, who took me under their wing. They showed me the real New York, the best parts and the seamiest, on an extended tour that no casual visitor or tourist could ever have expected to experience. Happy days."

## Brian Phillips – radio/radar mechanic

"Having handed over our 809 Squadron Sea Hornets we were given the option of staying at Culdrose, or going to Yeovilton with the squadron which most of us did. There we picked up Sea Venom FAW.20s and flew them for about six to eight months, until they were replaced by FAW.21s. The Sea Venom was a lot easier to service than the Sea Hornet because the radios were in an easier location. But the radar was a pig; the receiver and display were huge.

"One of our pilots, after having engine failure, landed a Sea Venom on the canopy of the New Forest – he had tried to stretch the glide. It was a canopy of tall

*No. 809 Squadron with 'Venomina' at Yeovilton. (Brian Phillips)*

trees, mainly oak and the like. He simply climbed down, and we got the aircraft back. Strangely enough although there was some damage to the underside panels and the tail, it flew again.

"One night we 'liberated' a nude statue from the local Yeovilton sculptor; we accidentally broke her arm off, so we had to pay for it. It became our property and we called it 'Venomina'! I'm not sure what happened to it. It was outside the officers' mess at Yeovilton, maybe it should go to Marham ready for 809 Squadron to reform.

"On 13 November 1955 we took the aircraft to Malta. Hal Far was having a new runway laid, so luckily we were pushed over to RAF Ta Kali. We flew from there most of the time, being the first squadron to move back into Hal Far until we left the island in March '56. It snowed while we were there, the first snow they'd had in Malta for about 60 years."

### Tony Pinney – pilot

"I was 891 Squadron's duty officer when we had an incident in *Centaur* when transiting from Singapore to Hong Kong and we were entering a typhoon. We couldn't get all the aircraft into the hangar so we had five on deck in the lee of the island superstructure. Due to the wind it was too dangerous for the maintenance personnel to attach the cockpit covers. In the absence of commander air or 'LittleF', who had retired because we weren't flying, I asked the captain if the ship could be manoeuvred to reduce the wind effect to make it safe for the covers to be fitted. The ship's navigator insisted that we had to maintain the ship's course and the captain supported him. The problem with the Venom was that the canopy seal would not inflate when closed without power on the aircraft. We tried to attach duct tape without success (the conditions were extremely dangerous for the maintainers anyway). Consequently all five cockpits were saturated, as were the multi-plugs on their lower right panels. This put the aircraft out of action until they could be re-wired. Having heard that the 891 Squadron CO had reprimanded me for not getting the covers on, the captain took responsibility and put him straight on the matter."

### Mark Thomson – pilot

"In November 1961 I was at Culdrose in 831 Squadron; our aircraft were all optimised for electronic warfare. My observer Chris James and I were tasked to fly a Sea Venom to Turin in the middle of winter – 615 miles. This was to take part in a two-week electronic warfare exercise with the US 6th Fleet. For the Sea Venom 615 miles was a very long way, the flight time would be two hours 20 minutes.

"We flew in cloud most of the way, arriving overhead Turin in thick cloud at 40,000 feet. It was clear that Turin ATC were in absolute chaos getting aircraft down in very bad weather. Landing aids were quite primitive then, and our fuel state was very low. They put us into the holding pattern at high altitude in cloud, which meant just going round in an orbit until each aircraft below had landed. We had a flameout at 30,000 feet while Turin ATC kept telling us to maintain altitude but we managed to relight at 15,000 feet.

"We were increasingly focused on our very low fuel state – I told ATC that we had ten minutes of fuel remaining. I declared an emergency – usually this enables ATC to give priority for an immediate descent to jump the queue of aircraft waiting to land – the response from ATC was total silence. So I repeated the emergency with seven minutes fuel remaining. We were given an immediate descent towards Turin airport (the approach to the runway was over the centre of Turin). We came out of cloud very low, and in poor visibility, over a sea of beautiful terracotta roofs.

"I could just see the runway in the murky distance and was concentrating on flying the approach, but with the fuel gauge very close to zero I told Chris to prepare to eject. I had this vision that I'd come all the way through fighter pilot training, had a near-death experience in a Sea Hawk, and I just couldn't believe that I was going to die on a terracotta roof in Turin. We were cleared to land, and by the grace of God, we touched down. We were in shock. ATC asked us to expedite turning off the runway as there were many aircraft behind us waiting to land. We had just partially turned off when the engine stopped. As the tail of the Sea Venom was sticking out into the runway no aircraft could land. A Jeep arrived with a lot of very excited Italians and we managed to push the aircraft off the runway.

"About four years prior to this four Sea Hawks flew from the UK to Italy in bad winter weather. Air traffic control were unable to get them down so all four pilots ejected when their fuel ran out. Rumour had it that the government funds destined for new approach aids had never arrived."

### Jonathan Tod – pilot

"I came off 800 Squadron and they said I was going to the first Buccaneer squadron.

However I was in the unhappy position that it was only going to have six aeroplanes, and they had seven lieutenant commander pilots – I was to be the one lieutenant. They decided they could only find four Buccaneers to fly. They had to get rid of one pilot, so they sent me off to Hal Far to hold over for a year. Whilst there on 750 Squadron, I flew the Sea Venom for the first time (on 21 April 1964). I had a wheels-up landing in a Sea Venom on 12 May 1964 [see Mike Norman's account in Chapter 2].

"The Sea Venom was a pleasant aircraft to fly. The whole thing was smoother; it was much nicer than the Vampire which, when you did a landing, sort of bumped and ground along. It had stiffer oleos, whereas the Sea Venom which was made for landing on aircraft carriers probably had better springing in the oleos. The Vampire was good fun for doing aerobatics, and the Sea Venom just seemed a bit more leisurely over the whole thing. It had the advantage of a much better view than the Vampire, the cockpit of which was very cramped with tiny little quarter lights to look out of. When you had the Vampire at full speed you got so much buffeting on the ailerons; the only thing that worked to bring you under control again was the air brakes. The Sea Venom had a much more comfortable approach towards the sound barrier at Mach .94 – or something like that."

*The retirement of the Sea Venom, as the Sea Vixen arrived, heralded a new era of high-performance fighters for the FAA; one which produced more than its fair share of challenging situations and tragedies.*

*Sea Venom FAW.20 WM513 BY-010 Airwork FRU St Davids, 1957-58. (Wynford Richards)*

## CHAPTER SEVEN

# SUPERMARINE SCIMITAR

*Scimitar F.1 XD236 038 FRU over the Isle of Wight, 5 June 1968. (Adrian Balch)*

*The FAA's first swept-wing single-seat fighter, the Scimitar, was born out of a series of earlier Supermarine prototypes. It was designed as an interceptor, reconnaissance aircraft and for low-level nuclear strike. Innovations included powered flying controls, and blown flaps to reduce both the landing speed and the speed needed off the catapult. Despite this it was a challenging aircraft to operate off the smaller carriers. It entered service in September 1957 and was withdrawn from squadron use in October 1966. However, a small number flew on with the FRU at Hurn until February 1971.*

*Squadrons: 700X, 764, 800, 800B, 803, 804, embarked on* Ark Royal, Centaur, Eagle, Hermes, Victorious. *Airwork FRU, RN Test Squadron ('C' Squadron A&AEE), Maintenance Test Pilot's School.*

## Allan Tarver

"I was a maintenance test pilot at Brawdy in '66; it was a routine thing for engineers that flew and we had a mini squadron of about six pilots. There was a maintenance unit there, mainly working on Scimitars and Vixens, and we checked out the aircraft. The Scimitar was a real 'hot rod' for its day – the Americans wondered how an aircraft could have so much power but not go supersonic (in level flight). It was heavy and had only small wings, however it didn't go quite as fast as people expected. It was nice enough to fly, but you'd be lucky to get it up to 40,000 feet. The engineers carried hammers and walloped it if something wasn't working! It had no radar, so what you could do with it was somewhat limited. It probably should never have been allowed to leave the drawing board, but the RN was short of aeroplanes."

## Brent Owen

*Brent Owen.*

"The Scimitar was a complex and exciting challenge. I was so delighted to have been selected to fly it; the rather negative aspects were irrelevant. It was big – the biggest single-seat aircraft operating from a carrier at the time. It was the last FAA aircraft with guns, four 30-mm cannon. It could carry four 1,000-lb bombs and had a nuclear capability. Some versions had a five-camera nose for high-speed low-level photo reconnaissance – that was my preference.

"Its two engines produced 23,000 lbs of thrust, and it weighed up to 42,000 lbs. It could be operated down to 32,000 lbs weight, which made for a very spritely acceleration. The rate of roll was said to be 540 degrees/second, but I have to admit that I never actually counted them. In order to operate it from one of our carriers (*Centaur*) it needed various lift-improving devices; leading edge flaps and trailing edge/fuselage flaps. It also had blown flaps, where high pressure air was bled from the engine compressor and blown over the trailing edge flaps. This reduced the approach speed by something like 10 knots.

"There was no VNE or never exceed speed, although the drop tanks were limited to 710 knots. I have never come across another aircraft without a VNE. Unkind people claimed that it developed too much drag at high speed to be able to hurt itself! Once, in a fit of exuberance, I did try a vertical dive at full power to see what would happen. I was only able to get 1.25 Mach – it was interesting how quickly the world seemed to get bigger, though.

"It had an uncomfortable habit of producing strange bangs, clicks and other noises at odd times. It could be counted on, when taking off in a four-ship formation, to find some reason to activate some warning system or other, with bells and flashing lights across the glare shield. One soon learned to silence the noisy bits (the cancel noise button was just within finger reach of the throttle) and wait until an appropriate moment to glance at the reason for the alert on the centralised warning panel. There were something like 17 sources of alert.

"There was a sort of simulator, but it was more of a cockpit trainer than a real simulator. It was claimed that the aeroplane was a good introduction to the simulator rather than the other way round! I remember my first take-off quite well. At the briefing in the bar (which as we all know is the true source of knowledge) I was warned that on take-off a firm rotation was the way to go. The other comment was, as the performance was so dramatic, no-one raised the undercarriage until 10,000 feet after the first take-off. This obviously couldn't happen to me, so a rather crafty idea formed. I will apply partial power to bring it back to Hunter performance, raising the wheels immediately after take-off thus impressing all as the 'Tiger of the Skies'. Unfortunately, when one gives it a little more thought than I did at the time, a firm rotation at reduced power is not the best combination. The wing dropped briskly on rotation – followed by a quick kick of rudder and the throttles being slammed far forward! At about 10,000 feet, when the eyelids finally relaxed, I retracted the wheels in the normal fashion.

### WHEN AIR-TO-AIR REFUELLING WENT A TAD WRONG!

"As a new Scimitar pilot on 736 Squadron at Lossiemouth the briefing was for a simple air-to-air refuelling (AAR) practice. The refuelling probe was to one side of the nose which made connection quite straightforward, normally not problematic. I had taken the fuel and was slowly drifting back from the tanker aircraft – the maximum disengagement rate was something in the order of seven feet per second.

"We had been having some problems with the system and when the probe appeared to disengage from the hose earlier than usual, I thought the tanker pilot needed to be informed. Foolishly I moved back behind the tanker to have a closer look for him, and just as I took position the hose was released. There was a rather large and heavy metallic basket affair attached to the hose (wherein to plug the probe) and this hit my aircraft a mighty blow. It shattered the outer windscreen and deposited debris into both engines, doing assorted damage. Not satisfied with that, the hose lodged under my refuelling probe and whipped over the canopy, making a mighty commotion. The forward windscreen and both engine intakes were badly damaged.

*Scimitar F.1 XD232 after the refuelling incident, 5 June 1964. (Brent Owen)*

"Unfortunately, about then

the port engine fire warning made its presence known – visually the starboard intake had much more damage! The Scimitar had no manual control reversion, meaning that at least one engine was needed for control. Ejection wasn't an option due to the hose being firmly lodged over the canopy. I had no confidence in the damaged right engine continuing to run, so after a certain amount of pondering I decided to ignore the fire warning and keep both engines running. Apparently the aircraft was trailing heavy smoke from the left side in a dramatic fashion, but since I couldn't see that, a simple fire warning light in the cockpit isn't nearly as frightening as it would have been had I been able to see the smoke.

"As I couldn't see much through the windscreen, it was necessary to form up on the tanker aircraft which led me to an uneventful landing. The fire rescue folks soon had the hose unhooked from the canopy, and the fire extinguished. After being towed back to the squadron I was met by our captain, David Kirke – a wonderful man. He told me how happy he was to have the aeroplane back, and what a splendid fellow I was. It made me feel quite good about the world, and about ten feet tall. He then went on to say, 'Owen, I was listening to your radio transmissions. When acknowledging a call, you said 'Rog'. That may be acceptable to our transatlantic cousins, but *not* to the Royal Navy! The correct acknowledgement is 'Roger', please remember that.' He totally brought me back down to earth, I had disappointed a man I very much respected. I never forgot that.

"Had this happened when I was embarked, I think I would have been hard pressed to land back on board; although I did manage one landing on the *Ark*, with a completely blinded windscreen, using voice aid from the deck landing officer. In a sense, landing in such conditions can be easier to the deck than to a runway, in that once on the deck you have stopped and don't need to keep straight.

"Very occasionally we were able to intercept one of the very long-range Bears which were frequently probing our air defence zone limits. The crew members always seemed pleased to see us, and on occasions would display, with big smiles, some kind of centrefold 'lovely'. Years later, during one of my forays into Lithuania, I met one of the Bear pilots and compared notes. He said they didn't like the job because of the tedium of flying back and forth from the far east of Russia. Far from being intimidated, they enjoyed the occasional interception to break the boredom, and of course they always took their own photographs. Above all else they were aviation enthusiasts, and interestingly, despised Russia and Russians.

"As a measure of how seriously we took the various missions we had Operation Teamwork in 1964. We were attempting to intercept an American task force, about 400 miles east of Iceland and the same distance north of Scotland. We had to air-to-air refuel to get to the search area and to get back. The weather was terrible with heavy cloud and heavy seas in the search area. We flew up there as a two-ship unit, my flight leader letting down on a forecast barometric setting. The last few hundred feet made my toes curl – I was rather tense about the whole idea – but we actually found the fleet, and treated them to a very noisy deck-level fly-by with me hanging on to his wing very tightly, then climbing back to altitude. An F-4 Phantom attempted to interfere with us, but it was no contest. Then a beautiful F-8 Crusader tried his luck, but in those days the US military was not trained in air-combat manoeuvring, and we were trained to be very aggressive."

### Jonathan Tod

"Of the two types I was flying at the time the Scimitar had the power, whereas the Hunter had the manoeuvrability to turn inside it. But if the Scimitar was getting into trouble he could just open both the throttles and disappear at 40,000 feet. There were 76 Scimitars built, and we managed to write off 39 of them. It really was quite an interesting period – we were moving seriously into the jet age. It was the first really fast jet fighter – the E-Type Jaguar of the skies. It had extremely powerful engines, and before that we only had a single engine in a Hunter. It could pull 7.5 g and go supersonic. What was not keeping up with it were the facilities within the aircraft; we had a huge number of hydraulic failures. The system pressure was 4,000 psi. If you were pulling 7 or 8 g fairly regularly there was all sorts of bending and twisting in the aeroplane – the fittings just couldn't stand up to it. If you couldn't get the wheels down you had to eject because the nose-up attitude on landing wheels-up was just too high.

"The aeroplane used to leak like a little puppy dog. When you put it into a hangar you had to put drip trays underneath because fuel was dripping out in all directions due to the amount of airframe stresses. With high-speed flight the aircraft actually increases in length; so how on earth do you make junctions in fuel pipes, hydraulic pipes, fuel tanks, etc.? The Scimitar was built heavy to take the stresses of going onto a ship. It was really a big step in technology progressing to a supersonic fighter.

"The old carriers were designed to take things like the Seafire and Sea Fury, with a landing speed of about 110 knots and weighing in at about three tons. Suddenly you had the Scimitar weighing in at 20 tons and coming in at 150 knots. As far as the carriers were concerned, what we were doing was 'putting new wine into old bottles'. So many times I've done a 'this is a minimum speed launch', and a 'landing in the emergency settings'! The four wires across the deck have got a series of settings depending upon the weight of the aircraft coming back. Sometimes you actually had to exceed the normal maximum landing weight, and go into the emergency overweight situation. That used to happen very regularly; particularly when you were up in the Persian Gulf it was always right on the limits. You couldn't launch a Scimitar with full fuel there; you were launching and then plugging into a tanker straight away, which would keep you airborne for about an hour. The tanker was another Scimitar, or sometimes a Sea Vixen.

"I found daytime deck landings were great fun, one of the greatest sports invented by man. It really was enormously satisfying when you did a nice one. But by night, every inch of any experience, any ability I had – everything went into

*Scimitar F.1 XD270 R-191 807 Squadron* Ark Royal, *landing on* Centaur *in the Med and showing the nose high attitude.*

those night deck landings. It was bloody terrifying – to put it mildly. Gosh, you had to concentrate. I didn't enjoy night deck landings at all.

"With the angled deck you are coming across the ship's turbulence. When you're coming round on the cross-wind leg, you crossed behind the ship and went through the turbulence. Then you come back in again, and just as you're getting very close towards the touchdown, you pick up the turbulence. That final turn round, especially in the southern oceans, always used to be where the Albatrosses waited on the corner. Coming off an aircraft carrier (just off the centreline), were two great vortices which the birds rode. So as you came round the corner you were eye to eye with an Albatross! Amazing birds they would stay with the ship for a week, two weeks, something like that.

"As you picked it up fairly late, I don't think the turbulence worried people too much – it was just a bit bumpy. You are focussed on the 'meatball', so subconsciously you rode it. You knew that if it tipped you a bit left, it would then tip you a bit right – it was the up and down that worried you. You didn't really look at the deck, you just had to concentrate on the 'meatball' and one orange centreline.

"*Hermes* being a small carrier was a bit more difficult, and flying Scimitars off her was quite tight. Later on, when you then found yourself on a Mk.2 Buccaneer on *Ark Royal* that was just luxury. I once cross-operated with the USN on the old

USS *Essex* which had a wooden deck. We quite often had Americans coming over to us, and they were always impressed with how small the ship was."

### Jock Mancais

"I got back to Lossie in May 1960, back to 736 Squadron, it was OFS1. We had eight Scimitars and 12 Sea Hawks which got you used to the faster aircraft. We had a communications problem with the Scimitars – half the radios were on UHF and half on VHF, so we got along fine with hand signals. The navy eventually got it all sorted out.

"I then took over 800 Squadron where there were a number of pilots who I'd trained in 736, but who hadn't done deck landings. One of them was Colin Morris who years later flew Concorde for British Airways. 800 was born out of 803 and 807 Squadrons which had six aircraft each, so we became a 12-'plane squadron moving up to 15, the biggest squadron in the navy at that time. Jonathon Tod joined us when we came back from the Far East.

"The Scimitar was designed to reach altitude quickly – you could climb to 50,000 feet easily. It was good at ground attack, but its range was horrible – it gulped the fuel like fury. My squadron was qualified to deck land at night; in case you got caught out coming back late to the carrier. However the aircraft was not cleared operationally for deck landings at night; the attitude for landing meant the tail was well down, and the cockpit was high in the air which made it dangerous. I got two dusk landings and two at night – it wasn't easy and that was enough. This was one of the limitations of the carriers, and with an approach speed that was about 130-135 knots there was very little room for error. We managed with *Centaur*, but we had to launch with much reduced fuel loads – that's how we got round it, just a thimble-full load of fuel.

"We were very proud of what we did on Scimitars. We were 'one-armed paper-hangers' by the time we finished, we had a nuclear role, photo recce, Bullpup missiles, rockets and bombs. But in a shooting war we would have been very restricted range-wise. We also had a nuclear role in the Far East and were told: 'After your LABS (low-altitude bombing system) manoeuvre you'll find us (the carrier) in a certain position, but if you have to ditch you'll be picked up.'

"No. 800 deployed in *Ark Royal* to the Far East and we went to Singapore, south-west Australia, Japan, Philippines (Cubi Point) and Hong Kong. We cross-operated with USS *Hancock*, but she b*****ed off halfway through the programme as she was one of the first carriers involved in the Vietnam War. We used to take off and fly for just half an hour before landing on, unless it was for real when we could do flight refuelling from the Sea Vixens. Later on in the Scimitar's life it also became a tanker."

### Bill Stocker – apprentice

"Those 'wet' wings on the Scimitar carried most of the fuel. There were no tanks as

*Bill Stocker.*

such, the rivets and joints were sealed over the fuel-containing section of the wings. The wings were filled and pressure tested at the appropriate time, and they invariably leaked around the rivets. We generally removed the offending rivet and replaced it with one coated in some foul-smelling 'gucky' sealer. This was generally carried out with the aircraft up on jacks. Lowering onto its undercarriage invariably created a new batch of leaking rivets which we set about resealing again. Given that this was a carrier-borne aircraft the Scimitar must have leaked fuel like a sieve after a few deck landings. What really sticks in my memory though was the smell of the sealer. It was appalling and you just couldn't get it off your clothes or skin for seemingly weeks. No chance of a date at weekends, and that was a real issue for a 19-year-old!

"The Scimitar had three or four small fuselage fuel tanks that fitted between the engines, with access from the top. These required taping and doping from the inside, generally carried out by the smallest, skinniest apprentice that happened to be around (often me). In you went, just hoping you didn't get cramp. No protection or breathing apparatus. Health and safety just didn't exist in the '60s.

"Another task filled with excitement was adjusting the rudder actuator. This was located in the fin just above the all-flying tailplane. It was a straightforward task and generally only took a few minutes. So if you were on a piece work/bonus system, why would you bother to gather and assemble the necessary scaffolding to get up on to the tail (about 15 feet up when it was on jacks)? The normal procedure was to get the tallest stepladder in the shop, stand on the top of it behind the tailplane and, holding on to the leading edge, pull yourself up on to it. This worked well if you were over six feet tall. I'm 5 feet 7 inches so I had to make a little jump to reach the leading edge. Coming back down was even more exciting!

"Engine changes: I'm sure it must have been the same for any British twin-jet of the '60s, Buccaneer, Javelin, Sea Vixen etc. The first engine went in fairly easily in the Scimitar, but the second required a masterpiece of co-ordination between the crane operator and about four fitters, all conducted by the foreman standing on a stepladder above the engine bay. The second engine had to be positioned above the engine bay with extreme precision then lowered inch by inch with the fitters checking for interference. With the engine located on its mountings all the connections for pipes, hoses etc., had to be made. My skinny arms were handy for reaching down between the two engines, but they were covered in scratches from wrist to elbow by the time we had finished. We were doing all this under almost ideal conditions in a roomy hangar with a good overhead crane and all the other

Top: *No. 801 Squadron on HMS* Illustrious. *From left to right of front row: Willie Hackett (8th from left in leather jacket), Danny Stembridge (9th from left), Martin 'Jak' London (10th from left), Henry Mitchell (centre), Neil Bing (8th from right) and Dave Ritchie (7th from right).* (Steve Bond collection)

Bottom: *No. 803 Squadron Scimitar over the round-down to land on Ark Royal, 1965.* (Mel Evans)

Top: *No. 890 Squadron ashore from Ark Royal at Changi, 1966. (Mike Garlick)*

Bottom: *No. 892 Squadron line-up at Leuchars prior to final embarkation to Ark Royal, 6 April 1978. From left to right: Flt Lt Ken McKelvie (N), Flt Lt Pete Budd (N), Flt Lt Steve Riley (P), Flt Lt Tim Wright (N), Lt Cdr Neil Thom (P), Flt Lt Tim Hewlett (P), Lt Cdr Bernie Steed (SOBS), Flt Lt Andy Lister-Tomlinson (N), Lt Paul Bennett (P), Fg ( Dick Lotinga (P), Flt Lt Murdo Macleod (P), Lt Cdr John Ellis (CO), Lt Cdr Andy Auld (SP), Flt Lt Selwyn Rodda (N Lt Cdr John Eyton-Jones (P), Lt Twiggy Hansen (P), behind him – Lt Pat Gravitt USN (P), Lt Taff Davies (O), Lt C Dave Braithwaite (P), Flt Lt Bill Alexander (N), front Flt Lt Bob Rowley (P), rear Lt Dave Bunnell USN (O), Lt Barr Nocker (O), Flt Lt Trevor Newby (N). (Steve Bond collection)*

Top: *No. 893 Squadron Sea Venoms in Fly 1 HMS* Eagle *at the time of the 1956 Suez crisis.* (Derek Peskell via Martin Grant)

Bottom: *Ark Royal 1965 'catch-up Sunday'.* (Mel Evans)

Clockwise from top left: *Busy 1960s' deck scene on HMS Eagle, with two more carriers following behind (Steve Bond collection); Royal Canadian Navy Sea Fury (Pat Martin); Deck hockey, Ark Royal, 1965 (Mike Garlick); HMS Ark Royal (CVS) hangar deck. (Steve Bond collection)*

Clockwise from top left: *Nigel McTear and Phil Norris brave the elements on HMS* Illustrious. *(Chockheads); Dave Eagles standing next to a Grumman F9F-4 Panther, Kingsville Texas in August 1955. (Dave Eagles); Phantom FG.1 of 892 Squadron on take-off from* Ark Royal, *late 1970s. (Chockheads); Stirring the Christmas pudding, HMS* Hermes, *early 1960s. (Tim Lewin)*

Top: *F-35B on HMS* Queen Elizabeth, *October 2019.*
*(defenceimagery.mod.uk)*

Bottom from left to right: *Royal Canadian Navy Firefly (Pat
Martin); Sea Hawk FGA.6 806 Sqn HMS* Eagle *(Andy Copeland);
Sea Venom FAW.22 893 Sqn HMS* Victorious *1959. (Dave Eagles)*

Top: Ark Royal *from the rear. (Chris Bolton)*

Middle: *HMS* Hermes *homecoming from the Falklands, Portsmouth, July 1982. (Tim Lewin)*

Bottom: *Sea Vixen FAW.1 893 Sqn HMS Victorious 1965. (Adrian Balch collection)*

Opposite, top: *HMS Invincible returns home to Portsmouth from the Falklands 17 September 1982. (Steve Bond collection)*

Opposite, bottom: *HMS Victorious deck scene 1959. Dragonfly, Gannet, Scimitar, Sea Vixen and Skyraider. (Steve Bond collection)*

Top: *Kim Sharman's first attempt at his final launch from* Eagle. *(John Eacott)*

Middle: *Crowded deck on HMS* Victorious. *(Dave Eagles)*

Bottom: *HMS* Victorious *leaving Portsmouth. (Steve Bond collection)*

Top: 'Roughers'. HMS Ark Royal in a storm. (Steve Bond collection)

Middle: Phantom FG.1 R-013 of 892 Squadron launching from Ark Royal. (Tim Woodman)

Bottom: Phantom FG.1 of 892 Squadron being loaded up with 500-lb bombs on twin ejector by 'bomb heads' (armourers). (Steve Bond collection)

Top: *Scimitar F.1 XD330 R-034 803 Squadron Ark Royal, 1966. (Mike Garlick)*
Bottom: *Sea Fury F.10 TF944 at Culham in 1947. (Pat Martin collection)*

Top: *Sea Fury FB.11 VX727 NW-114 805 Squadron RAN Nowra, 1957.* (Dave Eagles)

Middle: *Sea Harrier FA.2s of 800 Squadron* Ark Royal *en route from Nellis to Bangor 2003.* (Robin Trewinnard-Boyle)

Bottom: *Seafire 17, 805 Sqn HMS Ocean, doing ADDLs at Hal Far 1947.* (Peter Hiles via SB)

Top: *Sea Hawk FB.3s of 738 Squadron at Lossiemouth in April 1956. (Dave Eagles)*

Bottom: *Sea Hornet NF.21 VW957 J-481 809 Squadron HMS* Eagle, *sometime between 2 September and 22 October 1953. (Adrian Balch collection)*

Sea Venom FAW.21 WW221 V-461 893 Squadron HMS Victorious, 1959. (Rob Faulkner)

om: Sea Venom FAW.22 XG612 V-461 893 Squadron HMS Victorious *during Blue Jay (Firestreak) trials in*
*mber 1958. (Rob Faulkner)*

Top: *The last launch, HMS* Ark Royal, *24 November 2010. (Robin Trewinnard-Boyle)*

Middle: *893 Sqn line-up HMS* Victorious *1957-58. (Rob Faulkner)*

Bottom: *Sea Vixen FAW.1 XN708 R-244 890 Squadron HMS* Ark Royal, *1963. (Mark Thomson)*

facilities. Imagine doing an engine change in the cramped hangar of an aircraft carrier, while being pitched about on the ocean, and being alternately frozen or roasted depending on where you were. I continue to have nothing but admiration for naval artificers and fitters who did all this at sea."

### Tim Thorley – naval air mechanic

"I started on 736 Squadron, which was a Scimitar training squadron. During that time I was working in ARS, the aircraft repair shop, which used to do the deep maintenance on them. For me as a youngster, it was very enjoyable. I always remember, having signed for the servicing I'd done on my first aircraft at 17½ years of age, watching it charge down the runway at Lossiemouth thinking that that thing was flying on my signature. From an engineering point of view the Scimitar was fairly straightforward. There was nothing funny about it, servicing was OK. It was started with a Palouste starter and that was it. It had a gaseous oxygen system rather than liquid oxygen. It was just a normal type of aircraft.

*Tim Thorley.*

"We were losing aircraft all the time. We had one come in which was low on fuel. We knew he wasn't going to make the runway, and he crashed on the golf course at Lossiemouth. We saw it come down, we saw the pilot bang out and there was a great big thump and then two Avon engines came over the boundary fence!"

### Anon pilot

"We flew out in misty weather and landed on board *Ark Royal* off the Isle of Wight. The weather forecast for the next few days was poor. A decision to steam quickly to the Gibraltar area, using RAF North Front as our diversion, seemed a good idea. Unfortunately, the expected good weather (closer to Gibraltar) had not arrived; solid cloud stretched right up to 30,000 feet with poor visibility beneath. It was Sunday, and the first day of the work-up. There was some command anxiety in getting started, but eventually conditions were judged to be acceptable so off we went. It was a prudent decision to limit the number airborne to four Scimitars, four Sea Vixens and a Gannet.

"The flight of four Scimitars led by me completed our high-level exercise controlled by ship's radar, and we joined up above cloud prior to starting a controlled descent to the ship. It was then that everything started to go wrong. An ominous radio transmission 'Conserve, there may be a delay' had everyone looking at their fuel gauges; not a problem at this stage. The ADR (air defence room) controller finally ordered our formation to commence a descent. Leading the first pair of aircraft we quickly plunged into thick cloud followed a couple of miles astern by the second section. It was dark and extremely turbulent, the wingman hanging in close so as not to lose contact.

"Safe flying in cloud depends on a constant scan and assessment of the primary flight instruments. Water had apparently frozen in the pitot static line, and at about 15,000 feet the sight of the ASI needle slowly unwinding from 250 knots back to zero was extremely disorientating. The ensuing change of formation, handing over lead to my wingman in heavy cloud, was a pretty tense exercise for us both. We eventually dropped out below the ragged cloud base at 600 feet into totally grey surroundings. Forward visibility in heavy rain was perhaps one to two miles; this featureless scene was only enlightened by the occasional flash of white from a breaking sea below.

"Radio directions from *Ark Royal*, which had been growing fainter, now ceased altogether. Scimitars had a single navigational aid, TACAN (tactical air navigation), a radio directional set. This was useful at sea, but rarely compatible with shore equipment. The needle still pointed ahead, so we kept hopefully on course. *Ark Royal's* dark shape finally appeared through the rain-distorted windscreen. I took the lead again, as my ASI had now unfrozen, and led the formation into low orbit overhead. The situation was not improved by the sudden appearance of four Sea Vixens out of the rain, also trying to stay below cloud and keep the ship in sight. At least we had all got back safely to the ship, and there only remained a deck landing in poor visibility to finish off a rather fraught first day. The ensuing pause seemed endless while all aircraft continued to circle awaiting the order to land.

"Finally a weak radio transmission; there had been a serious fire on board, all aircraft to divert immediately to Gibraltar. Bloody hell just when we were looking forward to getting back on board for a hot bath and a drink. The ship's position was known when we launched, but now an hour later could be anywhere up to 20 miles from that point. Land had to be away to the north-east so the formation, now a little more spread out so that everyone could look ahead, set off in that direction straining to see through the trailing tendrils of cloud, which sometimes reached right down to the sea. The only remaining navigation aid available in a Scimitar cockpit was a map strapped to the pilot's knee, somewhat smaller than an A4 sheet, which covered the whole Iberian Peninsula – Gibraltar was merely a carbuncle on its backside.

"With observers to navigate them, the radar-equipped Sea Vixens climbed high into cloud to conserve fuel, and had no problem in finding the Rock. The Gannet also had radar and plenty of fuel. Only the Scimitars were forced to remain visual at low level. Without knowing how far it was it was impossible to calculate whether our fuel state was sufficient to reach North Front. Doing any calculation which meant eyes down in the cockpit, was really not a safe option. The Spanish coast to the west of Gibraltar is made up of a series of high cliffs – vital to see them in time to turn safely away.

"Minutes passed as the formation flew on at 500 feet in the murk, the visibility varying as the aircraft flew through rain showers. The fuel gauges slowly unwound.

The coast was sensed rather than seen when it first appeared, a darker shadow in the mist which quickly grew into a vertical rock face disappearing into the cloud base. In a steep bank the formation turned starboard to fly parallel to the cliffs, now hopefully heading east towards the Rock. Quite suddenly the four aircraft broke out from this vast area of frontal weather emerging into a gloomy cavern of higher cloud; visibility improving to several miles. It was still raining heavily but reassuringly ahead was that unmistakable landmark, the crouching lion of Gibraltar.

"A first radio call to North Front – 'Four aircraft inbound on diversion, short of fuel and requiring an immediate landing!' – brought no answer. A second more emphatic transmission seemed to disappear into silent space; no welcoming response giving the usual details, runway in use and clearance to land. Gibraltar airfield lies on a narrow isthmus of land between the Rock and the Spanish mainland. It is crossed at its mid-point by the main road; closed before aircraft land. The runway itself is rather like an extended carrier deck, the approach from the sea over a threshold wall and there is a vertical drop into the water at the far end. Our fuel state was now so low that the Scimitars either had to land immediately or their pilots eject out to sea.

"As we spread out downwind preparatory to landing, the runway was temporarily hidden behind the Rock. Then the glistening tarmac came into view as each of us turned on to finals, 136 knots, gear and flaps down. At the very last moment a 'clear to land' call relieved the possibility of meeting Sunday afternoon traffic crossing the runway. It became apparent that the runway was flooded, and the aircraft touched down into great pools of water.

"It was practice to hold the nose up for a short while after touchdown, allowing aerodynamic drag to slow the aircraft, but the first attempt to brake after lowering the nosewheel had little effect. Maxaret brake units detect when wheels are aquaplaning, and automatically release brake pressure. The remaining runway was fast disappearing under the nose with speed decaying slowly. My hand hovered over the undercarriage retract lever as a last desperate measure to drop the aircraft on to its belly, rather than run off the end and fall into the sea. Thankfully, at a late stage, the brakes began to bite and the Scimitar came to a juddering halt with its nose almost hanging over the far cliff edge.

"Quickly clearing the runway, concern was now for the others. The second swerved off the runway under hard braking and stopped right at the end of the landing area. The same thing happened to the next, but luckily it swung to the left, also safely coming to a halt. The fourth pilot, warned by radio, managed to do a better job and stopped in good time. Shaken by all that had occurred, we taxied clear of the runway and sat watching the Sea Vixens arrive. Two of them burst tyres under heavy braking and reeled off to finish crippled well down the airfield. The smug Gannet arrived last, full of fuel, to begin its approach. After touchdown it rolled sedately along the runway throwing up a sheet of spray from the nosewheel which entered the jet intakes and put out the turbine flame. The massive contra-ro-

*Scimitar F.1 XD215 611 736 Squadron Lossiemouth, Yeovilton, 3 July 1965. (Steve Bond)*

tating propellers slowly wound down, and the aircraft trundled to a stop exactly in the middle of the road.

"A soaked flight sergeant, the only man on duty, ran out to meet us and came to a standstill in shocked silence at the sight of aircraft spread out over his airfield. He came over as we climbed wearily from our cockpits. 'Gentlemen, you are in real trouble. Didn't you know the airfield is closed on Sundays?' Our uncontrollable laughter, a mixture of relief after a truly stressful day, and genuine mirth at its comic ending, must have persuaded him that all naval aviators were mad. The signal from the navy requesting diversion facilities at Gibraltar had got lost somewhere on the way.

"When the Scimitar entered service, it was immediately obvious that it carried so little internal fuel that it was barely operable ashore, and quite unable to operate from a carrier – great carrier asset! So the inevitable addition of drop tanks as standard increased drag and reduced performance. It was yet another UK product of a reasonable aerodynamic design, although critics pointed out that the engine power should have made it supersonic."

## Alan Reed – apprentice

"I was involved with the Scimitar as an apprentice, then as a tradesman in the major overhaul and repair of airframes. I took part in a complex fuselage repair of an aircraft which had ventured over the side of an aircraft carrier. This involved the complete rebuild of the underside of the airframe, aft of the nose undercarriage. A major inspection of the engine bays with the engines and jet pipes removed, revealed temporary riveted repairs of a cracked heat shield – using flattened corned beef cans! Desperate measures no doubt employed by a hard-pressed, but resourceful, ship's company. Major modification programmes were undertaken to install 'Q' feel units to assist pilot controls, and 'Blue Silk' Doppler radar units to enhance navigation.

"The Scimitar was found to have limited range for its required duties, and a modification programme was instigated to increase fuel capacity. This involved the fitting of new rubber fuel tanks in the smallest equipment bays within the fuselage. There were only two fitters small enough to work in those confined spaces. Luckily I was one of them and this enhanced my take-home pay considerably. It also gave rise to a little jealousy. One day my breathing mask hose was clamped in a vice whilst I was inside a small tank bay using trichlorethylene cleaner. Unconsciousness, and a trip to the sick bay for oxygen treatment was the result.

"Another job was the fitment of modified air brakes, comprising petal doors around the jet effluxes. Having completed and functionally tested these hydraulically operated doors the whole job was approved by the inspector. On clocking off this job I was stopped by the union representative. He explained, rather forcibly, that I had completed the job in under a quarter of the rated time, and that to clock off would ruin everyone else's wages. So I spent quite a few hours working on my 1936 MG TA behind the hangar until I could safely clock off – problem solved."

## AEROBATIC TEAMS

*Over a six-year period between 1958 and 1964 Scimitar squadrons were selected to represent the Royal Navy at some of the major annual air shows (only missing 1963). These included the SBAC (Society of British Aircraft Companies) show at Farnborough and the Paris Air Show at Le Bourget.*

### Anon pilot

"This is a tale of simple folk who unexpectedly found themselves on centre stage. The 800 Squadron aircrew were the usual mix with a small number of experienced pilots, while the remainder were coming to the end of their first operational tours. The squadron had just disembarked after nearly a year at sea and was due for a period of rest and reorganisation. We were to be joined by a number of new boys straight from OFS.

"The signal from the Admiralty was brief; 'You are nominated as the navy's aerobatic display team for 1961' – 'What us? The old duffers must be joking!' Of course there could be no appeal, so a retreat to the bar did something to lessen the shock. What to do? Our mount, the Scimitar, was not an ideal aerobatic aircraft. It was a powerful twin-engine machine with relatively high-wing loading, and thus unsuitable for making tight turns within an airfield boundary. It did however have good low-speed stability (a carrier attribute), and was able to hang down lots of things including an arrestor hook, at the same time making lots of noise. At the other end of the scale it could well exceed 600 knots low level, arriving in advance of its own shock wave enveloped in a large balloon of condensation, trailing dirty

*Lt Cdr Keith Leppard and 807 Squadron's Scimitar aerobatic team at Lossiemouth in 1959. (Adrian Balch collection)*

smoke and exhibiting considerable PIO (pilot induced oscillation)!

"A display routine was slowly developed round these characteristics. Practice started with aircraft first flying in pairs, then fours and finally a formation of nine. Efforts were given a keener edge on learning that the RAF had put up a Lightning squadron, flown by experienced pilots, in competition with the navy. There were setbacks along the way. An innovative engineer designed and installed a smoke-making system, which was new in those days. Operated by the gun trigger, oil from a small tank pumped into the jet exhausts produced white smoke. This was followed by adding coloured dye.

"After starting engines any pilot would be disconcerted to see the ground crew making incomprehensible signals to him. Was the aircraft on fire, or had he left his sandwiches behind? The situation was soon explained – figures in white overalls, liberally coated in blue spots, appeared from behind the aircraft. In his mirror he could see a blue cloud spreading out and drifting towards the wardroom car park. Modifications were made. 'The boss', a fine ETPS (Empire Test Pilots' School) trained pilot, brought them all along, experienced and sprog alike, with calm confidence. He led the display largely by reference to flight instruments. A level entry at 360 knots with 88 per cent power, followed by a 4 g pull-up keeping the wings level on the attitude indicator, ensured the formation went over the top of a loop at not less than 200 knots, slow but safe.

"The boss [Lt Cdr Mike Norman] was forced to eject from his aircraft [XD264], at a critical moment during a Friday practice, before one of the first shows of the season. One of the main undercarriage legs had failed to lower, and there was concern that a wing might dig in and the aircraft turn over on landing. The recommendation was to leave it. He was shaken and bruised but otherwise uninjured. After a swift reorganisation the show went ahead with the deputy leader (me) taking over at short notice to lead what was now called the 'Red Blades' team. Thankfully the CO was soon fit for the next event – there were days of tension! There were parties after the show – Paris next.

"The main recollections are not of the show itself. The Scimitar's TACAN navigational aid was not compatible with civilian equipment. There were few air traffic restricted areas in those days, anyway most naval pilots were not too well up in such matters. Leading a nine-ship formation at low level while looking for Le Bourget airport, the boss got lost in the Parisian smog and unexpectedly ended up rounding the Eiffel Tower somewhat below the top gallery!

"Farnborough Week was to be the high point of the season. The flying committee required a preview of all display routines, so the team flew in on Friday, in advance of the arrival of the ground crew. Pilots were 'QS', qualified to sign for first-line servicing, removing overnight bags from the ammunition tanks on top of the wing, and proceeding to prepare for the display flight. After lining up in formation on the runway, the first group of four Scimitars accelerated away. At about 100 knots there was a sight like leaves in an autumn gale, as unsecured ammunition panels fluttered away. Same for the next section – bad show (don't breathe a word of this in case the RAF should hear).

"On Monday the weather was at its most sullen – a steady drizzle with a 200 feet cloud base and half a mile visibility. The flying committee decided to cancel all displays. However, the CO had ex-ETPS friends in the tower and persuaded the committee to allow the navy to put on a show. He took off alone in a cloud of spray and immediately disappeared into cloud, reappearing five minutes later out of the murk hook dangling, to catch the runway arrestor gear. Minutes later telephone lines from the Air Ministry were red hot demanding to know why the RAF had been outdone by the navy.

"Thankfully the weather improved during the week, and the show went on. Once, at the top of a loop, it became obvious that the only cloud in the sky, a large cumulus, was sitting right over the centre of the runway. Our next sequence was an outward fan break from the vertical. As the formation

*No. 800 Squadron at Farnborough, September 1961.*

entered its dive the team plunged into cloud. For the first and only time the break was carried out on instruments, a sort of individual pull for your lives!

"A company seeking marketing publicity lent the team Lambretta motor scooters. They were invaluable in getting round the Farnborough perimeter. They might not have been quite so pleased to know of an alternative use. Late one night, the boss astride the white centreline of the old A3 road, led the team in diamond formation back to the mess. The busy summer came to an end at last: our white overalls and funny hats were put aside. The squadron next reverted to a more routine task; practising nuclear attack on distant Russian naval bases."

### Jonathan Tod

"I was the staff officer and ferry pilot for 800 Squadron's aerobatic team at the Farnborough air show. We had just started using coloured smoke. This was made by getting a 40-gallon drum of diesel, mixing in biro ink and prussic acid, then stirring the whole thing up by putting it into a rotating jig. There were two little tanks just by the jet pipes letting the stuff out into the exhaust, so we could do red, white and blue. Unfortunately on a rehearsal day, one of the pressure relief valves in the tanks stuck open, so it didn't discharge into the jetstream and burned. It discharged over half of Hampshire, all over Monday's washing. We got a whole series of letters from people complaining. One was from a Farnborough councillor saying 'Dear Sir, I'll have you know I had my baby out in the garden and he was covered in 48 spots of biro ink.' Being a foolish young sub lieutenant I drafted a reply for the boss saying, 'Try a recount, the navy's paying on 50 spots or more' and enclosed a bar of soap. He threatened to stop my leave!

"Bringing back a spare aircraft from Yeovilton, I was allowed to join up with the display team after their bomb burst, which was always the last thing we did. You shot down the runway trying not to go supersonic, which you weren't allowed to do. There was a dry-cleaners right at the far end of the runway, with a great big glass window, and every year it was cracked. Somebody dropped a supersonic bang – I'm not saying it was necessarily the Scimitars. It was great fun; we were so young and foolish, it was simply marvellous."

### Bob Edward

"My second Scimitar tour was second-line training in 736 Squadron at Lossiemouth. CO was Lt Cdr Pete Newman, senior pilot Lt Cdr John Kennett, AWI myself, QFI Pete de Souza, tactical instructor Paddy Anderson and simulator officer Maurice Hynett. I was there from 12 January to 20 December 1962. Our primary role was as Scimitar operational flying training, providing conversion for both pilots and maintainers.

"The normal student load was three courses of three trainees. These were from OFS (ab initio pilots) to COs-designate of the four front-line Scimitar squadrons. The training task continued until 24 July, at which stage the air station went on summer leave. Flying recommenced on 14 August with a reduced student load.

"For the 1962 Farnborough display, we were tasked to provide a four 'plane formation aerobatic team to act with a singleton. The whole was to be coordinated with a five 'plane aero team from a front-line Sea Vixen squadron from Yeovilton. The leader was Pete Newman, No.2 (port wingman) Paddy Anderson, No.3 (starboard wingman) John Kennett, No.4 (box) me and the singleton Pete de Souza. Initial practice commenced on 1 June 1962 with the display scheduled for 3 September. Three months of training was deemed to be sufficient time.

"In addition to practising formation aeros, teaching students air warfare tactics and weapon delivery, two major inter-service firepower demonstrations were carried out. 'Saucy Sue' was an international demonstration in the English Channel, and 'Noisy Nora' was a UK demonstration including foreign military attaches on Salisbury Plain. These involved coordinated attacks on splash targets and smoke floats in the channel, and mock-up military targets on the Larkhill range.

"In June I flew 25 formation aerobatic sorties, chiefly in the evening after student day flying was completed and before night flying. Night flying at Lossie in the summer was commonly called NEWDs – night exercises without darkness! In July I flew 21 sorties and 18 in August. This included a press display, and a display at Abbotsinch (now Glasgow airport).

"On 20 August we moved to Yeovilton for full-time working up with the Sea Vixens. On the 30th we moved to Farnborough where we lived in the ETPS mess, and were made most welcome and comfortable. On 1 September we had a final rehearsal before the seven-day SBAC show. On the final day, after being interviewed by BBC Television, Pete Newman ended their programme by marching down the runway into the sunset playing the bagpipes.

"The RN display started in mid-afternoon with a combined loop of five Sea Vixens along with four Scimitars forming a box nine. When we were at the top of the loop the singleton roared in at .97 Mach, and took a photograph of the VIP enclosure. This was then developed by the RN photo team, and about half an hour after we landed, copies were given to the startled VIPs – with their heads back, mouths open, watching the loop. On pull out from the loop there was a coordinated display of rolls, twinkle rolls, tight turns and a slow pass hook down before the Scimitars landed – the Vixens went back to Yeovilton.

"Our routine was very relaxed. In the morning admin, then a visit to the trade caravans. Lunch was kindly given by various firms and was quite super, but one did have to limit the alcohol intake. Then over to the hangars at the north of the runway, brief, start up and go. On completion of the display we returned to the firms' caravans to start the serious business of drinking – Horse's Necks made with Courvoisier brandy.

"We used motor scooters for 'runs ashore' as well as about the base. We had all had to obtain motorcycle licences, for which a certain amount of training was required. The RN provided the training on large dispatch riders' bikes at Lossie, and our tests were passed (no failures) in Elgin.

"The following weekend 736 did a five-aircraft display for Battle of Britain shows at RAF Acklington, and RAF Leuchars. That was the end of the 736 Squadron 1962 formation displays; a lot of work and a lot of fun."

## A spectator

*As a teenager the author attended these Farnborough shows – the Scimitar teams are among my abiding memories. The 807 Squadron team's finale in 1959 had a pair and singleton landing from opposite ends of the runway – folding wings as the singleton passed between the pair. After lunch in my father's company chalet, the pilots kindly signed their menu for me – a prized possession.*

## CHAPTER EIGHT

# DE HAVILLAND SEA VIXEN

*Sea Vixen FAW.1 XN707 R-242 890 Squadron Ark Royal 1963-64. (Mark Thomson)*

*The Sea Vixen grew out of de Havilland's DH.110. That and the Gloster Javelin vied for an RAF order for an all-weather fighter – the Javelin won. De Havilland navalised the aircraft as the Sea Vixen with which to replace the Sea Venom. The FAW.1 entered service in November 1958 and the FAW.2 in 1964. The last squadron, 899, disbanded when Eagle was retired in 1972. However a small number of Sea Vixens continued to fly with the FRU and FRADU at Yeovilton until January 1974.*

*Squadrons: 766, 890, 892, 893, 899, embarked on Ark Royal, Centaur, Eagle, Hermes, Victorious. FRADU, RN Test Squadron ('C' Squadron A&AEE).*

## Anon pilot

"The Sea Vixen cockpit was an ergonomic nightmare. There were various warning 'dolls eyes' and lights, scattered seemingly at random, and the modification state was always changing. The nosewheel steering was on the centre console between the pilot and observer, so the observer could use it despite the fact he couldn't see forward. Although he could put his arm through the hole between the two cockpits, and reach up on the pilot's right console, he couldn't quite reach or see the last panel for'ard, which was the radio. There was a repeat read-out just below the pilot's coaming but that didn't help a lot. So radio frequency changes entailed taking your right hand off the stick to fly with your left, reach forward, look down and change

*The Sea Vixen cockpit. (Kim Sharman)*

the frequency digit by digit with four rotary switches, with the observer unable to help. On one of my final OCU sorties the leader had radio failure. I ended up as the lead of a three ship of instructors. We went up through cloud topping out at 25,000 feet – with an aircraft on each wing I took my right hand off the stick to change radio frequencies whilst flying with my left.

"My instructor was a sub lieutenant observer, deemed to be very experienced because he'd survived a tour at sea. On one occasion I became extremely disorientated in pitch during a night GCA. My observer shouted, 'Power, power, push the sick forward, push harder!' He undoubtedly saved the aircraft, and probably us, since we were at 600 feet in cloud. Another time, on a still day, I was fourth in a four-aircraft formation coming round left-hand finals when I hit slipstream. We rolled right over 90 degrees and nose down, requiring full left rudder to recover – with me shouting, 'I've got it, I've got it' to my observer before we overshot to shakily go round again. Had I used the slightest bit of aileron I doubt we would have survived.

"The wing produced so much lift that its stall speed was way below its land-on speed; the latter was partly dictated by how much you could see over the nose. Later Mk.1s had a bubble canopy. You could raise your seat that little bit higher to see over an increased nose attitude, allowing about a five-knot decrease in speed. The amount of lift made landing on a runway slightly problematic. Since you couldn't apply the brakes above 90 knots (they would fade by the time you reached the end) you had initially – very gradually – to use aerodynamic braking. Watching first solos was fun. Having pulled the stick back slightly too much, new pilots would often get airborne again after touchdown. They wallowed down the runway at about 20 feet trying to get down – and often went round. Landing technique got better until you knew you'd cracked it when the tailbooms touched the runway – there were pieces of sacrificial metal on the bottom of them (spectacular at night – lots of sparks).

"On the OCU, I flew Mk.1s and Mk.2s – the Mk.2s first because the modification state was more up to date. There were 16 booster pumps, ten main and six standby, all electrical – just imagine the sheer weight of metal. A clean Mk.1 was probably as good as a Phantom to 10,000 feet, but then it fell out of the sky – the Phantom just kept on going. We had a simulator of sorts but it was only good for trying to understand the vagaries of the fuel system. The first time you flew the 'plane was the real deal, with the observer in the right-hand seat only able to see half the picture.

"I arrived in Singapore to join *Hermes*. There was a delay in getting an onward visa (*Hermes* was in Hong Kong) so I stayed in Singapore for three weeks. I asked the Naval Aircraft Support Unit (NASU) at Changi if there was anything I could fly, and I spent a week flying up and down Malaya in their Hunter T.8B.

"I joined the ship and made my first deck landings just off the Cocos Islands (North Keeling Isles) with an observer from my Dartmouth Entry. Shortly afterwards, the ship called into Fremantle and the junior aircrew – including me – were flown back to the UK while the ship made a direct fast passage back. In November '67 we re-embarked en route the Indian Ocean. We were then told the squadron was to be reduced to six aircraft, and become 'Simon's Sircus' aerobatic team. Since I was one of the new boys, with comparatively few hours on type, I was given the choice of returning to the UK to join another squadron, or transfer to 899 on *Eagle*, also in the Indian Ocean. I and two observers chose the latter, arriving on my second squadron on my 21st birthday with a ferocious hangover, having been rather too royally entertained by the senior rates mess who'd got wind of the occasion. I was awoken next morning by one of them at some ungodly hour with a steaming cup of coffee and with hindsight I thought, a rather malicious grin on his face as he said, 'Good morning Sir, your chopper leaves in 15 minutes.' I made it, just.

"We proceeded eastwards and two weeks later I had my first on board 'incident'. It was a hot, windless day and we were to fly an aircraft with a history of single generator failures. Maintenance assured us that the problem had finally been fixed. We launched but had only gone a few feet down the catapult when the generator tripped offline. My observer just had time to radio, 'Single generator fai....', when the other one also tripped. Now the problem of having ten electrical booster pumps kicked in. It was drummed into us that the main battery would go flat if the electrical load wasn't shed immediately. You would be left with no means of getting rid of fuel, be above max land-on weight and unable to land. You switched from the main to the standby battery via a rotary switch on the right-hand side on the panel between the two cockpits, which the observer could neither see nor access. Almost as we left the deck I switched hands on the control column, using my right hand to select the emergency battery and deselect eight of the ten booster pumps, then got the gear up. The main radio only worked on the main battery so I selected the standby radio, which took about 30 seconds to crackle into life. The first thing we heard was FlyCo saying, 'Pull up!' (in a slightly agitated tone). Over a glassy sea, if you were at all low, you could leave a 'wake' on the surface. Apparently the people in FlyCo were having kittens as we seemed to be flying using not much more than ground effect. We were given a 'steer' for Gan, 150 miles away, the nearest airfield. Aiming for a small island with a failing battery did not appeal, so we elected to land back on board. The maximum time for this sort of event with a fully charged battery was 20 minutes. After jettisoning the drop tanks and dumping fuel we landed back on board with one minute to spare.

"The engine performance was such that if for example, you were on CAP flying for endurance, it was more fuel efficient to fly with one engine shut down and this we did fairly often. Halfway through the sortie we would light up the engine, and shut down the other, keeping engine hours even. The day came when the engine would not relight, and since there was no diversion airfield, a single-engine land on was the only option. This was going to be a novelty to say the least.

"I flew a practice circuit at height to remind myself of the lack of power available before flying the approach. What started off as a good stabilised approach led to me getting low on the glidepath, and slightly slow at about ¼ of a mile. I sat there with full power just hoping the aircraft would respond. It finally did as we came over the back end of the ship sending the aircraft high on the glidepath. A very large cut of power started it descending again – too late, I thought, to catch a wire. I was already applying power in anticipation of the bolter, when we caught the last wire – an airborne 4 wire – which plucked us out of the sky and slammed us down onto the deck. The standard operation procedure for a single-engine landing required going to full power as soon as you hit the deck, otherwise the aircraft would not have enough speed to remain airborne if you missed. Since the good engine was the right one, full power effectively slewed the aircraft to the left. We stopped with the left mainwheel about a foot from the deck edge – a bit more excitement than I'd bargained for. But for the observer, who could not see out, it must have been a nightmare, as all he could hear was the LSO calling 'Power, power' (there was no more), and 'You are low on the glidepath'. Observers were either nerveless, or had nerves of steel. Incidents fall into two categories, those in which you have some sort of control over the outcome and those where you don't; this was definitely one of the latter.

"Late one morning the aircraft were ranged for the next launch, Buccaneers on the port side aft in Fly 4 and Vixens on the starboard side aft of the island in Fly 3. Both types facing inboard, 'echelon starboard' for the former, and 'echelon port' for the latter, all with wings folded, their back ends overhanging sea – and most armed with 2-inch rocket pods. We manned our aircraft, about fifth down the line, and began our start-up routine. I saw sheets of flame coming from one of the engines of the aircraft to the right of us which had a 'wet start', nothing really unusual in that – but the next thing was. An aircraft first or second up the line started an engine which caused the drop tanks to pressurise. Unfortunately the filler cap of one tank had not been secured and it blew off. There was always a wind over the deck and a fountain of fuel about 30 feet high cascaded onto the aircraft downwind. I immediately closed the canopy, but not before I had been soaked in fuel. My observer could not see all this but remarked on the very strong smell of petrol! We sat there waiting for something to 'blow', fortunately it didn't. I'm not sure what we would have done, but in extremis would probably have had to eject – not good with a seat where 90 knots were needed to ensure the parachute opened before you hit the deck, or probably in this case, the sea. The launch was cancelled. While we didn't exactly laugh it off, we didn't take it too seriously, the whole thing was just 'one of those things that happen at sea'. However, we had to scrap our flying suits and life jackets as they were soaked in fuel."

### David Allan – pilot

"It was decided to fit an underwater ejection system to the Sea Vixen. Prior to that, if an aircraft went over the side and the speed was less than 90 knots, the chances of the automatic ejection system working before the crew entered the water were slim. If the seat was fired underwater the water pressure on the body would probably be fatal – besides which the canopy would probably still be in place. If an underwater ejection was to be survivable, the rate that the seat accelerated had to be considerably reduced from that sustained during a normal ejection. The system had automatically to force the crew to the surface – the pneumatic system would be used to power occupant and seat out of the aircraft. The aircrew had to remember to release the canopy first to clear the ejection rail, then instigate the underwater ejection system by a separate lever – not the normal ejection handles. Both pilot and observer had separate firing handles for their respective seats and the observer's lever has three positions. The aft position is OFF/SAFE, the mid position is ARM (pneumatics to both seats), and the front position is FIRE. The mid position is selected for take-offs and landings. When safely on board it is selected to OFF.

"The Sea Vixen involved in the following incident is number three to land on. The first has taxied right up to the bow, and maintainers are rushing to attach chains to the landing gear. Number two has landed 40 seconds behind rapidly clearing the landing area. God forbid you fail immediately to follow the orders, and directions, of those with the yellow shirts; they are the experts. Deck space is always at a premium.

"Our Sea Vixen hits the deck and the throttles are idled. The pilot feels the aircraft being pulled back slightly by the wire. He applies the brakes, adds some power, selects hook and flaps up, folds the wings and looks to his right. The 'Y' director (marshaller) is encouraging a rapid departure from the landing area – a Buccaneer is not far behind. Power is up, brakes released, follow directions.

"We enter Fly 1 at a speed slightly faster than normal. The 'Y' director hands over taxiing responsibility to the next yellow shirt, who looks up the deck to see the second aircraft has not reached its parking spot, and indicates that we are to stop. The brakes are applied immediately, the aircraft gives a little bow and then – Oops! The observer, Norman Browne, had the firing lever out of the ARM position ready to move it aft to off when the pilot applied the brakes. This rapid stop threw his arm forward which fired his underwater ejection sequence. The seat started to travel up the rail, and the observer's straps and leg restraints were released. Bladders inflated behind his back and under his seat, as did his life jacket. He got squeezed hard against the radar scope. The aircraft continued to its parking spot, engines

*A Sea Vixen observer's narrow escape.*

are shut down and the pilot and maintainers see there's a problem.

"As the frangible hatch, above the observer's seat, has remained in the locked closed position it had stopped the seat from going any further up the ejection rail, however it had partially broken through. Some frangible material was lodged under the wire that initiated the normal ejection sequence via the seat's top handle. The observer pulls out his survival knife and commences to stab his life jacket and bladders to deflate them (later saying it 'wouldn't cut butter')! This gave him a little more space – while the engineers and armourers pondered how to make the seat safe. The Sea Vixen pneumatics were not renowned for maintaining pressure, and as it slowly drops, so does the seat. However all parts of the frangible hatch stay in the same position, including under the wire. This starts to pull the initiating cartridge wire in the same way as the top handle does.

"The observer becomes aware, trying to mould himself as far away from the seat as possible. As everybody stands back the seat fires, shatters the hatch, and continues with the observer riding it for a few seconds. It vanishes over the side, while the observer does a couple of somersaults and lands on the deck – unhurt! The only casualty was one of the engineers, who fainted. He thought the observer's helmet, which came loose during the induced aerobatic display and rolled down the deck, had his head in it.

"No. 893 Squadron were selected to help the RAF defend Cyprus. On 18 April 1968 we leapt into our Sea Vixen at Yeovilton, departing along with another ten, for 11 days of sun and fun in the Med. The RAF had laid on Victor tankers, the first over the English Channel to top us up with enough fuel to make it to the next, north of Malta, and from there direct to Akrotiri. Five hours flight time, piece of cake, now relax and let the RAF enjoy all the flying they want. We'll hit the beaches, followed by the odd run ashore.

"However, after a quick familiarisation flight around the island and a long sleep-inducing brief we (along with Lightnings), were allocated a continual alert status. This required two crews to be strapped in our aircraft at all times. We spent several uncomfortable hours attached to the ejection seat, never sure if our legs would work when required. At night we dozed off, and woke with a start wondering why we weren't lying on the grass outside the 'Lamb and Lark' in Limington. During the day, we figured that April weather in England was better than melting in this non-air-conditioned aeroplane.

"Then: 'Launch the fighters, traffic inbound…' Starting the engines took a bit longer than the Lightnings but once we got going air conditioning was available. We launched to 'intercept' the inbound – Buccaneers, Canberras, the odd V-bomber, etc. Having been airborne for about 20 minutes control would ask for our endurance, we would say one hour plus – the Lightnings 15 minutes! Not fair, having carried out his flight for the day, the Lightning pilot would be in the bar well before us. Over the next ten days I launched ten times for exercise traffic including two at night. I also attended a mini-squadron run ashore.

"On 29 April we planned to return to Yeovilton. Victor tankers would be available west of Cyprus, and north of Malta. We would then fly west of Italy on a northerly track, French airspace to the English Channel, then Yeovilton. Whilst in Cyprus, some of the V-force had arrived for a stop-over, and we noticed their crews always exited the 'nutty' shop with arms full of goodies (chocolate, biscuits, orange juice, fruit, etc.). As we were on a long-haul flight, could we obtain the same amount of in-flight rations? Having discarded all RN insignia, my observer, the great 'Bones', convinced the 'nutty' keeper that he was a poor flight engineer on a V-bomber heading to Gan. He needed the maximum 'nutty' allowance to keep the pilots, who were a bunch of tossers, occupied throughout the trip, and not bothering him too much.

"Our brief was simple, the aircraft would depart in pairs and we were the last pair to leave (I was a wingman). Bones had loaded the coal hole with 'nutty' for the flight, and I had the odd bottle of Kokinelli stashed away – what could go wrong? After take-off I locked onto my leader's wing until about 1,500 feet, then eased out to a couple of wingspans for the transit. All went well until 8,000 feet in the climb, when the leader said his pressurisation system wasn't working and he was returning to Akrotiri.

"Akrotiri vectored us towards the first Victor and we filled to the gunwales. I took a heading of roughly west asking Bones for a more accurate heading – silence. I eased my straps to look into the coal hole, and my view was blocked by a large NAAFI cardboard box. I heard a gurgling sound and a voice saying, 'the orange juice is really nice, want to try some?' 'Okay, but have you got the nav plan for this leg to the north of Malta?' 'Not really, I thought we'd follow our leader – didn't you copy it?' I replied, 'I'm flying this aircraft, you're supposed to navigate, have you got a map?' 'Not really, have you got one?' I reached down to the large pocket on my right lower leg and pulled out a map. 'Sorry Bones, all I have is an out-of-date "half mil" of Southern England. How about you?' 'Still looking.'

"Eventually he found one. 'Great where did you find it?' I asked. 'In the bottom of my nav bag'. 'What is it?' 'It's a Collin's Diary!' On a double page of the diary Bones drew a track from Cyprus to the north of Malta, and from there to a position near Toulon on the south coast of France, and thence direct to Yeovilton. The two pages covered from 100 miles out west into the Atlantic, to Jordan in the east!

Approaching Malta we had luckily written down the frequency for the Victor tanker and filled up again.

"We transited up the west coast of Italy trying to speak to somebody without success. Crossing the southern French coast we tried a few more frequencies, again without success. Shortly afterwards we entered cloud. With all the 'nutty' spread throughout the coal hole, Bones could not even see the radar scope to help with avoiding other traffic. Much later, guessing by dead reckoning that we may have left French airspace and entered UK airspace over the Channel, I called Southern Radar on a frequency we had found somewhere. I mumbled a rough position, in response to which the controller asked us to turn right for 30 seconds, and then left for another 30 seconds. Without asking he gave us a vector to Yeovilton. We were only about 20 miles out in Bones's calculations! We landed without divulging any of the problems we had en route, other than we were both suffering from drinking too much orange juice.

"We were non-diversion flying off *Hermes* in the Indian Ocean, off the east African coast, and were about 45 minutes into practice low-level intercepts under Gannet control, when we were advised to 'maximum conserve'. This didn't faze us at the time as we were flying with the idea of conserving as much fuel as possible, within the constraints of the exercise. However the lead decided to stop the exercise, and we transited back overhead the ship. Again we were told to 'conserve' – not normal advice – and for about 20 minutes we couldn't figure out what the problem was. Deck operations looked normal from our bird's-eye view, so we descended into the low 'wait', with two Buccaneers in the 'wait' above us.

"Then a little earlier than normal (we thought) *Hermes* started to turn into wind, and FlyCo advised us to standby for an amended 'charlie' time. A Buccaneer launched, and FlyCo said, 'The Buccaneer tanker will refuel the aircraft in the wait. At this time the aft lift is stuck down.' That is when we took notice, because the aft lift is in the centre of the landing area.

"The two Buccaneers, followed by us, refuel from the tanker. The tanker now joins the other Buccaneers in the high wait. Whilst *Hermes* turns out of wind questions are asked about our fuel states. I suspect we all subtracted a couple of hundred pounds from the actual figure. Thankfully, the Gannet (which did not have airborne refuelling capability) had at least another two hours endurance. We had conversations about the temperature of the water, sharks, the ejection sequence, and what height would we choose to eject…

"*Hermes* turned into wind again, launching another Buccaneer. 'That's the last tanker. No more aircraft will be launched' says FlyCo. This tanker refuels the initial two Buccaneers, then ourselves, and joins the three Buccaneers in the high wait. FlyCo says, 'The engineers are working hard to raise the lift manually'. We continue to peer into the black hole in the middle of the landing area. Will it be six aircraft abreast for a formation ejection? Will we individually eject close to one of the ship's boats, or will we plan to be picked up by the 'plane guard? We thought the formation ejection might be spectacular. Slowly we could see the gaping hole on *Hermes* reducing in size, and after about 15 minutes she turned into wind and invited us to come aboard. I was number two to land, taking interest in the leader's arrival in case he ended up in the hangar."

### Paul Bennett – pilot

"I was briefed for LLAI (low-level airborne interception), under the control of one of 'mother's' Gannets, somewhere in the Med about 100 miles from *Eagle*. The other Sea Vixens failed to launch, so I was by myself. This was not a serious problem with regard to the observer's training as the Gannet became the 'target' – its observers directing us towards themselves. The Gannet pilot had the most boring job, as they double-cycled across two launches and recoveries of the carrier. As they were first airborne, and last to recover, they spent close to four hours flying an almost straight and level endless racetrack pattern, allowing the observers to do their jobs detecting low-level targets threatening the carrier (often Buccaneers). When the Gannets were a target, they started quite dramatic manoeuvring to avoid us getting onto their tail – relieving their boredom. It was also beneficial for the Sea Vixen crew, as the slower Gannet could turn quite tightly, and getting on its tail was a challenge. The Gannet's smaller jet exhausts meant that getting the missile to 'acquire' it required you to be closer to them. Both crews were having fun – one lost the plot with regard to distance from the ship and 'charlie' time. Being the only Sea Vixen airborne it was my responsibility to make that time.

"When I eventually headed home I was running late and the only operating engine was put up to maximum power. The Vixen responded well – I was soon in excess of 500 knots. So fast in fact that the airflow into the non-running engine was too great to allow relight. I would have to slow down considerably to relight and allow me to increase to the Sea Vixen's max 610 knots – no time, so I continued on one engine. When I arrived I aimed ahead of the ship immediately to turn downwind into the circuit at 600 feet. There I was, engine at idle, full speed brake, trying to get the other engine started, getting flaps and landing gear down when at the limiting speed, flying a tight circuit, turning onto finals at the correct position and getting at the correct power, speed and attitude to approach from about two miles final. I did it and successfully hooked on at the first attempt. The deck crew directed me to a position near the bow, and having shut down, completed the checks, put in the seat safety pins, I clambered down onto the deck like a steaming wet jelly fish."

### Paul Chaplin – pilot

"I think most pilots have good memories of the Sea Vixen; it had a lot of character. The observer understandably may have had a different viewpoint. Obviously when you compare the two types, the Phantom was much more ergonomically designed

*Fg Off Dave McNamara and Paul Chaplin 899 Squadron Eagle, 1971. (Paul Chaplin)*

for pilot and observer, very practical and had a lot more ability; the Vixen was a little bit 'old school'. Putting the observer down in the coal hole was not as effective as having another pair of eyes up top.

"People complained about the hydraulic system, but it did the job. I didn't have any more failures with its hydraulics than I did with the Phantom. I was on the last Vixen squadron, and a lot of experience and much effort had been put into flight safety, training and maintenance. The utility and flight control systems each had a back-up – also the ram air turbine (RAT) could operate the flight control system. If the pilot 'stirred the stick' too much on finals, the pressure drop could trigger the flight control system low-pressure audio warning, because the pumps couldn't keep up. You could always tell this was occurring if a pilot happened to transmit his 'finals' radio call as the low-pressure warning was ringing in the background. He was not achieving anything by rapidly moving the stick around. It meant each flight control input was opposed by the next, and the aircraft remained rock steady.

"The teams we had maintaining the aircraft were absolutely brilliant – I had full confidence in them, and never had any worries. Nobody wanted to make that last cruise memorable for the wrong reasons. Mike Layard was the boss, followed by Dusty Milner. It was all very well run, a tight ship.

"I joined 899 Squadron in 1970, and stayed there until the end of '71. Apart from work-ups in the Mediterranean '71 was almost all in the Far East, with trips to Australia and New Zealand. When we were in the vicinity of Singapore or Australia, they took the opportunity to send their air forces to exercise with us. Alternatively we could be making our way across the Indian Ocean for maybe two weeks (passage-making with no time to go to flying stations). This was a good opportunity to get on with much needed maintenance, deck sports and even get the aircrew to clean their own aeroplanes. On average we probably flew about 15–20 hours a month, maybe 15 hours in three or four days."

### Bob Crane – observer

"The Sea Vixen airframe was very clean, and 'under-dragged'. Its two Rolls-Royce Avon 208 turbojets, which provided a total of 22,460 lbs static thrust, could push the Vixen beyond its maximum permitted indicated airspeed of 610 knots at sea level. They enabled it to climb fairly easily up to its service ceiling of 48,000 feet. Designated FAW the Vixen was actually a strike fighter possessing an excellent attack capability. It had three pylons under each wing, with the outboards dedicated to fuel tanks, each holding 1,000 lbs of fuel; a 'buddy' refuelling pod could

*Bob Crane.*

also be carried. Weapons carriage included combinations of up to four Firestreak or Red Top missiles (the latter with a head-on capability against supersonic targets), four pods of 24 x 2-inch rocket projectiles (RP) in each, 500-lb, 1,000-lb or 2,000-lb bombs, (including the 'nuke' variety) and a reconnaissance pod. The observer had one small window on the right-hand side of the fuselage. The only consolation of sitting in this 'radar environment' was that he could view the main instrument panel in the pilot's part of the cockpit.

"*Hermes* sailed her last months as a conventional carrier between September '69 and June '70, split into two one-month work-ups off Scotland and a five-month Mediterranean cruise. She was stretched to the limit when operating high-performance aircraft. She had two parallel catapults, the port longer than the starboard. On such a narrow deck, this allowed two aircraft to be hooked up simultaneously. The Vixen settled a little after launch from the starboard catapult. On a hot day with little natural wind we'd pray that we'd get the port cat for the extra end-speed. The cats were fitted with CALE (catapult alignment equipment) – the aircraft was taxied to a position with the nosewheel centred on the catapult track whilst the main gear on a system of rollers automatically aligned the aircraft for link-up. *Hermes* also had a deck-edge lift, a rarity on British carriers.

"There were two ready-rooms, one shared by the fixed-wing squadrons, the other for the helicopters. Normal flight ops comprised seven or so fixed wing, and two or three helicopters launched on each cycle by day – roughly half that by night. Although there were constituted crews all observers took their turn to experience the wonder of night launches and landings. The bit in between, for Vixen crews, could include high and low-level intercepts, bombing/RP attacks employing Lepus flares, and night formation and tanking.

"A Sea Vixen observer developed a 'sense and feel' as to what the aircraft was doing (I could always tell when the undercarriage was down – without seeing the pilot's 'doll's eyes' – from the slight 'boomp-boomp' as it locked into place). On final approach your job was, amongst other things, to monitor airspeed. The airflow at the rear of the ship is somewhat disturbed. For *Hermes* this resulted in the formation of a low-pressure area. As an aircraft passed through this 'low' the ASI reading would reduce momentarily but immediately recover – on most occasions. I've never fancied a ramp strike, so my eyes were always glued to the ASI. Once on final approach with an inexperienced pilot the ASI 'flicked' but didn't recover immediately – not to my satisfaction anyway. Given that I couldn't see forward, I had visions of us hitting the ship's stern. I shouted 'Power!' to the pilot, and simultaneously started to pull the lower ejection handle. For some reason I stopped, having pulled it up half an inch or so – before I knew it we had arrested. Following a call to FlyCo, the crash crew gingerly opened the hatch, encouraged a very scared observer to let go of the ejection handle and helped him out of his cockpit!

"HLAI (high-level airborne interception) was conducted at around 25,000 to 30,000 feet. Given that the Sea Vixen largely carried out stern intercepts because of the limitations of its air-to-air missile fit, the D (directing officer) would aim to set up a 180 by 8, i.e. with the fighter on a reciprocal heading to the target, displaced by eight miles. This equated to the diameter of the turning circle of the Sea Vixen with 45° AOB (angle of bank) at .85 Mach. The target would normally be at the same speed as the fighter.

"The AI 18 radar was pulse-only but had a PPI (plan position indicator) display, rather than a B scope, with a +/-90° scan. It could, with sector-scanning, detect a fighter-sized target at about 25 miles. The display consisted of two separate scopes – one for target elevation versus azimuth (C scope), the other range versus azimuth (PPI scope). A hand controller allowed the observer to vary radar-scanner elevation, moving the cursors over the display to lock on to the target.

"The D would call the position of the target, in terms of azimuth and range, relative to the fighter. Although the target would be operating in a known height band, its height was not normally given. Once the observer had detected the target, and was content to run the intercept, he transmitted 'Judy'. He then gave the pilot directions, e.g. 'port 30' to increase displacement if it was less than eight miles. The aim was to arrive at the final turn-in point on a reciprocal heading, with the target 40° azimuth and eight miles displaced. If all went well, the fighter would be positioned behind the target, co-speed at about one-and-a-half miles for a simulated missile launch. Generally, using the observer's directions, the pilot would ease or harden the final turn to maintain the correct amount of lead to roll out line astern. This was all practised day or night, VMC (visual meteorological conditions) or IMC

*Sea Vixen FAW.2 XN691 and XJ518 892 Squadron* Hermes, 1962.

(instrument meteorological conditions).

"The pilot would aim the missile using his PAS (pilot attack sight) ensuring that the missile seeker had acquired the target (indicated by a light in the cockpit). 'In range, clear to fire, splash one target!' With the radar locked to the target, the Red Top missile's seeker could be slaved, making it easier to achieve acquisition.

"Red Top also possessed a head-on capability against supersonic targets, detecting the heat generated by an aircraft due to its high speed. The tactic was relatively simple – the observer locked on to the target as early as possible (hopefully 20 miles minimum), and the pilot 'flew' the target marker in the PAS. This would apply the correct amount of lead for a missile firing in the front quarter of the target. Red Top wouldn't fire without acquisition. The pilot kept the firing trigger pressed and the missile launched as soon as its seeker 'saw' the target. This head-on option was rarely, if ever, practised because of a lack of supersonic targets. Theoretically RPs could also be fired at an airborne target, although in night/IMC conditions the fighter would have to be positioned dead line astern locked-on at a few hundred yards range, and the pilot would have to use his PAS very accurately for the correct aiming.

"Occasionally a jamming target would be available against which to practise interceptions. It denied range information to the fighter, normally masking itself with 'noise' which appeared on the fighter's radar as a 'spoke' at the target azimuth. The fighter would 'co-alt' (corresponding altitude) the target and then step down, say 5,000 feet and use spoke azimuth and angle-ranging (e.g. 5° target elevation and 5,000 feet below = ten miles target range) to run the intercept. The observer had to be a good mathematician!

"LLAI would be conducted with the target at 250 feet (day/VMC), 1,000 feet (night/VMC) or 2,000 feet (night/IMC), and target/fighter speeds of 350/400 knots. The D, or Gannet control, would aim to set up a 180 by five miles; because of the much lower height (and therefore thicker air) the Sea Vixen's turning circle was smaller. By day the intercept would be performed as for high level, although the target would not normally be detected by the observer until about ten miles range – due to 'sea clutter'. At night the 'scare' and 'wide-eyed' factors were off the clock, because LLAI was carried out well away from land and often in total blackness. Naturally, instrument flying was paramount, as was the observer devoting half his time to running the intercept, and the other half watching the altimeter and other instruments.

"Occasionally, besides Sea Vixens and the odd Buccaneer or Gannet, other target aircraft would make attack runs at the ship, especially during exercises. Once, off Malta, 23 Squadron Lightnings on detachment provided us with good practice. Sea Vixens flew low CAPs at 5,000 feet and 250 knots, with one engine shut down to conserve fuel. A Gannet was also searching for the Lightnings, running in as singletons at about 550 knots at 250 feet. As soon as one was detected, it raised the tempo inside the Sea Vixen cockpit. Well-rehearsed actions: re-start the other engine, speed up to 450 knots. A rapid descent to 250 feet to avoid being spotted by the target, and to reduce the effect of sea clutter on the pulse radar – set up and

*Sea Vixen FAW.1 XJ572 893 Squadron* Victorious *down low during a detachment to Nairobi in 1964.* (Mark Thomson)

control the intercept. Against such a fast target, it needs to be carefully run. Passing the '90' (degrees to go to target heading), push the speed up to 600 knots; one mile line astern, give him a Firestreak or Red Top. 'Splash one Lightning!' but, rather than break off to intercept the next one, stay in his 'six' until he passes over the ship. You can almost hear the cheers from the crew standing on the flight deck watching the show.

"Low-level 'navexes' in a Sea Vixen were a bit of a joke – the observer obviously couldn't map read very easily. Nevertheless, routes were planned so that major features could be seen from his window. He did his best, given his limited view, and normally the whole process relied on him reading from map to ground and confirming (or otherwise!) with the pilot on features he could see.

"For reconnaissance the Sea Vixen could carry a 'Phot' pod, which pointed to the left, equipped with day-only cameras. Recce runs were flown at low level for best picture quality. 'Aiming' the pod to get the correct image on film meant that the pilot 'flew' the target along the left canopy rail – quite sophisticated.

"Occasionally during exercises Sea Vixens were tasked to act as an anti-ship missile, guiding to a target. This enabled the ship to practise acquiring, locking on and firing its defensive weapons. A Sea Vixen would rendezvous with another, normally larger, aircraft such as a V-bomber at medium altitude. At a pre-determined point (between about 50 and 100 miles), it would 'launch' from the V-bomber, having detected the target ship on radar. It would then descend rapidly at high speed to simulate the flight profile of a missile – flying over the target at low altitude.

"Under-water ejection was, God willing, an action that you hoped you would never have to carry out. The compressed air used by the system was insufficient to force the seat through the observer's hatch – to be jettisoned first. Had an aircraft toppled over the side, or suffered a 'cold' cat shot, and sank before the crew got out with the canopy and hatch still closed, this (supposedly) is what the crew should have done:

1.   Sit calmly whilst the aircraft descends. At a given over-pressure, the observer's window implodes and water fills the cockpit (the canopy and hatch will not release until the pressure inside is equal to that outside. This point is reached when the water rises to the pilot's neck, the observer's head by now under some three feet of water)!

2.   Calm down, dear – by now you'll be on pressure breathing.

3.   Release the canopy and hatch; operate the under-water ejection system on each seat; inflate Mae West as soon as you are clear of the cockpit; release air through your mouth as you ascend to the surface.

4.   Once on the surface; deploy dinghy and await rescue (the ship will, hopefully, already have passed overhead).

"One Sea Vixen observer, who was a stickler for procedures, suffered such an incident. On his ascent to the surface he met the rescue diver descending through 100 feet! Whenever I was sitting in an aircraft on deck I kept my fingers through the 'D' of the hatch jettison handle – I was *not* going into the sea in an aircraft with the hatch on. Maybe I couldn't eject (the Sea Vixen didn't have zero-zero seats) but I could have escaped from the coal hole fairly quickly.

"Carrier flying provides an eternal action-packed spectacle, and the flight deck has often been described as 'the most dangerous place on earth'."

### Dave Eagles – pilot

"I went to 766 Squadron with the Sea Vixen, which I had been looking forward enormously to flying. Twin Rolls-Royce Avons, Firestreak missile-equipped for the air-to-air role, and a solid air-to-ground RP and bombing platform. The boss was Pete Reynolds who was 'Fred' in the 'Fred's Five' aerobatic team – I became his No.2. I served as the AWI in 766 Squadron for a year and then joined 892, and went back to *Victorious* in the Far East.

"The Vixen had a very spongy pitch control. It had a gear change coming down to landing speed, but the roll control was not crisp. By day you hardly noticed it but by night, when you were trying to line up with the centreline (which was moving sideways) you were continually making small corrections. Many people loved the Vixen – I always found I had to stay sharp.

"If there was no natural wind on approach at around 300 feet you had to fly through the ship's superstructure 'burble'. Whereas if there was a wind, the captain would head the ship in such a way that the net wind was straight down the angled deck. It was very disconcerting; by day you could see 'it' and handle 'it', but at night you never knew when 'it' was coming. In the latter stages you never quite knew how far away from the ship you were. It all speeded up quite quickly when you were close in; it was slightly hair-raising at night if the funnel gave a blob of soot in the middle of this lot."

### Tony Hayward – observer

"I had no problems with the Sea Vixen; its performance was an incredible advance over the Sea Venom – you felt slightly privileged that you were there. I started with 890 Squadron on the first commission of *Hermes*, then returning to her with 892 Squadron.

"I was asked to sit in on a pilot's first night deck landing, which was off Malta. His first pass was too high, the second pass was too low, and on the third approach I said, 'If you don't make it this time we'll have to divert to Malta.' He was absolutely perfect, plonked it into the wires, the hook bounced and he missed them all. We shot off the end and the boss said, 'Get refuelled, get back out here tomorrow morning first thing.' I was telling the pilot to turn this pump off, that pump on, open the cross-feed while radar was giving him a course to steer to Malta. I looked at my airspeed – 140 knots, I looked at the height – 200 feet. The power was 100 per cent and nothing was changing. We were about to enter a super-stall condition – I yelled, 'Speed Pete!' He got the nose down and we climbed away. That was my only exciting time in a Sea Vixen."

### Doug Macdonald – observer

"I joined 893 Squadron in *Centaur*, and we went off to do the Northern Express exercise in August 1962. I was crewed with Roy Richens, a youngster also on his first squadron. In those days, two new guys usually became a crew, but in the later '60s and early '70s crews became more balanced. It didn't bother me being down in the coal hole. I loved the job until I got a bit older. With small aircraft carriers and very powerful jet aeroplanes, two or three guys I trained with were killed in accidents in the 1960s. We had 15 Vixens to start with, then it was reduced to 13 and then 12, which became the standard.

"I did two years on 893, switching to *Victorious* in the Far East. She became the Far East carrier for about three years, based in Singapore. We got involved in the Indonesian Confrontation taking over from RAF Javelins at one stage when we were in Tengah. We did a couple of weeks' worth of sitting on the end of the runway – I think we were scrambled once, although we didn't intercept anything.

"I came back to the UK in 1964 and joined the first Mk. 2 squadron, 899. The weapons system was upgraded. The Red Top system was integrated into the radar

HMS Eagle *entering Mombasa harbour in 1966. (via Tony Smith)*

which was then called the AI 18R (R for Red Top). It didn't make an awful lot of difference to be honest. The weapons system was much more fun, it was much more variable; it did head-on attacks, beam attacks and of course stern attacks. I was involved in the Red Top trials against supersonic targets and we got a couple of intercepts on a Lightning out of Boscombe Down. We also did intercepts of Concordes from Filton. This was arranged because Concorde did a lot of its supersonic testing along the FIR (flight information region), north/south up the Irish Sea.

"*Eagle* was a newer ship than *Ark Royal*, she was better laid out. The briefing room facilities were much better, they were quite palatial. You could disappear into the back row and sleep undisturbed. We were back and forth between Aden, Singapore and Mombasa for about nine months – then back home to 'Blighty'. My next posting was on 766 at Yeovilton for 21 months. In the 1960s we were always short of aircrew, and consequently trained quite a lot of RAF pilots and navigators who did a tour at sea. In '66 or '67 one squadron had three or four RAF crews. They were all young and the more senior navy guys realised that this might not be so much fun; a lot of them left because they couldn't see any way forward.

"Mike Blackwood was my pilot when we went to the Paris air show in '67 with a Vixen Mk. 2, along with half a dozen ground crew. We left after ten days as we could not talk to the French air traffic controller. When we got back Yeovilton was in fog, so we had to divert to Boscombe and spend the night there. It was at this time that 766 were moving to Brawdy, so we were told to go there. They were digging up and strengthening the Yeovilton runways for the Phantoms; it was closed for about four months.

"I then went back to 893 on *Hermes* qualified as an electronic warfare instructor. We did the same old thing – the Far East – via Cape Town where we stopped for a few days, and then across the Indian Ocean. No wind; we didn't fly for at least three weeks. The captain of *Hermes* was Doug Parker, and the commander air was Rowan Thompson. Even though we were an extremely experienced squadron, they wouldn't let us fly,

"Our next flight was disembarking to Changi. We were east of Singapore all the time: Hong Kong twice, and Manilla Bay using the amazing air-to-air and air-to-sea American ranges. We went down to Sydney to work with the RAAF and RAN flying from Nowra, doing a lot of low flying. Lots of high explosive weapons were released; *Hermes* was trying to get rid of them all before going home."

## Terry McDonald – radio/radar technician
"I went to 766 Squadron in March '65 on a Sea Vixen radar course, and in July I joined 899 Squadron. In August we joined *Eagle* and did our tour around the Far East, returning to Yeovilton in August '66.

"The Sea Vixen was an easy aeroplane to work on, except that the hydraulically driven radar scanner was a problem. When you shut the system down it did a quick flip left, then right, banging down so that when you opened the nose cone it was out of the way. If it was left pointing forwards you couldn't get the nose cone open. It was of similar construction to a satellite dish, having a U-shaped channel across the back which was bolted to the hydraulics; the bang used to crack it. When it was swinging backwards and forwards trying to locate something, it would bang from side to side, but once it was locked on it wasn't so bad. When it picked up

*Sea Vixen about to leave the catapult on* Victorious. *The howdah can be seen under the Buccaneer's wing.* (Victorious FB)

a target the system would see if the target was tracking right or left, up or down, and the head rotated to follow it.

"The biggest problem was the observers who didn't know how to use the radar. They always forgot to switch something on or off. I was flight deck crew. When an aircraft on the catapult had something wrong with the radio or radar, I'd get called to it – pulled up on the cat! With two Avons thundering away you had to climb up on top of the aircraft to speak to the pilot, or observer, who had their hatches open, then try to sort out their problem. In the 'howdah' (a small glass-sided compartment raised up from the deck) was the stoker who pressed the button to fire the cat. The FDO stood waving his flags; dropping them down was the signal for the stoker to fire the catapult. I wondered what would happen if the stoker pressed the button while I was on top of the aeroplane. I really didn't like doing that.

"We went up on deck to do daily checks. As electricians and radio electricians we had four nominated aircraft, whereas the airframe and engine guys, as 'plane captains, had just one each. They dealt with whatever was needed on that aircraft. Usually just leading hands, they made one of the young A&E guys a 'plane captain. He was chuffed – that was prestigious for a young 'erk'. They were moving his aircraft on deck, three handlers forming the crew plus the tug driver. When they were parking it they were supposed to leave the tug attached until they'd chocked and chained it. They'd just chained the front, but didn't put the chocks in, and unhitched the tug – the 'plane captain was in the cockpit. The ship staggered, snapped the chains on the nosewheel, the aircraft rolled and ended up with the port wheel in the catwalk. It was teetering on the edge of the deck with the young lad in it; he thought he was going over the side. Fortunately they got the tug back on to hold it and the crane recovered it – the poor kid was as white as a sheet.

"'Jumbo' the aircraft crane was parked at the aft end of the island with its jib up, facing aft. Watching aircraft coming in to land, if they were on the correct flight path, they would be just above Jumbo's jib. If they were high, you'd think, 'He's going to have to go round again', but if he was too low, 'He'd better get up a bit otherwise he's going to hit the round-down'. Our CO, Lt Cdr Kirby, came in one day very high indeed, and we thought, 'Bloody hell he's not even going to try!' But he did, bouncing down on the deck, missing all the wires and did a bolter. They landed all the other aircraft and kept him up until last.

"When he landed his starboard wheel broke away, rolling all the way up the deck and through the parked aircraft. It missed everything, ending up in the very front of the starboard catwalk. The aircraft's wing went down on the deck and the oleo collapsed. We had a forklift truck with two men and a driver in fire-suits, and a platform on the forks ready to go in, spray foam and pull the crew out. They were a bit enthusiastic and punched the forks through the side of the aircraft – the observer had a fork prong either side of his head! The aircraft stood in the hangar for months until they sent some CPOs out from Fleetlands to repair it. We used it as a 'Christmas tree' in the meantime, robbing it for spares; we even sang Christmas carols around it."

### Richard Moody – pilot

"I converted onto the Sea Vixen and joined 899 Squadron in *Eagle*. That meant a lot to me as my father had been captain of the previous *Eagle* on the China Station leading up to World War 2.

"Landings on *Eagle*'s angled deck, and the thrill of the steam catapult launches off the bow, were very exhilarating. Launches involved the aircraft hurtling down the catapult track from a standing start, being slung into the air and hopefully achieving a flying speed of around 150 mph by the time the Vixen reached the end of the 150 feet track. Landing involved three variables – line up on the centreline, accurate airspeed (dependent on the aircraft's weight), and the correct glidepath to catch the ideal number three wire. Visual glidepath information was provided by the green meatball on the projector sight. A high approach and the meatball would ride high, a low approach and the meatball would go low, a very low approach would cause the meatball to turn red and if very, very, low the meatball would start flashing. A very, very, low approach would result in the aircraft hitting the round-down. During my two-year Vixen tour I achieved 188 deck landings of which 44 were at night.

"My observer was a South African with an eye for a gamble – we ran a book in the wardroom as to where *Eagle* would spend Christmas. Hot favourite was Singapore with Hong Kong a close second but we suckered the punters into placing bets at long odds on such as Perth, Australia, the Cocos Islands, Christmas Island, Penang and other unlikely venues. Needless to say it was Singapore but we still made a profit.

"One exciting deployment was to RAAF Pearce in Western Australia. Not only was the low flying in the outback quite sensational, but my cousins lived on the nearby Swan River and lent me a car for the duration. I was able to visit Aboriginal towns, and explore the Margaret River area where fine white wines are produced. *Eagle* also operated with the USN off the Philippines. We disembarked our aircraft to Cubi Point, while *Eagle* docked in Subic Bay. It was in the officers' mess at Cubi Point that I learned how to lose at Liar's Dice – a game I've never played since.

*Maximum concentration as an 890 Squadron Sea Vixen approaches* Ark Royal *in c.1963. (Kim Sharman)*

"After returning home and a short period of R & R, *Eagle* headed to Iceland, and then to the top of Norway to intercept Bison and Badger bombers coming down from northern Russia in displays of strength and intimidation. Many of our pilots hooked up with the Russians – always in a peaceful fashion, nothing unpleasant happened, there was no animosity among the opposing pilots. On one interception, my Vixen had a photographic pod fitted and I flew alongside a Badger at a distance of no more than 50 feet snapping pictures. One of our crews displayed a *Playboy* centrefold from his cockpit to the Russian bomber crew, much to their delight."

### Colin Morris – pilot

"*Eagle* August 1965–August 1966. This cruise was characterised by its continually changing plans. We had two carriers in the Far East, the other being *Ark Royal*. She was having a lot of problems with her catapults, condensers and engines, so we were having to do more than our fair share. The situation in Aden continued to bubble under, and towards the end of 1965 a major political storm broke in Rhodesia. Far East station tours were usually 12 months, with a pattern of approximately two weeks at sea and ten days ashore – it depended on the powers that be and the political situation. The 'hot potato' at the time was Africa's reaction to the possibility of Rhodesia's UDI (Unilateral Declaration of Independence).

*Colin Morris.*

"We were off Aden on 20 October – coming into there is spectacular. You've been through the Mediterranean, which can be lush and civilised, and two days later having gone through the Suez Canal there's what looks like the surface of the moon ahead of you – the most breathtaking sight. As usual, as soon as we got to Aden, the RAF Hunters came up and 'attacked' us as we defended the ship. We then did the traditional 'we've arrived' mass flypast. We had a fleeting visit followed by a fast passage to Singapore. *Ark Royal* was there, about to leave, when she had a fire in the engine room which put her back four weeks.

"Once I had to take a Sea Vixen ashore to Changi. Because of the ship's slow speed (we were tooling down the Singapore Straits at maybe five to ten knots) I needed the catapult to produce the whole shebang, so I was launched from the second, bigger catapult. On a normal launch the ship was going flat out at 28 knots, so you had that airspeed to start with. It was surprising how much extra punch that cat gave – a most exhilarating experience, and a good show for the little boats that came out to greet us. Changi had a very active officers' club which was fantastic fun. It was lovely doing your day's flying, then going to the officers' club still in uniform to enjoy a foaming pint of Anchor.

"The political unrest in various places, coupled with having to cover operations that might have been carried out by *Ark Royal*, meant we were flashing backwards and forwards across the Indian Ocean. On 11 November 1965, the prime minister of Rhodesia, Ian Smith, declared UDI. We had to get all our Sea Vixens armed up and ready to go to Ndola in Zambia to protect the Kariba Dam (strategically important for power supplies to Rhodesia and Zambia), and to show force. However the Labour government had just cancelled the construction of two new aircraft carriers, so were reluctant to be seen to need the FAA. They wanted instead to deploy the RAF Javelin squadron based at Akrotiri; it took them a fortnight to get all the necessary permissions. Meanwhile we were sitting in total secrecy off the coast, with all the aircraft armed up with missiles and rocket pods, our suitcases packed, ready to go the moment the British government gave the nod. We were tearing our hair out because they wouldn't use us. Eventually the Javelins arrived and we were stood down, leaving us feeling frustrated and pretty hacked off.

"That December we were in Khormaksar, Aden, again. We did a huge amount of night flying, which we weren't expecting. Someone once said there are two sorts of people – those who have night deck-landed and those who haven't. The former will never be able to explain matters to the latter. Flying from the ship is great fun in daylight, but there is not a person in this world who will tell you it's fun at night. When landing you're flying totally on instruments as the radar director guides you in: 'You're at five miles, you should be passing 1,500 feet…five degrees left…hold your heading…you should now be passing 1,200 feet' then at 300 feet he says, 'Look up for the sight, and land'. You look up and there is this tiny little projector sight with a meatball in the middle, and three or maybe four centreline lights on the deck of the carrier. The rest of the ship is in complete darkness. At night you have no depth perception, and no idea when it's all going to happen, then suddenly it's WHOOSH BANG – you hit the deck, hope you pick up a wire with your hook, and if you do, breathe a huge sigh of relief.

"The pilots were getting fed up with having to do two sorties a night. A night deck landing left you both physically and emotionally drained – there was no rest, it was off to the briefing room then back out to do it again. As I was more senior, some of the pilots asked me to complain. I was basically told to wind my neck in; we only had a limited period of time to get in a certain number of hours' night flying. Our location meant that, if needed, we could at least divert to Aden – so it was a case of 'get on with it'.

"It was during this time that I came the closest I have ever come to departing from an aeroplane. I'd got a little high on the approach, and started to pole forward, but the problem then is that your speed starts to rise, so you must come back on the throttle. If you're going to miss the wire, and do a 'bolter', you have to know pronto so that you have time to hit the power, and get airborne again. You wouldn't know yourself until it was too late, so you rely on the deck crew. As I was coming in for final approach, suddenly FlyCo shouts 'Bolter! Bolter!' and a red Very light is fired. I'd got myself into the worst possible situation, throttled right back, and missed the last wire. I pushed forward hard with the throttle, but the problem with a jet engine is you haven't got instantaneous power – it must 'spool up'. The lower the revs the longer it takes to accelerate. We touched the deck, then...nothing, we're in complete blackness, probably only 50 feet above the water, the engines still spooling up. In daylight you have a visible horizon, instant reassurance that you're climbing and not going suddenly to pitch into the sea. At night there is nothing but your instruments. Just as I was on the point of instructing my observer Bryn Moore, to eject, the power came up and we rapidly gained altitude. As calmly as I could I said, 'It's OK Bryn, not a problem, we'll just go around' all the while checking we had enough fuel to re-attempt a land on. 'Probably one more poke at that, we'll get it right next time.' Later, Bryn told me that was the only time he'd ever heard me sounding nervous. Whistling in the dark.

"Flaps are very valuable for carrier aircraft because you can carry a higher power setting on the approach, giving you a better response from the engine. The Sea Vixen's shortcoming was the limited full flap – you couldn't have high power settings on the approach. We did some trials on a modification which made it a little bit easier to land at night – the 'donkey drop' – a pigtail of lights dropped down the back of the ship and lined up with the centreline lights (if you got off the centreline you got an angle on the donkey drop). Another improvement was the introduction of a low red floodlight across the landing area. This meant that you'd got a little bit of depth perception when you came to that last few seconds. These changes made it a bit easier, but didn't take away the fear factor.

"Critical to night deck landing is the role of the ship-board radar director. He has little slots on his radar that he uses to bring you in and turn you onto final approach, making sure to get the spacing right to give you time to land and clear the deck. As part of his calculation he must be able to predict where the ship is going to be. One night I was the first back on, from the last launch of the night. It was inky black, but I could just make out the wake of the ship enough – it wasn't where I wanted it to be. With about a mile to go, I could see the wake snaking around as the ship went hard on its rudder to settle into the wind. It lined up just as I came over the round-down. Phew!

"We were involved in the blockade of oil shipments to Rhodesia through Beira. Our terms of engagement were to spot oil tankers coming out of Durban. We were not to attack any ships, just plot and report positions. A Gannet would go up at night and map all the shipping in that part of the ocean. We would then go up during the day, take the names of the ships, return to *Eagle* and wire their positions to the Foreign Office.

"During the Beira Patrol my looker Greg and I set a long-range record. We re-fuelled from a Scimitar tanker, enabling us to go 560 miles down to Durban and back, taking a photo of a tanker or two at the other end. Although it became a daily occurrence we were the pioneers, for which the captain bought us a bottle of champers.

"We found one tanker sitting around 300 miles south with a Royal Navy frigate latched on her tail, presumably awaiting instructions. Intelligence gave us a list of suspects, and we were signalled when they left harbour so we knew their approximate ETA in the area and their names. What we would do if one just forced on through nobody knew. On one occasion – our fifth early morning on the trot, Greg and I failed to get airborne for the first time in the operation – we had a restriction in aileron movement. Instead we flew the last one of the day. Only half of the squadron were flying at that time because of quite high winds, with the deck heaving up and down in the swell. This meant experienced guys only, so we were having to work even harder. This cruise also saw me involved in setting a record for time spent at sea in an aircraft carrier during peacetime – ten weeks.

"I had more or less made up my mind to leave the navy. The attrition rate for FAA pilots was too high for comfort. Roughly 20 per cent of Sea Vixen crews were killed, something few people were aware of, especially as it was peacetime. With the numerous political situations requiring our presence, we were working extremely hard with no shore leave, and I wasn't enjoying this tour much either. The Labour government was busy scrapping the FAA which meant that soon the airline market would be flooded with redundant pilots. Perhaps this was the opportunity for me to leave?"

**Henry Parker – engineering officer**
"I was on a 766 Squadron detachment with four Sea Vixens on *Eagle*, testing the newly fitted ADA radar system. I was often tasked with removing and fitting gear in the booms, as I was small and agile enough to get halfway through the hatch in the side. Joining at night in Weymouth Bay, with a darkened ship, up scrambling nets

from a boat was an experience.

"Via a rather rough Bay of Biscay we had a couple of weeks in the Med. Being a small detachment, we worked both in the hangar and on the flight deck. Toward the end of our time in the Med there was an announcement to say that our four Sea Vixens were going to come in at low level from port side to overfly the ship. They were so low that wing vortices were sweeping

*No. 899 Squadron Sea Vixen FAW.2s beat up HMS* Eagle. *(Kim Sharman)*

off the sea behind them. The CO leading, pulled up to get above flight-deck level and turned sideways to fly between the funnel and aerials (rumour said a tailplane change was required)."

### Tony Pinney – pilot

"You could fly non-stop in a Mk. 2 Vixen from Yeovilton to Malta, and then from Malta to Cyprus, but it was decided that the Victor tankers couldn't get airborne with enough fuel to refuel us. We had to take off from Yeovilton and fly north to Birmingham, pick up Victors and refuel because the French wouldn't allow us to do so after we'd crossed the FIR boundary, halfway across the Channel. We would arrive off Sardinia with enough fuel so that Victor tankers could get airborne from Luqa and refuel us again.

"Just as we had refuelled over Birmingham we were told that the Victors from Luqa were already airborne and we were asked to expedite our transit to the next refuelling area – we had to fly flat-out across France. We worked out how much fuel we would need to take from the tankers to get to Akrotiri, and they said we could take as much as we liked. We topped up to full and turned left across southern Italy. We knew there were Lightnings ready to intercept us approaching Akrotiri, and because we had plenty of fuel the best tactic in a Vixen is to run the Lightnings down to low level and run them out of fuel. On the run-in to break at Akrotiri, we let the Lightning pair lead us. The RAF wanted to court martial the flight lieutenant leader for unauthorised formation flying. I was flying as No.3 in a four-ship led by Bob McQueen the CO of 893. He made himself very unpopular with the RAF, when he went to see the group captain flying to tell him that if the court martial went ahead he would refuse to be a witness and we would return to the UK. There was no court martial.

"During the Beira Patrol, I was the first to find a tanker, the *Joanna V*, running north – which really p****d off the hierarchy of the Buccaneer squadron. It was

480 miles from the carrier; top up from a Scimitar tanker and fly out to 600 miles from the carrier to 100 miles off Durban. There were no diversions, we weren't allowed into South Africa, the edict was: 'if something went wrong with the aircraft just eject and we'll find you if you're lucky.' When we returned to Singapore Dennis Healey came on board. The captain cleared the lower deck of all officers who could be spared, into the wardroom, and told us that if there were any questions of Healey nobody was to ask one. After Healey had spent time waffling to us and asked if there were any questions, nobody said a word. He then asked why there weren't any questions, to which the captain replied, 'Secretary of State for Defence – how can you justify to my officers that they are no longer needed after what my ship has done for you?'"

### Richard Sheridan – pilot

"My appointer asked what I wanted to do. I said 'front-line flying', and he asked 'Vixens or Buccs?' I preferred Somerset to Lossie, so off I went to 766 Squadron. Pilot's Notes in one hand, and some poor unsuspecting observer from the staff – a few circuits and that was it. I didn't have any trouble with it. Of course, when you're a young man, you don't think about all the people who have been killed.

"After the course I went to 893 Squadron to be the QFI. I joined the squadron in Changi having been told to be there before Christmas, but when I arrived I was told I wasn't expected. So I did a lot more MADDLs, more drinking, and embarked in early January. My observer was a young midshipman. I said, 'this is your first deck landing isn't it?' 'Yes', he said, very quietly. I said it was my first one in six years, and he went even quieter. But we managed to get on board and hook a wire. They'd had one or two incidents with new boys, so they delegated night flying to those who'd been to sea before. Therefore I spent most of the time night flying, which was fine because you got used to it.

"The approach speed for a Vixen was about 125/126 knots depending on your weight. This wasn't a problem on *Victorious*. However 893 Squadron spent a few weeks on *Hermes* afterwards, and that was quite small – you didn't have to be far off the centreline to hit something. When I was on 766 Squadron we went out into the Irish Sea to do some 'touch-and-goes'. I showed my observer the ship from 5,000 feet and he said '****!' You had to rotate as you came off the end of the deck after launch. One night I slightly delayed doing so, and got ticked off by 'wings' who said he lost sight of me for a while. I didn't realise I'd come that close to the water.

"We flew our Sea Vixens out to Akrotiri for an exercise. We had to refuel air-to-air, picking up a tanker north of Malta (my observer thought he had the tanker on radar, and called for it to turn onto east, but it didn't – it turned out to be a Scandinavian Airlines 707!) Meanwhile the tanker had turned and was about 100 miles ahead of us so we had to chase it, catching it up with only 2,000 lbs of fuel remaining. Luckily we managed to plug in quickly."

*Sea Vixen FAW.2 XS580 V-253 893 Squadron* Victorious, *1967.*

### Tony Smith – pilot

"As Yeovilton was having runway work done, 899 Squadron temporarily relocated to Boscombe Down in May 1967. As the runway at Boscombe is much wider than most, to facilitate similar conditions for night flying, the runway edge lights were positioned at the normal runway width. We were practising formation landings in pairs during the day. As the runway was so wide we took up whatever space was required to land both aircraft at the same time. When landing as a pair, and using the whole width of the runway, we touched down bringing our aircraft up into the aerodynamic braking position. If number two was a little too far across from the centre his tail bumpers would come down onto the runway, smashing the runway lights. Boscombe was not pleased. We destroyed quite a few, and were ordered to go back to landing one at a time.

"On 11 July 1967 I flew from Yeovilton, with Ian Argyle as observer. Following our leader Mike Layard we headed for the Aberporth range in Cardigan Bay to test fire the Red Top missile – we were the first operational crews to do this. The target was a Jindivik target drone towing a UV flare, controlled by crew on the ground at RAE Llanbedr. Mike had a go, and we were then directed onto the target until Ian picked it up on radar. The procedure then was for me to arm the Red Top – a small yellow light duly appeared to confirm this. Next was to activate the firing button so that, as soon as the missile acquired the target, it would automatically fire. Ian got us into the correct position and suddenly, without any further warning, the missile fired and left the aircraft with a very spectacular woosh. This slightly panicked me – I had not sighted the target, and here it was streaming off into the 'luft', and me not at all sure where it was going. I was only able to pick it up as it hit the UV flare behind the Jindivik. What a relief! This at least proved you didn't have to see the target for it to be a successful strike, all you needed was a serviceable missile and a competent observer, which Ian was.

"John Lewis was one of a small number of RAF aircrew seconded to the Royal Navy at that time. On 26 September 1967 we were flying off *Eagle* in the Indian Ocean, south of Gan, and John had to divert there with a problem. As he touched down he realised his brakes had failed and called over the R/T: 'Barrier, barrier'. This would normally have been the signal for ATC to activate a barrier at the end of the runway. Unfortunately, nothing happened, and John ran off the runway and ended up in the sea with the wings level with the waves. Luckily both he and his observer [Lt C A Chase] got out completely unharmed, if a bit damp. We had all been briefed that there was a barrier at Gan, but what they had was a spray arrestor gear located halfway down the runway. This had been installed for 74 Squadron Lightnings transiting out to Singapore. If we had known this, John would have been able to use his hook and the spray arrestor gear to stop. There were a few comments from the RAF about their runway not being long enough for naval pilots – until they realised it was an RAF pilot!"

*The Sea Vixen was XN691 which was shipped to RNAY Belfast for repair.*

"Prior to us pulling out of Aden in November 1967, *Eagle* was ordered to position off Aden with the rest of a substantial fleet in case of trouble. The brief for the fleet was not to be seen, or give the Yemenis any idea that we were there, so we carried out our training well to the south. The flying was considered to be non-diversion. On one occasion, whilst carrying out high-level interception practice, we suddenly got the message from 'mother' that we should divert to Salalah on the south coast of Oman. This was a major surprise to us as, if we had diverted we would have blown our cover. We were only about halfway there when we got another order to return to 'mother', and all the aircraft ahead of me landed on. I touched down and picked up the wire, feeling the whole aircraft give a distinct shudder as it came to a halt – it felt as though the ship was shaking itself to bits. Soon the shaking stopped and the ship went silent as her engines were shut down. Divers went down to investigate. A large steel fairing had become detached from a stanchion, holding one of the ship's screws in place, and wrapped itself around one of the blades causing considerable imbalance, and thus the shuddering. The loose fairing was removed, and we had no further problems.

"On 2 February 1968 we were again using Gan as our diversion. I was scheduled for night 'duskers'. Unfortunately, my aircraft went u/s before launch and I was re-scheduled for a later flight when it was properly dark. As there was nothing actually planned for us, Terry Fletcher and I were directed towards another Vixen which had an in-flight refuelling pod under the wing. We carried out a number of practice dry-run approaches to fly the probe gently into the basket. This exercise was not simple in a Vixen, as the refuelling probe was located about 12 feet from the centreline of the aircraft sticking out from the port wing. As you approached the basket, any minor adjustments involving use of the ailerons meant that the probe would bob up and down. You had to be very accurate with your approach especially at night.

"After a while we realised that we would need to take on fuel in earnest to complete the sortie. Could I then get the probe back in? No, it took several more attempts eventually to take on fuel. We broke away, returning to the ship to do a CCA for a final landing. As I approached I picked up the projection sight, and flew the rest of the landing visually. As I got close to the round-down I realised my speed was a bit high, so I eased back on the stick. However I was quite close in so my aircraft lifted that bit too much – I missed the number 4 wire and had to 'bolt'. I went back into the circuit to set up for another CCA. Unfortunately the exact same thing happened, and I bolted having missed the number 4 wire again. I was then instructed to divert to Gan.

"As we approached Gan we heard an RAF VC10 coming in from Singapore, watching as it landed ahead of us. We landed and taxied to where the ground crew were ready for us. Terry and I went to the transit lounge. As we set ourselves up with a good stiff drink, the VC10 passengers came in. Lo and behold in amongst them was my wife Vanessa and our good friend Jo Argyle, Ian's wife! They had been with us over Christmas in Singapore, and had been able to get an indulgence flight back to the UK. So Vanessa and I spent a few moments together before I went back with her to the steps of the VC10 to see her off.

"The next morning we flew back to *Eagle*. I got a call to see Bill Hawley, commander air. He asked me if I had seen my wife when I diverted to Gan. I nodded and he asked me if I had known beforehand that she was going to be there. I of course said 'No' which he knew as there was no way I could have known. He then told me to 'bugger off' in his usual manner. Later on I found out that Gan's CO had sent a signal to *Eagle* expressing his displeasure that one of our pilots had intentionally diverted to Gan to meet up with his wife. He made some half-witted excuse that they may have had to divert the VC10! But what this group captain did not know was that we had a more senior officer on board, RAdm Ashmore. Following Bill Hawley's questioning of me, a return signal was sent to Gan's CO from the admiral requesting his reasons in writing as to why he should insinuate that one of *Eagle*'s pilots would divert there on purpose.

"Apparently I was missing the number 4 wire by only a few inches, and Bill Hawley knew there was no way one could do this on purpose even if I had planned to divert to Gan. The reason I made a bit of a hash of my landings was two-fold. Firstly, by the time we came back to 'mother' I was getting tired, and secondly, I don't think I had the volume of the airstream direction detector turned up enough to advise me of the correct speed on my approach. This was a visual and audible system designed to show when you were at the right speed for that particular weight, and when airspeed was either low or high.

"We suffered an engine failure on 23 April 1968 over the Indian Ocean, south of Aden. My 'looker' Don Perman, and I were carrying out an anti-aircraft gun direction and firing exercise with the ship's guns. We were coming in at about 300 feet for their radar directors to pick us up when a large noise was felt rather than heard coming from behind the cockpit. It wasn't a bang, more a very large GER-RUMP! Immediately the starboard engine's RPM was going down, and the JPT (jet pipe temperature) was rocketing up. I shut down the engine, pulled back the stick and put maximum power onto the port engine to get some height.

"I called 'Pan' to the ship which immediately decided to recover us back on board. This caused a bit of chaos on the flight deck as they were in the process of moving aircraft around, not expecting any land ons for a while. The ship eventually turned into wind and FlyCo cleared us to join downwind. I made the call, 'Downwind, undercarriage going down in the Red'. This was to remind FlyCo that I had remembered to use the red hydraulic system to lower the undercarriage (the normal green system would have been u/s with a dud starboard engine). I kept the port engine's RPM up to about 92 per cent and carried out a normal low-level circuit approach to land on. After climbing out I looked up the starboard jet pipe, which even then was radiating a lot of heat. I could see thousands of little splatters of molten metal dotted all around the inside of it. A compressor blade had detached making a real mess inside the engine."

### Jim Speirs – aircraft handler

"I was drafted to *Hermes* as an aircraft handler but, because I had obtained a good qualification from Shawbury, I ended up in ops doing flying control and flight planning, which I enjoyed. However it was a 'softy's' job, and it would have been more exciting to work on the flight deck. When the squadrons disembarked to Changi I went too, acting as liaison in ops, doing flight planning and as translator for naval lingo into RAF-speak. A Vixen had an incident where it apparently bounced off the sea during night flying. The pilot, Lt John Eyton-Jones, reported that the aircraft had suffered an explosion on his port wing. I was in ops and thought that it may have been his drop tank exploding, but that was most unlikely. He got his undercarriage down, although he had no hydraulics so used the RAT for emergency hydraulic power, but had to land fast without flaps. He had no brakes so took the wire at the far end of the runway. Despite denials by 'E-J' and his observer, when the maintainers lowered the flaps, sea water emerged. The aircraft must have bounced like a stone skimming on the surface of the sea, so the crew were very lucky. 'E-J' was later killed while operating from *Invincible* during the Falklands. I was on board at that time and had served on three carriers with him."

*Lt Cdr John Eyton-Jones and Lt Alan Curtis were lost in May 1982 during the Falklands War when their 801 Squadron Sea Harriers apparently collided in mid-air during an operation in bad weather.*

## Mark Thomson – pilot

"In June 1963 I was in 766 Squadron. One week I was invited up to London and the opening night of a new nightclub – Annabel's. I arranged to stay the night in London and planned to return early the following morning in time for the weather briefing at Yeovilton. There was no greater sin than to be late for this, which was always the start of a busy flying day.

"Annabel's was the greatest London nightclub there had ever been. I'd had virtually no sleep, and had drunk too much wine. Oh dear! When I woke up the sun was up. I looked at the time and thought I could never get to Yeovilton (120 miles from London) for the weather briefing by 08:20. Motorways there were not, but there was much less traffic.

"I drove the race of my life in my E-type Jaguar, covering 120 miles in 120 minutes. I just got to Yeovilton with minutes to spare, into the briefing room and nonchalantly flopped down into an armchair in the front reserved for instructors. They all thought I'd spent the night in the wardroom. After the weather man, the senior pilot gave us the flying programme for the day. I remember looking at my feet and feeling worse than death, and thinking 'please God, don't make me fly until at least this afternoon'. The senior pilot said the first sortie would be a four-ship, led by me, with three student pilots and observers. This would be two pairs practising interceptions, and air-to-air combat at 40,000 feet, for an hour-and-a-half. I thought perhaps I was being deliberately punished. I did the pre-flight briefing with the seven aircrew, and we climbed to 40,000 feet on a nice sunny day.

"We started our interceptions, which is hard work with four aircraft, and about halfway through the sortie I fell asleep. When I woke up I immediately looked for my wingman – there he was on my port wingtip. We were just over the vertical, heading downhill very, very fast. We were almost supersonic, and I could see the north coast of Devon directly beneath us – it was a terrific fright! We climbed back to 40,000 feet, and got it all going again.

"We landed back for the usual post-flight debrief (just as important as the pre-flight briefing). I went through the sortie 'post mortem' with coloured chalk on a blackboard, and then asked for questions. A hand went up from one of the student pilots. He said, 'Sir, about halfway through, I think you did a manoeuvre which wasn't covered in the pre-flight briefing. What was that manoeuvre?' I told him it was a standard manoeuvre if you have a MiG 19 on your tail. 'Any more questions?' Another student put up his hand and said, 'Excuse me sir, when can we do that manoeuvre again?' I replied: 'When you get to this manoeuvre in Week 16 in the flying syllabus, which is in about four months' time, and it will be very clear to you.' Nobody ever knew and I couldn't tell them.

"Being an instructor on Sea Vixens had its perks. Every year the army (who we always called 'Pongos'), ran a firepower demonstration on Salisbury Plain for NATO dignitaries. The idea was to invite the defence attachés of all our NATO partners to see what the UK armed forces could do against ground targets.

"On top of the only hill on Salisbury Plain was a large white marquee, in front of which was a row of all the NATO flags fluttering in the breeze and, in front of that, rows of chairs where the dignitaries would watch a wide range of ordinance against varied targets. Below this small hill there was a long plain of military land as far as the eye could see on which some Russian tanks, buildings and bridges were laid out as targets.

"I was tasked with leading a flight of four Sea Vixens, all flown by instructors, and we were suitably armed for ground-attack targets. As there is a lot of rivalry with the RAF, we had practised our weaponry for a few weeks. In the pre-flight briefing I had briefed how we would do a fly-by, if requested by the 'Pongos'. As the dignitaries were on top of this hill, I thought it would be more interesting if we flew towards them in formation at a modest speed but so low that they were looking down on us as we approached them. As we got to the marquee, we would go to full power and rotate into a very steep climb over the marquee. We dropped our rockets and bombs satisfactorily on the targets. We were just setting course back to Yeovilton when: 'Tango One, can you navy boys do a fly-by for the colonel?' came over the radio from a senior 'Pongo'. So, we did the fly-by as briefed.

"We landed back at Yeovilton. The senior pilot of 766 Squadron was Chris Comins; he and I had been together in 893 Sea Vixen Squadron on *Victorious*. I could see Chris standing on the grass as we taxied in towards dispersal and folded the wings. When you've been flying together you've just got to look at your friend's face – it says everything, you know what he's going to say. Chris had a funny sort of look on his face and, as we wandered over to the crew room, he asked me to come into his office and shut the door.

"He asked me whether we had done a fly-by, so I told him we'd briefed for it, and it was fine and safe, and they'd asked for a fly-by, so what was wrong? Chris said, 'I've had some Pongo colonel on the 'phone and I had to hold it three feet from my ear because the guy was yelling at me for about five minutes'. I asked what his problem was. 'Well 'Boysie', they didn't mind you doing a fly-by, but why did you have to blow the marquee down when the general was inside, on the bog and having a crap?'"

## Adrian Tuite – observer

"A bright spring morning in the Atlantic, somewhere south of Faro, Portugal. The ship was homebound after a year in the Far East. The squadrons were disembarking, spirits were running high. The previous evening's celebrations were noisy and late, and some crews would not pass even the most perfunctory sobriety check. Two Sea Vixens were ranged for launch to fly back to Yeovilton as a pair. Engines were running and all was ready, when our leader declared an engine snag. He was removed from the cat, instructing his No.2 to proceed independently.

"No.2 launched, headed west and climbed to height. At the top of climb (TOC) the observer (O) called the pilot (P) to turn north, which he did. After some min-

utes P asked O to confirm their position and was reward-
ed with – 'West of Portugal'. Sometime later, after several
such requests, and as many vague replies, P asked O to
show him the chart extending his right hand down into
the coal hole. O prevaricated. P insisted, and was told to
wait until it (the chart) was updated. After a short time O's
left hand appeared by P's knee waving what appeared to
be a flattened Benson and Hedges cigarette packet. On the
back, in ballpoint, was a sketch map showing the Iberian
Peninsula, the Bay of Biscay, Brittany and England as far
north as the Severn. In the ocean, many miles west of
Finisterre was a large cross and the legend 'You are here'.

*Adrian Tuite.*

They recovered to Yeovilton safely, if not sheepishly. The story only leaked out when
the 'chart' appeared later in the squadron line book."

## Paul Waterhouse – observer

"I had a 'pierhead jump' (unexpectedly and suddenly joining a ship) to 891 Squadron on *Centaur*. I had to go to Yeovilton to do a Sea Vixen conversion course – I
don't know how many hours I already had in it, but I had not done a formal course.
In five days I did ten trips with Mick Fieldhouse, who became the senior pilot of
891 Squadron. I got to Malta and was flown on to *Centaur* to meet up with my
pilot who was the AWI. Normally I would have joined a front-line squadron. with
a junior pilot. With the AWI I would be flying with the third-ranking pilot in the
squadron. *Centaur* was a bit small, being about 24,000 tons compared with *Eagle*
and *Ark Royal* which were 50,000. The Sea Vixen wingspan was 50 feet, so on the
smaller carriers it was a bit of a squeeze.

"When we got into the Mediterranean we did some cross-deck operations on
the USS *Forrestal*. After *Centaur* we couldn't believe we were landing on an aircraft
carrier, we thought it was an airfield. We had to go and see *Forrestal*'s captain, and
we were made honourary members of one of their squadrons. We would have liked
to hang around for a few beers, but there's none in the US Navy, so we flew back.
The most interesting thing was when we launched off their forward catapult. On
the *Centaur* these were 130 feet long, on the *Forrestal* they were about 200 feet. As
we had turned into a fairly stiff breeze, there was a substantial windspeed over the
deck, and *Forrestal* moved along quite happily at 25-30 knots. As we were nearly
all the way down the catapult and still holding on the deck, I shouted to the pilot:
'Watch the flaps!' – there was a limiting speed for the flaps of about only 170 knots.
For the first time in all the years I knew Dusty he swore and said, 'I haven't got any
******* flaps down!' We shot off at probably nearly 200 knots into a 30-degree
climb away from the ship. On *Centaur*, going flat out, we would just hit 130 knots
as we went off the end.

"I went back to Yeovilton as an instructor on 766 Squadron, quickly followed by another 'pierhead jump' to 890 Squadron. When they had disembarked, their AWI and his observer, were killed in a night Glow Worm or Lepus flare attack in Lyme Bay. My new pilot Dick Lord, was an AWI, and I had flown with him on occasions on 891, so we got on very well together.

"We did a missile firing off Aberporth with a Firestreak. We fired one missile, and came back with the other one on board. When we hooked up it launched itself straight down the deck; fortunately it was an angled flight deck. I just happened to look out of my window as we passed the island and watched it launch and disappear over the side.

"We set off with *Ark Royal* into the North Sea. Sadly one of our pilots over-rotated off the catapult, and as the Americans would say he 'rode it in'. The observer was an RAF guy and he ejected safely (but did his back in) – the pilot perished. We went via Cape Town to Singapore at the time of the Indonesian Confrontation, doing close air support of our ground forces in Borneo, who had forward air controllers. Due to the threat from surface-to-air missiles we used to run in from offshore. It was a bit tricky finding these guys in the middle of Borneo because the maps weren't all that good, but we managed it most of the time. We could have used 500-lb bombs, but best was the pod of 24 two-inch rockets. However although called in frequently, we didn't need to discharge any of our weaponry. We also used to lead the Scimitars because they didn't have any navaids – working on dead reckoning (DR) only.

"We were later diverted towards South Africa for the Beira Patrol. We were there to provide surveillance as best we could. The AEW Gannets had quite a long radar range, about 200 miles. If they couldn't identify any ships themselves, we would go and have a look. One night, we weren't anticipating flying, but the ship had a signal from the Admiralty saying a frigate was trying to intercept a vessel that was heading towards Beira. It was going so fast that they couldn't close the gap, so they wouldn't have caught it by the time it reached Beira. The ship was asked to send an aircraft to go and have a look. Dick and I got airborne, flew about 300 miles and picked up the frigate. He then directed us to this target that they couldn't catch.

"We came down to 5,000 feet, identified the vessel and ran in at low level – about 1,500 to 2,000 feet. Then in a slight turn we loosed off a Glow Worm rocket. We came round and had a look. It could only be described as an Arab dhow – it was quite large, but obviously wasn't a tanker. You could see the whites of their eyes because they were quite surprised to be illuminated. We said farewell and came back to *Ark Royal*. However, unbeknown to us the ship had turned south to close the gap with us, because we'd gone out a long way. It hit rough water but we had to try and get back on board. There was so much pitch that as we landed the deck came up to meet us. Fortunately we hooked on safely, but it shook the aircraft and broke one of the oleos. Typical of the navy, there was no pat on the back for what was a pretty tricky thing to be sent out to do.

"Out of the blue I was asked to go back to the Sea Vixen in '69. The senior observer on 899 Squadron had ejected from a Vixen in the past and his back was not that good, so he had to come off aircraft with ejection seats. The squadron was getting ready to go off again on *Eagle* – it was a bit of a shock to get back into the coal hole. Because I knew the CO, Mike Layard, I went relatively willingly – we had been on the Venom course together. After him it was 'Dusty' Milner, who I was on the same course with at Linton-on-Ouse.

"When I joined the squadron, ten out of 13 observers were RAF navigators, but then it whittled down to six. They excelled in their new post away from the stifling RAF discipline – finding the navy very different. As far as becoming 'navalised' they moved into it very well, they just became naval officers on board ship – which speaks quite harshly of the RAF at the time. Although it was coming to the end for the Sea Vixen and *Eagle*, we still had a job to do and just got on with it right up to the final flying off.

"The Vixen was very comfortable to fly in and had an excellent radar. It had all the attributes that the Venom didn't have as far as the radar-controlled intercepts, and the Red Top missile – it was well ahead of its time. However it wasn't the best aircraft to land on an aircraft carrier. With the Fowler flaps it was necessary to maintain the engine power in the mid 80 per cents on approach. There were a lot of accidents in the Vixen."

### David Webb – observer

"Our squadron occasionally disembarked to Luqa. On one occasion some USN aircraft were parked on our flight line. An interested American pilot came over to see the Vixens and asked how on earth did such ugly aircraft continue to fly?

"Operating out of Akrotiri, Cyprus, provided some exciting flying, especially at night with a high-flying Vulcan as our target and Mount Olympus radar providing control. It was a dangerous exercise, especially as it was flown 'lights out' and once radar contact was made you were on your own. You really needed a beer after that sortie. Low-level intercepts at night were not without their problems, one Vixen landed on with seaweed in its flaps [see page 200]. It was thought that could only have occurred if the aircraft had bounced off a wave crest. As a Sea Vixen observer/navigator it was a thrilling and exciting era to have been part of the Fleet Air Arm – I enjoyed every minute of it."

### Denis Woodhams – 'plane captain

"I joined 893 Squadron on its formation. We spent the initial period getting to know the aircraft, and its systems, under the supervision of experienced senior rates. We were worked up by 25 November when we embarked in *Ark Royal*. The ground crews joined her in Plymouth with the aircraft arriving a few days later in the Channel. Fast passage to Gibraltar for a few days, then into the Mediterranean. We made passage to Malta where the aircraft, ground and aircrews disembarked to Hal Far for bombing and rocketing practice on Filfla Rock (off the south coast of the island). We lived in Lister Barracks just outside the airfield, and enjoyed the facilities of Ronnie's Bar by the airfield gate.

"More working up in the Med with visits to Toulon and Lisbon, then across the Atlantic and up into the Davis Strait, between Greenland and the North West Territories. Here we were subjected to cold soak with temperatures rarely going above -35 degrees. You would not dare touch any metals with bare hands, but we had good quality Arctic clothing including three layers of gloves, silk, woollen and large mittens. It was possible to perform nearly all of the flight deck tasks without removing gloves, including connecting the Palouste starter, strapping in the aircrew and refuelling. The one task not possible was replacing the small screw cap on the oxygen re-charging point. It was easy to spanner off but you had to remove your glove to replace it, and in seconds your fingers were painfully frozen. We were fortunate there were no accidents. For a considerable time the surface of the sea was not visible because of 'Arctic sea smoke', a thick mist, which would have rendered the finding and rescuing of downed aircrew virtually impossible.

"Then we went into New York before sailing home and disembarking to Yeovilton for leave in February 1961. By April we were embarked in *Centaur* for another five months in the Med, spending a lot of time in Malta, with visits to Istanbul and Sicily, all great fun. In September we were back at Yeovilton for six weeks. Then off again, this time to the Middle and Far East to experience operating in high temperatures and humidity.

"Exciting times as we disembarked to Khormaksar, Tengah and had a visit to Hong Kong, Mombasa (for Christmas), Subic Bay Philippines, Trincomalee Ceylon and a very hot period of several weeks in the Persian Gulf. This was when Iraq was threatening Kuwait. We spent our time off the coast with 100 per cent serviceability, every aircraft clean and no flying. I had the deepest sun tan I've ever had.

"On 23 January 1967 *Hermes* was on commission in the Mediterranean steaming towards Malta whilst 892 Squadron was conducting flying exercises. As a Sea Vixen was launched off the catapult the observer ejected. The pilot was unable to eject, and was with the aircraft on impact with the sea. The 'plane guard helicopter immediately went to the rescue, but it was hit by the ship and crashed along with the Sea Vixen. The pilot of the Sea Vixen was lost, and so was the heroic pilot of the helicopter. The Sea Vixen observer was saved."

"There were many injuries among the helicopter crew that survived. The SAR 'plane guard involved was a Wessex HAS.1 XS883 crewed by Lt John Betterton (pilot), NA Dennis Hodgson (crewman) and NA Jamie Bauld (SAR diver). They were also carrying LA Photographer Chadwick who was there for an air experience ride. An anti-submarine sonar helicopter on a mission nearby, flown by Lt Harding and crewman Dave Wrigglesworth, also went in to assist at the tragic events that ensued.

"This is testimony to the bravery of SAR crews who flew alongside a carrier at flying stations by day and night ready to rescue downed airmen. They flew within a precarious flight envelope called 'Deadman's Curve', which meant that in the event of an engine failure they would hit the sea like a brick unable to make a controlled ditching. The SAR divers were trained to jump from a considerable height from the helicopter, with specialist breathing equipment in order to affect a quick rescue and help the airmen escape as the aircraft sank."

*According to the accident record for Sea Vixen FAW.2 XJ564 H-314: 'Ship executing a high-speed turn; aircraft rotated to a critical nose-up attitude on launch.' The pilot was Lt J R Smith and the observer Lt P S J Love.*

### Tim Thorley – engineering officer

"I went to Yeovilton and finished up working on 766, and then 890 Squadron which was the last one. It was funny because I actually locked the hangar doors at Yeovilton when the Sea Vixens were withdrawn. I returned the keys to the guardroom, only to draw them again three months later when I came back from Culdrose with helicopters. That was it, the end of the Sea Vixen world.

"I used to change engines on them, and could ground-run them. I had no problems with the Sea Vixen really, but they did have *some* idiosyncrasies. Basically it was fine and was quite exciting."

*The Sea Vixen's last hurrah at sea came with Eagle's final commission. In January 1972 899 Squadron flew off for the final time and was disbanded at Yeovilton. Eagle was paid off in Portsmouth that same month.*

### Alan Key – naval air mechanic

"At the age of 17 I was one of the youngest to serve with a front-line Sea Vixen squadron. About a dozen of us left Arbroath in early 1970 to join 766 Squadron and gain our qualified to service (QS), and qualified to maintain (QM) on Vixens. The intention was for us to stay on the squadron until it disbanded in 1971. An A&E naval air mechanic was urgently needed on 899, and I was asked if I wanted to go. *Eagle* was going out to New Zealand, and would be away for a long period. As all my good friends were on Blue Watch, that's where I wanted to be and where I ended up.

*Alan Key.*

"It was a fabulous squadron, very career-minded, everybody was pushed to take their qualifying exams for the next rank. The aeroplanes were good to work on when they were serviceable; but some became 'hangar queens' for months! It was quite dangerous on the flight deck, hard work, but enjoyable. Our senior chief was Vic Redwood who was among the first WOs in 1971 – we were known as Monty

Redwood's Flying Circus.

"Off Scotland on 'Black Friday', 23 November 1970, the sea was quite rough and we were working up. One aircraft [XP955] went off the port cat and dropped, as they all do. We called 'pull it up', which the pilot did, but he stalled and the left wing hit the sea. The observer, Fg Off G Hamlyn, banged out, but unfortunately Lt Bruce Harrison tried to but was drowned. That was the first fatal accident we'd ever seen – you just have to get over it and carry on.

"In the Far East the Vixen's air conditioning was used a lot. The air control unit was behind the pilot's cockpit low down, with only a small access hole. It was only myself and 'Brum' Hardman who could fit in there, so between us we ended up doing nearly all the air conditioning unit changes. I was 4'10" and weighed seven stone in those days.

"There was a LOX plant fire on board one afternoon. We were just going on watch and heard 'Fire, Fire, Fire', then 'Hands to Emergency Stations', so went up to our muster position on the flight deck. The fire burned until midnight. We heard one pipe 'Padre to the Bridge' – two chaps had lost their lives – and another for anybody in overalls because they were needed for fire-fighting duties. Squadron crews didn't do fire-fighting training, so that was left to the ship's company. The fire was put out and the damage was to both the LOX plant, and the dentist's surgery above it. The model railway set in his surgery was destroyed – he wasn't happy. The captain said the ship needed to affect repairs; we would be returning to Singapore – not going to Australia and New Zealand. However, I don't think he'd even put the mike down before the admiral, who was FOF2 (Flag Officer Far East Fleet 2), said over the tannoy that we would be going to Australia and New Zealand, affecting repairs en route.

"On landing the undercarriage of one Sea Vixen folded, and the missile under one wing came hurtling down the deck. We had been trained to stand still and let the shrapnel go round us because if you try to evade it you put yourself at risk. Then another Sea Vixen took the barrier on *Eagle's* last commission.

"Despite its reputation I certainly never had any hydraulic problems on my two aircraft, but we were forever changing parts and engines. You had your own aeroplane and three AE mechanics, one for each of the three watches, and your job was to look after that aeroplane. The watch between midnight and 6 a.m. would do a full daily inspection, which took about 2-2½ hrs, followed by a before-flight. We kept everything topped up all the time, so the inspection didn't take so long. I like to think we kept the

*Hermes hangar in the early 1960s.*

aircraft in tip-top condition.

"The ship was exercising off Hong Kong when we were told that a crew would have to go to Singapore to receive two replacement aircraft; '125' with a cracked tail-boom, and the one that had taken the barrier, had been offloaded there. Nine of us flew to Singapore to receive the aircraft, which we then had to take by road (over two nights), to RAF Tengah. It took about four hours for each aeroplane, as part of our escort duties was to stand on the aircraft using sticks to push tree branches, on the side of the road, out of the way.

"I was doing a check on one and noticed some corrosion on the No.1 frame, where the radome closes onto the fuselage. I scraped it with a screwdriver and it went all the way through – the frame was completely corroded. With only five months to go there was no point in affecting a repair so we removed bits as spares. I took the flap motor out from the back end of the port engine bay – there were 50 bolts to undo. I was told not to bother and use an axe! We left the aircraft at Tengah, donating it to an engineering school.

"On the way home we approached the CO (Lt Cdr Milner) to ask, as we were the last Sea Vixen squadron, whether we could decorate the aircraft. He said, 'Yes, but nothing obscene', and to use washable emulsion. British warships don't carry emulsion so we acquired as much gloss paint as we could from the ship's store. We painted flowers on my aircraft with 'Key's Kite' on the port intake. The aircrew helped – the whole squadron was doing it. An advance party had gone off to Yeo-vilton to receive them and get them ready for the final flypast. They didn't know anything about the painting and when the aircraft arrived they were gobsmacked!"

## Kim Sharman – pilot

"I was on *Eagle*'s last commission with 899 Squadron. Off Cape Town the ship did 'Procedure Alpha' where the sides are lined with sailors. The officers were in the bow and I was fortunate enough to be one of them. I shall never forget the sight of Table Mountain emerging from the dawn and changing colour as the sun came up. One disadvantage of mooring in the docks there was that all the ship's tannoy announcements were reflected and amplified by Table Mountain. The good citizens of Cape Town were delighted to be informed by the ship that 'the forward heads were unserviceable'.

"Off to Singapore, and we were doing night flying in the Malacca Straits. Every-one was diverted to Butterworth, but we weren't expected there. 'You're staying the night and going back on board tomorrow chaps.' 'Oh, err, where do we stay?' 'Well, the navy's arranged some accommodation for you, in the local brothel!' We had no money so it was all right.

"We went on to Hong Kong and disembarked to Kai Tak for two weeks. When we left we flew round to the south of the island, joined up in formation and came back for a flypast over the harbour. I looked up and saw the top of the Mandarin Hotel going past. We went out through the gap, round to the south of the island,

*Kim Sharman's last launch from* Eagle. *(John Eacott)*

broke out of formation and joined up in line-astern. We came in a stream like the bats out of hell, 500 knots at low level down the harbour. About 40 years later, when I was with Cathay Pacific, *Ark Royal* came to Hong Kong and we were all invited on board for the cocktail party. I asked one of the guys whether they were going to do a flypast before they left. He said, 'No!' so I asked him why not. He said: 'Forty years ago some twats beat the s\*\*t out of the place!'

"The ship stopped in Malta for a couple of weeks on the way home, and we disembarked to Luqa. We were flying at night and my aircraft decided to dump all its fuel overboard – a not uncommon occurrence in the Sea Vixen. As a result I was down to about 10 to 12 minutes' fuel. I came back to Luqa and declared a Mayday – 'No, you can't land here'. 'Why not?' 'Someone has blown his tyres and is blocking the runway'. I flew over the runway. I can't remember what sort of aircraft it was but I thought there was no way I was going to jump out over the Med at night. I thought I could get away with it – so I landed. As I approached the obstruction I folded my wings and went round the side. I put the starboard wheel in the grass, and there was a bit of grass in the undercarriage when I looked – no-one said a word. They didn't say 'well done' or anything like that, but I wasn't castigated because I had saved an aircraft.

"We were on the last ever day of flying from *Eagle*. I was the leader of a pair with P V Lloyd (who was one of the few guys to transfer to the air force). We were going round in formation to join the ship. Normally I would lead it in and land, and he would land second. But I pulled rank and told him to go in first, for his last deck landing. I was then the last person ever to deck land a Sea Vixen. On the last launch we were going back to Yeovilton – my aircraft went unserviceable. All the rest launched, and eventually I was the last one away. That was the last cat launch, and all the boys thought I was swinging it!"

> *The Sea Vixen was a major advance on the Sea Venom, although it was not without its challenges. Of the 145 aircraft built no fewer than 55 were written off in accidents, of which 30 were fatal (21 of those fatal to both aircrew). Thus Sea Vixen operations led to the tragic loss of 51 pilots and observers – a very heavy price to pay.*

> *'Epitaph to a Vixen' from 899 Squadron's line book*

> *"Farewell old friend you've done us proud*
> *Praise we cannot sing too loud.*
> *Despite the song of A25[4]*
> *And other ditties of staying alive;*
> *Of men with whom you aviate –*
> *only a 60% disaster rate.*
> *Of illness in the right-hand seat,*
> *Emergencies and other feats to test and try*
> *The men whose whim it is to fly.*

> *"But on reflection over gin and beer*
> *The Devil got the Vixen – and man that's rare!"*

---

4.  Accident report form.

CHAPTER NINE

# McDONNELL PHANTOM

*Phantom FG.1 XV586 R-003 892 Squadron Yeovilton, 5 July 1972. (Stephen Wolf)*

*In the early 1960s the Royal Navy began to look for a Sea Vixen replacement.
The carriers intended to operate the next generation fighter, alongside the
Buccaneer, were the two largest — Ark Royal and Eagle — together with
a planned new carrier CVA-01 to be named Queen Elizabeth.*

*Initial thoughts had turned towards a 'catapult capable' two-seat version
of the Hawker P.1154 (a supersonic variant of the P.1127/Harrier, with a
single-seat variant being proposed for the RAF). Ultimately, the navy's
insistence on two seats compromised performance, and they opted for an
'anglicised' version of the F-4 Phantom fitted with Rolls-Royce Spey engines.*

*The original intention was to buy 140 aircraft, sufficient to equip squad-
rons to serve on all three carriers. However CVA-01 costs continued to
spiral leading to a decision to cancel it in the 1966 Defence White Paper.
This left just Ark Royal and Eagle as potential homes for the Phantoms.
Despite initial carrier trials taking place aboard Eagle, costs – and politics
– once again got in the way, and eventually only Ark Royal was modified
to take them. As a result the FAA Phantom fleet was limited to 28 aircraft.*

*Operating units: 700P, 767, 892 Squadrons, Phantom Training Flight
(PTF), embarked on Ark Royal, trials on Eagle. No. 892's motto was 'Strike
Unseen' – otherwise known to the others on Ark as 'Lash Out Blindly'!*

Anon pilot

## NIGHT CARRIER OPERATIONS

"Despite the flight deck being lit by red floodlights, set high up on the island, it is a very different scene at night, gloomy and rather mysterious. The dayglo centreline and the coloured surcoats of deck personnel fade into greyish tints. Aircraft parked away from the lights appear as large shapes in the shadows. Aircrew walk down the flight deck carrying helmets under their arms and disappear into darkness.

"There is little wind over the deck as the ship steams downwind before turning to launch aircraft: 'Stand clear of intakes, jet pipes and propellers, start the jets.' A vibration can be felt through the deck announcing that the ship is increasing speed and starting to turn. Wands light up briefly, held by barely visible marshallers, circle and then shut off – the signal to start engines. Dim navigation and fuselage lights come on, indicating that engines are running. A pair of wands suddenly click on in the gloom beckoning the first aircraft from the range. It waddles forward; its under-belly light reflecting from the deck. The wands point forward, and immediately another set come on directing the pilot towards the bow. The lights move in a wide fan, and the navigation lights follow as its wings are spread.

"A marshaller standing astride the catapult track, with wands upright, gives small signals to ensure that the nosewheel is aligned correctly. Dim figures appear and crawl under the aircraft's belly, then scamper clear. The lights point towards the centre of the deck and suddenly snap off. A new set comes on. The FDO, leaning against the wind, carefully raises his wands high and with concentrated care rotates them slowly. This is the signal for the pilot to go to full power. The jet pipes, which were merely faint glowing circles, now grow into two long incandescent spears of flame reaching out behind the Phantom. They beat against the jet blast deflector, whilst the deck immediately behind the aircraft begins to glow with intense heat.

"Its navigation lights become brighter, the signal 'ready for launch'. A sense of raw power only just held in check continues for a few brief seconds. The controlling wands descend to the deck in exaggerated slow motion so as to make clear they were not dropped accidentally. A couple of seconds later the catapult fires hurling the Phantom forward, its fiery tail sweeping along the deck. The aircraft disappears immediately into darkness leaving only twin glowing circles, and navigation lights, soaring upwards. As its afterburners cut out the flames are suddenly extinguished. The next Phantom moves forward onto the catapult."

**Tony Pinney – pilot**
"*Eagle* had been given a thorough refit. Prior to that she had been an unhappy ship, mainly due to overcrowding and poor interaction between parts of the air group

*Ark Royal leaving Plymouth on her last deployment 5 April 1978, passing the retired* Eagle.

and the ship's officers. She was in good shape and had been fitted with 984 and double 965 radars. Then the 1966 Defence Review dismissed the idea of global influence, and the power projection that only the carriers could provide. Though in some ways vulnerable carriers did not require overflying permission and could move 700 miles in a day. The decision meant that once the East of Suez withdrawal was complete (the modernised *Eagle*, *Victorious* and fairly new *Hermes* could handle that), it was pointless spending money on them.

"Despite the body blow it had been given the navy had apparently started to plan *Ark's* refit after her return to Devonport, and de-storing. I understand the refit was stopped before it was started. There were areas of the country that the Labour government deemed needed extra financial support due to lack of work. It was soon realised that the cancellation of the modernisation would reduce the dockyard work. It would trigger Plymouth becoming one of those regions, costing more than the refit to cover only one commission. After being stopped for ten weeks it was re-started. That was fairly common knowledge at the time, and was confirmed to me by Captain Lygo.

"The ship's company, the naval staff and the dockyard did their best. However refitting a carrier in 1967-70 with some machinery salvaged from very old ships was not ideal. Most importantly *Ark* was not fitted with 984 radar; she was given two double 965s. They could only operate singly as no money was allocated to synchronise them – to save each blasting the other. This led to coverage gaps.

"The modernised *Eagle* was kept to be robbed for spares – until *Ark* sailed for her last commission. It is of note that the cost of fitting *Eagle* to take the Phantom was deemed to be £5 million – whereas *Ark's* refit was pegged at £35 million. The fact that *Ark's* ship's company worked tirelessly to the end of her extended life is more a demonstration of the spirit of pride, and sheer bloody mindedness, than anything else."

### John Dixon – pilot

"No. 892's lifespan with Phantoms was relatively short; nine years from when the squadron first went to sea on *Ark Royal* in 1970, to decommissioning in 1979. The primary role was fleet defence – but how well equipped were we to deal with the Soviet threat?

*John Dixon.*

"When I joined the navy in 1957 the Soviets possessed a vast array of air-launched nuclear stand-off weapons. These weapons were the threat to our carrier fleets in the '50s and into the early '60s. Launch ranges were roughly 50-150 nautical miles, and with limited guidance and target acquisition, the early stand-off weapons could more accurately be described as glide bombs. The granddaddy of the bunch was the Kangaroo. Based on the MiG-19, 49 feet long and weighing 26,000 lbs, it had a selectable yield of up to 3,000 kT (kilotons), or 3 MT (megatons). Big and ugly, it needed something equally big to carry it. The Tu-16 'Badger' could carry one, but it was designed around the Tu-95 'Bear' which could carry three.

"In the mid 1960s things became notably more serious with the introduction of the Sukhoi Su-24 'Fencer', and the Tupolev Tu-22 'Backfire'. Both were supersonic and formidable opponents, especially the Backfire. At the same time a new anti-shipping stand-off weapon was brought into service, the 38-feet long AS4 Kitchen. It replaced the previous range of out-dated weapons, with the exception of the AS2 Kelt which continued in service until 1990. Although the Fencer could carry the Kitchen, it was the marriage of Kitchen and Backfire that caused considerable concern. The Backfire carried three. Against a prime target, such as a carrier task force, it was expected

*Tu-22 'Backfire' with Kitchen missiles. (Russianplanes.net)*

to ripple off two or even all three. Launched at a range of up to 320 nautical miles from the target – this gave us the problem. The carrying aircraft needed to be destroyed before this point. Once the Kitchen was in its cruise, either high at 89,000 feet and Mach 4.6, or low at around 1,000 feet and Mach 3.5, it would be virtually impossible to intercept.

"In 1970 most of the southern European countries, Ukraine, Romania, Bulgaria, Hungary, Serbia etc. were under Soviet control, and all with airbases a short flying time to the Med. In the 1970s Soviet strategic planners recognised the importance of the Med, basing 300 Tu-22 Backfires in the southern Soviet states alone. No surprise then that the Med was one of *Ark Royal's* launch areas for mounting our own Buccaneer nuclear strikes. But unless 892 Squadron could deal with the Backfires, expected in streams and making their way towards 'mother', the worst prediction was we had about four hours to get the Buccs armed and airborne before *Ark* was mortally wounded or sunk. Not the sort of good news that was pushed out on *Ark's* TV channel!

"We re-equipped from Sea Vixens to Phantoms to give us the best opportunity to intercept the Backfires before they reached their release points. Air-to-air armament was four AIM-7E Sparrow semi-active missiles, plus four AIM-9D Sidewinder infrared missiles on the inboard pylons. You would think that fleet defence would be well within the Phantom's capability, given that in its interceptor role with its excellent Pulse Doppler radar, it was as good as anything else at the time. The aircraft was certainly up to the job, but there were other issues which affected 892's ability.

"In a head-on situation with high closing speeds, the Sparrow could be launched at a range in excess of 20 nautical miles. Rmax was about 22 miles, and the aerodynamic range Ra, about 28 nautical miles – not bad. But to use it we needed two things; a reliable missile, and a weapons-free environment so we could let loose at long range. We didn't get a reliable Sparrow, and a weapons-free environment was never going to be a given.

*An RAF Phantom showing the missile fit. (via John Dixon)*

"The long-range Sparrow/radar combination has never been used effectively; this was partly because the environment in which the F-4 found itself was far different from the original concept of being a Mach 2 interceptor launched into the path of Soviet bomber streams. The main problem with the AIM-7E was the seeker head. Being a semi-active missile, it relied on the F-4's reflected radar returns off the target for guidance. In ideal conditions, on beautiful clear days at medium altitude, it generally worked fine. But in extreme weather, or in a look-down environment into clutter, or in a jamming environment it was 'iffy' at best. We did some training in a jamming environment; but nothing like the intense barrage and spot jamming we could expect from dedicated Badger aircraft, with their enormous electrical power swamping the combat area. All 892 missile shoots were to provide crews with the experience of getting a missile away. Nothing wrong with that, but the idea was never to waste a missile by putting the seeker head to the test.

"Sparrow trials carried out at Aberporth showed what we already knew – the AIM-7E seeker head wasn't up to the job. In the mid '70s the UK developed an entirely new seeker head, gave it a better anti-jamming capability, renamed the missile Skyflash and introduced it into the RAF. As by this time *Ark* was within three years of the end of its working life, 892's 7E model Sparrows were never replaced. Although an improved version of the Sparrow, the AIM-7F was available, the squadron continued with the 7E model to the bitter end.

"From the beginning of US Operation Rolling Thunder in March 1965, to the end of operations against North Vietnam in January 1973, only two beyond visual range kills were officially recorded out of 597 Sparrow firings. The Yom Kippur War (6–24 October 1973), was a much shorter conflict but the air-to-air combat was intense. During the 18 days of fighting the Israeli air force claimed to have downed some 172 Egyptian and 162 Syrian planes. Despite the large amount of air-to-air combat Israeli F-4s only fired 12 AIM-7 Sparrows, claiming a single be-yond visual range kill.

"Why was the exploitation of the technical capability to fire from beyond visual range so rare? In my opinion the overriding constraint was not so much rules of engagement (ROE), but more a matter of human preference. Fighter pilots are understandably reluctant to shoot unless they are confident, if not virtually certain, that the target on the radar scope will not turn out to be a friendly aircraft. This was especially so when you consider there were a lot of friendly aircraft airborne at any one time. As well as shore-based USAF, South Vietnamese and RAAF aircraft, there were as many as four carriers operating in Vietnam's Tonkin Gulf simultane-ously. For a short period in 1972 six were deployed on Yankee Station.

"Another reason for their reluctance was the poor performance of the AIM-7D and E Sparrows in use at the time. During the course of the Vietnam War, 1965 to 1973, of 612 Sparrows fired depressingly only 59 scored hits, a kill factor of less than ten per cent. To narrow it down even further, during the 'Rolling Thunder' period (1965-68) of 330 Sparrows fired by air force and navy 'planes just 27 scored hits. The rest either failed to guide or suffered mechanical failure, such as premature detonation or motor failure. Only eight of the navy's 54 kills during this entire war were made with Sparrows. The AIM-9D Sidewinder had become the primary weap-on. Although not an all-aspect weapon during the Vietnam era, it was agile and once you had a 'growl' it was a 'fire and forget' weapon. The Sparrow was not as you had to continue roughly towards the target to maintain radar illumination.

"However the Sparrow was probably better than the figures suggest. Yes, there were too many failures, but the AIM7 was not designed for the hurly-burly of close combat with wildly manoeuvring targets at high 'g' and crews rippling off two or three in impracticable situations in the hope of getting a kill. But what lessons could we learn from Vietnam?

"Did the rules of engagement affect beyond visual range firings? Surprisingly, not as much as you might think. A VID (visual identification) was part of the ROE right from the start. After a 'blue-on-blue' the ROE were tightened up removing any ambiguity, especially with regard to the controller's (direction officer's) instructions and clearances. The need for a VID could only be relaxed when strict requirements were met; for the first two or three years of the war those requirements were hard to meet. Gradually American advances in electronic intelligence equipment meant that the stringent requirements were met more often. This gave air controllers greater opportunities to relax the VID requirement, clearing aircraft to fire. Even so it was rarely given.

"Lockheed EC-121 and Boeing EC-135 aircraft orbiting over Laos, Thailand and the Gulf of Tonkin carried Vietnamese-speaking specialists monitoring voice comms between the MiGs and their controllers. This information was supplemented by an ELINT (electronic intelligence) EC-135 in the Gulf, a navy EC-121 'Big Look' aircraft monitoring SAM (surface-to-air missile) activity among other things, navy EA-3Bs and E-2 Hawkeyes. All this info was fed to 'Red Crown', a naval tactical data system (NTDS) equipped ship in the Gulf, enabling it to provide a positive identification radar advisory zone (PIRAZ). The complete air picture of both friendly and enemy aircraft throughout the region was transmitted into the combat information centre of carriers and ships by 'Link Eleven', a secure data transmission system. By 1969 air controllers had a pretty good air picture of MiG activity all the way up to Hanoi.

"Little known was a capability to trigger the IFF (identification friend or foe) system of the MiGs. Called 'Combat Tree' this nifty bit of kit was integrated with the AWG radar of some air force F-4Ds and Es. Triggering the Combat Tree, even with the F-4 radar in standby, would show all MiG IFFs on the radar screen in the direction of the antenna out to about 40 nautical miles – even if, as was the norm, the MiG's IFF was selected off! This was a hell of an advantage for the F-4s, pinpointing MiGs down in the ground clutter where they preferred to operate, whilst not transmitting oneself. The MiGs could thus be tracked without their knowledge.

"Perhaps the Sparrow success rate would have been better if employed in the manner originally visualised, head on against bombers in a weapons-free environment. This was not where the F-4 found itself. Luckily it was a pretty good all-rounder, in capable hands, and engagements of the classic kind became the norm. There was a lack of confidence in the early models of the Sparrow when forced to VID before engaging. By the time F-4 crews had seen their 'bogey' (often smaller than the Phantom) the bogey had seen them, even if the Phantom was in minimum afterburner to reduce smoke. By now the bogey was already close to, or even inside, the Sparrow's minimum range (roughly 1.7 nautical miles). If the crew did manage a Sparrow shot, the time from lock to launch was an eternity, and there was always a strong possibility that the missile would fail to track. This problem was still with us when 892 reformed in 1969. A US Navy RIO (radar intercept officer), who did three tours in Vietnam, told me that one F-4 squadron wanted to dispense with the Sparrows completely. This had the added advantage of saving 2,000 lbs in weight and making the aircraft more manoeuvrable. The idea was vetoed by the air boss.

"What could 892 have done in the '70s? Would it have been any different from what was going on in Vietnam? If a weapons-free environment could not be satisfied, because of a VID requirement, then one way round the problem of having to VID and destroy the target would have been to operate as a pair of F-4s on each CAP station. One to VID, one to hang back and position as shooter, a tactic developed by Top Gun in 1973. But this requires practiced teamwork, and unlike the Americans, we never had the resources. On *Ark* we only had room for 12 F-4s, perhaps 14 in war time. Without exception, both on Vixens and F-4s I have always been on a CAP station as a singleton. We have to come to terms with it – size does matter!

"It's a slightly depressing story but you can only work with what you have. This was not helped by the lack of intelligence fed down to the sharp end, the crews. In an all-out conflict the expected stream of Backfires would probably have ensured at least one weapon got through, even with American and French carrier support. I never gave *Ark Royal's* chance of survival any better than 50:50. It was a prime target as carriers have always been, and I don't think that things have changed much in the ensuing 50 years. The Backfire is still with us in 2020, perhaps not in the same numbers but updated and still very potent.

"The AS4 Kitchen is also still with us, updated with the latest EW and navigation technology and equally potent. The latest version only came into service in 2017; it has greater range – the launch point has moved out to 630 nautical miles, up from 320. If our new *QE* carriers are working in conjunction with an American carrier, that 630

*No. 892 Squadron's last departure for* Ark Royal, Leuchars, *6 April 1978.*

nautical miles is outside the combat radius of both their F-18 Super Hornet and our F-35B. The Kitchen now cruises a lot higher too, up to 130,000 feet in the stratosphere. Its terminal dive onto the target at Mach 4.6 is near vertical from directly overhead – just where any ship-borne self-defence missile system (including Sea Viper) has the most difficulty, and is at its most vulnerable.

"To add to the excitement, lightweight decoys can be strapped onto the Kitchen. In the stratosphere weight hardly makes any difference to the trajectory, so released late in the cruise you could have nine potential targets raining down onto you if all three Kitchens are rippled off. With a wing of three Backfires doing the same, as would more than likely be the case, I'll leave the Sea Viper combat management system to do the sums – I don't think it will like the numbers. It has still only been tested at Mach 2.5, the fastest target drone available. For a variety of reasons I'll downgrade survival odds for today's carriers to 60:40 against."

### David Allan – pilot

"Here we are, strapped into our Phantom, attached to the waist catapult on the *Ark*. We are somewhere off the north of Norway, poised to launch as the 'alert 5 minutes', or whatever. My body is starting to ache, even although I have eased the straps. I haven't heard from my observer for about 20 minutes, I think he's asleep. We have been here for over an hour. That is not the worst of it. As we are taking part in a NATO exercise, we are required to carry reams of paper. There are restrictions everywhere, worse than the rules of golf!

"I feel the vibrations through the ship increase, and she starts to turn. The wind across the deck initially blows from in front of the island, and then across the deck as she turns onto a flying course. I get a lung full of funnel smoke, having been a bit late lowering the canopy. The observer coughs – he's now awake. A voice on the intercom says that there is a Russian inbound, and to shadow as required. Forget about all of the interesting bumf for the exercise, just operate on the *Ark's* comms – the gods are on our side.

*No. 892 Squadron Phantom 007 formating on a Norwegian F-5, David Allan up front.*

"Twenty minutes later we are 'attached' to the right wing of a Tu-16 'Badger G' from Russian naval aviation. We have introduced ourselves to the cockpit crew by flying ahead of the wing, giving them a wave, and then back to a more normal formation position. This puts us opposite the aft blister window of the Badger, and another wave to the occupant. It is so easy to see practically every ship in the NATO fleet from this

*Tu-16 and 892 Squadron Phantom low pass over* Ark Royal.

vantage point, and together we visit just about every one of them. At times, when we enter thin layers of cloud, my visible world becomes restricted to the wing of the Badger. Having read tales of Russian aircraft reducing speed, and suddenly turning into their escort causing them to stall, the brain sitting behind me monitors the what, where, and when of the instruments, just in case.

"After about an hour airborne, *Ark* calls us with a 'charlie', to be some 25 minutes later. Just as my observer says, 'she is left 30 degrees at 80 miles', the Badger turns in that direction. Foolish not to see where it takes us! The Badger lines up on *Ark*'s into-wind recovery course and drops to 600 feet. I lower the hook about a mile from the *Ark*, flying just aft of his right wing and opposite the blister window. We fly close to the carrier down the starboard side through the 'slot' and, 200 yards in front of the bow, the Russian in the aft window smiles and waves me away into the landing circuit. Throughout my flying on the wing my observer has been updating all the usual safety items including the time to 'charlie' etc. As I pull up over the Badger into the landing circuit, he says that if I am late, it is my fault! It was only five seconds."

### John Keenan – artificer

"My first time at sea with the Phantom was on the USS *Nimitz* – I was detached there before joining 892 – anchored off Edinburgh. A group of us were conveyed from Rosyth in a tug. In my holdall I had a bottle of whisky, not realising that US ships are 'dry'. Having been told by a USN officer that I couldn't take it aboard, the only option was to drink it. So the three of us, including the tug's Scottish master, did so on the bridge. I certainly felt the effects of it but the American officer was absolutely pie-eyed; I had to help him up the gangway.

"We were on *Nimitz* to familiarise ourselves with their Phantoms; it was fascinating having experienced life on the older British carriers. Although ours only carried about 20 to 30 aircraft, we launched every 30 seconds or so from two catapults. US carriers, with four catapults, only launched ten aircraft to our 24 in the same amount of time. On the flight deck, wearing a headset and plugged into a USMC aircraft to check for any problems, I couldn't understand a word of the clipped-speech used by aircrew and deck crew alike. So, I transmitted, in my best English voice, that I wished them all to speak clearly and fluently, enunciating their vowels. Everybody was looking at me, including the air boss in the island who was howling with laughter. It worked a treat.

"When our aircraft embarked there was a problem with one of the engines and we had to set up the BLC (boundary layer control) sensing. To get the BLC sensing and Delta P (pressure difference) figures you have to go into and out of reheat, so that you can make adjustments. The aircraft was straddled, in the dark, across the outboard waist catapult – we just got on with it. I was in the cockpit reading my graphs and another 892 engine mechanic was on the deck tweaking the BLC sensing. Having corrected the problem, I was waiting whilst the engine idled for a minute or so when the mechanic said there was a guy running across the deck towards us. The guy gestured to me, so I shut down the engine and exited the aircraft. He said the FDO wanted to see me PDQ, and I was to get over to flight deck control in the island. I did so, but after finishing the paperwork because they wanted the aircraft for night flying. The FDO was sitting, puffing on his cigar, behind the table which represented the flight deck. He said, 'Hey, a********e, I've been calling you on the goddamn radio. You've been illuminating the side of the goddamn ship, and all the submarines have been popping off their goddamn flares (we were in the middle of a big exercise) and firing their (simulated) goddamn torpedoes at us. The captain is goddamn angry!' I knew I was in trouble, and pointing to my chief's epaulettes said, 'I am a chief petty officer in Her Britannic Majesty's Service, and I serve the Queen. Nobody, but nobody other than the Queen calls me an a******e. If you had given me a radio as I had requested, you could have called and stopped me, so don't you ever be so impertinent again.' This was all in my best English. You could have heard a pin drop in the following silence. I spun on my heels and walked out, thinking 'Keenan, it's the cells for you'. However whilst walking away I was given a radio headset to wear on the flight deck.

"The Phantom was a magnificent aeroplane, although early on its Spey engines proved very problematic. They fitted into the belly, and all the stressed skin panels had to be removed to change an engine. During a change we used a specially designed trolley. This allowed the engine to be manoeuvred in all directions so as to fit snugly with the trunnions, and line up with the 'MacPherson Strut' (the pillar that transmits the engine thrust to the airframe) inside the fuselage. 'Wilf' Graham, Ark Royal's captain, would occasionally appear walking around the ship in his white overalls to see what was going on. We were attempting to fit an engine but because of the ship's motion, and with the aircraft resonating with it, we were having difficulty lining the engine up with the MacPherson Strut. About a dozen guys of all trades were helping with the job. Whilst I was looking into the bowels of the aircraft using my torch, Wilf's head appeared under my armpit. He asked: 'Are we having a bit of a problem here, chief?' to which I replied, 'With all due respect, Sir, why don't you 'eff off'. He burst out laughing and wandered off. A few days later, he asked me how it went.

"We once did an engine change in Malta whilst the ship was tied to a buoy in Valletta harbour. On Phantoms we used 816s. This was a process sheet for an engine reheat run with a lot of graphs to refer to when making adjustments to the sensors and acceleration controls. I was underneath the aircraft making adjustments and Ted Hatton was in the cockpit. The harbour authorities only allowed one hour in which to do the job because of the noise created in reheat, and we were having problems. We lowered the arrestor hook and put a clamp around the hook point. The clamp was fixed to the deck stopping the aircraft from moving whilst running up engine power. We were going in and out of reheat. Ted calling out the figures while I was making the adjustments.

"One of the lads ran over to me, grabbed my shoulder and pointed. The OOW was standing in the middle of the flight deck, in his white uniform, gesturing 'cut, cut, cut' to me – I turned my back, pretending I hadn't seen him. I asked Ted whether he'd seen the OOW, and how much more there was to do. He said he hadn't, but there was only one more reheat selection to finish the job. We were racing against time, but the OOW started berating me. The squadron AEO turned up, and the ship's senior commander was hovering in the background. Ted climbed out of the cockpit, having shut down the engines. The OOW told us to accompany him to the forward part of the flight deck, which overlooked the catwalk, and pointed at the chain connecting the ship to the buoy. As we had been using reheat so much, we had been driving the ship round and round so that the chain had become knotted. The buoy had been lifted ten feet out of the water, exposing the chain with which it was secured to the seabed. The OOW was apoplectic, the commander didn't say much and the AEO just stood there with his pipe in his mouth so we knew he wasn't too bothered.

"They launched a Gemini sea boat crewed by the chief bosun's mate and some seamen. The OOW told us that the ship had had to flash up its boilers and be held by its propellers, and we had to un-shackle the buoy. The chief bosun's mate ordered one of the seamen to climb on top of the buoy, calling to him: 'Here's a sledgehammer, it's on my slop-chit so don't drop the b*****d.' The idea was to use the hammer to remove the pin on the chain's swivel link. After several strikes of the hammer the pin was eventually removed, and the buoy dropped back into the water with the young seaman clinging to it, and the chief bosun's mate shouting at him to keep hold of the hammer. Problem solved, but the AEO said to us, 'I think you're in the poo.'"

## Chris Bolton – pilot

"The RN stopped training fixed-wing pilots in 1968, so they had to borrow crews

*Chris Bolton.*

from the US Navy. As people left the navy, the numbers were augmented by RAF volunteers – there were no pressed men. I was volunteer number four, two had gone before me from Coningsby and one from Leuchars – it all sounded great fun to me. I spoke to people in the bar particularly navigators who had done time with the navy on Sea Vixens. The Phantom was due to enter service but the navy lacked two-seat air defence navs.

"I was posted to the PTF at Leuchars. It was run by the navy and although the boss was an RAF squadron leader, he was ex-navy. The PTF didn't teach me to fly the Phantom – I was already trained – it taught me to do things the navy way. Some of it was significantly different, lesser fuel requirements to land, and the way they did air intercepts was not the same. I hadn't done many anyway so I was open-minded. The other bit to make me navalised was doing deck landings. We did MADDLs at Leuchars where they painted a dummy deck and put a projector sight on the port side of the runway – it was almost like the real thing. The only difference was that the Phantom was low wing, virtually delta. As you got in close you'd hit the ground effect, so you went higher close in; that wasn't going to happen aboard ship. 892 Squadron had a secondary role with two-inch rockets, not dissimilar to the 68-mm SNEB, slightly less accurate, but with more per pod, and bombs. We did practice weaponry on Rosehearty and Tain ranges, which were handy for Leuchars.

*PTF Phantoms XT861 V and XV569 X get airborne from Leuchars.*

"Before going to sea we were required to do catapult shots, for me the first time ever. This was done at Bedford, so I flew down there with a QFI in the back. Taxi up onto the ramp, have a bit of a briefing, the aircraft is now cocked and ready to go. If you had a tail wind you'd get an almighty kick, 5g or thereabouts. As the wind was down the catapult that was not to be. On navy Phantoms the nose leg extended pneumatically by 40 inches, which gave an incidence of 9° to avoid having to rotate so much at the end of the catapult. You're at full flap, full after-burner and the guy on the ground is waving a little flag at you. You put your hand up as if to say 'I have power, the aircraft is serviceable' and he puts his flag down. The guy in charge of the catapult acknowledges that – he's been sitting with his hands on his head, so that he doesn't inadvertently shoot the thing – and fires the catapult. Bang, off you go, that's a thrill, and there you are at 1,000 feet and you turn downwind. You make an arrested landing on the runway, and taxi back onto the catapult. Three catapult shots made, after the third it's straight back to Leuchars.

"Navy Phantoms had an SPD (stick positioning device), a little cylinder with a wire coiled around it. You de-clutch the cylinder and put it into the stick, holding it de-clutched until you've got the right angle on the stabilator on a cockpit gauge. A guy on the flight deck tells you that you have the right incidence for the aircraft to achieve a good transition from take-off to climb position. You release the SPD once airborne. The idea was that the stick would not come back into your belly with the 4/5g shot causing you to over-rotate.

"Having done all the cat shots and MADDLs (almost) to everyone's satisfaction, the last thing was a briefing from the LSO Peter Sheppard. He briefed all the things that can go wrong when landing on. Every take-off and landing is filmed, so the horror shots were there to illustrate other people's errors to make sure that, me, the new guy wasn't going to f**k up similarly. There's late line-up, wingtip touches the deck (and the aircraft goes over the side), too low, hitting the ramp, bits falling off…and so on.

"I'm signed off at the PTF and join the ship. There's only one guy who's more nervous about this than me and that's my observer, despite him being experienced on Sea Vixens and Phantoms. There was no such drama for my first catapult shot from the ship – you just go, it's out of your hands. Coming back is where my judgement is going to make his day exciting.

"When we joined the ship for the first time it was not by air, but by jack-stay transfer. When they do replenishment at sea (RAS) there's a tanker to provide furnace oil and aviation fuel. It goes into formation with the carrier, fires a line over and then the fuel lines are pulled across to refuel. We were on board the tanker and transferred over on a wire in a little cage. This was my first day on board *Ark Royal*, with the remainder of the morning up in FlyCo; 'Little F' (lieutenant commander flying) and wings (commander air) operated from there. It's a great spot for me to observe the deck and operations before my afternoon flight. So after watching all that stuff, getting briefed again, I'm now on my way.

"Down to the ACRB – a little greasy spoon in the island where you can get a great bacon butty and a cup of tea. Our ready room is also in the island, with what look like lots of second-hand airline seats. I get briefed for my trip which will be a high-level radar intercept sortie – the exciting bit for me will be coming back and landing one hour and 20 minutes later. Walk out, crew the aeroplanes. The Buccaneers will be going off first, and coming on last; they don't use fuel as quickly as we do and therefore have longer sorties. Then it's our turn, hands shaking, knees almost under control, watching the marshaller in front of you who hands you over to the next one on your way to the catapult. They put me on the waist catapult which is about 195 feet long, the bow cat is very short. The guy on the catapult is marshalling me with the nosewheel on the cat track, slight bump as you go over the launch shuttle, then brakes on. They fit the bridle which is looped around the shuttle, and then attached to the catapult hooks underneath the fuselage. Having attached the hold-back they tension the catapult and extend the nosewheel leg, via a switch in the port undercarriage bay. The incidence required for the stabilator has been determined by the end speed of the catapult. The waist cat will give you 118 knots end speed. Add to that the ship's speed and the natural wind, which combined should be about 30 knots. So 148 knots wind over the wings is what you're going to get at the end of the cat shot.

"A guy on the deck checks the stabilator angle by using the painted marks at its leading edge on the back of the fuselage. When he's happy, I'm happy – I can see the stab angle on the cockpit gauge – we're 'hot to trot'. The FDO is waving his flag, which means wind up your power, so we do and rock the throttles outboard into reheat. Everything is stabilised and when I'm happy I accept the launch by holding up my hand, he acknowledges it, looks up at FlyCo and checks the green light. He checks everything is clear, including ahead of the carrier, and puts his flag down to the deck. The guy operating the catapult fires it, at which point about half a ton of superheated (about 600°) steam is fed to the catapult and off you go. For two-and-a-half seconds it's a vibrating, exhilarating ride with your head forced back against the head rest. Then it's all over, you're free to fly, disconnect the SPD, get the flaps and undercarriage up, trying not to overstress and the nose leg automatically retracts from the 40-inch extension. On occasion it doesn't so you have to divert ashore with it still extended.

"I join up with the other two aircraft, and off we go to play bat and ball in the sky. I'm not paying much attention yet, just going where I'm told – my bit's coming up at the end of the hour. Now back to the carrier. We're over Lyme Bay so they know that if I screw it up I can go to Yeovilton. We join the 'wait' for our turn and then we're cleared to 'slot', which is a run in and break at 270 knots, not the 420/450 knots that we do ashore. We break at ten-second intervals, speed reducing, gear down, full flap – holding that configuration until you land. It's a nice day, you're downwind and there's the carrier. You're aiming for a mile and a quarter abeam, then you start the turn, maintaining 140 knots. Into the straight-way, with the carrier ahead of you, you call 'on sight' looking at the projector landing sight. Hopefully the 'ball' is green and in line with the datum lights for the right approach angle – maintain line-up and airspeed. You've got indicators in the cockpit, the observer's calling the airspeed and there's the audio angle of attack. If you're fast it's beeping fast, if slow it's beeping slow; if you're 'on speed' it's a constant tone – I only heard that once! The LSO is talking to you, 'roger', 'you're low', 'power'...things like that. There is a lot looking after you, not least self-preservation. Holding a steady attitude and a 700-800 feet per minute rate of descent, you're going straight into the deck, no flaring – that's a roller, my first approach to the deck. Following comments by the LSO and my observer, it's round for another one. Not wonderful. Then for a third – this time FlyCo calls 'hook down'. There are four arrestor wires, No.3 is the target for the Phantom providing sufficient clearance over the round-down. The Buccaneers were a bit further back because it was a flat approach aeroplane.

"I hit the deck and catch No.1 wire. A lot of twittering from the LSO, but who gives a s**t? I'm down, so hook up, fold wing, marshallers everywhere, taxi to Fly 1 which was very crowded by the end of the day. Pilots were not responsible for clearances from other aircraft, the marshallers were, manoeuvre slowly, stop, shut down the engines, the aircraft is tied down with chains and out you get. After every arrested landing you get debriefed by the LSO, or his deputy from the squadron. Four colours were used to assess the landing. Blue meant a very good, steady approach, Green – good, Yellow – rather workman-like, and Red (which I got that day) – dangerous, low, with no corrections. It wasn't that dangerous, I walked away! Everyone's there to hear how badly you did; you can imagine how many spectators there were when someone is doing it for the first time.

"Usually a deployment was six months at a time; embarking the aircraft in Lyme Bay. First down to Gibraltar, you could be going round the Med, so Malta would be a popular spot to go to, Toulon, Barcelona, or Transatlantic. It was four days crossing to the Caribbean, exercising with the US Navy a lot. If the ship required a bit of maintenance, the air group disembarked to various naval air stations, flying with host squadrons, whilst the ship had the 'barnacles scraped'. All ship-shape we'd re-embark three weeks later and off we'd go again.

"On one sortie I flew an aircraft (in a standard fit with two drop tanks) which required an engine air test. I climbed to about 40,000 feet to do slam tests on the engine; when completed we had lots of fuel remaining so we did a sight-seeing tour of the Western Isles, then let down to low level. As I was flying up Glen Tay, quite low and fast, there was a big bang – no tele light captions illuminated. I pulled up and did a slow speed handling check on the way back to Leuchars. After landing I could see sailors pointing at the aircraft. An electrical loom had frayed and fired all the electrical release units; so the pylons, drop tanks and dummy missiles had all come off near the Tindrum Hotel! It was a few minutes of fame on the national news that night. Of course I was to blame, until they did the volts check to prove that I hadn't pressed the 'clear wing' button.

"On occasion we would be in company with a US carrier, which if necessary, could be used as a diversion. That's a two-way street and cross-decking, as it is known, was not uncommon. It wasn't done intentionally, but if one deck was fouled you could go and land on the other. Our systems were compatible, the only difference between our Phantoms and theirs was that our 40-inch nose leg extension pointed the jet pipes right down on the deck. Thus, in 'burner that made their deck very hot (on *Ark* we had water-cooled jet-blast deflectors). They had a longer catapult stroke, about 300 feet, off four catapults, so it was a gentler process. Cross-decking was popular – the prize to get was the US Navy leather flight jacket, the more badges the better, especially in bars ashore. What we had going, which they didn't, was a bar. If they stayed overnight they could 'fill their boots' and get a submariner's sweater, something much prized by the USN. Flying with US carriers we did dissimilar air combat training against their A-6s, A-7s and Phantoms. We held joint briefings on either their ship or ours to make sure we all knew what to do, where to operate etc.; it wasn't just a free-for-all. We were controlled from air defence/air direction rooms.

"Generally there were two fleet auxiliaries in company with us, one was the oiler which carried furnace and aviation fuel, and water. *Ark Royal* carried about 6,000 tons of furnace fuel, which they liked to maintain at 70 per cent capacity. This gave the ship about ten days-worth of sailing. She also carried 1,500-1,600 tons of aviation fuel. This may sound a lot, however each aircraft sortie would consume at least eight tons of fuel and we were launching three or four waves per day. That probably equates to 20 hours flying per aircrew per month, but it was all high-pressure stuff.

"There was a designated night team of four or five pilots – these were the ones with grey hair and a twitch. The RN made night flying a big drama. For example you didn't night fly, unless you had flown that day or the previous night. The USN qualified all its pilots at the end of advanced flying training, and night-qualified them at the end of type training. For the latter they had to complete ten day and six night arrested landings. Getting back aboard at night was always off a CCA. Visual cues were very limited – there were about ten lights along the centreline, and three lights, the donkey's plonker, down the back of the ship. You're being talked down, then you see the projector sight and call 'on sight' as normal, the LSO then continues with the talk-down. I never saw a happy person step out of an aeroplane, they'd been particularly unhappy walking out, but coming back in they were nervous and needed a cigarette. Regardless of whether the bar was open or not there would be booze available."

### Another anon pilot

"Of the first six UK-trained crews three remained on 767 Squadron as instructors, and three – four lieutenants and two sub lieutenants (my observer and myself) – joined 892 Squadron. The senior members of the squadron, who had all been in the USA, were taking part in the *Daily Mail* Transatlantic air race at the time. My observer's and my claim to 'fame' regarding the event was flying two of the aircraft from Wisley back to Yeovilton – well somebody had to do the less glamorous stuff.

"The Phantom was an entirely different beast to the Sea Vixen. British aircraft, the Hunter included, were designed, and then they thought,

*Phantom FG.1 XV587 R-005 892 Squadron en route* Ark Royal *to Yeovilton, 15 December 1970.*

'Where shall we put the crew?' – particularly the Vixen with the observer stuck in his coal hole. My shoulders were fairly broad, touching the canopy rails in the Hunter GA.11 – the Sea Vixen wasn't much wider. The F-4 was built for a 6'5" Texan. The seat was like a big armchair with loads of space, all the knobs and switches were typically American – big. The gear handle was a large lever with a large knob on the end. It flashed red at you when the gear was up below a certain speed and height, or was in transit, the hook lever likewise. There was a centralised warning panel on the right-hand side which had every warning in one place; it was repeated in the rear cockpit. In addition there were two radio panels, one in the front and one in the rear; you could give/take control of either. The instrument panel seemed quite a bit further away from you compared with the Sea Vixen. In the Vixen you sort of snuggled down in the office, night flying with subdued red lights all around you, quite cosy. I was initially quite disorientated in the Phantom because the instruments were so far away, but you soon got used to it. All the knobs and switches were easily reached and logically placed.

"The only downside was the engine response. Unlike the Vixen's Avons, which were very fast to respond, the F-4 engines were twin spool and much less responsive, particularly with reheat selection. In the early days they took about 2½ seconds to select from minimum to maximum reheat. You first had to select min reheat to ensure it lit, then gradually accelerate to maximum. The upside was that they were much more fuel efficient. I remember one of my flying instructors pointing out two black trails, about 30 miles away, coming towards us and saying, 'they're Phantoms, just you watch'. They were, American ones with very dirty J-79 engines, whereas ours were clean(ish).

"For the first year or two we had no simulator – nor did we use 'two stickers', so your first solo was the real deal. The navy took the pragmatic view that if you could deck land, you could certainly fly another aircraft type. The acceleration down the runway was phenomenal, and there was automatic flap retraction at 235 knots. The thing on first solos was to try and beat this auto flap retraction – I don't know anybody who did. Your first reheat climb was also an eye opener, you really had to try to keep it subsonic by keeping the nose up. We initially amused ourselves by calling Eastern Radar, immediately after take-off, to request a climb to flight level 350 – just over a minute later call 'level' – stunned silence, except for: 'Say again'. Eventually they got used to us with this newfound ability to climb.

"I took part in deck trials aboard USS *Saratoga*. Having flown an aircraft with three tanks on from Yeovilton to Sigonella, in Sicily, we had to dump 500 lbs of fuel to get below landing weight. While the transit was uneventful, the approach was anything but. The weather was appalling, rain with cloud tops around 25,000 feet and a 400-foot base. The Italian controller tried to steer us into Mount Etna! We ignored him and continued our own approach into the gloom using our radar combined with the Tacan to creep in on the runway heading. We had a lightning strike as we descended – just to keep us on our toes.

"We were flown onto the ship, along with loads of bags of mail, in a C-1 Trader which seated about ten passengers facing backwards. By comparison our COD Gannet seated two passengers, one facing backwards, and not very many bags of

*USS* Saratoga *and 892 Squadron cross-decking 17 October 1969.*

mail. *Saratoga's* landing area wasn't much longer than British carriers, but the parking area was huge. On ours you could get a few aircraft into Fly 1, but often you would come out of the wires, get turned right through 150°, and park pointing backwards by the island in Fly 2. This had the added 'advantage' of you being able to see the next 'large lump of metal' hurtling towards you, and crashing to a halt 40 feet or so away – occasionally not if the pilot missed the wires.

"Early on I had a double-engine flame-out. Because of the need to go into min reheat, to make sure they lit, you got used to looking at the engine gauges like a hawk. On this occasion I selected min reheat, and then after a delay, started to open the throttles with the result that both turbine gas temperatures started to go off the clock. I had no option but to shut down both engines, and it all went quiet (the jet didn't glide too well). Unlike most aircraft the Phantom didn't have a battery. Instead it had a RAT to generate electrical power so I deployed it. It took about 30 seconds to wind up. With the generators offline the intercom failed. The first thing I heard from my observer as the RAT spun up was, 'Hey, the radar's gone offline'; I told him we had a slightly bigger problem than that. Luckily, we were at height. I tried to relight the engines twice, each time with the same overtemp – eventually one lit at about 15,000 feet. After landing at Yeovilton the starboard engine jet pipe was completely white where all the turbine blades had melted. The other one was grey-ish/white where only half of them had. This was what had kept us airborne for 80 miles.

"It was a terrific aircraft to fly. It was built for deck landing, stable on approach, with a big wide track undercarriage which could take a real beating. It would climb like a rocket – down to 5,000 lbs of fuel – you definitely had more power than weight. A real thrill to see the ship or runway getting smaller and smaller in your rear-view mirrors as you passed 30,000 feet still climbing."

## Paul Chaplin – pilot

"When I went to the Phantom I was an experienced second tourist. We had a lot of RAF crews on loan. Mostly volunteers, they were keen to give it a go and find out what all the fuss about deck flying was about. They all integrated superbly proving to be most adept at the job, handling the Fishheads' banter in the way it deserved. They seemed to enjoy their time with us. As they couldn't be expected to get involved in night deck operations until experienced, we navy boys went straight into the night team for the whole of the cruise. I did back to back night flying on Phantoms, and after the 892 Squadron cruise I went straight to a US Navy carrier squadron, so I did four consecutive years as night crew.

"Your mind is much more focussed at night. Nobody really looked forward to it, but it was very satisfying to say you'd done it. But to me going cold from briefing, up to the deck, sitting in an aeroplane, and taking off day or night, especially if you were getting a bit rusty and hadn't flown for a while – that was almost more thought inducing. There are many areas that can go wrong, but only one of them is you pulling the stick back at the right time. The rest – the ship and aircraft serviceability, the deck handling, the catapult, the steam pressure, the waves – were all amplified at night. If there's no moon you can't see a thing. Going off into the black, you know that at the end of the shot you're only just above the sea. You'd gone for a briefing, you'd probably have had a meal at the last minute, then up to the windy flight deck. When you come into land you've been in the flying atmosphere for an hour and a half, you're all switched on and up to speed, you're there. Whereas on the catapult launch, all of a sudden you're woken up by this big kick in the back. To me the night launch was probably more thought provoking than the night landing – the landing was more down to me than the launch.

"Going to the US Navy was great. It was nice to be offered it, and you think you must be OK to be a representative. We almost always had our training crews on their training squadron VF-121, because in the mid to late '60s the navy did our conversions with the US. It was only after Vietnam that they sent an RN exchange guy to a carrier, if it was wanted – we needed to keep people flying. A contemporary of mine, Paul Bennett, did the first front-line exchange for many years, on the USS *Kittyhawk* – I replaced him after his tour. Obviously it was very exciting going from Scotland to California. The job was very similar, apart from a few different calls in the circuit. The way we operated the 'plane was exactly the same, albeit with different engines, different avionics – really it was being one Brit amongst 4,000 US crew, and the challenge was holding your corner in a proper and humorous way. Our US counterparts were ultra-professional, with a similar outlook on life, and their population held them in high esteem.

"I'd flown off the *Nimitz* the previous year. We'd seen it being completed alongside us when we were in Norfolk, Virginia with the *Ark Royal* – it was huge. A few months later it was on its first shakedown cruise, coming down the North Sea with a skeleton USN and dockyard crew. They invited us to send four aeroplanes to come aboard for five days, and I was lucky enough to go. But later, when on USN exchange duty, after I'd finished my three months 'Americanisation' onto their Phantoms, I was sent to VF-191 attached to the USS *Coral Sea*. It was nice to be a founder member of the squadron. The ship was about the same weight as the *Ark Royal*, about the same age, and just as knackered. But from the piloting point of view, although the big American carriers had much bigger flight decks, it was much the same whether you were landing on the *Nimitz* or the *Hermes* – you were still aiming for the same degree of accuracy."

### John Dixon

"It is sometime in 1970.

"'Y'know, if this carries on we'll be up here all night!'– this to my back seat. We were tooling around holding over *Ark*, at a conserving speed, while the flight deck 'badgers' tried to get the arresting gear to reset – and by the sound of things from FlyCo without too much success.

"We were the last aircraft to recover, the other three F-4s all safely aboard. Not that it had been a flawless recovery by any means. We had launched as a flight of four, I was the number four, for a night Lepus/two-inch RP event on the splash target. As the event was the last of a busy day's flying programme, ours were the only aircraft airborne. Night exercises on the splash target were occasionally programmed this way, as it gave the opportunity for the ship's company to come out onto the flight deck and watch the fun.

"On deck it was quite warm. Our operating area for the previous couple of days had been somewhere mid-way between Sardinia and Italy, in the Tyrrhenian Sea. Naples Airport, which also had a US military presence, was our diversion airfield. At 'charlie' time the visual recovery started off okay, but after the second aircraft landed the number three and ourselves were waived off. Apparently, there was a problem with the arresting gear not resetting.

"After holding in the 'wait' for about six or seven minutes, we were cleared to recommence recovery. Ahead of me number three touched down okay, but before I had completed my finals turn, I was waived off. And hold. The arresting gear had gone on walkabout once again. So there we were, tooling around in the 'wait' getting ever closer to Bingo fuel – when we would have to head on in to the beach.

"'This is not the first time this has occured.' 'What do you mean?' 'Well', I recalled, 'I remember a few weeks back, when I was squadron duty boy in FlyCo for the recovery, the same thing happened.' We were non-diversion flying that day, which meant we always arrived back at the ship with extra fuel, even if we had to dump some to get down to landing weight. But it did add a lot of pressure to wings, especially if the wind over the deck was light, as it was this day. I could see that wings, Derek Monsell, was getting a little edgy with the on/off situation with the arresting gear. Under these sort of worrying situations Derek would get a little flustered, relapsing into his own particular vernacular remembering when you couldn't dump fuel but would have to burn it off. 'Okay guys' this over the radio from wings no less, trying to reassure those airborne on that occasion. 'Problem fixed. You can start burning off now.' Another aircraft landed on, and yet again a problem with the gear. 'Okay guys, conserve!' This went on a couple of times, 'conserve', 'burn off', 'conserve' and I could see that wings had lost the picture. He called up to Nick Kerr, the squadron boss, circling overhead and said, 'What's your situation, Nick?' An obviously very pissed off Nick dryly answered, 'Well to tell you the truth I'm conserving on one, and burning off on the other!'

"So here we were, 'a few weeks later', and as another five minutes or so had gone by with no sign of a clear deck becoming available any time soon, we decided that although there was still a couple of hundred pounds of fuel or so in the bank before Bingo state, it was best if we set off for the beach. On the way to Naples we couldn't raise them on the radio on any of the usual frequencies. As we got closer to where I thought the airfield should be, I couldn't see any runway lights either. This was odd I thought, as we could plainly see the lights of the city to the

*Coming home to 'mother'. (Richard Dickinson)*

east of the airfield. Added to that Naples was also an international airport, albeit traffic was light, so what was going on? I could see what I thought were terminal and apron lights, but the rest of the airfield was in darkness. It was about 22:45; if civilian flights weren't that frequent at night, perhaps they conserved power by switching off all the lights? But surely the tower would be manned?

"After a few more calls on the radio a voice answered. 'Ah! about time' I thought, but then I realised it was not an air traffic voice. He seemed very unsure of himself, and there was no procedure in the way he talked. 'Hello', he said, 'we're closed.' 'What d'you mean closed?' 'We're closed at night, but open during the day for VFR (visual flight rules) traffic.' 'So why closed at night? I'm a navy aircraft diverting to you short of fuel, and I need to land!' 'Sorry. We've been closed at night for a couple of weeks now. We're replacing all the runway lights, approach lights, VASIs (visual approach slope indicators), everything.' 'What's the situation on the runway then? Contractor's vehicles, equipment, rubbish, that sort of thing?' 'Well the runway itself is clear. We haven't started on that yet but you can't land. There are no lights. All the power is off.' 'Don't you worry about that. We've brought our own light, and we *are* going to land. So can you please get out to the runway, make sure it's clear and stand by for a military jet to land.'

"It was a dark night. In fact very dark with no moon at all. The hazy, goldfish-bowl type conditions out at sea with no horizon had slowed our exercise on the splash down such that I still had one Lepus flare left. We quickly talked over the plan, made switches and ran in over the Bay of Naples at 500 feet, pulled up in a programmed 'loft' manoeuvre, turned downwind, landed off the flare on the single runway and taxied into what was the US military side of the airport. On shutting down a USAF sergeant came out to meet us, and showed us to transit accommodation to get our heads down for a few hours.

"All in all, the diversion seemed pretty run of the mill. No excitement, no drama, apart from being short of fuel, and no night flying nosh. The splash exercise was far more exacting. As to use of the Lepus, I'm sure with the available light from the aprons and nearby city we could have landed without it, but it was reassuring in making sure that the runway was truly clear. Back on board *Ark* next day there were profuse apologies and red faces in ops, for nominating a diversion field that had been NOTAM'd as closed at night. As it happened no-one else had diverted ashore during the previous couple of nights."

### Tim Gedge – pilot

"I joined 892 as the QFI in 1969. The problem for the Phantom on *Ark Royal* was that the limitations for operating it were pretty tight in terms of deck movement. The original intention was to have both *Ark Royal* and *Eagle* modified for the Phantom. In terms of size there wasn't much in it, and although there were differences in equipment, there wouldn't have been any in terms of deck operation. We spent a lot of money putting Rolls-Royce Spey engines, and Ferranti radar in the Phantom, plus various other changes. Despite the extra cost, they didn't make it a better aeroplane. Although most of that was unnecessary, the argument was that as we had a slotted tailplane, we would be able to fly the aircraft slower for landing aboard smaller UK carriers. For launching we had almost a double nosewheel leg extension. We would have been better operating the American version which would have been about one-fifth of the cost off-the-shelf. This was brought home to me in 1975 when the USS *Independence* successfully cross-operated their F-4s aboard *Ark Royal*.

"It was well suited to both the air-to-air and air-to-ground roles. However one of the problems was that we were limited to 42,000 feet, considerably lower than the Vixen. Unless you were supersonic it didn't handle very well at altitude, the Vixen had a better high-altitude turning performance but couldn't go as fast. The only aircraft which could out-turn a Sea Vixen at altitude was a Vulcan. The Phantom could physically fly higher, but there was a danger of over-temping the engines. It was a combination of things which made it difficult to achieve the primary role

*The US Navy's revenge, 892 Squadron at NAS Oceana, August 1978. (Bob Crane)*

of intercepting high-flying Backfires and Blinders.

"My stand-out memory was trying to keep the squadron in flying practice, particularly at night. Flying an aircraft to the deck by night is about ten times more difficult than by day. It needed a lot more practice, people needed to be in-practice to do it confidently – to know what they were doing. One of the limitations was deck movement, especially in pitch. If it exceeded 1½° you were getting to the limit of what was possible, +/-1¾° was an absolute limit. The US Navy worked to the same sort of limits, although its bigger carriers could endure higher sea states and still be within those limits. If you consider the deck movement of the carriers we had in the Falklands, we were operating in +/- 4 or 5°, a different order of magnitude. Had there been a conventional carrier down there, such as *Ark Royal*, we would have been out of limits a lot of the time. The Americans concluded that even *Nimitz*-size ships would often have been out of limits. Thankfully, the Sea Harrier was not limited in deck movement very much at all!

"It's pretty logical if you're coming down a 3° glidepath, and the ship pitches up 3° you'll fly into the aft end. What you can't do in a conventional aircraft is time your approach to the ship to counter the deck movement. In a Harrier you could stop over the deck, and land in the quiescent period when the ship wasn't pitching. Approaching in a conventional aircraft, if you're on that 3° glidepath and are a bit low, so it reduces to 2°, plus any other effects – that's where the 1¾° limitation comes in. You could increase the glideslope to 4° but the aircraft's undercarriage then becomes a limiting factor."

## Doug Macdonald – observer

"I opened up the training lines of 767 at the end of 1968; we had the RAF as our guests as well. I qualified within about two weeks but we had the most tremendous job to do. The aeroplanes were working and were just dying to be flown, but we were short of maintenance men. My senior pilot, who was later my CO, was Nick Kerr with whom I was great friends latterly.

"The Phantom and Sea Vixen were 'chalk and cheese'. My first flight, sitting in the back, seeing everything that was going on as we thundered off Runway 27 at Yeovilton was quite extraordinary; I've never forgotten it. The weapons system was more complex than the Mk. 2 Sea Vixen, although I'm not convinced it was any better. I thought the AI 18R/Red Top combination was a very good system.

"We rapidly found out that because it had quite a long range, you had to identify something before you fired Sparrow – it was not liked. I know this to my cost; whilst on 892 Squadron my pilot and I managed to damage a US Navy A-3 Skywarrior on the Atlantic Fleet weapons range. We were doing a weapons exercise – it was more or less a free-for-all. The A-3 was launching BQM target drones (he had one under each wing). He launched them into the middle of the range then, instead of quickly getting out of there, he hung around for a bit. The American controller guided us on to this target, and cleared us to fire. As the visibility was not great,

*XT863 of 767 Squadron starts its display at Abingdon, 18 September 1971. (Adrian Balch)*

we certainly had not identified the target. We fired the Sparrow from about four-and-a-half miles astern of the target, and it flew right through the A-3's starboard engine! His Mayday stopped everything and the A-3 limped home.

"We were sent for court martial. I was woken up at two o'clock the next morning; the news had got back to the UK, and an admiral's staff officer told them to put us under close arrest. Looking slightly perturbed, the CO told us we were not allowed to leave our cabins. It was cleared up quite quickly because the Americans realised that the controlling authority was at fault. We didn't hear much more about it, but I had a nervous 24 hours.

"I then went back to 767 as an AWI for another six months to the summer of 1970, then off to 892. We went to the Med several times, but mainly it was the North and West Atlantic. Good flying, but not a lot of it because we were always on the move. Lots of passage time, which was always a bit of a bore. But during 1972's Exercise Northern Express, I was shadowing some amazing Russian aeroplanes. We got Bears and Badgers which were commonplace, but I was fortunate to intercept three Bisons; the lead was a tanker. We didn't know whether they were Russian naval aircraft or Russian air force, and where the other two were off to we never did discover.

"At the end of Northern Express I had to dash home to pick up my wife and children to catch an aeroplane to San Diego. I did two years and four months with the US Navy's VF-121 at Miramar. The Vietnam War was still on and I ended up as the operations officer, which was the No.3 job on the squadron. I did carrier qualifications about four times. They knew how to operate their carriers; it was non-stop and noisy. I spent a couple of nights aboard one of the carriers and was billeted beneath one of the catapults; as they operated around the clock you didn't get much sleep.

"The Miramar squadron had 38 aircraft, 36 F-4Js and two F-4Bs; we had 120 students at any one time, with about 65 to 70 instructors. Their F-4s had the same weapons systems as ours. We concentrated mainly on air-to-air, and the Top Gun squadron was round the corner – we did a lot of work with them. I had as much flying as I wanted – I found it very difficult to take any leave.

"I came back to the UK in February '75 to PTF at Leuchars; there were some great guys there. Although by this time, I had more than a thousand hours in the F-4s, but they taught me how to fly again! I re-joined 892 in August; just before the next Northern Express. My CO was Hugh Drake, super guy. 'Sharkey' Ward was senior pilot, and I was the senior observer – but I was senior to him so he couldn't boss me around. I did 18 months of that, in and out of Leuchars, on and off *Ark Royal*. I left in early '77 – that was the end of my fast jet time."

### Reg Maitland – engine technician

"I joined the engine bay at Yeovilton in January 1971, working shifts because the

*Reg Maitland.*

Phantom's Spey 203 was not very well. After 18 months I was drafted to Leuchars, by which time the engine was getting better with Rolls-Royce modifications. After about two years I joined the PTF, and a year later 892 Squadron on *Ark Royal*. By then the engine was performing very satisfactorily.

"For ground runs at Leuchars the Phantom was pushed back onto the running site then two chocks, each of about three feet in height (Alameda chocks), were positioned one in front of each mainwheel. If during the ground run you noticed that the fuel in the main centreline tanks was getting low, you could select fuel transfer from the wing or overload tanks.

When the main tanks were full the float switches would operate and switch off fuel transfer, but if the fuel transfer was still selected then once the level of fuel dropped the float switches reactivated fuel transfer. The reason I mention this is because of the difference between the two Phantom ground running sites.

"At Yeovilton the Phantom test bed was on a ramp, so the back end of the aircraft was higher than the front, and there were two doors at the back which were closed in front of the stabiliser. After 892 Squadron left there for the last time to go on board *Ark Royal*, there was one Phantom left behind in NASU with both engines removed. When the aircraft was rebuilt it required ground running with reheat. As it was rear uppermost, and the float switches in the main tanks were situated at the aft end of the tanks, the fuel vent apertures were at the front of the tanks. When an inexperienced operator noticed his fuel level was getting low he selected fuel transfer. This was fine except the rising fuel level reached the fuel vents before the float switches operated. You could not see the back of the aircraft because the doors were closed. The fuel vent nozzle was situated just above and between the two engines – the aircraft was venting fuel which nobody could see. The operator selected reheat – there was an almighty 'whoosh' and the back of the aircraft was engulfed in flames. There was nothing in the book about not selecting fuel transfer while tethered on the test bed!

"A pilot at Leuchars reported no acceleration on the port engine, caused by the CASC (constant acceleration and speed control) unit malfunctioning. You could change this unit in-situ on the starboard engine, but not the port one. So we changed the port engine, did the ground run, and handed the aircraft over to the aircrew. Another pilot taxied out to the end of the runway and immediately returned to the line saying port engine acceleration was good, starboard engine acceleration rubbish. We changed the starboard engine CASC, and everyone was happy. The original pilot turned up next day and one of his mates had written on his port glove *left*, and on the starboard glove *right*.

"In 1977 *Ark Royal* was returning to Devonport for a six-month mini refit. Just off Land's End the Phantoms were being readied for launch back to Leuchars. I was asked to be on hand so I was on the 'goofers' deck watching the flight deck activities. All 12 of the Phantoms were ranged on deck, and the launches continued using both catapults. I noticed one of them, on the starboard rear of the *Ark*, was not moving. A naval airman came and told me I was needed.

"I borrowed an aircraft handlers' headset and spoke to the pilot. He said he couldn't start his starboard engine, although the RPM on attempted start was sufficient. When we were ashore we used AVTUR (standard military jet fuel), but when we were on board *Ark Royal* we used AVCAT (this had additives to make it less volatile to reduce the fire risk at sea). I suspected partially blocked burners – a known fault. The remedy was pumping a substance called LIX into the fuel-burner system, letting it soak for four hours then restarting. The whole procedure took about five hours, time we didn't have as we were due to dock immediately after we finished launching. I had the starboard engine intake blank refitted, had the handlers turn the aircraft into wind and removed the blank, telling the pilot to press his relight button when it reached 50 per cent RPM. There was a great 'whoosh', a pile of black smoke came out of the jet pipe and the engine settled down. The pilot took the aircraft on to the catapult, did all his checks, and flew it off to Leuchars."

### Paul Waterhouse – observer

"I came back to Yeovilton in 1968 to join 700P Squadron the Phantom IFTU

*XT859 from 700P Squadron Yeovilton over Pembrokeshire in 1968. (Steve Bond collection)*

(intensive flying trials unit). The UK Phantom –it was a good aeroplane ruined! The powers that be insisted on British engines, so that meant a lot of modification – it also affected the size of the air intakes. Then, would you believe it, because our runways were relatively short, compared with the ones in the States which were always 12,000 feet long, they had to put bigger and fatter tyres on to cope with the relatively short and wet runways in the UK. These bigger tyres meant that the undercarriage doors bulged out underneath the wing. The combination of the bigger intakes and the bulges under the wing slowed the aircraft down somewhat. In the American Phantom we could easily do Mach 2.5 – you might have made Mach 2.3 in a British one. There were problems with the Spey engine which were eventually sorted out – however it was a fine engine. The avionics were the same as the American Phantom, although after I'd left they fitted more sophisticated passive radar detection kit.

"I then became a founder member of 892 Squadron, and we did flight deck trials. The boss of 892 (an ETPS graduate), did all the F-4K trials in St. Louis; I went with him to *Ark Royal* to do the initial deck trials. Some earlier trials had been done on *Eagle* by Boscombe Down test pilots.

"After finding myself back on the Sea Vixen (before 899 Squadron was disbanded), I returned to the Phantom again in 1972. They'd just started to set up a small unit at Leuchars, the PTF, at first known as the post-operational conversion unit, but the title 'POCU' was not considered a good idea. I had a quick refresher on the Phantom, then straight up to Leuchars for, would you believe – an RAF appointment. Politically it had to be an RAF unit, but the only RAF person on the unit was the CO, Matt Walker, who just happened to be an ex-naval lieutenant commander and Sea Vixen driver. The aircraft were F-4Ks, which the navy had handed over to the RAF. They kindly allowed us to put a design on the tail – which was very much non-RAF.

"I finished on PTF in early '74, and my final flying appointment was with the NFSF at Yeovilton. That was a one-off in the sense that I was an observer, but NFSF was basically for pilots. It converted people back onto fixed wing who'd gone from say, Vixens to helicopters, or had gone to sea. I did a bit of snooping around of any observers, but the reality at that time was just 892 Squadron. That lasted for six months after which I left the navy."

## Richard Moody – pilot

"I took up my duties with the US Navy at Miramar on VF-121. Fortunately I was in the right place at the right time when the Navy Fighter Weapons School – Top Gun – was formed. I was asked to join the team of instructors, for which I qualified on the A-4E Skyhawk. Top Gun took top quality pilots from their squadrons and trained them to the highest level of air combat manoeuvring (ACM). The initial kill ratios in the early days of the war against North Vietnamese pilots, flying MiG-17s and 21s, were poor. Top Gun was designed to improve greatly the success rate by training pilots who went back to their squadrons to train the others.

"In ACM training it's important to 'fight' against aircraft with dissimilar performances, and the A-4E, known as the Mongoose, was the ideal aircraft to train against since its performance was similar to that of the MiGs. In addition the F-4 did not perform well fighting in the horizontal, which the MiGs did, and so a method of fighting in the vertical – known as energy manoeuvrability – was developed. The power of the F-4's engines would easily allow the F-4 pilot to get above his opponent and perform slashing downward attacks before screaming skywards again. I flew many hours as the 'aggressor' pilot.

"One of my fellow aviators there was 'Goose' (his call sign). Along with 'Viper' and 'Cougar', his was one of only three original call signs used in the film. He was from Wisconsin and subsequently flew with me for a year on board *Ark Royal*. When it was time to leave Top Gun we were appointed to 892 Squadron, and I was made senior pilot. The majority of our operations were in the Mediterranean, and in NATO shows of strength off northern Scandinavia. A lot of time was spent 'cross-decking'; I would take a flight of four Phantoms on board a USN carrier for two weeks. We also spent time flying with the German navy's F-104s, and the French navy's F-8 Crusaders. During my time operating the Phantom off *Ark Royal*, I carried out a further 214 day deck landings and 50 at night. This gave me final figures of 483 day deck landings, and 144 at night, a total of 627 deck landings in all – flying the Gannet, Sea Vixen and Phantom off various aircraft carriers. And I lived to tell the tale!"

## Murdo Macleod – pilot

"Phantom OCU at Coningsby for a brief 39 hours before joining PTF for a spirited month's flying to include everything the Phantom ever did (41 hours), and thereafter release to the Fleet on 892 Squadron. Then on 27 November 1978, accompanied by Lt Dennis McCallum in XT870/R-012, I flew the last ever catapult shot from an RN carrier – *Ark Royal*."

*With the passing of 892 Squadron, together with 809 Squadron Buccaneers and 849 Squadron Gannets, fixed-wing carrier operations in the Fleet Air Arm came to an end. Ark Royal returned to Devonport for the last time on 4 December 1978, and decommissioned on 14 February 1979 – leaving no*

*decks for her aircraft. Just over a year later, in July 1980, fixed-wing op-
erations restarted but this time with a very different aircraft – the Sea
Harrier – and with much smaller ships.*

*Murdo Macleod and Dennis McCallum make the final catapult launch from Ark Royal. (Murdo Macleod)*

CHAPTER TEN

# BAE SEA HARRIER

*Following the demise of the 'large carrier' fleet, the navy had no air-defence capability, until the advent of a new fleet of three small carriers (initially referred to as through deck cruisers), from 1980. However, the style and size of these carriers meant that conventional fixed-wing aircraft were not an option. The solution was the Sea Harrier, an extensive adaptation of the RAF's Harrier, which served from 1980 until its premature retirement*

*Sea Harrier FA.2 ZD613 L-002 801 Squadron Illustrious North Sea air refuelling area waiting to tank from a VC10, 15 July 1999. (Chris Lofting)*

*in 2006. It proved to be a formidable aircraft, and was a major asset in the Falkland and Bosnian campaigns.*

*Operating units: 700A, 800, 801, 809, 899 Squadrons, Joint Force Harrier, Sea Harrier OEU (Operational Evaluation Unit), embarked on Ark Royal, Hermes, Illustrious, Invincible, trials on Eagle.*

## Bill Covington – pilot

"Despite the prophesies of many so-called experts the Sea Harrier delivered fighter air superiority during the Falklands War. This small, single-pilot, single-engine, single-radio, subsonic aircraft became iconic, defeating a numerically superior land-based air force.

"The core of naval pilots that made up the early Sea Harrier squadrons were highly experienced, coming from Sea Vixens, Phantoms and Buccaneers. Once they overcame learning to fly this V/STOL aircraft, they were very well placed to understand its capabilities, and importantly, its weaknesses – so they knew how to exploit its war-winning capabilities. However its accident rate was

*Bill Covington.*

disappointing; in most years the Sea Harrier force lost an aircraft, and occasionally the pilot. I believe it was in part the challenge of the Harrier, its legacy from the Falklands with its hard-won focus on operational effectiveness, in part the demanding challenges of the Cold War, and partly the never-ending requirement to prove the value of the Sea Harrier, when so many still seemed to find it difficult to recognise its effectiveness.

"So-called 'viffing' (vectoring thrust in forward flight) for the Sea Harrier was almost a myth. The real benefit of V/STOL was that the jet could deploy, from ship or land, to places where conventional aircraft couldn't go. Without that we would not have gone to the Falklands, it was a fantastic capability. There were moments in the air when you could use 'viff'. Modern air combat doesn't really align with stopping in the air – you lose your kinetic energy. Jet engines suffer with altitude, so although the Harrier can hover at sea/ground level, it is limited to low altitude and low fuel weight. At 10,000 feet for example its hover ability is zero, and at 40,000 feet all performance was poor. But 'viff' was useful on occasions, especially if you'd got yourself into a dogfight and you used the nozzles effectively. You could improve your turn rate and ability to pitch through the vertical, or slow down to get the enemy to fly out in front of you. But it didn't happen as in the movies, where they show aircraft going one way, and then instantly the other way. Modern fighters don't want to dogfight, they want to kill the opposition from long range. There may be occasions in the fog of war where you suddenly find yourself in close proximity to an enemy aircraft, and where the nozzles come in useful. However they are not a capability driver.

"By the late 1980s the FRS.1 was limited as a fighter and needed updating. The Sea Harrier FA.2, introduced in 1994, was a much more complex aircraft with a complete update of the avionic and weapon suite. The pilot-led development of the HOTAS (hands on throttle and stick) system and cockpit man-machine interface, pioneered particularly by Cdr Simon Hargreaves (the lead BAE test pilot), centred on the AMRAAM (advanced medium range air-to-air missile) and Sidewinder producing a hugely capable air-defence fighter. The Ferranti Pulse Doppler radar was a major step forward, and most people had no comprehension of just how capable it was. Although the FA.2 retained its fairly basic nav system, constant improvement meant it still allowed easy shipborne alignments of ever-more complex systems, giving the ability to take off in well under five minutes when necessary.

"The term 'dogfighter' implies lots of 'turning and burning', whereas if you title the FA.2 a 'tactical fighter' it had huge capabilities. So much so that when first deployed in *Illustrious* for operations over Bosnia (Operation Grapple), we had difficulty impressing on the JFACC (joint force air component commander) how capable 801 Squadron was. Finally, after showing videos of its radar picture, and the situational awareness it generated, the American JFACC general declared to his staff, 'Gentlemen, if a Sea Harrier says it can see a target believe it. It is a little aircraft with a 'big dick' radar.'

"For the newer pilots, the multi-role aspects of the fighter, reconnaissance, strike aircraft were very challenging. It was a small-winged fast jet with complicated take-off and landing procedures. But once the aircraft was mastered it had many advantages. It was the first UK aircraft with digital avionics. Its head-up display (HUD), weapon and navigation systems were straightforward to work, designed to operate in the carrier environment, especially around the Sidewinder AIM 9L. Operating off the ski jump, and stopping before landing, made take-off and landing much more straightforward than when using catapults and arrestor wires. Although it did not carry huge fuel loads its fuel burn rate was low and predictable; long-range fuel calculations were easy to keep up to date. Fuel requirements for recovery were ridiculously low by jet standards, and the ability to operate in poor weather and rough seas was impressive. Performance at high level was poor, at intermediate levels OK, but at low level it was excellent. The aircraft did not spin and stalled benignly. In sum, while it did not excel in many areas of combat it was surprisingly competent in most, and with practice the pilot could confidently extract every ounce of performance out of it."

### John Keenan – artificer

"The first time I saw a Harrier was on the *Ark*. We all thought it was wonderful, but very tricky to fly. Everybody in the squadron, down to the lowest rating, knew it wasn't a suitable aircraft for the FAA; then we are talking about the generation which had the Scimitars, Vixens, Buccaneers and Phantoms. When we saw the Harrier with John Farley landing it on and taking off, we thought, 'Yes, very nice, we hope the crabs enjoy it, but it's not for us.'

"I was drafted to Yeovilton in 1978 where I was to set up the Pegasus engine bay in preparation for the Sea Harrier. Lt Cdr 'Sharkey' Ward was the CO of the Sea Harrier IFTU 700A Squadron. When our first Sea Harrier was delivered he took it up to about 25,000 feet, which was quite high for it, and when he pitched up the engine pop-surged – which didn't impress him very much. It also flamed out, but he managed to re-light it. He wouldn't accept the aircraft because the engine pop-surged at high Alpha (angle of attack). The engine was removed so that I could borescope it – there was no damage. Sharkey contacted John Farley at Dunsfold to explain what had happened. He was told that it was an unfortunate side effect in the Sea Harrier, with its large keel area, that at high Alpha, with even a little rudder deflection the Pegasus will probably pop-surge – Sharkey was livid. The problem having been raised at high political and service levels, was eventually solved. In the meantime we had no option but to continue accepting aircraft deliveries.

"Lt Cdr Dick Goodenough, who had previously been a chief on 801 Squadron Buccaneers on *Hermes* with me, ran the Sea Harrier Special Maintenance Party at BAe Kingston and Dunsfold. He 'phoned me one day to tell me I was coming onto 'his' squadron, 801; he was to be the AEO. I joined the squadron in January 1981, although at that time we had no aircraft; the great majority of the engineers had no fixed-wing experience. We were bright-eyed and bushy-tailed when we received our six aircraft, destined for *Invincible* (which only had space for that number).

*Invincible's hangar deck.*

Sharkey was the CO and along with Dick we embarked shortly after we had formed. For several years, ratings' training had concentrated solely on helicopters, so we had to stop flying for a day to instruct them on fixed-wing procedures. The lads were all keen as mustard, but the manuals were rubbish and had to be re-written completely; as was the air mechanics' training syllabus. We had time in the Mediterranean, working up and trying to iron out various problems. Though the hangar was used for various sports activities we needed every square inch of it for aircraft maintenance so they weren't happy with being told to 'b****r off'!

"The squadron having settled in well, I returned home on Easter leave. I was at home on 1 April 1982 when the 'phone rang – I was told that I had to report back aboard because Argentina had invaded the Falkland Islands. Thinking it was a joke ('April Fools' Day') I told the chief to 'do one' and put the 'phone down. He rang again – I got the message! Having been stood down for Easter, the squadron quickly fired up and got all the aircraft ready for embarkation ASAP.

"On 4 April with several others we piled into a Wessex 5 for transit to our ship. *Invincible* was a hive of activity with the loading of stores from queues of lorries. Just after we left 'Pompey' the ship's reverse coupling gearbox blew up. Ordinarily it would have had to enter dry dock to be fixed, but the stokers decided they could fix it in situ; in the meantime we would be driven by only one propeller. We managed to do some flying as part of our work-up to a war footing and the Sea Harriers fired Sidewinders at Lepus flares. Sharkey flew a sortie with some two-inch rocket pods, legacy weapons from the earlier fixed-wing era, which had not been cleared on the 'SHAR' (Sea Harrier). Afterwards he said that we shouldn't use these weapons because if you ripple-fired them the engine would flame out, due to its large intakes ingesting the gases.

"One of the early changes we made to the aircraft was to paint the undersides grey. They had originally been white, with the top grey, but when the aircraft rolled and the sun caught the white, it produced a 'twinkle' effect which wasn't tactically sound. Once the reverse coupling gearbox had been fixed the ship transited at high speed, and we continued the work-up with almost constant flying. However, when we crossed the equator all the inertial navigation systems went u/s because they had been set up for the northern hemisphere. Ian White, the chief 'greeny' (avionics) arranged for the requisite programming equipment to be parachuted to us – retrieved by Sea King. In the meantime the aircraft had to rely solely on the ship's

TACAN for navigation. The Sea Harrier's radar was a fairly basic system. Pick-up ranges were between six and 12 miles, but the 'pinkies' (radar techs) managed to 'tweak' them to achieve 20-25 miles on a fighter-sized target.

"With aircraft sitting permanently on deck, on Alert 5, the inertial systems began to fail as a result of the high humidity in the South Atlantic. Ian White obtained some cling film from the galley to protect the control panel – this worked a treat! Although the Sea Harrier had a probe it couldn't air-to-air refuel because there were no tankers; the aircraft couldn't carry the 'buddy' pod because of weight consider-ations (it had very limited fuel to give away anyway). Thus it only had a 150-mile radius of action, including a 30-minute loiter time – an enormous disadvantage.

"When we arrived at Ascension Island we loaded weapons and other equipment; this included the more advanced 9L seeker head for our Sidewinders, which had originally been fitted with the 9G head (all the 'kills' during the war were obtained with the 9Ls). An Argentinian 707 had been monitoring the Task Force; we want-ed to shoot it down but weren't allowed to because of the on-going US diplomatic process trying to end the crisis. We were on a war footing, and were quite prepared to do whatever was necessary to avoid the 'Argies' gaining intelligence. It was frustrating to be restrained because of the diplomats' toing and froing. As soon as the Argies realised that these diplomatic efforts were not going to succeed the 707 missions stopped.

"We had employed a peacetime, flexible servicing schedule for the aircraft up until we went on a war footing, after which we used the wartime schedule. Having read the manuals covering this, we suggested to Dick that we should take one aircraft down to the hangar each night and perform a basic (3-hour) service on it, including cockpit cleaning and topping up of pressures, to keep it up to scratch. This paid dividends, but our sister squadron on *Hermes* didn't do this, paying the price in unserviceabilities.

"Having commenced a war-footing watch system, a 'damage-control' state (one step down from action stations) was declared throughout the ship. That meant you couldn't sleep on the mess deck (where I shared a cabin with three other chiefs). I commandeered a cockpit cover which became my bed in the hangar, and even if I wasn't on watch I could help fix any u/s aircraft which had been moved to the hangar. When off watch our lads were sent down to spaces on 12 deck, up for'ard, and 'closed up' there as part of a damage control team – pretty grim. I tried to put only the single guys down there, but eventually I also had to include the married ones. They stayed 'closed up' there for eight hours and were relieved by another group coming off watch. They then worked in the hangar for the next eight hours, followed by eight hours back on watch. We had 'action messing' where the food wasn't all that good. As the war progressed, food choices became pretty restricted – mostly soya which I can't stand. The bakery never closed so I existed on cups of chocolate and cake.

"We went to war on 1 May. Because we had prepared the aircraft well, we had

a high level of serviceability. In the ship's island we stored some of the most important spares, such as INUs (inertial navigation units) and weapon-aiming computers, which enabled us quickly to fix aircraft which needed them. There was
much excitement when the aircraft launched on their first war sorties, although to
our frustration they did not see action. I was in the mess that evening (our chiefs'
mess bar never closed) and the 'fishheads' were taking the mickey out of us because
we, apparently, hadn't achieved anything. The 'phone rang – we had shot down
our first aircraft! Everybody was jubilant, then the 'phone rang again – we had shot
another down!

"From then on flying took place pretty much non-stop, but by day only. We
were quite relieved there was no night flying, because it meant that full servicing
could be carried out. We were a very close-knit squadron, having formed with six
aircraft we had then increased to eight with additional aircrew. We were only half
the size of squadrons in the conventional carrier era, and we had a very close relationship with the aircrew.

"The Task Force was attacked many times and several ships hit – it was pretty
frightening the first time we went to action stations. I was on the hangar deck, and
as the fire curtains were lowered I threw myself to the floor. The PWO (principal
warfare officer) tannoyed: 'Brace, brace, brace, incoming.' I lifted my head and
looked at a bulkhead labelled 'Sea Dart Magazine'. I said to a mate lying beside me,
'If we get hit we're doomed so if you arrive at that big bar in the sky before me get
the beers in quickly because there'll be a long queue!' There were three or four
lads holding on to my overalls for dear life and I asked them what they thought
they were doing. They said, 'No-one's going to kill you chief, so we're staying close
to you!'

*Sea Harrier FRS.1 ZA177 of 809 Squadron landing on*
Intrepid *during the Falklands War.*

"We launched a Sea Harrier,
piloted by Charlie Cantan, to intercept airborne targets detected
approaching us. Then we
steamed into a very thick fog
bank, the top of which was about
400 feet. Recovering from what
was a long sortie, the pilot
couldn't see the ship and we
couldn't see him. We deployed
flares which he eventually ob-
served, and following the ship's
wake he was able to make a careful approach. He suddenly appeared out of the fog and immediately plonked the aircraft down
onto the flight deck, obviously

very shaken. After climbing out and giving a quick, gruff acknowledgement that the aircraft was serviceable, Charlie went straight to the crewroom for a stiff whisky. The 'plane captain told me how much fuel the aircraft had taken on refuel – I said the Sea Harrier couldn't take that much – but it had.

"Every day a re-supply Argie Hercules flew into Port Stanley. Various pilots had tried to detect and engage one without success. Eventually Sharkey Ward was adamant that he was going to 'get it', so he and Steve Thomas launched. Sharkey detected the aircraft on radar and manoeuvred into position to engage. He fired a Sidewinder which buried itself in the aircraft's starboard wing root. Frustrated that the Herc wasn't apparently going to crash, he emptied his full load of 240 x 30-mm HE rounds into it. The Herc slowly rolled and pitched down, cartwheeling into the sea. The ship steamed at flank speed towards the Sea Harriers, because we knew they would be low on fuel. Steve Thomas had landed on, and Sharkey appeared over the horizon pointing straight at the ship, rather than joining the circuit, and also landed on. He opened the canopy, put both thumbs up, and found himself airborne again – the aircraft just leapt into the air as if in jubilation! He quickly landed it again, and we carried him on our shoulders to the ship's island. Such was the relationship between aircrew and ground crew.

"We spent 166 days at sea. 801 Squadron completed 599 missions, with only one where we failed to get an aircraft off the deck. We dropped 56 1,000-lb bombs, expended 3,061 rounds of 30-mm ammunition and fired 12 Sidewinders. We shot down three Mirages, a Canberra, a C-130 and a Pucará. 'Probables' comprised two Mirages, a Canberra and a Puma."

### Tim Gedge – pilot

"As all the people who first got involved in the Sea Harrier programme were from Phantom and Buccaneer squadrons, they were all current in fighter and strike flying. We were almost over-borne with experience. This meant quite a lot in terms of the people we had around us in the Falklands in 1982. We had a lot of quite highly qualified people, and more AWIs than we would normally have on squadrons – this of course was highly fortuitous.

"We had 700A Squadron, the IFTU, which turned into 899, and the first front-line squadron was 800. It was a new squadron which I formed from a blank sheet of paper; we hadn't reformed from a previous one. That was in March 1980. Forming a new squadron from scratch was

*Sea Harrier FRS.1 XZ451 700A Squadron Yeovilton, landing at BBC Pebble Mill studios Birmingham in 1979, flown by Lt Cdr Sharkey Ward. (Tim Thorley)*

very interesting. Air Publication (Navy) had a chapter devoted to how to form a new squadron in the FAA. I read this, and followed it to the letter. It had an excellent chart which worked back about 80 days from your commissioning day. It gave you instructions on what to do on each day, working up to the big day itself, including writing to all the personnel who were going to join the squadron – maintenance as well as officers – which I duly did. I had feedback from some junior maintenance personnel who said it was a nice surprise for them to have received a letter. So we went through the process, we got aircraft and started flying them. Thinking back to those days I was surprised that I didn't receive any real direction in how much flying I was required to do. So we modelled the daily/weekly flying programme on what we had previously been used to.

"We took as a guide the fighter/recce/strike Sea Harrier FRS.1. We didn't have radars or a navigation system at that time, however we certainly got stuck in to the fighter side of things. Air-to-air combat was modelled on our time in Hunters, and the fact that a number of us were AWIs. So we developed our Hunter tactics for the Sea Harrier, and practised the recce mission using the F95 camera mounted in its nose. We also started dropping weapons, although the nuclear strike role was something that I seriously wondered how we were going to achieve. In those days, to do anything in the strike role you had to have done the 'Z' course. You weren't allowed to tell anybody you had done the course, so other than those on the course with you, nobody knew how many were qualified to undertake the role. It was assumed that all the AWIs were (it was part of the AWI course). Although we considered it, we never really came to any serious conclusions as to how we were going to practise the strike role – there was no direction from the MOD either. The role was removed a year later, so we just practised the fighter and recce roles.

"We practised air-to-air with 899, but also tried to involve other types whenever we could. This included F-16s on detachment at Lossie and, when in the US we utilised the USN aggressor squadrons. During the two years I had command of 800, up to 1982, we had practised air combat against most aircraft types in the western world, including Phantoms, Lightnings and Skyhawks. Only the Mirage III and V were missing from the list, which was a bit unfortunate for obvious reasons.

"Most of the time we had no radar so were simply visual/day fighters. Many of us had flown Phantoms and we knew, by manoeuvring and placing it on our beam (90° off our heading), how to break the lock of a Phantom with its doppler radar. We employed that tactic against opposing fighters; although they may have been able to re-lock onto us, it was too late for them to engage us with a missile. I would say that we didn't lose many fights but then we didn't necessarily win them either. We capitalised on all this training in the Falklands War. This gave us quite an advantage because we knew the limitations of the aircraft, what we could do and, more importantly, what we couldn't do.

"We first embarked, in *Invincible*, in May 1980 which was only a couple of months after we'd formed the squadron. The transit over to the States gave us a lot of deck experience, and it was the first time we had seen the Sea Harrier when embarked; we were breaking new ground in terms of how we wanted to operate it. We did the same the following year in *Hermes*, transferring the deck experience to her and developing it. This was also a learning curve for the ship companies, although things worked pretty well. The surprise for me was that the *Invincible* design hadn't taken on any of the requirements of an aircraft carrier. For example, the storage for quite delicate Sidewinder missile seeker heads was underneath the quarterdeck. This suffers the highest levels of vibration of the whole ship, so maintenance personnel would have to step outside, possibly in bad weather and/ or sea state, and go down several ladders to retrieve a delicate spare seeker head – ridiculous. This was among a number of problems which had to be ironed out after the first embarkation. The briefing rooms were nowhere big enough for our needs; totally inadequate, they had been designed around a small number of helicopter crews. Another factor was the island superstructure. It had things about a foot long, sticking out of it at exactly the same height as a Sea Harrier wingtip – it was very tricky avoiding denting the aircraft. All those extensions had to be removed and re-positioned elsewhere. Although this was straightforward it reflected the lack of ship design to cater for fixed-wing aircraft. The original complement was based around eight Sea Harriers. You just couldn't get enough people into the briefing rooms.

"After just inside two years in command I handed over 800 Squadron. I went to Flag Officer 3rd Flotilla (FOF3) in Portsmouth as the fixed-wing aviator on the staff. I managed to stay in flying practice; although I was there for less than two months I manged to fly the Hunter at Yeovilton once a week or so.

"On the Friday that the Argentines invaded Stanley the admiral called a meeting for all the aviation staff in the Portsmouth area. The purpose of this was to announce the redundancy programme, with brown envelopes being handed out. I was called out of the meeting, rather publicly, to answer a telephone call from C-in-C Northwood's staff, who told me to report to the C-in-C in half an hour – I was in Gosport at the time! I drove to Northwood and heard the news on the radio. On arrival I was ushered into the conference room full of many senior people. I was asked if FOF3 deploys on operations, how many carriers and Sea Harriers would he wish to take with him? I replied assuming it was the Falklands – there was stunned silence in the room. I wasn't cleared to know where the operation would be, and although I'd heard it on the BBC news in the car, the operational location was highly classified. We'd want to take all the carriers (there were only two), and all the Sea Harriers, of which there were 20. Asked how I would allocate the SHARs I replied eight in *Invincible* and 12 in *Hermes*; I felt that I could speak with authority, having operated the SHAR from both ships. I returned to Portsmouth and alerted the SHAR squadrons; one was on leave, and one was about to go on Easter leave. All leave was cancelled, and the squadrons ordered to embark, which they did on Easter Sunday and Monday. It was a frenetic weekend. I was at the staff location on Portsdown Hill, and to my surprise I was the only aviator left behind because all the operations staff had moved to Gibraltar to join FOF1's staff. FOF1 was Sandy Woodward, a submariner, so he had limited aviators on his staff. I seriously questioned this move of staffs, it was FOF3 who 'owned' the carriers and the amphibious ships *Fearless* and *Intrepid*, and whose staff were worked up in carrier and amphibious operations. It was totally illogical to place these ships under a different admiral, and to me this was one of the very big mistakes of the Falklands War.

"The ships sailed on the Monday morning. That evening I received a telephone call from Flag Officer Naval Air Command (FONAC), Ted Anson, asking if I'd like to form another SHAR squadron, to which I replied in the affirmative. He told me to be in his office at 08:00 the next morning, so I drove up to Yeovilton that night. Ted Anson gave me a very simple remit which was to gather all the aircraft, pilots and maintenance personnel, and be ready to go to war in three weeks. I commandeered the 899 boss's office, and got on with the job.

"We'd already sent 800, 801 and almost all of 899 (the training squadron). No. 899 had deployed as a front-line squadron, its aircraft allocated to 800 and 801, and its commander acting as an additional CO. I formed 809 Squadron – our aircraft came from all over the place. Some were in deep maintenance at Yeovilton, some came from Dunsfold and St Athan, and one from Boscombe Down. We ended up with eight aircraft, and needed eight pilots. The pilots also came from everywhere. Three were brought back from tours abroad (one from USMC base Yuma, Arizona, one from USN VX-4 Point Mugu, California and one from Canberra, Australia). They each flew back on the next commercial flight, leaving their families to return in slower time. Three other pilots, including myself, were in various jobs

around the UK. Totalling six at that stage, we were two pilots short. I spoke to Adm Anson, telling him I needed two experienced RAF Harrier pilots as we'd run out of Sea Harrier pilots. These had to be second tourists, perhaps Lightnings and then Harriers, and there were two who fitted the bill. Apparently they were in the bar at RAF Gütersloh when their boss told them he had good news and bad news. Leaving them to decide which was which, he said they were going to war and it would be in a Sea Harrier with the RN.

"My next question was how we, as a squadron, were going to get down there as the two carriers had already deployed, only to be told that wasn't my concern – the means would be provided. *Atlantic Conveyor* was

*Hermes's flight deck during the Falklands campaign.*

made available; on a Saturday morning three of us were walking around the deck noting what would need to be removed to make it an effective aircraft carrier. We decided to leave the containers down the side, and the forward wave breakwater and foremast, but we had steel plates welded over the forward hatch. The ship's beam was about 90 feet, so I asked for a landing pad 92 x 92 feet which was the size of the MEXI pad used by the Harriers in Germany. We couldn't put markers either side of the landing area because they'd simply float away. In order to land the aircraft we could hover and point the aircraft's nose at the top of the foremast and then descend vertically – you'd then land on the deck. There was quite a bit of discussion as to how that would work so, on the way back to Yeovilton, I asked for a crane with a 70-foot jib to be parked at the end of one of the runways. The jib was angled at 10° off the vertical to simulate the *Atlantic Conveyor*'s foremast. On the Monday morning I practised the landing manoeuvre in a Sea Harrier – it worked a treat. I then practised three or four vertical landings from different directions onto the pad on her deck, after which I radioed back to Yeovilton to say that she was clear for sea and to receive the squadron's aircraft. Because I was short of fuel I landed at Plymouth Roborough airport to refuel, which was on a Sunday morning, and returned to Yeovilton. Eight days after we had initially inspected *Atlantic Conveyor* she had sailed for war, en route to Ascension Island initially.

"About ten days later the squadron deployed; the question being whether we would in-flight refuel or stage. It was decided we would air-to-air refuel; my concern was flying the Sea Harrier for the nine hours it was going to take. The maximum flight time we'd experienced up until then was about two hours. We knew that the Harrier had flown for that time but it had a different oxygen system, as well as other differences. So, with AAR we flew six hours down to The Gambia and a further three-and-a-half hours on from there. To my annoyance we had to deploy a week before the *Atlantic Conveyor* would arrive at Ascension Island. We weren't told why, but on arrival at Ascension Island we found the airfield full of Victor tankers, ready for the first of the Vulcan raids on Stanley – the 'Black Buck'. My

view of the effectiveness of the Vulcan raids was coloured – they got in the way of many other things that were going on. I have admiration for the planning and the way the missions were conducted, but they were of limited value (probably zero), and screwed up many other things – not least the management and organisation at Ascension Island and the enormous quantity of fuel used.

"Although we were at Ascension

*Tim Gedge landing on* Atlantic Conveyor.

for six days before *Atlantic Conveyor* arrived, everywhere and everything was taken up by the Victors and Vulcans etc., so we decided not to fly practice missions. Along with six aircraft of 1 Squadron RAF under Peter Squire, we then deployed aboard *Atlantic Conveyor*. All the aircraft were wrapped in specially made covers and 'put to bed', except one which was for air defence of the ship if needed. We were on passage for 12 days, keeping the one Sea Harrier on alert. We were concerned about the Argentine military 707 which was using its cloud-avoidance radar for sea mapping to detect ships. At the time we didn't have approval to shoot it down, although we gained that later, but the Argies must have been tipped off that the rules had changed because we never saw it [see page 247]. I was itching to get airborne and shoot it down. It would have been a first – a V/STOL aircraft which had launched from a container ship shooting down a commercial airliner. To improve the Sea Harrier's range, given the VTO requirement, we had unloaded the guns and other equipment from it. Obviously it was temperature, and pressure-dependent but I reckoned we had a maximum radius of action of 170 miles.

"We flew off transferring all the Harriers, and half the Sea Harriers, to *Hermes* and the other half to *Invincible*. I initially flew to *Hermes* and then to *Invincible*. As the war progressed I flew about 43 operational sorties. There was a general sense of the unknown initially. At Yeovilton I'd asked for a briefing by the Defence Analysis Centre at West Byfleet, only to be told by an idiotic senior civil servant that we would lose all of the Sea Harriers by Day 2 of first contact. He was apoplectic when I asked him to leave; he had wanted to give us (eight pilots) all of his carefully-prepared brief – but I didn't want to hear what he was saying, and furthermore it wasn't true. This wasn't based on my own inflated view of my ability. We'd trained against many other types of modern fighters, and even though we may not have 'shot them down' – they hadn't 'shot us down' either.

"We didn't know what the outcome would be when we met up with the opposition aircraft, however the reality was it quickly became apparent that they were not particularly skilled at what they were doing. Had they flown large numbers of aircraft against us, we would have had a problem; in the event they flew in what I called 'penny packets'. We had intel about the numbers of their aircraft taking off, and when they were. We were probably 30 minutes flying time to the east of the Falklands and the Argies were 45 minutes to the west of the islands, give or take. So, we had time to launch aircraft to be on station as they arrived. Although there was nothing wrong with their aircraft, for example the Mirage III (which Israel had used very successfully), their tactical thinking was seriously flawed. The Argies really should have got better results than they did. The aircraft I saw were all at a distance, it was the luck of the draw; pretty well every time we saw Argie aircraft they were in retreat. I think they got the message that they could not win if they 'mixed it' with Sea Harriers.

"I split the squadron in two at this stage. Most of my flying was done from *Invincible* with 801 Squadron, the other half working with 800 on *Hermes*. The integration was a success. All the maintainers that I had taken down had adapted very well within their respective units, with each operating effectively as a single squadron. As to the numbers, we lost six aircraft (taking us down to 22), none in air combat – but we shot down 24.

"The aircraft was astonishingly successful. The availability and serviceability was nigh on 100 per cent; out of the 1,500+ sorties/missions flown, only two were cancelled for unserviceabilities. This was because they were new-ish aircraft, two years old at the most, and it was a relatively simple and well-proven aircraft. However flying with live missiles throughout several cycles of launch and recovery, meant the missiles became soaked in sea water before firing, and this had not been trialled. Not surprisingly, there were unserviceabilities in the electrical interface between aircraft and missile, the electrical plugs. On *Invincible* the routine was to remove the missiles' seeker heads and dry them out, often in the ship's bread ovens. Unfortunately this upset the bread-making routine! The other thing we hadn't done was to expose cockpit instrument and switch panels to sea water. We were often operating in very rough, huge seas with water running into the cockpit as soon as you opened the canopy. Equipment such as the Ferranti inertial system and radios suffered; we had not thought to ask the manufacturers to make them saltwater-proof. The solution was to unscrew the covers, put cling film on, and replace the covers. This worked extremely well; cling film was also used to wrap missile plugs and other systems.

"As a closing point, the Sea Harrier really was a delight to fly, in the very best tradition of Hawker aircraft. I likened it to the Hunter; it was real pilot's aeroplane and did what you wanted it to – that was the great success of the aircraft. If you couple its flying ability with the much-upgraded radar, and missile fit plus ECM in the FA.2 version, it became a world-beating fighter aircraft. Being small it was also difficult to see. Its capability was quite incredible. I could never understand why it was ever taken out of service, and why we didn't manage to sell it to other nations after the Falklands War. We had shot down 24 aircraft without any air combat losses ourselves – it spoke for itself."

> *Two 800 Squadron aircraft were lost; XZ450 on 4 May shot down by ground fire over Goose Green, Lt Nick Taylor killed; and ZA192 on 23 May crashed into the sea off* Hermes, *Lt Cdr Gordon Batt killed.*

### Steve George – engineering officer

"In 1988 I was appointed to Yeovilton as the AEO on 801 Squadron Sea Harriers which were embarked in *Ark Royal*. We lost a couple of 'planes (one to aircrew error during a flying display, and one to a jammed control) – thankfully both pilots ejected safely, but it was a tough trip. In 1990 I was appointed again to Yeovilton, this time as the station's senior aircraft engineer – a less grand job than the title suggests. I was working for an outstanding commander as a lieutenant command-

*Steve George.*

er looking after around 120 aircraft on the station. Subsequently, it amused me at Strike Command when RAF planning staffs said that they couldn't put more than 32 aircraft at a station. It was a very interesting, demanding and rewarding job and involved preparing aircraft to participate in Gulf War 1. This included getting Sea King 4s and Sea Harriers ready to go out to the Red Sea, and we had to get many hundreds of aircraft modifications done in a really short time. Although it was absolute pandemonium, I had the time of my life. I was privileged to work with some absolutely outstanding engineers and technicians.

"Amazingly I then got another appointment at Yeovilton, to a post in the engineering authority for the Sea Harrier. As well as looking after the existing fleet (including their weapons, engines and avionics) my small team also brought the Sea Harrier FA.2 into service. I am proud to have been a part of that. For ten years the FA.2 was the best fighter in the Western world – it could beat anything, including F-15s and F-16s. It was probably the first fighter in the history of the British aircraft industry that entered service with a radar that worked on day one! Not only that but it worked magnificently, and the integration with the AMRAAM was fabulous. The guys from the US who made the missile said that the FA.2 was the best platform the missile had at that time, and we were ahead of any other aircraft by some distance. The only thing that came close was an F-16 Block 60.

"By 1992 we were the first coalition aircraft to be declared swing-role (off the coast of Bosnia). We had Sea Harriers launching with a 1,000-lb bomb, two AMRAAMs and a very good F95 camera. We were declared in three roles at once – I don't know of any other coalition aircraft that was. Quite an astonishing achievement, and one that reflected huge credit on the UK companies and FAA personnel involved."

## Andrew Neofytou – pilot

"I joined 899 Squadron in 2002. On my course was Nathan Gray (F-35B test pilot), later to be joined by Dan Denham. It's unusual hovering the Harrier because you're hovering between 75 and 90 feet. You've got an ejection option if the engine fails, but you still have to be really quick. Your references are a bit further apart, I was flying off 'charlie' pad, which was the biggest pad at Yeovilton. You just sit there, put the nozzles down, do your checks, go for full power and you feel all its energy. I was being watched from the tower by 'Jak' London (prior to the Wittering accident mentioned on page 37), but I couldn't really hear what he was saying to me. I somehow managed to do my first hover and land without breaking the aeroplane.

"I was on the air combat work-up, doing 'one versus one' basic combat stuff. We'd done one air combat sortie in the morning, and another one chasing the weather east with the intention of landing at Wittering, then a further one and transiting back to Yeovilton. The weather deteriorated towards the end of the second sortie so we landed at Wittering. The staff pilot decided it would be a good opportunity for me to lead my first pairs formation flight back to Yeovilton.

"During that transit through the Westcott radar corridor, just north of Heathrow, we'd often transit airways at 90 degrees at a level which was at least outside the vertical separation minimum. On this particular day we were at something like 24,000 feet and in the middle of the Westcott corridor when my engine failed – I had a 15,000-feet glide with about six relight attempts. I went down to 9,000 feet with a huge amount of vibration and a huge workload in the cockpit, IMC in the middle of an airway!

"When an engine fails, other stuff fails, you have no primary nav and so on. Finally, the engine relit, but wasn't producing much power, but it was enough to fly back to Wittering. However it was not enough to do any form of landing that I'd been taught. The most common approach flown in the Sea Harrier was a fixed-power, variable-nozzle approach, otherwise known as a 'nozzley'. Depending on the aircraft weight, the pilot would set a fixed power between 80-85 per cent RPM, then control the rest of the approach with a combination of nozzle adjustment (plus pitch with the normal flying controls) to maintain a constant 'alpha' on the approach. But I couldn't get the engine to produce more than 69 per cent RPM without very large, unsatisfactory noises emanating, plus a great deal of vibration. This posed two issues, namely that I couldn't set enough power for a nozzley approach, and with the power setting at only 69 per cent the nozzles had to remain further aft – meaning the aircraft wouldn't slow down. Having just dealt with a major emergency, this was another complexity I could have done without. I had just over 50 hours total time on the Sea Harrier, but I had only flown five hours in the preceding five months. However I did land it OK, albeit only two knots below the tyre limiting speed – about 178 knots over the threshold! When I landed I went into power-nozzle braking, but as I increased the power the engine gave up and I went through my own ball of flame. The engine seized, I stopped – the fire crew were already there. I was subsequently awarded a Green Endorsement.

"I drove back to Yeovilton and the very next morning I was flying up to Edinburgh for the International Festival of the Sea. I was with a staff pilot who was going to be doing a display there – I was flying the spare jet. The ethos of the Sea Harrier world at that time – sometimes for the right reasons, sometimes not as much I think – was 'just get on with it'. I think we've seen things change since then.

"On the penultimate OCU trip, which was a two-versus-two, I was trying to catch up with my wingman somewhere over the Bristol Channel in pretty murky conditions at altitude, when my canopy failed. It was an explosive decompression at about 29,500 feet and Mach .9, and it shut down the engine which pop-surged. I restarted it and landed at St Athan after a torrid set of approaches.

"Halfway through the course, 899 embarked on *Invincible*. Unusually we embarked a T.8 two-seater, and some Sea Harriers. I got to see a deck landing in the T.8, and I was the first to go off on a ski-jump launch on my own, having not seen that before. After a bit of a torrid time that was great and for me a confidence boost – I absolutely nailed the first deck landing. At the end of the course I joined 801 Squadron.

### FLYING THE SEA HARRIER

"From a general handling point of view I always prided myself in my control through basic and advanced jet training. I really didn't find the handling of the Harrier a problem, there was just so much more to do in it. It wasn't just the handling, you were working with a HUD which you'd never seen before, so I had to get my head around that, and flying a V/STOL aircraft. The biggest challenge in the handling was probably the transitioning between hovering flight, conventional flight and vice versa. The wing would dump most of its lift at about 100 knots, so you were decelerating to the hover. Fly the circuit, do your downwind checks, and at the point where we would get to 100 knots you would check whether you'd got performance from the engine to hover. In the HUD there was what we called a 'hex' (a hexagon – six sides). If we had three slats or three sides of that hexagon or less, that said you were at 100 knots and could hover, then transition back to conventional flight again.

"That period of transition from 100 knots to the hover was complex. The Sea Harrier had rudder pedal shakers, and there was a weather vane on the nose showing whether we were into or out of the wind. The idea was to keep the vane aligned

*Sea Harrier FA.2 ZE693 714 899 Squadron Yeovilton, 22 March 2004. (Chris Lofting)*

with the fuselage, and in the HUD there was also a slip-ball which you made sure was kept in the centre. Imagine if, for example, you are looking straight out of the aircraft and the pad you're going to land on is left of your nose, and the wind is quite brisk from the right. As you decelerate you've got gradually to move the nose of the aircraft round to the right, and transition sideways to the left to position yourself over the pad keeping the nose into wind. If you didn't do that the Sea Harrier would suffer from a phenomenon called intake momentum drag – effectively one side of the intake became blanked. This induced a gyroscopic effect that would manifest itself in a rapid yaw, and the secondary effect of that was to roll – the aeroplane would be upside down in a couple of seconds. Your only option then was to eject. A number of people back in the early days of the Harrier died as a result of that.

"That transitioning from conventional flight to the hover was tricky, and the same was true when transitioning away from the hover. You'd take off first into the hover and then select the climb attitude. One of the HUD displays was for V/STOL flight, so you selected that mode, put a bit of power on and then start hovering out and moving the nozzles backwards. As you began to accelerate the stick forces would start at about 30 knots, and again you had to be very careful. On my first attempt at this Rob Schwabb, my instructor, was sitting in the tower watching me and said: 'It's very windy mate, just make sure you keep the vane in the middle.' I nozzled out a bit too quickly and the next thing I felt was the aeroplane descending. At the same time, around about 30 knots, we had an audio alpha gauge and we could hear what alpha the wing was at. It had three tones; a constant tone, a high-pitched 'beep..beep..beep' and a lower tone to warn of the biggest threat, which is high alpha – and that was what I was hearing. As someone said, 'If it all goes wrong, undo the last thing you did'. So I slammed the nozzles back to the hover stop and as it started to nozzle out, I went sort of vertically upwards and forwards and accelerated away.

"I flew downwind, decelerated to the hover, then accelerated away from it again, then did it once more. So I'd done it perfectly twice and then landed. At the debrief, the instructor asked me, 'How did that go?' I said, 'Well I screwed up the first one' and he said, 'Yes, I was close to the crash button to tell you to bang out! But you probably should have just landed when that stuff happens.'

"Launching from the ski jump you have the nozzles at the slow stop. You have three sets of nozzle stops – the slow stop which you could set at an amount of degrees based on your weight and the atmospheric conditions, and the hover stop (about 81 degrees). The third one is the brake stop (98 degrees), for which you lift the nozzle lever, go over the hover stop and into the brake stop.

"We had a demineralised water-injection system (to help cool the engine and give extra engine performance), which gave 90 seconds of water. At the early stages when you've got very light jets you don't need water, but when you start flying with drops tanks and weapons you need water to counter the extra aircraft weight.

The water would start flowing prior to getting to the hover. Particularly when coming back to the ships, you find that as you decelerated water would start flowing probably at around 100 knots, just after wing lift is lost. You would probably arrive alongside with maybe just over a minute of water left, so you'd not got long to get yourself sorted and transition across to the deck.

"I was doing an air combat sortie which was going quite nicely, until I went to select the boresight switch. You could link the Sidewinder to the radar, or you could just tell it not to do its normal scan – just point exactly where I tell you to. If your opposition was a sitting duck, that would put all its energy straight to that aircraft. That's what I attempted. In the cockpit's ergonomic nightmare, the boresight switch was almost co-located with the water flow switch. I was obviously looking outside the cockpit, so the first I knew was the flashing amber caution lights going off that I'd got 15 seconds of water left! I was operating from the ship, and clearly if there had been no other option but to land on I would have done so and risked putting a lot of life counts on the engine. But that wasn't the case so I diverted to Newcastle airport. I then had to fly back to Yeovilton to get some de-mineralised water, and flew back to the ship. I was greeted by the captain on the quarterdeck with a glass of water.

"Most of the hard yards on the Harrier came from working the aircraft – this was where the really serious effort came on the OCU. We could do three roles; reconnaissance, bombing and strafing, and air combat. Our main role of course was air intercept with the AMRAAM, and Sidewinder if you got closer. As the two-seat T.8 Harrier didn't have a radar, our radar practice was limited to the simulator. This gave you quite a clear picture on the radar because it was synthetic, whereas the radar in the aircraft was subject to the normal atmospheric clutter.

"Learning how to use the AMRAAM missile with the Blue Vixen radar was demanding. You had to build a picture in your head of what was happening in the air; the fighter controllers were trying to give us that information, usually with a reference point called 'bullseye'. Imagine a dart board with the bullseye in the middle and everything related to a range and bearing from that position. Both the pilots, and the fighter controllers, would reference calls to this bullseye position – a randomly selected point. Enemy forces wouldn't be able to relate our calls to any known position. The Blue Vixen radar display took some getting used to, moving a cursor that resembled a set of goal posts to the called bullseye position and scanning with the radar to get an idea of the 'picture'. Having put the radar in the right place, we would acquire and designate a potential target, then manoeuvre the formation and depending on what the mission was, if it was hostile – engage. Sometimes we would be tasked to VID a target before engaging. In this instance, one of the formation aircraft would fly by the aircraft at an oblique angle, possibly identify it, and then if VID'd as hostile another member of the formation would shoot it with an AMRAAM from a distance – very satisfying.

"Doing that with multiple targets of all sorts of different types – F-15s, Sea

Harriers, Jaguars, Tornados – was extremely demanding; flying the aircraft, working the formation, the tactics, the weapons systems and the radar! Basically people got to the Sea Harrier OCU because they had that level of situational awareness. Tenacity and the ability to take on all these tasks, and not 'lose it', was so important. Then of course, at the end of all that (average sortie length was about an hour), you've got to go back and land on a ship.

"Sorties were extendable with air-to-air refuelling. We had a fixed probe which was a pain in the arse. We hated turning left with the probe on, it just didn't want to roll left – it acted like a wing; I would invariably try to roll right all the way and pull. People talk about viffing; if you're in a turning fight, and invariably it's a circle of some sort, you can either out-rate the other aircraft, or out-radius it. Out-rating is the speed at which you go round the circle (in any attitude). Out-radius is flying a smaller circle, where you need slow speed, flaps down, etc. You bled energy every time you manoeuvred, so ending up at a fairly slow speed. If someone else is going round the circle faster, even if you could out-radius them, you couldn't get the nose round quickly enough. You might have one last ditch attempt to bring the nose up to fire off a Sidewinder and at that stage you might viff. But, as soon as you viff it kicks you by about 20 degrees, but only for a second; you've lost even more energy, and really you're a sitting duck.

"Another manoeuvre was a brake-stop barrel roll. You try to force another aeroplane to fly through your six o'clock at 90 degrees. You pull the nose up, roll inverted over the top, and pull in the nozzle to the braking stop whilst upside down. This would effectively kill all your energy and your forward momentum – they then flew out in front of you and you could shoot them. Great if you get it right, if you don't you 'depart' the aeroplane.

"In an air combat environment it would have been advantageous to have afterburner to get the energy, also it would have been nice to pull any amount of 'g' without worrying – it wasn't a high 'g' aeroplane. It was challenging to operate; it was a very dangerous environment in the transition. Although it only had one engine which, as I discovered on more than one occasion, would present its own issues, I found the Sea Harrier really good fun."

## Jim Speirs – aircraft handler

"At the start of the Sea Harrier era Boscombe Down had carried out flying trials on *Hermes*. I joined the *Invincible* just after she had finished building at Barrow-in-Furness – I was in a porta-cabin alongside – and we did the ski-jump trials. The ship's operations officer threw me three volumes of air orders from the old *Ark Royal*, telling me to take the meat out of them and re-write them for the *Invincible*. When I looked at them and realised that they described catapult and arrestor gear, and other related ops, I threw them in the bin and started from scratch.

"I was drafted from *Invincible* to *Illustrious*, which was being built at Wallsend. I had engineered the move, having talked to the commander (air)-designate and

others. Nobody had operated a flight deck like the one on *Invincible*, so they wanted my experience. The plan wasn't for me to go to sea on *Illustrious* operationally,
it was more a case of ensuring that everything such as logistics came together
properly. We had previously had problems on *Invincible*. However, the Falklands
War fired up and *Invincible*'s captain said, 'I'm not going without you', which was
a compliment. I received a call from my drafting officer who told me I was to remain
with *Invincible* and go to the Falklands.

"The ship was stuffed full with some people even sleeping in the hangar. We
took a 'war fit' of stores and had extra Sea Harriers on board; the squadron normally had five but had been reinforced with an additional three. We remained at
sea for 166 days, most of it working a 24-hour flying regime, with an eight-hour
on, eight-hour off shift system; as opposed to the engine-room guys who were
doing four-hour shifts. The flying programme was intensive, there was always
something in the air, especially helicopters. Even if they weren't flying, Sea Harriers would sit at Alert 5 (five minutes to get airborne) with pilots in the cockpit
ready to go.

"We lost four Sea Harriers including two which were believed to have collided. Four SHARs had been due to launch but one went u/s, so only three went off
in what was pretty awful weather. Apparently they picked up a low-level contact
on their Blue Fox radars, probably a ship, and two of them went to investigate
whilst the third stayed above the cloud layer. The two were 30 miles apart when
they entered cloud – we never heard from them again. It was thought that what
they had detected on their radars was the floating hulk of *Sheffield*, but this is
only supposition.

"One aircraft, piloted by Flt Lt Ian Mortimer, a 'crab', got shot down by a Roland
SAM. He was returning from a CAP and decided to overfly Stanley airfield at height
in order to carry out a recce so that he could report on any aircraft activity there.
He saw the missile being fired at his aircraft but was confident that it wasn't a threat
because he was at 18,000 feet – theoretically beyond the missile's reach. Although
he selected full power and initiated a climb the Roland hit his aircraft as it was
passing 19,000 feet. He ejected and landed in the sea just off Stanley's runway. He
heard a helicopter and, realising that it was Argentinian, he switched off his SARBE.

He was in his dinghy for several hours, and despite the
order being given by the admiral to cease all searches, he
was found by an RN helicopter
– they had ignored the order
and rescued him. The RAF
wanted to court martial him
because he had deviated from
his briefed mission, resulting

*Flt Lt Ian Mortimer 801 Squadron* Invincible.

in the loss of a valuable asset. The first aircraft to shoot down an Argie (a Mirage) was one of our Sea Harriers piloted by Flt Lt Paul Barton."

> *The 801 Squadron aircraft lost were as follows: 6 May Lt Cdr John Eyton-Jones and Lt Alan Curtis in XZ452 and XZ453 lost in the probable collision mentioned above (see also page 200); 29 May Lt Cdr Broadwater ejected successfully when ZA174 started sliding uncontrollably across the deck prior to take-off; 1 June Flt Lt Mortimer in XZ456 hit by a Roland missile as described.* **Jim Speirs** *again:*

"Handlers got on with the aircrew pretty well in general. Our directions to them on the flight deck, which is a dangerous place at the best of times, were mandatory – as a chief I didn't have a problem pulling them up if they erred. Carrier flying ops have to be very slick. Once an aircraft had landed on they had quickly to clear the landing area and taxi over the safety line into Fly 1 to avoid balking the aircraft behind them. Thus, the need for directions to be mandatory.

"I think you'll find that most senior officers, and indeed the pilots, had great respect for us. I was CFD (chief of the flight deck) on *Invincible*, which was probably the best job in the world, and Sharkey Ward was the CO of 801 Squadron. Whenever he landed, especially after night flying, he would seek me out to say 'Thank you Chief'. To use an analogy, the CFD was the ringmaster to the flight deck 'circus' – he ran the whole operation there. Although commander (air), lieutenant commander (flying) and the FDO (who was normally aircrew), were above him, the CFD held the reins. I was based on the flight deck itself, running around shouting and balling at people, including aircrew, and kicking them up the backside when necessary.

"Despite being very busy and knackered during the Falklands, it was a very good atmosphere on board. During all that time at sea we never had any discipline problems. I can't even recall anyone falling out with someone, although I used to berate the pilots, especially when they didn't do as they were told!

"I was recommended for a BEM for service during the Falklands. Although the captain put me in for an award, they said you could only have two medals on the ship, one of which was the captain's DSO. However, he put me in for the Queen's Birthday Honours the following year."

### Tim Thorley – engineering officer

"I was moved into the headquarters of FONAC at Yeovilton. I was then due to go to Llangennech, a naval stores place, but instead went straight on to 700A Squadron, the IFTU. It later became the headquarters squadron, 899. I came into work one day to be told that I was to be the AEO on Heron Flight (the visiting aircraft flight), and the Historic Flight. The incumbent had been killed the night before in a road accident, and I had to go into his office, clear his desk and take over his job at an hour's notice. It turned out to be brilliant fun, especially with the Swordfish and then, lo and behold, I got posted to Lee-on-the-Solent.

"I was into a backwater training job, but then along came the Falklands War. I received a telephone call to 'get my backside up' to Yeovilton. I was to be the AEO of 809 Squadron, training some RAF people to use the ski jump. We still had some Australian and Canadian pilots, however their governments said they didn't want to get involved in the Falklands. I didn't go south – cursing like hell, I tried to get on board but I couldn't. The Falklands conflict came to a halt fairly quickly and I found myself back at Lee-on-the-Solent.

"I joined MARTSU (Mobile Aircraft Repair Transport and Salvage Unit) – equivalent to the RAF's 431 MU. Just as I thought I was going to be sent to Culdrose it all changed. How did I fancy a world cruise? I said that sounded good, what was involved? They said I was to go on *Illustrious* as one of the engineers on a global '86 exercise around the world – I consequently spent two years on board.

"It was the trip of a lifetime. We sailed from Portsmouth and our first port of call was going to be Acapulco. To get there we had to go round Cape Horn in order to call in at the Falkland Islands. We left Portsmouth at about 9 p.m. and then at about two o'clock in the morning we were doing a speed trial south of the Isle of Wight and the gearbox blew up. It was the biggest fire on a warship since World War 2.

"There was a horrible noise and then: 'Fire, fire, fire in the gear room'. I thought someone had set fire to some rags, and thinking nothing of it turned over. Ten minutes the same thing again, then the voice said: 'Do you hear there, this is the captain speaking. Prepare to abandon ship'. I thought I'd better get up! We were down to our last drum of AFFF (aqueous film-forming foam) to put the fire out – we just about did it. Statistically we should have lost 15 people that night – but we didn't lose anybody. We were straight back in to Portsmouth the next morning. A couple of aircrew on board didn't know anything about it. They came to my cabin door in their pyjamas and complained that there was no hot water! We were back in for three months, went out again and caught up with the fleet in Singapore.

*Sea Harrier FRS.1 after losing starboard outrigger, landing on mattresses HMS* Illustrious, *1986. (Tim Thorley)*

"When I arrived the captain was Alan Gross, but he was relieved in Singapore by Peter Woodhead. It was brilliant – a bloody holiday. They dropped me off on a deserted island off the coast of Malaysia; there I was setting up on the beach with everybody coming ashore – we had a banyan, a barbeque. The captain's wife was with me and she said: 'This is typical. Here I am on a deserted tropical island in the South China Sea with 600 blokes, and what am I doing? I'm cooking!'

"We did have a problem with an outrigger on a Harrier. The pilot caught it on the ramp and knocked it off, so had to do an emergency landing without the starboard outrigger. To take the weight of the starboard wing as he came in, we got a load of mattresses from the mess decks, put cargo nets over the top and secured them to the deck."

### Robin Trewinnard-Boyle – engineering officer

*Robin Trewinnard-Boyle.*

"HMS *Ark Royal* in 2003 with 800 Squadron. We embarked in the Mediterranean as we were returning from Operation Telic [Gulf War 2 in Iraq] because the RN wanted the ship worked back up as a strike carrier as soon as possible. The ship's company were not impressed and saw us as delaying her return to the UK, so everything was a bit tense. We flew off from *Ark* to Rota in Spain as she sailed past, before heading on to Torrejon AFB near Madrid for our next exercise.

"That summer we flew as aggressors alongside the USAF F-16s at the Red Flag exercise at Nellis AFB. Our biggest issue during this detachment was the cockpit temperatures – which got to around 60°C in the Nevada sunshine. It also caused concerns about the ejection seat cartridges 'cooking off'."

> *The premature retirement of the Sea Harrier in 2006 for economic reasons (the newest examples were only ten years old), once again left the FAA without an air-defence capability. The continued deployment of joint RAF/ FAA-operated Harrier GR.7s and GR.9s effectively offered ground-attack capability only.*

## CHAPTER ELEVEN

# LOCKHEED MARTIN F-35B LIGHTNING

*Squadrons: RN 809 (from 2023), RAF jointly manned 17, 207, 617, embarked on Prince of Wales, Queen Elizabeth.*

## THE RETURN OF AIRCRAFT CARRIERS

*Two new aircraft carriers, Queen Elizabeth and Prince of Wales were approved by parliament in July 2007, and construction of Queen Elizabeth began in 2009 at Rosyth. Originally intended to operate the F-35B, the SDSR in 2010 changed the plan to traditional 'cat and trap' ships to operate the conventional F-35C. However financial issues forced a re-think, and a change back to ski-jump carriers with the F-35B. This delayed operational service entry of the first ship from 2015 to 2020.*

*The crew moved aboard Queen Elizabeth in May 2016 under the command of Cdre Jerry Kyd. Following sea trials she sailed from Portsmouth on 18 August 2018 on Westlant 18 carrying three Merlin HM.2s of 820 Squadron, arriving at Norfolk, Virginia on 17 September to undertake tests*

*F-35Bs on Queen Elizabeth in October 2019. (defenceimagery.mod.uk)*

*with two F-35Bs of the Integrated Test Force. On
25 September two USMC F-35Bs landed on, with
Nathan Gray having the honour of being the first
to touch down. He then did the first take-off from
the ski jump – the FAA was back in the fixed-wing
carrier business. The first shipborne rolling vertical landing (SRVL) was undertaken on 14 October, this being intended as the primary method
of recovering the aircraft.*

*Jerry Kyd.*

*Two further trials deployments took place in
2019 and 2020, involving increased numbers of
joint FAA/RAF-manned aircraft from 17, 207 and
617 Squadrons. Queen Elizabeth will be declared operational in 2021 with
a mixed force of UK and USMC F-35Bs, the Prince of Wales following in
2023 (with RN 809 Squadron). Each ship can accommodate up to 36 F-35Bs
and four Merlins. The SDSR anticipated the routine peacetime deployment
of 12 F-35Bs, plus Merlins.*

*The background to the F-35 acquisition programme and an overview
of the current situation is provided by engineering officer* **Robin Trewinnard-Boyle.**

"Having started my FAA engineering career on the Sea Harrier FA.2, before moving
on to the Harrier GR.7 and T.10, the decision in SDSR 2010 to decommission *Ark
Royal* and retire the Harrier came as a massive shock. This cut my role as senior air
engineer on *Ark Royal* in half, dashing any thoughts of returning to Joint Force
Harrier (JFH) later in my career. The silver lining was that I was offered the opportunity to go to NAS Patuxent River, Maryland to join the F-35 ITF and subsequently moved out to the US with my family in July 2011.

"The other big announcement in the SDSR was the switch from the S/TOVL
F-35B to the cats and traps F-35C. At this time the F-35B was under US government
probation. However as the economic crisis grew and the development programme
costs spiralled, it looked like it might be axed. The USMC had literally 'bet the
farm' on the F-35B, and the UK order was seen as insurance that the jet wouldn't
be cut. Our switch of variants was taken personally by the corps, leading to exchange pilots being grounded and returned to the UK. At Pax River this meant that
the UK engineers, both RAF and RN, who had been working on the F-35B now
had to start thinking about wing-fold systems, arrestor hooks and a different undercarriage. The F-35C was sent to Lakehurst for its first ever catapult launch
using the electro-magnetic aircraft launch system (EMALS). An RN engineer was
sent with the aircraft to start learning the system that was to be fitted to the *Queen
Elizabeth* class (QEC) carriers. As the majority of the systems were common, I could
move the UK manpower from the F-35B to the F-35C with no issues.

Queen Elizabeth *in October 2019.* (*defenceimagery.mod.uk*)

"But 2011 was a critical year for the F-35B. Airframe modifications, and initial sea trials on board the USS *Wasp*, were required to prove that it was making significant progress and get it off probation. Most of the media reports were extremely negative and outside expectations were low, however for the test pilots, flight test engineers and maintenance team on the ITF it was just another challenge. Working six, sometimes seven, days a week to get the test points needed and the aircraft ready to embark, the initial sea trials went extremely well, proving that the F-35B could already operate to all the existing limits for the AV-8B Harrier. Modifications to reduce vibration in a critical area were designed, completed on the aircraft and flight-tested successfully. In early 2012 the US Secretary of Defense formally removing the probation, visited the ITF team to shake the hand of everyone who had worked so hard and hand out his personal challenge coin to all military personnel.

"By now the SDSR decision to switch to cats and traps was under severe scrutiny back in the UK; costs to change the 'flexible' design of *Queen Elizabeth* were proving to be extremely expensive, with the possibility that the UK would only be able to afford one of the two aircraft carriers planned. The F-35C was always going to be the third variant to be ready for IOC (initial operational capability). The date was likely to be around 2023 or later for the UK, leading to a longer than expected 'capability holiday' for the UK's strike carriers. The F-35C testing was also hitting a few problems (after all that's why we do flight test!), with the arrestor hook struggling to catch the arrestor cable consistently; due to a miscalculation of the distance between the landing gear and the hook point. The UK had already bought three F-35Bs that were being built. Questions arose as to what we were going to do with them, retain them as test assets, swap them with the USMC for F-35Cs, or try and sell them to the Italians (the only other country buying the F-35B at that point). The two ski-jump ramps for the QEC were already built, paid for, and waiting to be moved to Rosyth for assembly – what was to happen with them? With all these questions flying around and with the F-35B successfully proving itself at sea, the UK switched back to that variant – in my mind the correct decision. The strategic implications of only having one aircraft carrier would have led to issues similar to the French navy's *Charles de Gaulle* – no capability at all when she is in re-fit or repair. Also, the problems that the Americans were having with both EMALS and the advanced arrestor gear on the USS *George W Bush* showed that the technology remained immature and would have further delayed the UK's return to carrier strike operations.

"All of us Brits on the ITF (service and civilian) took a lot of banter from our US colleagues: 'make your minds up', 'make a decision' – but it was all good natured. The test aircraft BF-02, the second F-35B built, was always seen as 'the Brit jet'. UK personnel were involved with her construction at Fort Worth and throughout her time at the ITF, with a UK military crew chief and BAES flight test control engineer. She presented some unique challenges to the team, such as the fitting of a 'spin-chute' system for high angle-of-attack and engine-out testing. She received a John Deere-style silhouette 'mission marking' under the canopy after hitting a deer on the runway!

"The jump in technology for the maintainers, who mostly came from Harrier or Tornado backgrounds, was huge. Modern US types of connectors, significantly more fibre optics, touch screens, and low-observable coatings were among the challenges. Also learning to use the diagnostic computers and software to trouble-shoot problems added a level of complexity; similar to a modern car but very different from previous UK platforms. From the outset the F-35 had been designed to be maintenance friendly; elements such as changing the engine were significantly less work than changing a Pegasus on a Harrier. We were learning and developing the techniques and procedures as we went along; trying out new pieces of support equipment and making sure that processes and policies were not marked as 'US Eyes Only'. Initially there were no formal training courses. Everything was done 'in house' at Pax River by Lockheed Martin and Pratt & Whitney engineers.

"With our switch back to F-35B, we worked hard to get the UK-specific test points back into the F-35B schedule. As the build of *Queen Elizabeth* progressed the maritime capabilities of the F-35B became more important to the UK. Sqn Ldr Jim Schofield and I were heavily involved in the planning and execution of the second set of sea trials in October 2013. Although RAF and RN maintainers had gone to sea with the USS *Wasp* in 2011, at that point we were more interested in the elements we could read across to the F-35C. By 2013 we were already deep in

*F-35B BF-04 launching from* Queen Elizabeth *during Westlant 18. (defenceimagery.mod.uk)*

the planning for the first of class flying trials on *Queen Elizabeth*, and every aspect of testing the F-35B at sea was of importance. Key elements from an engineering perspective were: maintenance of low-observable coatings, transport, storage and, following recent fires on board Boeing 787s, charging of lithium ion batteries. Also the limitations of operating and maintaining the jet in a ship's hangar, performance of the Thermion protective flight-deck coating, positioning of deck crews during launch and recovery cycles; along with suitability of tools and support equipment in a maritime environment and many other things.

"With the first of class flying trials in 2018, and the operational testing on board in 2019 going so well, it is good to think that the work we were doing at Pax River and on board the USS *Wasp* played a key part in making them so successful. With the lack of a carrier and its jets impacting on the UK's response to the Libyan conflict in 2011, the future for FAA carrier aviation seemed a long way off. However, we are now on the brink of a truly 21st century carrier-strike capability, with the initial operating capability on track to be declared by the end of 2020."

> *The views of some former FAA personnel about the new carriers are quite varied. There is a mixture of regret at the loss of the traditional cat and trap capability and thus the reduced opportunities for cross-decking with US and French carriers, balanced by the excitement at the return of FAA fixed-wing carrier-borne aviation.*

### Jim Speirs – aircraft handler

"I think the new carriers are brilliant, I watched QE arrive in Portsmouth for the first time – I was very impressed. I've tried to get aboard but so far without success. My grandson is in the navy and even he can't get on board. I've been trying to contact the captain of the flight deck, to tell him that I was one once – even that hasn't worked. They're huge – with the acreage on their flight decks the job's going to be 'easy'."

### John Keenan – artificer

"I'm not for the F-35B, we should have had the cat and trap version for the new carriers, and bought three squadrons of F-18s – a tried and tested aeroplane with a bucket load of spares for the same money. The FAA needs to be a force – these F-35Bs will have to launch from *QE* and *Prince of Wales*. I was the senior airframes and engines chief on 801 Squadron during the Falklands War. We had enough trouble with the Sea Harrier's lack of endurance during the Falklands – the F-35B is no different. The Sea Harriers would fly 100 miles to a CAP and remain on station for 20 minutes before having to recover. They didn't have an in-flight refuelling capability and any V/STOL aircraft is limited by AUW to be able to get off the ramp."

### Tim Gedge – pilot

"I think the F-35B Lightning will be quite constrained in terms of how it can be operated – it won't have quite the flexibility that the Harrier did. Of course, it's vastly more capable, but being able to land on unprepared strips is something the Harrier/Sea Harrier did astonishingly well.

"I was involved in discussions about how you were going to control the F-35 whilst in the hover, whether you'd use the stick or throttle or a combination of both. There were quite heated debates back in the mid 1980s when RAE Bedford were doing the trials on the VAAC (vectored-thrust aircraft advanced flight control) Harrier. I was also on the staff of the British embassy in Washington DC, and was heavily involved in discussions with the USMC. There were quite a lot of differences of opinion about how you would control what eventually became the F-35B. I can imagine that someone with Harrier experience would find the F-35B quite different."

> *During the spring and summer of 2020 the Royal Navy has issued periodic updates on the progress being made to bring the F-35B and the two carriers up to a state of operational readiness.*

### Published: 7 February 2020

"Exercise 'Lightning Fury' training over the North Sea is aimed at ensuring 207 Squadron achieves essential carrier flying and Landing Signals Officer (LSO) supervisory qualifications. The exercise builds on successful trials completed on last year's 'WESTLANT 19' Carrier Strike Group deployment off the east coast of the USA.

"Defence Secretary Ben Wallace said: 'Few countries in the world have the capacity and technology to deploy fighter jets from an aircraft carrier in the North

Sea. These trials put the UK at the helm of 5th generation warfighting and cement the UK as a Tier 1 military power.'

"HMS *Queen Elizabeth* and HMS *Prince of Wales* will be the first aircraft carriers in the world to be designed specifically to operate the Lightning jet. The 'short take off and vertical landing' (STOVL) Lightning represents a step change in capability. With its advanced sensors, and stealth technology, the Lightning will provide the UK with a world-beating combat aircraft, which will be jointly manned by the Royal Air Force and the Royal Navy. Commander UK Strike Force, Mike Utley said: 'Operating the UK's Lightning Force from the deck of HMS *Queen Elizabeth* in UK waters is a significant milestone, and one we are delighted to have shown the Secretary of State for Defence in person. This training with 207 Squadron will set the conditions for valuable warfighting exercises later this year between the operational squadron and the ship. The future utility of these tremendous UK defence assets is gaining clarity each day as we push the envelope of their combined ability, leading to the first combined operational deployment of the carrier strike capability next year.'

"Once fully operational, the UK Carrier Strike Group will be a formidable force around the world, using a number of platforms to work alongside our allies and signalling the UK's position as a global player on the world stage. RAF Marham Station Commander, Group Captain James Beck said: 'It was great to welcome the Defence Secretary today. This was an opportunity for him to meet with personnel from the Lightning Force and to be briefed on the activity of the squadrons currently taking part in Exercise RED FLAG in America and carrier qualifications on HMS *Queen Elizabeth*.'

"The UK will declare initial operating capability for carrier strike by the end of 2020. The UK currently owns 18 aircraft, with an additional order placed for 30 jets. The first operational deployment for HMS *Queen Elizabeth* 617 Squadron and a squadron of US Marine Corps Lightning jets is due to take place in 2021."

### Published: 1 May 2020

"HMS *Queen Elizabeth* has sailed from Portsmouth today to ensure she is ready to conduct her first operational deployment in 2021. The Portsmouth-based aircraft carrier will undergo several weeks of training and assessment with the staff of Flag Officer Sea Training (FOST) to ensure the UK can deliver on its commitment to have a Carrier Strike Group ready to deploy from the end of this year. The continuation of this training has been agreed by senior leaders across defence.

"While many Royal Navy and Royal Marine personnel from the regular and reserve forces remain ashore supporting the current national fight against COVID-19, the ship's company of HMS *Queen Elizabeth* are focused on ensuring that UK defence remains prepared for future global threats. HMS *Queen Elizabeth* will be put through her paces in UK waters off the south coast, facing simulated battle damage, fires and floods, as well as warfare training and mission rehearsals.

"The training will include more qualifying training for UK F-35 Lightning crews, who will be conducting practice manoeuvres from her decks, giving vital experience to the aircrews and ship's company involved in air operations. This training will prepare the ship for further training later in the year with other Royal Navy ships to ensure they are ready to deploy as a task group next year.

"All personnel sailing with the ship have undergone testing for coronavirus. As a further precaution, HMS *Queen Elizabeth* will conduct a period of isolation at sea, before she starts her training with the FOST staff. She will be operating in waters close to the UK coast and the commanding officer has the discretion to cease the training if it is deemed necessary.

"HMS *Queen Elizabeth* has a key role to play in the defence of the United Kingdom and the Royal Navy will continue to conduct essential training ashore and at sea in order to fulfil its critical outputs now and in the future. Her sailing today marks yet another significant milestone in the regeneration of the United Kingdom's carrier strike capability."

## Published: 10 June 2020

"The decks of HMS *Queen Elizabeth* are roaring with the sound of F-35 Lightning jets as the famous Dambusters squadron landed on the aircraft carrier for the first time today. Pilots, engineers, cyberspace and mission support staff from 617 Squadron, the UK's operational strike squadron, embarked the carrier over the weekend during a quick stop in Portsmouth for supplies before the aircraft themselves landed on board this afternoon.

"It marks the first time 617 Squadron has fully joined HMS *Queen Elizabeth* as the UK prepares to deploy the next generation squadron of fighter aircraft to operate from the sea. The F-35 jets that landed on board today will be the same aircraft that will sail next year with the ship for her maiden Global Carrier Strike Group 21 deployment.

"Commander Mark Sparrow, the CO of 617 Squadron, said: 'We are excited to be on board the carrier and we have been training hard to be here. This is the first time the ship's operational squadron has embarked and worked together. The F-35 brings next generation capability to UK defence through its ability to find, destroy or avoid enemy air defences and enemy aircraft whilst gathering intelligence data.'

"Commander Ed Phillips is the commander air on board HMS *Queen Elizabeth*. Known as 'Wings', Cdr Phillips is in charge of flying operations on the aircraft carrier. He said: 'Today is a significant day for HMS *Queen Elizabeth* on the road to delivering carrier strike operations for the Royal Navy. We are at the heart of a world-leading capability for the UK and will soon have on our decks two squadrons of F-35s – from the UK and US – plus the protection of a strike group made up of destroyers, frigates and support ships.'

"HMS *Queen Elizabeth* will now enter an intense period of flying having just successfully completed four weeks of basic sea training. The aim is to demonstrate that the jets can successfully defend the aircraft carrier by delivering combat air patrols – launching from the ship to conduct strike missions against a target – and being ready to take off at short notice.

"After the initial qualification period, 617 Squadron will test their ability to work with Portsmouth-based HMS *Queen Elizabeth* and Merlin helicopters of Culdrose-based 820 Naval Air Squadron by conducting a number of complex training missions. This is all in preparation for their second embarkation later in the year when the squadron will join the carrier and her task group for a large multinational training exercise with US, European and NATO partners.

"The Royal Navy is transforming into a force centred around carrier strike – supporting the ships as they conduct carrier-strike missions, enforce no-fly zones, deploy Royal Marine Commandos, deliver humanitarian aid, and build international partnerships with our allies."

### Published: 2 July 2020

"Britain's biggest warship today returned home to Portsmouth for the first time as a fully-trained aircraft carrier. Future flagship HMS *Queen Elizabeth* has cleared her penultimate hurdle for front-line duties after ten hugely-demanding weeks around the UK, preparing for her maiden deployment in the new year. A final package of training in the autumn – working alongside NATO and US allies – will confirm her ability to act as a task group flagship, so that she can lead a potent carrier strike force on front-line operations anywhere in the world.

"Minister for the Armed Forces James Heappey said: 'HMS *Queen Elizabeth* is an extraordinary ship crewed by extraordinary people from both the Royal Navy and the Royal Air Force. They deployed at the height of the COVID-19 outbreak and have remained at sea for over ten weeks so that they could complete their operational training with the minimal risk of infection. They've put their duty to our country ahead of spending time with their families during the pandemic and in the process, they've taken us a step closer to, once again, having a carrier-strike capability with the capacity to project British influence across the globe.'

"In view of the size and complexity of the carrier, she received a dedicated training package, initially off the south coast, to test the ability of all 1,100 men and women on board to deal with everything they might expect to face in peace and war. The training package reached its climax with 18 fictional fire and flood incidents raging simultaneously – with the ship expected to continue flying operations while damage control teams toiled in the carrier's depths.

"'Given the sheer size of the ship, operational sea training has been a learning curve for all involved,' said Lieutenant Commander Si Bailey, one of the 46-strong team of assessors on board. It's been a challenging time for HMS *Queen Elizabeth*, but the ship's company and embarked personnel have been receptive to the training and advice – and have done so with a smile.'

"Having passed that assessment, the carrier shifted to the North Sea to welcome

F-35 Lightnings from 617 Squadron. It's the first time operational UK F-35s have worked with *Queen Elizabeth* and they faced a punishing schedule once aboard, completing a record number of landings on the flight deck. The future of carrier strike is a truly joint effort and the Royal Navy has worked closely with the RAF throughout the development of the carrier. 617 squadron – based at RAF Marham and comprising both Royal Air Force and Royal Navy personnel – progressed from qualifying pilots in the art of landing on and taking off from a moving warship by day and night all the way up to the first 'four-ship package': launching four F-35s on a combat sortie in rapid succession.

"The fighters shared the flight deck with submarine-hunting Merlin helicopters of 820 Naval Air Squadron from RNAS Culdrose. In all the fast jets and helicopters touch down on *Queen Elizabeth* 830 times in all weathers, at all times of day.

"The collective training ended with a five-day test of the ship to defend against threats in the air, on the sea and beneath the waves, herself using F-35s, Merlins and the frigate HMS Kent. In the 70 days since leaving Portsmouth at the end of April, the carrier has been almost exclusively at sea and clocked up 11,500 miles – the equivalent of the distance from her home base to Auckland, New Zealand. 'The ship's company have worked incredibly hard over the past 70 days, making every effort to surpass the high standards set by our assessors,' said Captain Angus Essenhigh, HMS *Queen Elizabeth*'s CO. They have come through with flying colours which means Her Majesty's Ship *Queen Elizabeth* has taken a huge step towards sailing on her maiden deployment, flying the flag for the United Kingdom and demonstrating that we are a global naval power with global ambitions.'

"HMS *Queen Elizabeth* will now enjoy planned maintenance in Portsmouth before task group training later in the year, which will also see the ship work with two F-35 squadrons for the first time."

> *The last word goes to **Bill Covington** who, as a former Joint Force Harrier commander, brings a very expert view to bear on the coming of the F-35B/ QE class force.*

"The dismay with which the RAF viewed the loss of cockpits to FAA pilots, meant the RAF enthusiasm for Joint Force Harrier and the Invincible Class carrier programme waned. They far preferred their natural comfort zone of Tornado and Typhoon aircraft, wholly under their control, operating from airfields they understood and were set up to support. In my view, these and other factors together led to the demise of the UK Harrier Force and the CVS carriers. One needs dedication and enthusiasm to argue the strategic case. If the perceived needs of the services do not align then the result is bad news for one side. What was interesting was that forward-thinking RAF officers could see they needed the *Queen Elizabeth* class carriers to underpin the procurement of the F-35 Lightning. I think it fair to say that there must have been stunned silence, when even without the Harrier, the FAA devised a plan to maintain the Royal Navy's fixed-wing expertise. In conjunction with the US Navy and Marines, and also other navies it has positioned itself, with its normal 'can do' attitude and innovation, to be very well placed to participate in today's F-35B Lightning Force and carrier operations – a formidable achievement.

"It should also be said that the F-35 is a totally new aircraft, very different from past UK aircraft. Gradually and sensibly building the Force up over time will avoid so many visceral issues that JFH endured. I hope so."

*After a gap of over ten years the entry into service of the* Queen Elizabeth *and* Prince of Wales *has placed the Fleet Air Arm very firmly back in the fixed-wing aircraft carrier business. The service's justifiable pride in both its heritage, and this new beginning, shines through from everyone who has contributed their stories – this book is for them.*

*F-35B ready to launch from* Queen Elizabeth. *(defenceimagery.mod.uk)*

# CARRIERS AND AIR STATIONS

Carriers in service August 1945, de-commissioned or US lend-lease return between 1945 and 1948 – 44, including operational, ferry and training carriers, excluding those on loan to other navies.

*Activity, Ameer, Arbiter, Archer, Atheling, Attacker, Battler, Begum, Biter, Campania, Chaser, Colossus, Emperor, Empress, Fencer, Formidable, Furious, Hunter, Khedive, Nairana, Patroller, Premier, Pretoria Castle, Puncher, Pursuer, Queen, Rajah, Ranee, Ravager, Reaper, Ruler, Searcher, Shah, Slinger, Smiter, Speaker, Stalker, Striker, Tracker, Trouncer, Trumpeter, Venerable, Vindex*

## Carriers continuing in service after August 1945 – 13

*Glory* R62 paid off June 1956, *Illustrious* R87 December 1954, *Implacable* R86 September 1954, *Indefatigable* R10 September 1954, *Indomitable* R92 October 1953, *Ocean* R68 March 1958, *Perseus* R51 January 1955, *Pioneer* R76 September 1954, *Theseus* R64 December 1956, *Triumph* R16 1953, *Unicorn* R72 November 1953, *Vengeance* R71 November 1952, *Victorious* R38 March 1968

## Total carrier fleet August 1945 – 57

## Carriers commissioned post-1945 – 11

*Albion* R07 May 1954-March 1973, *Ark Royal* R09 February 1955-February 1979, *Ark Royal* R07 November 1985-March 2011, *Bulwark* R08 October 1954-April 1981, *Centaur* R06 September 1953-February 1971, *Eagle* R05 March 1952-January 1972, *Hermes* R12 November 1959-June 1985, *Illustrious* R06 June 1982-August 2014, *Invincible* R05 July 1980-August 2006, *Prince of Wales* R09 2020, *Queen Elizabeth* R08 December 2017

## Royal Naval air stations August 1945 and date 'paid off' (closed)
Naval names in parentheses.

**United Kingdom**: Abbotsinch (Sanderling) October 1963, Anthorn (Nuthatch) February 1958, Arbroath (Condor) March 1971, Bramcote (Gamecock) November 1958, Brawdy (Goldcrest) April 1971, Burscough (Ringtail) June 1946, Crail (Jackdaw) April 1947, Culdrose (Seahawk) current, Culham (Hornbill) March 1956, Dale (Goldcrest) March 1948, Donibristle (Merlin) October 1959, East Haven (Peewit) August 1946, Eglinton (Gannet) February 1963, Evanton (Fieldfare) March

1948, Fearn (Owl) July 1946, Ford (Peregrine) November 1958, Gosport (Siskin) became Sultan for the RN Engineering School June 1956, Halesworth (Sparrowhawk) February 1946, Henstridge (Dipper) November 1946 but retained as a Yeovilton satellite until 1957, Hinstock (Godwit) September 1947, Inskip (Nightjar) July 1946, Lee-on-the-Solent (Daedalus) March 1996, Lossiemouth (Fulmar) September 1972, Machrihanish (Landrail) September 1952, Maydown (Shrike) 1947, Merryfield, Yeovilton satellite current, Middle Wallop (Flycatcher) April 1946, Milltown, Lossiemouth satellite September 1972, Nutts Corner (Pintail) March 1946, Peplow, Hinstock satellite end 1949, Portland (Osprey) March 1999, Predannack, Culdrose satellite current, Prestwick (Gannet), Culdrose 'tender' current, Rattray (Merganser) December 1947, Roborough civil airfield home to BRNC Flights until 2011, Ronaldsway (Urley) January 1946, St Davids, Brawdy satellite April 1971, St Merryn (Vulture) January 1956, Stretton (Blackcap) November 1958, Twatt (Tern), Lossiemouth satellite 1957, Worthy Down (Kestrel) March 1948, Yeovilton (Heron) current, Zeals (Hummingbird) January 1946.

**Overseas**: Archerfield Australia (Nabsford) March 1946, Bankstown Australia (Nabberley) March 1946, Changi Singapore lodger units 1965-May 1969, China Bay Ceylon (Bambara) October 1950, Cochin India (Kaluga) August 1946, Coimbatore India (Garuda) April 1946, Dekheila Egypt (Grebe) January 1946, Fayid Egypt (Phoenix) February 1946, Hal Far Malta (Falcon) September 1965, Kai Tak Hong Kong (Flycatcher) December 1947, Kalafrana Malta 1965, Katukurunda Ceylon (Ukussa) September 1946, Maryborough Australia (Nabstock) November 1945, Navy Point Falkland Islands (Sheathbill [unofficial]) 1982, Nowra Australia (Nabswick) March 1946, Piarco Trinidad (Goshawk) February 1946, Puttalam Ceylon (Rajaliya) October 1945, Ratmalana Ceylon (Seruwa) September 1946, Seletar Singapore lodger units until October 1960, Sembawang Singapore (Simbang) October 1971, Sollur India (Vairi) April 1946, Stamford Hill South Africa (Kongoni II) January 1946, Ta Kali Malta (Goldfinch) June 1953, Tambaram India (Valluru) December 1945, Tengah Singapore lodger units October 1960-January 1965, Wingfield South Africa (Malagas) May 1946.

# SELECT BIBLIOGRAPHY

Ballance, Theo, Howard, Lee and Sturtivant Ray, *The Squadrons and Units of the Fleet Air Arm*, Air Britain, 2006

Buttler, Tony, *The de Havilland Sea Vixen*, Air Britain, 2007

Jolly, Rick, *Jackspeak – A Guide to British Naval Slang and Usage*, Bloomsbury, 2011

Manning, Charles, *Fly Navy: The View from the Cockpit 1945-1995*, Leo Cooper, 2000

Morgan, Eric and Stevens, John, *The Scimitar File* Air Britain, 2002

Sturtivant, Ray, Burrow, Mick and Howard, Lee, *Fleet Air Arm Fixed-Wing Aircraft Since 1946*, Air Britain, 2004

# ABBREVIATIONS

| | |
|---|---|
| AA | Aircraft Artificer |
| AAR | Air-to-Air Refuelling |
| ACM | Air Combat Manoeu-vring |
| ACRB | Aircrew Refreshment Buffet |
| ADD | Airstream Direction Detector |
| ADDL | Assisted Dummy Deck Landing |
| Adm | Admiral |
| AEO | Air Engineering Officer |
| AEW | Airborne Early Warning |
| AI | Admiral's Inspection |
| AMRAAM | Advanced Medium Range Air-to-Air Missile |
| ASI | Air Speed Indicator |
| ASW | Anti-Submarine Warfare |
| ATC | Air Traffic Control |
| AWI | Air Warfare Instructor |
| BEM | British Empire Medal |
| BLC | Boundary Layer Control |
| BRNC | Britannia Royal Naval College |
| CAP | Combat Air Patrol |
| CCA | Carrier-Controlled Approach |
| Cdr | Commander |
| Cdre | Commodore |
| CFD | Captain of the Flight Deck |
| CFS | Central Flying School |
| C-in-C | Commander-in-Chief |
| CO | Commanding Officer |
| COD | Carrier On Board Delivery |
| CPO | Chief Petty Officer |
| DFC | Distinguished Flying Cross |
| EA | Electrical Artificer |
| ELINT | Electronic Intelligence |
| ETPS | Empire Test Pilots' School |
| F | Fighter |
| FA | Fighter Attack |
| FAA | Fleet Air Arm |

| | |
|---|---|
| FAW | Fighter All Weather |
| FB | Fighter Bomber |
| FDO | Flight Deck Officer |
| Fg Off | Flying Officer |
| Fishhead | Non-Air Group Member of the Ship's Company |
| Flt Lt | Flight Lieutenant |
| FlyCo | Flying Control |
| FONAC | Flag Officer Naval Air Command |
| FRADU | Fleet Requirements Air Direction Unit |
| FRS | Fighter Reconnaissance Strike |
| FRU | Fleet Requirements Unit |
| FRY | Federal Republic of Yugoslavia |
| FTS | Flying Training School |
| GA | Ground Attack |
| GCA | Ground-Controlled Approach |
| Gp Capt | Group Captain |
| GR | Ground-Attack Reconnaissance |
| HLAI | High-Level Airborne Interception |
| HMS | Her Majesty's Ship |
| HUD | Head-Up Display |
| IFF | Identification Friend or Foe |
| IFR | Instrument Flight Rules |
| IFTU | Intensive Flying Trials Unit |
| IMC | Instrument Meteorologi-cal Conditions |
| IOC | Initial Operational Capability |
| JBD | Jet Blast Deflector |
| JEM | Junior Engineering Mechanic |
| JFH | Joint Force Harrier |
| JPT | Jet Pipe Temperature |
| kT | Kiloton |
| LABS | Low-Altitude Bombing System |
| LLAI | Low-Level Airborne |

| | | | |
|---|---|---|---|
| | Interception | | Flight Deck Operations |
| LOX ................... | Liquid Oxygen | RNVR................. | Royal Navy Volunteer Reserve |
| LSO.................... | Landing Safety Officer | | |
| Lt ...................... | Lieutenant | ROE ................... | Rules of Engagement |
| Lt Cdr ................ | Lieutenant Commander | RP ..................... | Rocket Projectile |
| MADDL.............. | Mirror-Assisted Dummy Deck Landing | RPM ................... | Revolutions Per Minute |
| | | SAM ................... | Surface-to-Air Missile |
| MT ..................... | Megaton | SAR ................... | Search and Rescue |
| NAS.................... | Naval Air Squadron | SBAC................. | Society of British Aircraft Companies |
| NASU ................ | Naval Aircraft Support Unit | | |
| | | SDSR................. | Strategic Defence and Security Review |
| NATO................ | North Atlantic Treaty Organisation | | |
| | | SHAR ................ | Sea Harrier |
| NF...................... | Night Fighter | SNO ................... | Senior Naval Officer |
| NFSF.................. | Naval Flying Standards Flight | SPD.................... | Stick Positioning Device |
| | | SPRAG .............. | Spray Arrestor Gear |
| NOTAM ............. | Notice to Airmen | SRVL ................. | Shipborne Rolling Vertical Landing |
| OCU................... | Operational Conversion Unit | | |
| | | Sub-Lt ............... | Sub Lieutenant |
| OFS.................... | Operational Flying School | T ....................... | Trainer |
| OOW ................. | Officer of the Watch | TACAN.............. | Tactical Air Navigation |
| PAS.................... | Pilot Attack Sight | TGT .................. | Turbine Gas Temperature |
| Plt Off ............... | Pilot Officer | TT ...................... | Target Tug |
| PO...................... | Petty Officer | UDI ................... | Unilateral Declaration of Independence |
| PPI ..................... | Plan Position Indicator | | |
| PTF .................... | Phantom Training Flight | UHF ................... | Ultra-High Frequency |
| QFI ..................... | Qualified Flying Instructor | UK ..................... | United Kingdom |
| | | UN ..................... | United Nations |
| RAAF................. | Royal Australian Air Force | US ...................... | United States |
| RAdm................. | Rear Admiral | USAF................. | United States Air Force |
| RAE.................... | Royal Aircraft Establishment | USMC ............... | United States Marine Corps |
| | | | |
| RAF .................... | Royal Air Force | USN .................. | United States Navy |
| RAN ................... | Royal Australian Navy | USS ................... | United States Ship |
| RANAS............... | Royal Australian Navy Air Station | U/S..................... | Unserviceable |
| | | U/T..................... | Under Training |
| RAS .................... | Replenishment at Sea | VAdm................. | Vice Admiral |
| RAT .................... | Ram Air Turbine | VFR.................... | Visual Flight Rules |
| RATOG............... | Rocket-Assisted Take-Off Gear | VHF ................... | Very High Frequency |
| | | VID .................... | Visual Identification |
| RCN ................... | Royal Canadian Navy | VIFF................... | Vectoring Thrust In Forward Flight |
| REA.................... | Radio Electrical Artificer | | |
| RN...................... | Royal Navy | VMC................... | Visual Meteorological Conditions |
| RNAS ................. | Royal Naval Air Station | | |
| RNAY ................ | Royal Naval Aircraft Yard | V/STOL .............. | Vertical/Short Take-Off and Landing |
| RNEC.................. | Royal Naval Engineering College | | |
| | | WAFU ................ | Wet and (Flippin') Useless nickname for FAA member |
| RNEFTS ............. | Royal Navy Elementary Flying Training School | | |
| | | Wg Cdr .............. | Wing Commander |
| RNHF.................. | Royal Navy Historic Flight | WO .................... | Warrant Officer |
| RNSFDO ............ | Royal Naval School of | | |

# INDEX

# NAVY WINGS
## Inspire & Remember

Navy Wings aims to catalyse remembrance and inspire future generations by bringing together the aircraft, people and story of flying from ships, and we do this primarily by flying our heritage naval aircraft around the UK.

The Navy Wings Collection unites a range of owners and operators of historic Naval aircraft. This outstanding array of aircraft, when considered together, provides a unique insight into the full suite of Naval aviation achievements, from the very earliest days of flying aircraft over the water to the breathtaking technological advances that enable high-speed jets and heavy helicopters to land on the moving decks of ships at sea.

The core of the collection comprises the aircraft of the Fly Navy Heritage Flight, which are then joined at air displays and air shows, by other privately owned naval heritage aircraft under the Navy Wings Umbrella. This is achieved through the generous contribution Associate owners and this enables us to tell the truly impressive story of naval aircraft development.

These aircraft thrill hundreds of thousands every year at events across the UK. It is vital that these historic aircraft are supported to keep flying and so continue to honour the past and inspire the future.

You can support Navy Wings by becoming a Supporter, by shopping in our Flight Store or by playing our weekly lottery. Visit our website to find out more.